Inventions of D

Inventions of Difference

ON JACQUES DERRIDA

Rodolphe Gasché

HARVARD UNIVERSITY PRESS

Cambridge, Massachusetts
London, England
1994

Library of Congress Cataloging-in-Publication Data

Gasché, Rodolphe.
Inventions of difference: on Jacques Derrida / Rodolphe Gasché.
p.   cm.
Includes bibliographical references and index.
ISBN 0-674-46442-7 (cloth)
ISBN 0-674-46443-5 (paper)
1. Derrida, Jacques.   I. Title.
B2430.D484G36   1994
194—dc20   93-47595
                                                              CIP

Contents

Acknowledgments

I AM GRATEFUL to the Johns Hopkins University Press for permission to quote from Jacques Derrida, *Of Grammatology,* trans. Gayatri C. Spivak; to the University of Nebraska Press for permission to quote from Jacques Derrida, *Glas,* trans. John P. Leavey, Jr., and Richard Rand; and to Routledge for lines quoted from Jacques Derrida and Derek Attridge, *Acts of Literature.* I would also like to acknowledge the Humanities Press (Atlantic Highlands, N.J.) and Unwin Hyman, an imprint of Harper-Collins Publishers Ltd. (London), for permission to quote from G. W. F. Hegel's *Science of Logic,* trans. A. V. Miller.

Several chapters of the book have been published previously. "Deconstruction as Criticism" first appeared in *Glyph 8* (Baltimore: Johns Hopkins University Press, 1979). A shorter version of "Answering for Reason" appeared under the title "Postmodernism and Rationality" in the *Journal of Philosophy,* 85, no. 10 (1988). "Structural Infinity" first appeared under the title "Nontotalization without Spuriousness" in the *Journal of the British Society for Phenomenology,* 17, no. 3 (1986). "God, for Example" was previously published in *Phenomenology and the Numinous* (Pittsburgh: The Simon Silverman Phenomenology Center, 1988). "Yes Absolutely" appeared under the title "Yes Absolutely: Unlike Any Writing Pen" in *Identification and Political Identities,* ed. E. Laclau (London: Verso, 1994). Except for some minor, mostly stylistic improvements, these essays appear here unchanged.

Very special thanks go to Robert Bernasconi, John Caputo, Charles Scott, and David Wood, all of whom read, or heard, early versions of several of the chapters. Their insightful comments and valuable suggestions have helped me a great deal in rethinking some of my ideas. And finally, I am greatly indebted to Michele Sharp for her unstinting assistance in preparing the manuscript for publication.

Inventions of Difference

Abbreviations

Works by Derrida

D   *Dissemination,* trans. B. Johnson (Chicago: University of Chicago Press, 1981)

DMJ   "Deux Mots pour Joyce," *Ulysses Grammophone: Deux mots pour Joyce* (Paris: Galilée, 1987)

G   *Glas,* trans. J. P. Leavey and R. Rand (Lincoln: University of Nebraska Press, 1986)

M   *Margins of Philosophy,* trans. A. Bass (Chicago: University of Chicago Press, 1982)

O   *Edmund Husserl's "Origin of Geometry": An Introduction,* trans. J. P. Leavey (Stony Brook, N.Y.: Nicholas Hays, 1978)

OG   *Of Grammatology,* trans. G. C. Spivak (Baltimore: Johns Hopkins University Press, 1976)

P   *Positions,* trans. A. Bass (Chicago: University of Chicago Press, 1971)

SP   *Speech and Phenomena,* trans. D. B. Allison (Evanston: Northwestern University Press, 1973)

TWJ   "Two Words for Joyce," trans. G. Bennington, in *Post-Structuralist Joyce: Essays from the French,* ed. D. Attridge and D. Ferrer (Cambridge: Cambridge University Press, 1984), pp. 145–159

UL   "Ulysses Gramophone: Hear Say Yes in Joyce," in *Acts of Literature,* ed. D. Attridge (New York: Routledge, 1992), pp. 253–309

WD   *Writing and Difference,* trans. A. Bass (Chicago: University of Chicago Press, 1978)

Works by Hegel

A   *Aesthetics: Lectures on Fine Art,* trans. T. M. Knox (Oxford: Clarendon Press, 1975)

PR   *Philosophy of Right,* trans. T. M. Knox (Oxford: Clarendon Press, 1985)

SL   *Science of Logic,* trans. A. V. Miller (New York: Humanities Press, 1969)

Introduction

HOW DOES ONE APPROACH works of thought whose singularity has most often provoked either a violent hostility or a mechanical imitation that obscures them from our sight? From what angle does one look at these works, so markedly different from standard modes of thinking and exposition, which not only ponder questions of difference and singularity, but put these questions into action? How does one read works that do not limit themselves to making a point, but also perform and enact it? And finally, what do these works that foil and frustrate given expectations, that meditate on the rules of breaking the rules, expect from the critic? What place do they assign their readers? For what mode of relating do they properly call?

The essays in this book, composed over a dozen years, each, in one way or another, attempt to answer these questions in response to the works of Jacques Derrida. The first essay, "Deconstruction as Criticism," discusses the reception of deconstruction in North America, and was written at a time when, in the absence of any serious attempts to come to grips with the philosophical nature of Derrida's writings, the main task consisted in establishing minimal standards and guidelines for reading his texts. This essay, with only minor alterations, appears here in essentially its original form, not only to underline my sense of perplexity at Derrida's reception in North America, a perplexity that has motivated a significant portion of my research toward the clarification of various issues relevant to his work, but also because it articulates an account of Derrida's thinking distinct from that which I proposed in my earlier book. Although *The Tain of the Mirror*,[1] like "Deconstruction as Criticism," is concerned to differentiate Derrida's thought from an interpretation, especially by literary scholars, that saw it as advocating not only the primacy of literature and rhetoric over philosophy and conceptual

1

argumentation, but as conceiving of the specificity of the literary text in terms of self-reflexivity and an ironic debunking of conceptual opposites, it proceeds to make this point in a different way. Whereas *The Tain of the Mirror* seeks to situate Derrida with respect to the predominantly German post-Hegelian criticism of the philosophy of reflection, the earlier essay understands his thought from the perspective of Merleau-Ponty's interrogation of the aporias of reflexivity and the continuation, in the early work of Jean-François Lyotard, of this inquiry into the limits of reflection. This text, which presents "deconstruction" in a context different from the one developed in my earlier book, is thus an independent piece, and serves here to outline some basic aspects of Derrida's thought to be futher elaborated, and built on, in the essays to follow.

Despite the commonality of theme, each of these essays broaches issues not explicitly addressed in *The Tain of the Mirror,* making this a companion volume of sorts to that earlier book. They home in, directly or obliquely, on questions of singularity, alterity, and difference, and the affiliated topics of relating and responding. These are the issues discussed and performed throughout the writings of Derrida, and the mode of exposition chosen in all the essays is that of a reconstruction of the problematics in question. Each essay seeks to elucidate the "principle" that informs the development of these topics and to clarify the philosophical implications that derive from the singular twist to which they become subjected in Derrida's work. Yet given the specific styles with which Derrida engages philosophical conceptuality, some may object that such an approach risks a reduction of the radicality and force of this thinker's contributions. Yet any encounter worth the name presupposes not only encountering the Other in all his or her singularity, but recognizing this singularity in the first place. Paradoxically, even the most radical singularity must, in order for it to be recognized for what it is, have an addressable identity, guaranteed by a set of universal rules that, by the same token, inscribe its singularity within a communal history, tradition, and problematics. In the case of a thinker such as Derrida, this means that the force and radicality of his writings can be addressed only if one recognizes the rules invoked by the singularity of his "position," the rules which secure the intelligibility of this "position" to begin with. The identification of what makes the works of Derrida intelligible—his ties to a tradition of thinking and its discipline, argumentative structures, performative gestures, identifiable topoi, for instance—must be a prime concern for anyone who wishes to understand the singularity, the idiosyncrasy, of the "position" in question, so as to address, and if luck permits, respond to it.

Yet while the necessity of such an approach may have been acknowledged (however reluctantly) for Derrida's earlier work—given its explicit debate with major representatives of the philosophical heritage and the quite conspicuous presence of eminent figures of thought—the later, seemingly more playful, more literary writings, are deemed to thoroughly defy such an approach. If *Glas,* considered to be the first among the later works, is called "*the nec plus ultra* of philosophy's undoing at the hands of rhetoric and intertextual 'freeplay,' " it is seen not only to repulse all "categorial treatment" and "reading in straightforwardly conceptual or philosophical terms,"[2] but ultimately to have severed all identity-constituting references to established conventions and modes of thought. In these terms, a text like *Glas* escapes, as Richard Rorty claims, the sphere of the public, that is, the pedagogical and political sphere, altogether. To Rorty's eyes, this text shows Derrida adrift from all the great problems of the tradition, indulging in a private fantasy to be savored, at best, by only a very few. If, hereafter, my debate with this assessment invokes the names of Richard Rorty and Mark C. Taylor, it is not to find out who among us may "be somewhat squinty-eyed." Perhaps it is, as Rorty notes, too soon to judge the right angle on Derrida's thought.[3] The names of Rorty and Taylor stand here not only for attempts to address the singularity of Derrida's work, but for attempts that recognize that singularity is indeed one of the major stakes of that work. My argument will therefore be interested only in what in their responses to deconstruction transcends their individual points of view, and, as far as the treatment of the question of singularity is concerned, my interest is to elucidate what, being no one's singular property, at least up to a certain point, might be shared by all of us.

The main justification for distinguishing between an earlier and later Derrida, Rorty claims, is that, beginning with *Glas,* he stops being a philosopher with a public mission. Rorty writes: "Derrida's work divides into an earlier, more professorial period and a later period in which his writings become more eccentric, personal, and original." During the earlier period Derrida remains a metaphysician, a negative theologian, who not only continues the inherent modes of argumentative thinking, but, much like Heidegger, illicitly extends such thought by making an "*argumentative appeal* to the non-propositional." The early Derrida is also tempted to make transcendental arguments and to continue the search for "the mysterious transcendental 'conditions of possibility' dreamed up by Kant." He is said to be "in quest of the same thing Heidegger wanted: words which express the condition of possibility of all previous theory."[4] "Like late Heidegger, early Derrida sometimes goes in for word magic . . . he too, wants to find words which get 'us' beyond metaphysics— words which have force apart from us and display their own contingency," Rorty contends.[5] Is not the transcendental question "a thoroughly deceptive question"? he asks; and what are these "conditions of possibility" if not "ingenious gimmicks," "so many leaps into the darkness" rooted in the unreasonable belief that there is "a great big meta-vocabulary which will somehow get at the least denominator of all the various uses of all the various marks and noises which we use for . . . various purposes"?[6]

Needless to say, the "conditions of possibility" Rorty refers to are the Derridean terms of " 'trace,' 'differance,' and the rest of what Gasché calls 'infrastructures,' " which he characterizes as no "*more* than the vacuous nonexplications characteristic of a negative theology."[7] From the nominalist and pragmatic position espoused by Rorty, the whole idea of " 'conditions of possibility' sounds terribly metaphysical."[8] Although the search for conditions of possibility and transcendental a prioris is only part of Kant's critical philosophy, and thus only anticipates a metaphysics still to come, Rorty has a point of sorts. Indeed, even if one acknowledges, as one must, that Kant's conditions of possibility are merely those of a finite intellect limited to objective cognition and, hence, to an inherently finite kind of bedrock, the search itself continues to conform to the classical philosophical quest for a ground, an origin, a last instance. Philosophy in a transcendental perspective worries too, as did "the metaphysics of the tradition . . . about what is older."[9] But are "trace", "differance," and all those notions that I have called "infrastructures" conditions of possibility to begin with? Not only are they older "in a certain and very strange way" (*M,* p. 22), but they are, and Rorty never takes notice of this, at the same time *conditions of impossibility*. Rorty's negative appraisal of the infrastructures rests on his exclusive consideration of their enabling functions.

What then about infrastructures? I recall that the choice of that term to encompass the ensemble of "trace," "differance," "supplementarity," and so on, was strategic. It was motivated by the desire to demonstrate a relation, however critical, between Derrida's work and structuralism and phenomenology. Other terms would have served equally well, "undecidables," or "the law of the law," for example. But the choice of such terms would have required different expository strategies, and would have emphasized different strains of Derrida's critical debate with the tradition.[10] Rorty is right to remark that I "have taken seriously Derrida's claim that 'differance' is 'neither a word nor a concept' and [have] applied it to all the other Derridean terms which . . . [I take] to signify infrastructures."[11] Indeed, if one understands words as names, that is, as unities of sense and not merely as exchangeable and disposable tools or tokens for referring to something, and concepts as those representations that permit the unification of the manifold intuited with respect to a thing, and thus the comprehension of what a thing is, rather than as "just the regular use of a mark or noise,"[12] then infrastructures are neither words nor things. Although the Derridean infrastructures differ in significant ways from such Heideggerian terms as *Ereignis* or *Gestell,* it is not inappropriate to note at this point that *Ereignis* is not, as Rorty holds, "a magic word." Rather, and I follow here Heidegger's developments of the notion in question in *On the Way to Language, Ereignis* is a *singular* linguistic construction, possible only in German, hence untranslatable, that designates what unifies the different modes of Showing in Saying, as well as the various modes in which the human being is addressed and called upon by language to respond to what it shows in Saying. *Ereignis* as a linguistic construction gathers together the different, at times heterogeneous traits of these modes of Showing in Saying. Indeed, it ties into one, *eignen* (owning), *ereignen* (bringing about), *er-äugen* (beholding, conferring the possibility of seeing), *eigen* (own, proper), which has no linguistic affiliation with *ereignen, vereignen* (to allow to belong, to claim), which is a word that does not exist in German, and so on. Because of this odd construction, *Ereignis* is neither a word in a pragmatic sense nor simply a name. "This owning which brings . . . [all present and absent beings] there, and which moves Saying as Showing in its showing we call [*heisse*] Appropriation [*Ereignis*]," Heidegger writes. The construction in question designates, denominates *(nennen),* and it does so, Heidegger remarks, in a saying in which "we speak our own appropriate *(eigenen)* already spoken language."[13] *Ereignis* thus has the singularity of a proper name. It is the proper name in a specific linguistic idiom—in German— for how in that idiom, and in it alone, the different modes of Showing and the responses to it are unified. Consequently, it is not a concept either, since it does not possess the generality of such a representation. It does not grasp the event of Appropriation as such or in general, and yet this singular construction denominates something whose generality manifests itself always only in a singular manner, as a particular idiom. Derridean infrastructures differ from such Heideggerian notions as *Ereignis* or *Gestell* by the decidedly more heterogeneous nature of what they tie together; by the singularity of their combination, which is not limited to that of an idiom; by the non-dyadic arrangement of the gathered traits; and, notwithstanding the fact that they represent combinations, by their lack of a unifying *(einigen)* thrust. Yet, for reasons similar to those applying to Heidegger's terms, they are neither words nor concepts. Undoubtedly, simply to take this Derridean claim at face value is to compliment Derrida's words and, as Rorty puts it, to whistle in the dark.[14] But if, as I did in *The Tain of the Mirror,* for each one of the infrastructural arrangements, one establishes the nature of the traits that become woven into them, as well as the (*only* possible) kind of combination to which such traits can lend themselves, it soon becomes clear that the claim in question is solidly grounded.

Even so, if infrastructures are not words or names in the sense dominant throughout the philosophical tradition, they are not, for that matter, simply tokens. It is not a question of choosing between the Platonic alternatives of understanding words either as having truth or correctness in themselves or as being the results of convention and agreement. It is not a question of realism versus nominalism. Words, whether unities of meaning, or marks, signs, or tokens, are required to be recognizable, repeatable, entities that can be detached from what they named first and used in the absence of their referent. Infrastructures are not words in either of those two Platonic senses because they pertain to the conditions and limits under which a word can be either a unity of sense or merely a *sema*. They concern the laws under which words, in whatever sense, even as mere tools, can be intelligible. Let me also add that even if one holds that all words are ultimately undecidable or, following Maurice Blanchot, "that each moment of language can become ambiguous,"[15] infrastructures, because they are undecidables, are not for that reason simply words. Because they articulate the laws and limits of intelligibility, they have, compared with words, a certain privilege.

The traits that make up an infrastructure are without exception traits of pointing away from (themselves), being marked in advance by an Other, referring to an Other, and so on. Although these traits cluster to form an infrastructure, they can thus never give rise to a unity (of sense, of form, or even of a mark). The law articulated by an infrastructure applies to itself as well. It has an identity, that is, a minimal ideality that can be repeated only at the price of a relentless deferral of itself. Although each infrastructure is formulated with respect to a determined context and for a specific occasion with the result that the generality of the law that it articulates is marked by that context or occasion, the idiomaticity of the categorial infrastructural laws follows ultimately from the very nature of the traits that they feature. Whether those traits are those of pointing away from (themselves), being marked in advance by an Other, referring to an Other, and so on, they are the structural reason for the infrastructure's singularity. Yet infrastructural laws are not for that reason limited to one singular event. They are categorial laws that inscribe the event of their formulation, but above all laws whose generality does not obliterate the singularity that comes with ideality and iterability. What these laws establish, indeed, is that any ideality, identity, or generality, hinges on a prior doubling, pointing away from (self), and referral to an Other—in other words, on a prior singularization. In short, then, infrastructures are not words or concepts, because as laws of intelligibility of both words and concepts, they articulate not only the conditions under which the recognizable and understandable identity of both become possible, but also the limits of a word's meaningful unity, a token's identity, and a concept's unifying power. In their ensemble, which, because of everything that has been established about each one of them, is not a totality or a system, they represent a complex set of conditions which brings the ideality of a whole or a system both into reach and out of reach, and which articulates the limits—that is, that from which something begins but also where it ends—not only of words and concepts, but of just anything.

I recall that for Rorty the rationale for distinguishing an earlier from a later Derrida is that from *Glas* on, Derrida became "a private writer—writing for the delight of us insiders . . . a writer without a public mission."[16] "Content simply to have fun," Derrida was "engaged in self-creation," we are told.[17] Rorty writes: "I suggest that we read Derrida's later writings as turning such systematic projects [for instance, the transcendental project] of undercutting into private jokes . . . The later Derrida privatizes his philosophical thinking . . . He simply drops theory—the attempt to see his predecessors steadily and whole—in favor of fantasizing about those predecessors, playing with them, giving free rein to the trains of associations they produce. There is no moral to these fantasies, nor any public (pedagogic or political) use to be made of them."

He adds: "So I take Derrida's importance to lie in his having had the courage to give up the attempt to unite the private and the public, to stop trying to bring together a quest for private autonomy and an attempt at public resonance and utility."[18] Such writing, "less and less susceptible to the sort of reading Gasché offers,"[19] is for Rorty the only writing to radically interrupt and transfigure the tradition of metaphysics. No longer tempted to identify himself with something big, the later Derrida, by splitting the private from all public pretensions, not only succeeded in radically doing away with all claims to universality, generality, consensus, and so on, but also realized something that no one before had achieved, paradoxically something truly big, a privacy cut loose from all affiliation with, or incarnation of, something larger than itself. By writing books "which nobody had ever thought of before,"[20] by "forging new ways of speaking, not making surprising philosophical discoveries about old ones," and by inventing "a new, splendidly ironic way of writing about the philosophical tradition,"[21] Derrida achieved an autonomy whose originality derives from his no longer fitting into any conceptual scheme, and which would elude the descriptions that past philosophers or, to use a Husserlian term, "the civil servants of humanity" might have given of it. For Rorty, it is by "falling back on private fantasy" and "idiosyncratic obsessions," by "taking pains never to say the same thing twice,"[22] by treating the discourse as a joke, and thus making it "enigmatic rather than ubiquitous,"[23] that Derrida succeeds in creating himself, "creating his own language game, trying to avoid bearing another child by Socrates."[24]

Before evaluating Rorty's description of the later Derrida, it might be appropriate to evoke, however briefly, Derrida's discussion of the concept of invention. As he recalls in "Psyche: Inventions of the Other," for an invention to be an invention it must be unique. "Every invention supposes that something or someone comes a *first time*."[25] By definition, a radically new, noncalculable, even aleatory, invention must escape all programming. Invention thus implies an inaugural event. Without it there is no invention. Yet, and at the same time, an invention is such an inaugural event only on the condition that "its status as invention, let us say its patent or warrant, its manifest, open, public identification has . . . [been] certified and conferred." Its act of inaugural production must "be recognized, legitimized, countersigned by a social consensus according to a system of conventions." In addition to its certified uniqueness, an invention requires an "*advent (avènement),* if we take the latter to mean the inauguration for the future of a *possibility* or of a *power* that will remain at the disposal of everyone." Finally, an invention receives its status of invention only "to the extent that this socialization of the invented thing will be protected by a system of *conventions* that will ensure for it at the same time its recording in a common history, its belonging to a culture: to a heritage, a lineage, a pedagogical tradition, a discipline, a chain of generations."[26] What follows from this is that an invention cannot simply be private—it is the arrival of something new only on condition that it is publicly recognized as such. "For there to be invention, the condition of a certain generality must be met, and the production of a certain objective ideality (or ideal objectivity) must occasion recurrent operations, thus a utilizable apparatus . . . once invented, so to speak, invention is invented only if repetition, generality, common availability, and thus publicity are introduced or promised in the structure of the first time."[27] Paradoxically, then, an invention as a unique, first-time novelty that breaks all implicit contracts and consensuses only "*begins* by being susceptible to repetition, exploitation, reinscriptions."[28] It begins to be something original only if at the same time the invention is recognized and legitimized, it is subjected to the public and the generality that constitutes it, and is made reproducible and utilizable outside the place of its first occurrence and beyond its initial context. In short, an invention is an invention only if from the outset its originality and uniqueness are ruptured by its public recognizability, possible repetition, and reinvention.

Private fantasy, as characterized by Rorty in his attempt to account for Derrida's work since *Glas,* is "merely private," a complete rupture with "metaphysics, the search for generality."[29] He writes: "*All* that connects [Derrida] with the philosophical tradition is that past philosophers are the topics of his most vivid fantasies."[30] But although he admits that not everything in Derrida is clear-cut, and that in fact Derrida "betrays his own project" by trying to give arguments and offer rigorous analyses,[31] Rorty himself inexplicitly acknowledges that they cannot be radically cut off from all generality. First, if these exquisitely private elucubrations can be savored by an audience of connoisseurs, however limited, it is because they are not so private to begin with. Ultimately, Derrida will be "congealed (as eventually he must be) into one more set of philosophical views, suitable for doxographic summary,"[32] Rorty admits. Moreover, the whole tradition and "many transfigurations of the tradition begin in private fantasies . . . fantasies so original and utopian that they become the common sense of later time."[33] For Rorty, "metaphysics is, so to speak, irony gone public and flat."[34] Yet if all this is true, then private fantasies must in their very singularity (which is not to be called into question) already be inhabited by generality, by the public. Otherwise, they would not be recognizable, that is, intelligible, as what they are; nor would it be possible for them to become stale, to lose their force by gaining uses, or to be at the origin of a tradition by becoming public. Rather than being "special circumstances" or "difficult borderline cases"[35] that would remain exterior to the private/public split, private fantasies have an intrinsic relation to generality and repetition that is constitutive of the very possibility of something as private as a fantasy. The possibilities of recognizing a private fantasy for what it is, of turning it into a public acquisition, into something that can be imitated and reproduced, are not simply possibilities that can happen to it (and that therefore divide the merely private, too), but possibilities without which the private, the singular, the idiosyncratic could not exist. If these possibilities did not already haunt the private, it would remain unintelligible, as such. However, such blurring of the private/public split does not make this distinction irrelevant. Rather than being the result of what Rorty terms "a neat textbook dilemma" that could be easily dispelled by showing that in reality "things are just not as bad,"[36] the blurring in question is the condition under which a private fantasy can be thought in its difference from the public.[37]

Let me circle back to the distinction between an earlier and later Derrida. Derrida's claim that deconstruction is plural would seem to indicate a relation of continuity rather than of simple opposition between the earlier and the later work. Even so, the supposition of such continuity does not negate the value of the distinction between the early and later work. Still, is the distinction really between an argumentative thinker in search of infrastructural generalities and a private writer engaged in self-creation? Rorty claims that since *Glas,* Derrida has ignored argumentative discourse. But at the same time he quotes Derrida as saying that what he *does* in those later texts will no longer permit a distinction between "the 'symbolic' or the 'material' features of words," between words as signifiers or marks, and especially between their use and their mention. Yet, even as he blurs these distinctions, Derrida *makes* a point about their limitation and hence about the arguments which they structure. However nonpropositional it may be, does this not constitute an argument? More precisely, in *doing* what he does in these later texts Derrida undercuts the distinction between saying and doing, between argumentation and performance. To blur these rules is not to invalidate them and, as Rorty puts it,[38] is certainly to "expand the realm of possibility" in a kind of writing/discourse that "foregrounds," as it were, all these rules and distinctions. This operation of undercutting distinctions on which the possibility of argumentative discourse rests is no private exercise. Its "principle" can be reconstructed; its moves can be rendered intelligible. Moreover, what it achieves may itself be translated (though not without the inevitable loss that all translation entails) into argumentative discourse. In short, the later Derrida poses his philosophical concerns in action, rather than in a strictly discursive fashion. And stressing some of the consequences of such a deconstructive procedure will bring additional distinctive marks of the later work into view. First, the performative nature of deconstruction evident from *Glas* on—performative, however, in a way unlike the speech act defined by its opposition to the constative—increasingly makes Derrida's later works responses, active engagements or processes of negotiation. This explains the marked concern with questions of responsiveness and responsibility, the question of the Other, and the question of ethics in general that appears with increasing insistence from *Glas* on. Second, deconstruction's performative nature also brings its event quality into relief. Deconstruction in the later Derrida becomes occasional, and singular in every case. Such singularity implies, of course, plurality, and in particular the proliferation of genres, styles, voices, tonalities, formats, archives, and media that characterizes the later Derrida, a plurality that no *concept* of deconstruction could hope to totalize. Third, by virtue of their event-character and singularity, these deconstructive texts open themselves to the incalculable, unpredictable, nonprogrammatizable response by an Other for whose arrival they have opened the way. However, none of these traits characteristic of the writings of the later Derrida is entirely new. Any careful consideration of what I have called "infrastructures" would leave no doubt that these new aspects "only" make explicit and put to work what the early works already contained.

Yet, a lack of concern with infrastructures is perhaps the distinctive mark of the later writings. We have seen Rorty, for example, unable to carry anything, including infrastructures, away from those texts. Two remarks must suffice here. First: Infrastructures are not something that one could ever hope to bring home "cupped in one's hand or cradled in one's arms."[39] The very nature as well as the arrangement of the traits that make up infrastructures eludes all identifying fixation and hence all appropriation. The arche-trace, for example, defined as the inevitable mark of the Other born by a self-present or self-contained entity, the mark not of any constituted, particular Other, but simply the place marked for the arrival of the Other, the site of referral to an Other still to come, is an infrastructural principle of asymmetry that articulates "nothing" but the structural or vectorial feature of being marked by an Other and of relating to an Other. "Nothing" but a structure of pointing away from self, itself included, and of making room for the arrival of an Other, this infrastructure can never be turned into a result or conclusion. Yet, this impossibility of cupping it in one's hand does not exclude, but rather impels the elucidation and construction of this impossibility. Second: While infrastructures are perhaps less conspicuous in the later texts, their traits not always explicitly tied together in a specific term such as "differance," "supplementarity," "remark," and so on, it is simply not the case that the later Derrida is no longer concerned with infrastructures. In the later texts infrastructures arise out of the different performative operations constitutive of these texts. It is the texts themselves that become the articulations of what I earlier termed infrastructures. The example to be given in the following chapters of such performative linkage of the individual traits of an infrastructure is that of the problematic of stricture, restriction, constriction, constructure in *Glas*. But such discursive-performative or performative-discursive interweaving implies as well that infrastructural accounting for a manifold of heterogeneous items, issues, events, takes on, in the later texts of Derrida, a more occasional character. It becomes the singular response to differing demands. That such is the case is shown below in the essay about the *hearsay yes/ yes laughter* structure analyzed in a reading of "Ulysses Gramophone." With due respect to the undoubtedly significant differences that exist between the roles of terms such as "differance," "supplementarity," and "iterability" in Derrida's writings throughout the sixties, and in the work following *Glas,* one must not overlook the fact that the way in which infrastructures are set forth throughout the later texts—in a multitude of modes, as intrinsically singular responses, and often gathered together only through the various acts that make up the event, textual or not— is the very consequence, or rather the actualization, of the implications that come with the notion of infrastructure itself.

Since Rorty emphasizes only the enabling role of infrastructures, he is able to dispose of them as transcendentals. Mark C. Taylor, on the other hand, in "Foiling Reflection," briefly alludes to them as conditions of possibility *and* impossibility, in order immediately and exclusively to press the issue of their disabling function.[40] In this essay, Taylor sees them only as "interrupting," "shattering" or "infecting" the mirror of philosophical speculation and reflection in a way that causes the failure of reflection. But infrastructural limits are rather the unreflected borders from which reflection comes into its own. Notwithstanding reflection's inability to reflect them, they are the conditions which allow for the possibility of reflection, self-reflection, and speculation. Infrastructures thus do not shatter reflection at all, but simply mark the reflection's positivity with a limit. Although "to foil" also means to back, or cover with foil, to lay a thin coat of tin on the back of a mirror, thus enabling the mirror's mirroring play, Taylor's "Foiling Reflection" hints at a terminal defeat of reflection, philosophical reflection in particular. His account of infrastructural limits suggests that any attempt to philosophically reflect or interpret Derrida's writings must fail as well. "Interpreting Derrida *philosophically*," he writes, is not only to bring an unwarranted seriousness to the latter's work, and to miss its irony, but inevitably to present "a Hegelian reading of deconstructionism."[41] Philosophical interpretation is said to be homonymous with Hegelianism, yet, since *Glas* at least, Derrida has stopped taking Hegel seriously. "Ironic texts sound the disastrous *Glas* of philosophy," Taylor concludes.[42]

But how does Taylor understand irony? Quoting Sylviane Agacinski's study of Kierkegaard, he notes that irony "represents in an unsurmountable way the point of view of the writer."[43] The viewpoint of the writer manifest in the literary qualities (which Taylor understands quite conservatively as rhetorical and tropological in nature) of his or her texts is understood as irreducibly singular. Taylor, who like Rorty conceives of Derrida's radical subversion of philosophical thinking as a consequence of his writerly style, claims that the point of view, the "the distinctive trait" of Derrida's writing,[44] imparts its singularity to his texts in a way that renders their generic categorization impossible. By virtue of this irreducible singularity, the point of view and the texts that it informs elude any interpretive approach. Indeed, for Taylor, the singularity of the point of view sounds the death knell to philosophy's claim to universality. It is a blow from which philosophy cannot hope to recover. Putting to work a rather odd interpretation of what Heidegger has called the unthought, Taylor conceives the point of view as the unthought par excellence for philosophy in general, or the System, since it is what the

System is "constructed to forget."[45] As the mark of the writer's irreducible individuality, the viewpoint as well as the literary qualities in which it manifests itself is simply untranslatable. Any translation of "the inexpressible," the "unmentionable," which, as Taylor also puts it, "is *to a certain extent and in a certain way* 'sacred' or 'holy,' "[46] amounts to betraying the singularity in question by domesticating it.

Singularity present in the viewpoint or implied in the stylistic gestures of a writer must thus be protected from differences in translation or philosophical interpretation. Taylor believes that this can be achieved through "repeated inscription." He writes: "The task that (always) lies ahead is not simply translation into philosophical discourse but it is the repeated inscription of that which is untranslatable."[47] In the face of what he calls "Derrida's scattered writings," the task is not to "bring together differences that Derrida persistently holds apart," but to reenact with as little difference as possible, and in its full disruptive power, "the untranslatable remainder" that is the singularity of the viewpoint of the writer.[48] But understood in these terms, singularity, by refusing all translation and interpretation, becomes opaque, silent, or immediate in a nondialectical sense. It becomes quite simply thoroughly unintelligible. Such a singular would be a failure in its own terms. No longer identifiable, it could not be recognized, let alone repeated as a singular. For the singular to be possible as a singularity, it must pose itself as singular, that is, it must repeat itself in an idealizing doubling. Differently put, to be repeatable, the singular must translate itself, interpret itself as intelligible in its unintelligibility.

In "Schibboleth: For Paul Celan," Derrida argues that even an event as singular, as unique, as a date which "*comes* to mark itself as the one-and-only time"[49] and which thus is thoroughly alone and exempt from repetition, *must,* at the "risk [of] losing itself in readability," let itself be "transcribed, exported, deported, expropriated, re-appropriated, repeated in its utter singularity."[50] Such translation is inevitable—Derrida, interestingly enough, points to the need "to resituate here the question of the transcendental schematism of the imagination and of time, as a question of the date, *of the once*"[51]—since otherwise the ineluctably singular would become walled up and reduced to silence. Without running this essential, and hence necessary risk, by which the singular relates to the Other, it would not be a singular to begin with. Translation, while obviously carrying with it the possibility of loss, at the same time allows the singular to be recognized in its irreducible singularity and thus to be repeated. The singular *itself,* and necessarily, calls for translation. Of the date, Derrida writes:

> It is necessary that the mark which one calls a date be *marked off,* in a singular manner, detached from the very thing which it dates: and that in this de-marcation, this deportation, it becomes readable, that it becomes readable, precisely, as a date in wresting or exempting itself from itself, from its immediate adherence, from here and now; in freeing itself from what it nonetheless remains, a date. It is necessary that the unrepeatable *(das Unwiederholbare)* be repeated in it, effacing in itself the irreducible singularity which it denotes. It is necessary that in a certain manner it divide itself in repeating, and by the same stroke encipher and encrypt itself. Like *phusis,* a date likes to encrypt itself. It must efface itself in order to become readable, to render itself unreadable in its very readability. For if it does not annul in itself the unique marking which connects it to an event without witness, without other witness, it remains intact but absolutely indecipherable. It is no longer even what it has to be, what it will have had to be, its essence and its destination, it no longer keeps its promise, that of a date.[52]

From the ductus of this passage it should be clear that what we have to do with here is a necessary, quasi-transcendental law of singularity, a law that makes the singular dependent on a necessary idealization and universalization which at the same time betrays it. As a consequence, the belief that the singularity of the "point of view of the writer" must be shielded from philosophical translation and repeated without difference not only disregards the law of singularity—that is, the inevitable dissingularization through the repetition without which it could not hope to secure its singularity—but also dreams the dream of a singularity pure to the point that the possibility even of its "repeated inscription" becomes virtually unimaginable. Is this not the dream of an Other that rebuffs all (self-)alteration through relation to an Other?—in other words, the dream of a fully self-present Other?

Singularity, whether conceived as the writer's private fantasy or point of view, cannot be simply demarcated from the universal. As with the ciphers encountered in Celan's poetry, with the singular "chance and necessity cross and in crossing are both at once consigned. Within its strictures a ligament binds together, in a manner at once significant and insignificant, fatality and its opposite: chance and coming-due, coincidence in the event, what *falls*—well or ill-together."[53] It is thus imperative to acknowledge this *togetherness* of the unique, the one-and-only-time, of the utter singular's refusal of all possible repetition *and* necessity, ideality, universality, in order to do justice to the singular itself. For the singular to be understood as what it is, that is, in its utter singularity, the ligament that within it holds together, each time in a singular manner, contingency and necessity, sheer punctuality and universality, must, in one way or another, be acknowledged. "Repeated inscription" of the point of view, for instance, presupposes that the point of view be at least minimally identical, that is, constituted by conditions of generality that allow it to be repeatable in the first place. Or differently put, such repetition cannot preclude the possibility of identifying, recognizing, and remembering the signature of the writer in all his or her scattered writings, cannot resist recourse to a utilizable apparatus of conventions. Yet, if this is true, then the point of view, and the signature, are not exclusively singular. In addition, if the singularity of the Other requires a minimal universality to be itself and to be recognized as such, then the Other's point of view, or private fantasies, become repeatable, risk being lost by becoming entirely mine. Yet without this risk no justice can possibly be done to the singular; without it, the very possibility of something singular would remain irretrievably lost. And what one would deem to be a repetition of the singular would merely amount to an apology for one's own untranslatable singularity! If, consequently, a minimal identity of the signature is required which inevitably disappropriates the writer by making his writings readable to all, then all the scattered writings of Derrida—however different they may be in format, style, genre, or even in noncategorizable ways—must be interrogated with respect to the double bond, or testamentary structure, of all signature. According to this structure, a proper signature survives only insofar as it is counter-signed, and hence elevated to a minimally universal intelligibility. This structure, however, represents what Taylor derogatorily calls a certain "identity in the midst of Derrida's different writings."[54] It is (at least) one of the structures that gathers together and integrates his very singular texts. However, the identity conferred by such a structure is an identity very unlike what one commonly understands by that term. At the same time that it gathers together the singular works, it maintains the *reference*—that is, a trait of referral (which, in contradistinction to the singularity *itself,* is repeatable)—to the singular, which *as such* had to disappear for the singular to remain. This *reference* to the singular causes all such gathering through which the work becomes readable and intelligible to remain suspended, in its possibility and necessity, from the encrypted enigma of the singular.

Both in *The Tain of the Mirror* and in the following pages I pose this question of the unity of the work by highlighting the ways in which Derrida, in his own texts, weaves or gathers together a manifold of often "unrelated," underivable, untranslatable differences in configurations which are either "conceptual" or "textual," and by means of which these differences become readable in their very singularity. The title under which I develop this issue is that of the infrastructures. Indeed, infrastructures, by linking distinct and singular differences in an arrangement that by their very nature they mark with precariousness, are structures in which these differences acquire a novel, if not singular, intelligibility. Infrastructures achieve linkage between unlinkables, and thus secure their minimal readability. In short, they elicit a universal intelligibility from the singular through minimal contextualization. But by the very nature of what they tie together, such structures of gathering remain in their very generality intimately suspended from singularity. Hence, not only is their number (in principle) infinite, but they are generically different as well. There is not *one* specific genre of what is called "infrastructures."

Yet in the face of the singular, of a multifarious and scattered whole of texts or events, gathering may seem to some to be the objectionable undertaking par excellence. To address this point, let me turn to a text by Derrida entirely devoted to one singular person. Although a homage, more precisely a text in admiration of this one individual, this text, rather than giving into proclaiming or acclaiming the singular person in question, proceeds in all detachment to an analysis of what makes this individual the individual that he is. It is thus a text that, notwithstanding its admiration for that one singular human being, asks what it is that *forces* everyone, friends and foes alike, overtly or secretly, to admire the individual in question. The answer, in "The Laws of Reflection: Nelson Mandela, in Admiration," is that Mandela is a "man of the law."[55] But it is a text not only about the admiration that he inspires, but about something intimately linked to it, the admiration Mandela feels. "The two have the same focus, they reflect upon each other," Derrida writes. The hypothesis is that "he becomes admirable for having, with all his force, admired, and for having made a force of his admiration, a combative, untreatable, and irreducible power."[56] What Mandela, this one singular person has admired, is the law, and it is this admiration for something that by its very structure tends toward universality that makes him admirable. In this essay, Derrida is interested in deploying the law of this double, hence multiple admiration, that is also to say, this multiple mirroring, or reflecting.

Of the numerous facets that make up Mandela's admiration and reflection of the law analyzed by Derrida, I single out only the following. The
essay portrays Mandela as a man of the law, struggling against apartheid
from his admiration for the law, that is, for the tradition that begins with
the Magna Carta, the declaration of human rights, the parliamentary
system, and so on. Yet Mandela is shown to reflect the law, and not in
a simple speculative reversal of the political phenomenality of the law
owing to the fact that it is represented and usurped by the white minority
in South Africa. The struggle against apartheid is not an internal and
symmetrical struggle that the Western law carries on with itself.
Undoubtedly, in admiration of the law, Mandela "respects the *logic* of
the legacy [of the law] enough to turn it upon occasion against those
who claim to be its guardians." But if Mandela is a man of the law, he
is so also because he turns the law against its usurpers in order to reveal
"what has never yet been seen in the inheritance: enough to give birth,
by the unheard-of *act* of a reflection, to what had never seen the light of
the day."[57] With this a law becomes visible which is not imported, which
has no simply assignable origin, and of which the Western law is perhaps
only an example. Indeed, Mandela shows himself not only to be in admiration of, but even to be fascinated with the virtual presence of this law
in African societies before the arrival of the white man. Mandela thus
reflects upon, and reflects as well, a law that transgresses the determined
historicality of the law as Western law. This is, in Derrida's words, "the
law itself, the law above other laws," "a law beyond legality."[58]
    Since all these singular operations of reflection of and on the law—
"The Laws of Reflection" distinguishes many more—especially the one
that has a law beyond legality for its topic, make sense *only* within a
"reflecting apparatus," without, however, lending themselves to a speculative mirror play, it proves necessary to reflect on this apparatus "which
cannot be represented in an objective space."[59] "The Laws of Reflection," as a text, is itself this reflection in which the singular reflections
of and on the law are viewed, and hence unified, in "a sort of great
historical watchtower or observation point *(mirador)*,"[60] whose name is
Nelson Mandela. Mandela, universally admired, is the singular figure in
which all the singular operations of reflections are gathered together. His
is the name of the Law, of the laws of reflection.
    The essay on Mandela, to quote from *Memoires for Paul de Man*, is "a
non-architectonic *Versammlung*,"[61] or gathering, of a multitude of non-
symmetrical and nonspeculative reflections into a Law, that is, into some-

thing that by its very nature tends toward the universal, but whose name is that of a universally respected individual. Although on several occasions Derrida has made known his reservations regarding the Heideggerian motif of gathering, noting, for instance, that in such gathering there is always a question of being one with oneself, of indivisible individuality, of being always already with oneself, he has also noted "the force and necessity of the motif of *Versammlung* in Heidegger, especially since it never excludes difference."[62] Not only is the motif of gathering explicitly present in the essay on Mandela,[63] but the nonspeculative reflection apparatus sketched there is such a gathering in action. Yet gathering does not per se need to mean unchallenged unification, totalization, synthesis. "Things take place between *Versammlung* (that is to say also the *logos,* for Heidegger) and dissemination," Derrida remarks.[64] Let us note, first, that although in the text on Mandela he continues to gather a manifold of singular traits into one figure, he does not give this figure a name similar to those non-concepts that are "differance," "supplementarity," "trace," and so on, but calls it by a proper name. With this the "occasionality" of gathering multiple traits into an infrastructural arrangement is explicitly re-marked. Although it is true that this was already implicitly the case with infrastructures such as "difference," "supplementarity," "trace," and so on, "Mandela," as the proper name of the Law of reflection, stresses that all synthetic accounting begins as response. It takes place in admiration of the Other, as is the case in the essay under discussion. The thus re-marked occasionality of gathering also prevents infrastructures from abusive generalization, from becoming the "elementary words," the "unique names," the "conditionless conditions of possibility" Rorty dreads so much.[65] And yet, from what we have seen in "The Laws of Reflection," the apparatus of reflection not only is a universal structure marked by singularity, but also is universally admired under the name of Nelson Mandela.

Yet there is another, perhaps more essential reason that such gathering does not lead, necessarily, to a mastering totalization. Indeed, the very nature of what is gathered under the name "Mandela" in the "great historical watchtower or observation post" turns what is thus assembled into a very peculiar kind of unity. Speaking of Mandela's defense before the South African tribunal, Derrida writes: "To bear witness, to test, to attest, to contest, to present oneself before witnesses. For Mandela, it was not only to show himself, to give himself to be known, him and his people, it was also to reinstitute the law for the future, as if, finally, it had never taken place. As if, having never been respected, it were to remain, this arch-ancient thing that has never been present, as the future even—still now invisible."[66] Needless to say, "the presumption of unity" that comes with gathering can always produce "an effect visible and invisible, like a mirror, also hard, like the walls of a prison,"[67] but to reject all gathering because this always possible effect lets itself be appropriated is to misunderstand the sort of gathering here in question. One of the singular reflections woven into the apparatus set into motion in the essay under discussion is one that "lets us see, in the most singular geopolitical conjunction . . . the promise of what has not yet ever been seen or heard, in a law that has not yet presented itself in the West, at the Western border, except briefly, before immediately disappearing."[68] In other words, the unity of the apparatus of reflection is also re-marked by a reflection of the future and of future reflection. The very temporality of that reflection prohibits the closure of what nonetheless has been gathered so as to form one apparatus of reflection.

To conclude, then: To reject all gathering, because it can turn into self-identical individuality, totality, or System is to close the doors of reflection and philosophical interpretation. Is this not to abort what gathering still holds out for the future, to reveal a lack of respect for what is still to come, for what has never yet been present? To abandon all gathering because inevitably it would have effects of totalization is only the other side, the speculative inversion, indeed, of the effort that turns the manifold into a homogenous whole. Such renunciation of all gathering surrenders the still-open possibilities, the yet-invisible future of thinking. To relinquish all attempts at comprehensive, synthetic, even systematic presentation because they are totalitarian is not only to blind oneself to perhaps unheard-of possibilities of gathering, but also to miss the singular shape that synthetic and unifying thought has taken in a very determined historical conjunction, and what such singular recasting of gathering holds out for the future. Rorty is right to demand that Derrida "ought to be kept fluid a while longer before being congealed (as he eventually must) into one more set of philosophical views, suitable for doxographic summary."[69] One way to seek to secure such fluidity is to respond to what in his thinking, irrecuperably, tends to the future, the future of thinking. It cannot be a question of who is right or wrong, of simply deciding about the essential Derrida versus what of him has been appropriated and distorted. Rather the question is what in his very singular reworking of traditional forms of thinking, of the motif of gathering, for instance, always escapes for essential reasons any essentialist determination, and thus, implicitly, also the possibility of a distortion of the authenticity of his thought. One must seek in his writings precisely those structures that singularize, extend, and overflow any totalization. They are also the instances or places where Derrida's texts open themselves to an ever incalculable and unpredictable response. If, indeed, these structures make room for the Other, and for the countersignature of an Other, they also assure that no response may ever congratulate itself for being finally the correct or true one. And without this essential doubt, there can be no response at all.

Inventions of Difference is a book about singularity, first of all, on the singularity of the different philosophical concepts of difference that it broaches, and against whose backdrop Derrida's meditation and simultaneous performance of singularity are then discussed. To invent difference can, of course, mean simply to think it up, or fabricate it. But such invention, even where it is not idle, serves merely to domesticate a difference or differences that do not fit familiar schemas. Yet, to problematize difference from the perspective of its invention is, first and foremost, to account for its specificity or singularity against the horizon of intelligibility with respect to, and within which, difference, even in its most extreme form, must be consecrated. For a difference to make a difference, and hence to be one in the first place, its uniqueness must be wrenched from and negotiated within a system of conventions. The question concerning the invention of difference, therefore, refers especially to the irruption into the world of that difference which, according to a long tradition, initially institutes universally shareable generality and ideality. This is the difference that wonder makes, and with which the philosophical concept of difference properly speaking emerges. Invention of difference, consequently, proffers an invitation to think the singularity of the inaugural event in which communality, universality, legality, objectivity, ideality, and so on, arise as the context which by right precedes all thought and invention of difference. But given that this context also serves to program and fix the meaning of difference, and hence to stifle invention, the title *Inventions of Difference* hints at the thought of how unique difference, in its extreme singularity, *arrives,* breaking with the legality of the established codes on difference, and in particular the philosophical code, in a relentless, infinite negotiation to secure a possibility for its impossible status with philosophy.

1

Deconstruction as Criticism

IN SCIENCE, conceptual progress as well as "the wandering off into different fields," without which there is no such progress, leads to the impossibility of asking questions and explaining problems which were essential to the previous theoretical configuration. Indeed, such a loss is not considered a serious one, for "there is no need to possess such knowledge," since the only *one* thing legitimately to be demanded of a theory "is that it should give us a correct account of the world, i.e., of the totality of facts *as constituted by its own basic concepts.*"[1] What is true of science is, in principle, also true of literary criticism. If "the context of discovery" comes into conflict with "the context of justification,"[2] if the reading devices produce discoveries that the previous theories can no longer account for, and if in the eyes of the traditional critic it becomes undecidable "whether a new view *explains* what it is supposed to explain, or whether it does not wander off into different fields,"[3] then one may speak of what Paul Feyerabend calls the *incommensurability* of approaches. Yet, is this incommensurability as securely established as some of the Newer Critics—the so-called deconstructive critics—and most of their opponents would like to believe? Implicitly, a distinction such as Wayne C. Booth's between monism and pluralism (that is, liberalism) acknowledges that the seemingly mutually exclusive approaches to literature are about the same. What Booth's conceptual system implicitly vouches for—an intimate affinity between traditional academic criticism in all its forms and deconstructive criticism, a commensurability unknown to the critics (Booth included)—is one of the explicit presuppositions of this essay. However, rather than representing a conciliatory gesture in the direction of a "critical commonwealth" whose access depends on the critics' statements being seen as "a passport into the country of debate,"[4] and far from being a belief in the continuity of tradition, the stand taken here is critical of deconstructive literary criticism, and maintains that it is incapable of living up to its pretensions. For the problem of either thematic criticism or New Criticism (only disguised by a new and sometimes fashionable vocabulary) still dominates the post-structuralist approaches,[5] in spite of their rhetoric. Apart from this rhetoric there is no trace of what Gaston Bachelard called an epistemological break.[6] In no way does such a judgment disqualify or impair the contributions of modern deconstructive criticism. On the contrary: in the wake of New Criticism, deconstructive criticism has developed new, indispensable insights into the very object of literary criticism, the text. But just as science textbooks represent a sort of obstruction within the ongoing activity of scientific research,[7] much of what appears as deconstructive criticism contributes more to prolonging the impasses of traditional academic criticism than to opening up new areas of research. Hence the generalized discomfort about, in particular, deconstructive criticism. But the critical malaise of modern critics that makes them long for a "beyond-deconstruction," and simultaneously allows the attacks of the rearguard, stems in the first place from a mutual misunderstanding of the notion of deconstruction. It is precisely this misinterpretation that makes its accommodation by American criticism possible and, by the same token, transforms it into a mechanical exercise similar to academic thematism or formalism.

Before trying to clarify the misinterpretation of the notion of deconstruction, I must point out some of the *evidence* guiding so-called deconstructive criticism.[8] In the wake of New Criticism, which rightly showed that literary criticism was not derivative and was not simply a parasitic response to literature, but an autonomous discipline, it has become fashionable to conceive of literary criticism as *theory*. Yet, what does theory mean in this context except the all too often naive and sometimes even, given its uncontrolled and unwanted side effects, ridiculous *application* of the *results* of philosophical debates to the literary field? It is on this unproblematized and rarely justified application, as well as on the lack of any questioning of the applicability of such philosophemes to the specific levels of texts, that theory rests. It rests especially on a generally intuitive understanding of conceptual systems, situated as it is in the (institutionally motivated) absence of all rigorous formation in pilot sciences such as anthropology, linguistics, psychoanalysis, and especially philosophy.[9] In this, *theory* is no different from the impressionistic approaches and loose conceptual instruments of traditional academic criticism, which seldom reflect its own presuppositions. In fact, the unproblematized application of borrowed tools to the analysis of literary texts has already proven the affinity of deconstructive and traditional criticism. Indeed, not only is the newly fashionable *a-theoretical* stand which in the present configuration pretends to come to the rescue of literary, aesthetic, and ethical values by its very definition *violently* theoretical, but this hypocritical innocence in matters of theory stems from its blindness and an ignorance of its own presuppositions that are in the end dependent on various extra-literary disciplines such as psychology, history, and philosophical aesthetics. The origins of these disciplines in nineteenth-century philosophy are never admitted or made explicit.

If deconstructive criticism does not simply coincide with such an ill-founded application of conceptual tools borrowed from certain pilot sciences to the analysis of literary texts, its theoretical pretensions end with the elaboration of the cognitive aspects of these texts. Such an approach, however masterful it may be, by taking the information and knowledge explicitly or implicitly displayed by a text for granted or by taking the reflections a text confers about itself literally, not only fosters a theoretical eclecticism that raises the critic to the status of literary characters like Bouvard and Pecuchet, but also makes him subject to the same kind of criticism that Claude Lévi-Strauss directed against Marcel Mauss: that he tried to explain the Melanesian notion of *mana* with the help of a native theory.[10]

A second evidence predominant in deconstructive criticism is the conviction that everything is literature, text or writing. This evidence of Newer Criticism only radicalizes the purely aesthetic and ahistorical vista of its academic antecedents. It also continues the conservative function of traditional criticism by neutralizing and blurring the capital differences and critical functions between different kinds of discourses. In the case of so-called deconstructive criticism, this evidence originates in an illicit application of the Derridean notion of *écriture* to all forms of discourses. This precipitated application is made possible—as always—through a confusion of levels in a specifically philosophical debate with Husserl's phenomenology. These levels are in fact distinguished carefully by Derrida himself. The notion of *writing* (of text, and of literature, as well) as used by modern deconstructive criticism refers in general only to the *phenomenological experience of writing* as something present in all discourses and texts. Yet, in *Of Grammatology* Derrida clearly warned against mistaking writing (as arche-writing) for the colloquial meaning of writing. Indeed, writing as arche-writing "cannot occur as such within the phenomenological experience of a *presence*." The notion of the trace, he adds, "will never be merged with a phenomenology of writing" (*OG,* p. 68). Derrida's notion of writing and of the trace presupposes a phenomenological reduction of all the mundane regions of sensibility (but also of the intelligible). Being anterior (yet not as an essence) to the distinctions between the regions of sensibility, and consequently to any experience of presence, the trace or writing is not something which can be said to be *present* in all discourses. The regions of sensibility and of presence are "only" the regions where writing as arche-writing appears *as such,* becomes present by occulting itself. Thus, the evidence in question, since it confuses and is unaware of distinctions as important as those between appearance and appearing, between appearance and signification, consists of a fall back into a phenomenological apprehension of writing as something readable, visible, and significant in an empirical medium open to experience. However, criticizing this evidence does not entail (as will be shown) that there is a tangible outside to literature, to the text, and to writing, nor does the rejection of such an exteriority necessarily imply one's entanglement in the pure immanence of the text.

The major evidence of deconstructive criticism, also shared by its opponents, is its understanding of the operation of deconstruction. The evidences already mentioned, the priority of theory and the universalization of literature, are linked to modern criticism's understanding of deconstruction. According to these presuppositions, Derrida's philosophical work can be turned into a theory to be applied to the regional science of literary criticism as well as to the literature it deals with, without the categories of literature and criticism (and the institutions supporting them) being put into question. This naive and intuitive reception of Derrida's debate with philosophy, its reduction to a few sturdy devices for the critic's use, represents nothing less than an extraordinary blurring and toning-down of the critical implications of this philosopher's work.

Since it requires little more than skimming Derrida's major works to know what deconstruction *is not,* let me briefly enumerate what it certainly cannot be identified with. Deconstruction is *not* to be mistaken for a nihilism, nor for a metaphysics of absence, nor for a negative theology. It is not a demolition and a dismantling to be opposed by or calling for a rebuilding and a reconstruction. At the same time, deconstruction is not what is asserted by positive definitions in Newer Criticism. Here deconstruction is said to represent the moment where, in a text, the argument begins to undermine itself; or, in accordance with Roman Jakobson's notion of the poetic and aesthetic function, the relation of a message of communication to itself that, thus, becomes its own object; or, finally, the self-revelation and indication by the text of its own principles of organization and operation. Consequently, deconstructive criticism seldom appears to be more than a very sophisticated form of structural analysis. It only differs from structural analysis in that the diacritical principle of meaning, that is to say, its dependence on differentially determined opposites, on the correspondence and reciprocity of coupled terms, is applied in a negative fashion. Meaning, as well as the aesthetic qualities of a text, then spring forth from the self-canceling of the text's constituting oppositions.[11] But not only is this interplay of binary terms that parody and debunk each other called deconstructive; to increase the confusion, it is often also said to be dialectical.[12] Yet, in terms of logic, the diacritical relations do not even represent the threshold to (negative or not) dialectics, not to speak of deconstruction.

As a negative diacritical approach to literature and the text, deconstructive criticism consequently asserts and simultaneously depends on the idea of the self-reflexivity and the autonomy of the text. This assumption of self-reflexivity, a third evidence of almost all modern criticism, totally distorts the notion of deconstruction.

Here again, in order to avoid some all too hasty conclusions, a few remarks are indispensable. The self-reflexivity with its idea of a more or less infinite *mise en abyme* of the text, as well as the idea of its autonomy assumed by modern criticism, is not to be criticized from an, if you will, extrinsic approach. Besides, such an approach—whether historical, sociological, psychological, psychoanalytical, or otherwise—goes perfectly with the assumption of the text's self-reflexivity and self-referentiality as constitutive of its autonomy. Nonetheless, the contributions based on such a notion of the text cannot be minimized. Compared with the traditional approach, which in spite of its erudition is scarcely more than an unflagging effort to avoid the object of literary studies, modern deconstructive criticism has shown itself to be able to investigate the manifold linguistic density of the *work of literature itself*. Moreover, the self-reflexivity of the text is in no way to be denied. Undoubtedly, its self-reflexive strata *almost* constitute its entirety. But what is at stake here is this *almost*, the point of nonclosure of the reflexive space of the text.

In general, contemporary deconstructive criticism attributes this self-reflexivity of the text to certain specific totalizing emblems such as tropes, images, similes, and so on. Never questioning the nature and the status of *representation* in the text, deconstructive criticism conceives of these emblems of the whole as hyperbolically reinscribing the act of writing.[13] Through such images, the text *itself* (or the writer) is said to perceive "the act of constituting—that is, of writing—(its, or) his nascent *logos*."[14] This is certainly true, but this is precisely the problem as well. Indeed, as an especially modern aesthetic device, this self-reflexivity of texts depends on the totalizing consciousness of an author, or on an equally questionable assertion of a consciousness or unconsciousness of the text. Thus a textual reading would precisely have to account for these cognitive functions of the text, for the images or scenes where its production is staged and for its self-reflexive strata, by inscribing them into the *global* functioning of the text. Since the self-perceiving function of the text is subject to the same aporias which haunt perception and consciousness in general, since the act of production of the text will never coincide with its reflection through totalizing emblems (or concepts), such a move toward a global apprehension of the functions of the text becomes imperative. Yet since the (neither de facto nor de jure) overlapping of the two languages—writing on the one hand and its reflection on the other— never takes place, that overlapping or that identity, which is supposed to engender the text, would also call, in a global apprehension of the functions of the text, for another notion or concept of the text. The current notion of the text's autonomy and self-reflexivity only continues the claim of American formalism to a totalizing principle, to what is called the integrity of the literary form. The idea of self-reflexivity indeed reconfirms, but also—and this is its historical importance—represents the development of what makes the idea of contextual unity possible. Contemporary deconstructive criticism, a faithful offspring of New Criticism, significantly enough was able to formulate the mode of totalization of texts in terms of what makes such a unity possible by borrowing from European thematic criticism.[15]

A compromise between formal and thematic criticism on the one hand and a radical development of the metaphysical implications of the formalist's idea of contextual unity on the other, deconstructive criticism cannot hope to escape critique (usually dull, it is true) by its opponents. A more radical critique, however, is to be directed against deconstructive criticism (a critique that affects traditional criticism even more), which, by erroneously mistaking the reflexive strata and the cognitive functions of the text that it describes for the text as a whole, seriously reduces and restricts the play of the text, a play deconstructive criticism was one of the first to take into account.

Reassessing deconstruction thus involves several tasks. Besides the necessity of restoring its rigorous meaning in the face of both its defenders and those who argue against it, deconstructive criticism will have to break away from its formalist past and to resituate its legacy from thematic criticism, in order to open the notion of the text to its outside. That will not, however, mean that the text is to be precipitously connected to the real and empirical outside.[16] It is true that, far from being an operation *in the limits* of the text, deconstruction proceeds *from and at the limit* of the text. But the outside of the text, that which limits its reflexive strata and cognitive functions, is not its empirical and sensible outside. The outside of the text is precisely that which *in* the text makes self-reflection possible and at the same time limits it. While, on the one hand, the position which consists of criticizing the self-reflexivity of a text from one of its possible sensible and empirical outsides is still privy to what it criticizes, deconstructive criticism, on the other hand, is incommensurate with either of these symmetrically opposite alternatives. Proceeding from that limit which traverses the text in its entirety, deconstructive criticism reasserts literariness and the text as *play:* as the unity of chance and rule. In this perspective, the reflexive strata which constitute *almost* all of the text appear as *almost* parasitical in relation to the text and its play. In short, such a deconstructive criticism reaffirms all of the text. More complex than a totality solely based on a self-reflexive autonomy, the global situation of the text encompasses both the text's reflexive inside and that outside from which it proceeds, an outside which it harbors in its core. This approach to the play of the text (still called literature in the absence of a better term),[17] which, unlike conventional criticism, inevitably limits this very play by its mere investigation, accounts for its own desire to limit and induce changes in this play (*OG*, p. 59).

Thus, in the pages that follow, only one aspect of deconstruction will be analyzed. Indeed, even though Derrida's work provides a superficial reader with enough material to invalidate most of a critic's contentions, this one aspect in particular has misled philosophically untrained readers. This one aspect, more than obvious to the philosopher, is that deconstruction in the first place represents a critique of reflexivity and specularity. It is the lack of awareness of this essential feature of deconstruction that has caused the easy accommodation of deconstruction by contemporary American criticism.

Although Jacques Derrida was the first to introduce the notion of deconstruction (in the context of a debate on Husserl's phenomenology), for reasons soon to become clear, it may be convenient to start with an analysis of Jean-François Lyotard's use of this notion in *Discours, figure*.

However different Lyotard's work may be from that of Derrida, *Discours, figure* is a monument of deconstruction similar to *Of Grammatology*. Indeed, the notion of the *figural* which Lyotard develops in this book, a notion whose meaning shifts as the book unravels from what is at first a sensible connotation to a libidinal definition in order to finally be determined by the concept of difference, is the result of a deconstructive operation. The production of the notion of the figural takes place in two distinctive steps.[18] Setting out from one particular conceptual dyad structuring the discourse of Judaic and Christian metaphysics—the opposition of writing and the figure[19]—Lyotard first reprivileges the hitherto secondary and necessarily inferior term of the dyad, that is to say, the figure. This first step is achieved by *reversing* the hierarchy of the given dyad. The second step consists of *reinscribing* the newly privileged term. This reinterpretation of the notion of the figure takes place in *Discours, figure* through a moving away from phenomenology and a turning to psychoanalysis. This second step of deconstruction—the reinscription of the newly privileged term—is indispensable in order to prevent the naive solution of wanting "to pass to the other side of discourse," which is nothing but a simple inversion of metaphysical values. The reinterpretation of the phenomenological notion of the figure is achieved through an *extension* of its range and scope. No longer simply opposed to writing and discourse, the figure, or more precisely, the figural, now broaches them from the inside:

> The figure is both outside and inside . . . Language is not a homogenous medium, it is . . . divided because it interiorizes the figural in the articulated. The eye is inside speech because there is no articulated language without the exteriorization of something "visible," but also because there is at least a gesticulatory, "visible" exteriority at the heart of discourse that is its expression.[20]

Hence, the figural, which represents a sort of margin to discourse while already broaching it from the inside (and which, consequently, no longer corresponds to the notion of the figure, which remains caught in the dissymmetrical and hierarchical space of the initial dyad), becomes the very space of the inscription of discourse. Discourse, in this way, appears surrounded and undercut by the figural. This (double) inscription—a term whose meaning is strictly limited to the derivation of the central from the marginal—gives the final touch to the operation of deconstruction. Now, what is of interest here and what explains the detour through Lyotard's use of deconstruction is that he dates the necessity of an operation such as deconstruction back to what the late Maurice Merleau-Ponty called *hyper-reflection (sur-reflexion)*.

Before discussing the term *hyper-reflection* and its relation to deconstruction, let me, in a very succinct manner, recall the problematics of Husserlian phenomenology. The answer to the traditional question of the origin of the world, reformulated by Kant as a question concerning the conditions of possibility of a world for a subject, is rejected by Husserl. Indeed, for Husserl the transcendental categories are still mundane categories and will not explain the absolute origin of the world. Husserl, to the contrary, by bracketing the world, discovers its absolute origin in the subject of the *epoche*. This is a subject which, after having suspended the world, becomes evident to itself, evident in an apodictic manner. A mundane object no longer, and distinct from both the psychological and the transcendental subject, it derives this apodictic self-evidence from the gaze of consciousness at itself. It is a gaze which becomes possible only through an eidetic reduction. Although this apodicticity does not entail equality in content, adequation, or the certitude of self-knowledge, it represents the condition of possibility of a subject fully conscious of itself, which, no longer being a thing, is absolutely free in regard to the world, which, consequently, is contingent.[21]

Merleau-Ponty, however, in interrogating the primary openness upon the world in *The Visible and the Invisible* puts the very possibility of such an apodicticity of a subject into question. This interrogation of the gaze of consciousness at itself, a gaze which is different from every possible object-relation and which gives access to the new mode of transcendental existence as an absolute present existence, takes in *The Visible and the Invisible* the form of a critique of reflexivity in general and of all philosophy of reflection. This critique interrogates the very possibility of reflection. Such a critique becomes inevitable, indeed, as soon as one proceeds to question the problem of perception. Thus, while analyzing the perceptual and pre-reflexive faith (in *one* same world shared by all subjects) to which all sciences and (intuitive, reflexive, and dialectical) philosophies remain tributary, Merleau-Ponty ascertains that the opacity of the body of the subject of perception, that is to say, the distance or depth between me and the thing suspended at the end of my gaze, represents the condition of possibility of all perception of the thing itself. However, if it is true that my body as an opacity opens up the space of my glance, then this condition of possibility of all perception also entails the impossibility of self-perception. Merleau-Ponty gives here the famous example of the experience of touching and being touched: "If my left hand is touching my right hand, and if I should suddenly wish to apprehend with my right hand the work of my left hand as it touches, this reflection of the body upon itself always miscarries at the last moment: the moment I feel my left hand with my right hand, I correspondingly cease touching my right hand with my left hand."[22] Hence, the body, while opening the indispensable depth of perception, is equally the space where self-affection and reflexive conversion miscarry.[23] This impossibility will negatively affect all reflexive movements in general.

In order to prevent a too-hasty misunderstanding of Merleau-Ponty's critique of reflexivity, it will certainly not be out of place to underline the fact that this exhibition of the inability of reflection to engender a self-identity, does not imply a sacrifice of the intelligible universe of philosophical cogitata to the benefit of the irrational and the sensuous. It is absolutely necessary to realize that for Merleau-Ponty "the remarks we made concerning reflection were nowise intended to disqualify it for the profit of the unreflected or the immediate (which we know only through reflection). It is a question not of putting the perceptual faith in place of reflection, but on the contrary of taking into account the total situation, which involves reference from the one to the other."[24] No doubt, the movement of reflection remains inevitable: "in a sense it is imperative, it is truth itself, and one does not see how philosophy could dispense with it." Thus, if reflection is not only an unavoidable temptation, but also "a route that must be followed," the question becomes a different one. In light of the paradoxes constitutive of reflection, "the question is whether the universe of thought to which it leads is really an order that suffices itself and puts an end to every question." The question, consequently, aims at its presuppositions, "which in the end reveal themselves to be contrary to what inspires the reflection,"[25] in order to account for the total situation of reflection.

After having demonstrated how science and the philosophy of reflection remain tributary to perceptual faith, to the pre-reflexive openness upon the world which presupposes our participation in one and the same world, a world which in the case of philosophy coincides with the world of the spirit, Merleau-Ponty defines the philosophy of reflection as an attempt to *undo* the world in order to *remake* it.[26] This rebuilding of the world from "a center of things from which we proceed, but from which we were decentered," from a center that as *"a source of meaning"* is identical to the spirit, makes reflection a "coming back over the traces of a constitution." Yet, between this original constitution and the *après-coup* moment of reflection, between the movements of retraveling to the origin on a "route already traced out from that center to us," on a route that can only be used after one has already come back from the center, Merleau-Ponty discovers divergences so insurmountable as to impede all internal adequation. These divergences are, for Merleau-Ponty, of a temporal nature: "The movement of recovery, of recuperation, of return to self, the progression toward internal adequation, the very effort to coincide with a *naturans* which is already ourselves and which is supposed to unfold the things and the world before itself—precisely inasmuch as they are a return or a reconquest, these operations of reconstitution or of reestablishment which come second cannot by principle be the mirror image of its internal constitution and its establishment, as the route from the Etoile to the Notre-Dame is the inverse of the route from the Notre-Dame to the Etoile: the reflection recuperates everything except itself as an effort of recuperation, it clarifies everything except its own role." This left-over *(reste)* or blind spot of "the mind's eye"[27] that characterizes perceptual faith and consequently reflection, the massive "assurance that the things under my eyes remain the same while I approach them to better inspect them," and "according to which it is always *the same* thing I think when the gaze of attention is displaced and looks back from itself to what conditions it,"[28] coincides with the act of reflection itself. However, the temporal differences between the always belated movement of recovery and return, on the one hand, and, on the other hand, the originary constitution, their dissymmetry, forbid all contemporaneity of reflection with itself:

> The search for the conditions of possibility is in principle posterior to an actual experience, and from this it follows that even if subsequently one determines rigorously the *sine qua non* of that experience, it can never be washed of the original stain of having been discovered *post festum* nor ever become what positively founds that experience. This is why we must say not that it precedes the experience (even in the transcendental sense) but that it must be able to accompany it, that is, that it translates or expresses its essential character but does not indicate a prior possibility whence it would have issued. Never therefore will the philosophy of reflection be

able to install itself in the mind it discloses, whence to see the world as its correlative. Precisely because it is reflection, re-turn, re-conquest, or recovery, it cannot flatter itself that it would simply coincide with a constitutive principle already at work in the spectacle of the world, that, starting with this spectacle, it would travel the very route that the constitutive principle had followed in the opposite direction. But this is what it would have to do if it is really a *return,* that is, if its point of arrival were also the starting point.[29]

The aporia between the constitutive principle and reflection as a retrospective construction is nonexistent for the philosophy of reflection. Because it has nothing to say about this gap "since it is literally *nothing,*"[30] philosophy exempts itself from accounting for it, albeit, or precisely because, its foreclosure is constitutive of philosophy itself. Now, with Merleau-Ponty this *nothing,* this non-space of philosophy, literally becomes the space of *hyper-reflection. Hyper-reflection,* then, is that other "operation besides the conversion of reflection, more fundamental than it,"[31] that takes "the twofold problem of the genesis of the existent world and of the genesis of the idealization performed by reflection" seriously in order to account for the global situation. Therefore, *hyper-reflection,* by taking the paradoxes and contradictions of the reflexive conversion into account, becomes "not a superior degree at the ultimate level of philosophy, but philosophy itself."[32] As "another point of departure," *hyper-reflection* as "a philosophy of total reflection" assumes the task of not losing sight of the unsublatable antinomies of reflection as well as of the specific nature of the sides involved in this operation (these sides being brute perception and the transcendence of the world, on the one hand, and, on the other, the world of idealization) so as to be able to account for the total situation and for "the changes it introduces (itself) into the spectacle."[33]

In *The Visible and the Invisible* Merleau-Ponty distinguishes *hyper-reflection* from Hegelian dialectics. This happens in some remarkable pages where Merleau-Ponty shows why *hyper-reflection* is a "hyper-dialectics," that is to say, a "dialectics without synthesis."[34] Yet this *hyper-reflection,* which is fundamentally self-critical, which does not model itself after any historically given form of dialectics, which resists the temptation of being "stated in these, in univocal significations," and, thus, of becoming "what we call a *philosophy,*"[35] still longs for the rediscovery of "the being that lies before the cleavage operated by reflection."[36] The desire for such a pre-reflexive being keeps hyper-dialectics in the bonds of philosophy. It is not a philosophy, but, as Merleau-Ponty admitted, philosophy itself. Nonetheless, *hyper-reflection* came close to anticipating what is *strictly speaking* the no longer philosophical operation of deconstruction.

Merleau-Ponty's *hyper-reflection,* which phenomenology, weary of ruminating over intentionality, felt urged to develop, had already led, through its critique of the always retrospective and belated construction of reflection, to a reverie about the language of philosophy. In *Discours, figure,* Lyotard, while continuing this investigation of the language of philosophy, transforms Merleau-Ponty's reverie on language into a questioning of the language of dreams. Such a move becomes necessary if the linguistic conditions of reflexivity are to be explored. Remember that Merleau-Ponty had made reflexivity dependent on the opacity of the body and the transcendence or depth of the object suspended at the end of one's gaze. Now, since all reflexivity takes place in a language game, Lyotard can question discursive reflexivity in terms of what makes that play possible, that is to say in terms of the Saussurian notion of language *(langue)* as opposed to speech *(parole)*. But, it is precisely when trying to combine the negativity specific to speech and discourse (the spacing of referential transcendence, which, like the visual depth out of which the pictorial redoubling originates, makes reflection possible) with the negativity characteristic of language *(langue)* (its closed system of distinctive and differential features, which not only prohibits the transgression of the differences and the free play of the subject, but also forbids all reflection on that level) that Lyotard sees himself compelled to go beyond the distinction and, consequently, beyond linguistics altogether. Thus, taking up again Merleau-Ponty's idea of *hyper-reflection,* but reformulating it "in the shape of deconstruction,"[37] Lyotard posits a "third" negativity, which, however, is not the dialectical identity of the first two. This "third" negativity is the *figural,* which not unlike the death-drive silently constitutes both the reflexive discourse of speech as well as the nonreflexive system of language *(langue)* presupposed by all speech-acts as their condition of possibility. With this "third" negativity, deconstruction then seeks to account for the irruption of the extra-linguistic both into reflexive discourse and into its invariable system of differential traits. It is an operation that takes aim at elucidating the linguistic and nonlinguistic conditions of the possibility of reflection.

It is important here to remark that the negativity of the *figural* on which reflexivity appears to rest, a negativity that represents the limits of reflexivity, takes its most radical shape for Lyotard as poetry, as poetry, however, that assumes what Mallarmé called a critical function. This radical poetry, which is not identical with literature in general, is deconstructed language par excellence. It is deconstructed language because it is a language that, by delaying communication through the intervention of extra-linguistic procedures and by exhibiting *(faire voir)* the laboratory of the images causing the seductive power of poetry, accommodates what impedes its reflection by means of a "regressive flexion."[38]

The space of inscription of reflexivity that Lyotard calls the *figural* corresponds to what for Derrida is the text.

After having established how deconstruction with Merleau-Ponty and Lyotard takes the operation of reflection as its target not to destroy it, but to account for its antinomies, let me now consider the writings of Derrida. After Merleau-Ponty and Lyotard demonstrated how the mundane exteriority of the body on the one hand and the nonmundane exteriority of the figural on the other prevent all reflection from coinciding with itself, one could still dream the dream at the bottom of *all* of Western Philosophy of a pure reflection that would not have to rely on a nonproper mediator. This dream takes—in Husserl's phenomenology in particular and in philosophy in general—the shape of the idea of self-affection, of an auto-affection of the voice in the "medium of universal signification" that is the voice itself (*SP,* p. 79). This idea of self-affection is the matrix of all forms of self-reflexivity. Now, what Derrida's deconstruction has in view is precisely the undoing of the idea of self-affection and, consequently, of all forms of self-reflexivity.

Speech and Phenomena is a critical essay about Husserl's doctrine of signification, as developed in particular in the *Logical Investigations.* At first Derrida's critique of this theory comes close to resembling what one calls *immanent criticism.*[39] For instance, Derrida reproaches Husserl for insisting on the necessary absence of presuppositions while, in fact, constructing his theory of signification on the metaphysical presupposition par excellence: "the original self-giving evidence, the *present* or *presence* of sense to a full and primordial intuition" (*SP,* p. 5). In addition to this *implicit* contradiction, Derrida points out *explicit* contradictions. This kind of contradiction is either overtly admitted by Husserl himself or becomes visible through contradictory strata of description in Husserl's work. To give an example: one such stratum recognizes the idea of an originary presence while other strata cannot avoid linking presence to "an irreducible nonpresence as having a constitutive value" (*SP,* p. 6). Let me add to this inner turmoil and contestation of Husserl's philosophy from within the following critical move: by showing that Husserl privileges a certain region of language only, a region he raises to "the dignity of a telos, the purity of a norm, and the essence of a determination" by means of a simple *de facto* delineation "of the logical *a priori* within the general *a priori* of language" (*SP*, p. 9), Derrida not only pins down a contradiction between the philosophical necessity of foundation and a philosophy's discursive practice, but also specifies certain very precise *ethico-theoretical decisions* that are responsible for an actual discursive state of a particular philosophy, as well as of philosophy in general. It would not be very difficult to continue analyzing Derrida's critique of Husserl in terms of immanent criticism, though such a notion already becomes questionable since the survey of contradictions in Husserl's theory of signification is not undertaken with a view to establishing greater logical coherence in the discourse of philosophy, but in order to demonstrate that they are a function of the ethico-theoretical decisions constitutive of philosophy. But if this is so, then the contradictions Derrida has been pointing out are not simple contradictions but, on the contrary, *contradictions constitutive of philosophical discourse* in general, and of Husserl's philosophy in particular. They represent inevitable contradictions, contradictions which cannot be overcome, as long as the ethico-theoretical decisions they spring from privilege the idea of presence, the logicability of language, and so forth.

It is only after having emphasized the contradictions inherent in philosophical discourse from a position which, as could easily be shown, is not skepticism,[40] that the operation of deconstruction becomes possible, not to say imperative. In *Speech and Phenomena* it takes place in Chapter 4, entitled "Meaning and Representation."

Let me summarize as briefly as possible the argument of this chapter. Using several descriptions by Husserl concerning the nature of the sign and representation in general, descriptions which stem from different strata of Husserl's text, Derrida recalls that a sign as a necessarily ideal identity (ideal, because a sign must remain the *same* if it is to be repeated) always implies a threefold relation to representation: "as *Vorstellung,* the locus of ideality in general, as *Vergegenwärtigung,* the possibility of reproductive repetition in general, and as *Repräsentation,* insofar as each signifying event is a substitute (for the signified as well as for the ideal form of the signifier)" (*SP*, p. 50). Indeed, each effective discourse, that is, every discourse that uses signs and has, consequently, an indicative func-

tion must, in order to take place at all, set to work all these representative
modalities. However, Husserl, in his theory of signification, wants to
reserve the modality of *Vorstellung* (the locus of ideality in general) for
the inner discourse alone, for the soliloquy of the soul as a silent speech
independent of (even imagined) words, which is, according to Husserl,
a discourse of expression radically different from all effective and indicative discourse. Husserl needs the quality of *Vorstellung* conferring ideality
in general to be able to establish the purely representational and imaginary nature of the expressive inner voice. Yet, since Husserl has already
(in other strata of his text) implicitly attributed this particular modality
of representation to the sign in general, Derrida can rightly infer the
equally imaginary and expressive nature of the so-called effective or
indicative discourse. And, conversely, the discourse of represented communication which Husserl wants to be radically different from the discourse of real communication appears then to be as effective as the latter.
Consequently, a total blurring of the distinctions between expressive and
indicative signs, between representation and reality, takes place. Yet these
distinctions are essential to Husserl's whole enterprise, which consists of
trying to exclude all indication from expression so that the soliloquy of
the silent inner voice can achieve an unmediated and apodictically self-
evident presence to itself.

It has to be noted that the conflicts between the distinct strata of
Husserl's philosophical discourse do not represent a weakness of his philosophy. They cannot be ruled out through an attempt at greater logical
coherence.[41] They are functions of the ethico-theoretical decisions of
philosophy itself. Thus the question of why Husserl would sacrifice the
coherence of his discourse in order to be able to maintain his distinctions—an incoherence that coincides with the very coherence of philosophical discourse—and why "from the same premises . . . (he) refuse(s)
to draw these conclusions" (*SP,* p. 97), is to be answered by the "ethico-
theoretical act that revives the decision that founded philosophy in its
Platonic form" (*SP,* p. 53). This decision is the theme of full presence.
It is indeed "the obstinate desire to save presence and repetition," to
juggle away death and "to reduce or derive the sign" (*SP,* p. 51) which,
in the name of this *evidence* of philosophy (*SP,* p. 62), makes Husserl
maintain the differences between expression and indication, between
two kinds of signs, between representation and reality. Now, to suspect
that this very evidence of philosophy (the evidence being the privilege
of the present-now and everything it governs: sense and truth) gains its

life from an attempt at excluding the Other and death, becomes possible only "from a region that lies elsewhere than philosophy." Such an enterprise would represent "a procedure that would remove every possible *security* and *ground* from discourse," for such a security can be grounded only in the evidence of the idea of presence constitutive of philosophy as a whole.

Husserl, as remarked, tries to evacuate the sign from the living presence of the self-affecting voice. It is, indeed, an obstacle, a nonproper mediator to a pure act of self-affection. What Husserl tries is to reduce the sign's originality and originarity. This, then, becomes the precise moment when deconstruction occurs. Derrida writes:

> But there are two ways of eliminating the primordiality of the sign . . . Signs can be eliminated in the classical manner in a philosophy of intuition and presence. Such a philosophy eliminates signs by making them derivative; it annuls reproduction and representation by making signs a modification of a simple presence. But because it is just such a philosophy— which is, in fact, *the* philosophy and history of the West—which has so constituted and established the very concept of signs, the sign is from its very origin and to the core of its sense marked by this will to derivation or effacement. Thus to restore the original and nonderivative character of signs, in opposition to classical metaphysics, is, by an apparent paradox, at the same time to eliminate a concept of signs whose whole history and meaning belong to the adventure of the metaphysics of presence. (*SP*, p. 51)

A few lines later, Derrida notes that with such a restoration of a nonderivative notion of the sign, which simultaneously coincides with the elimination of its traditional concept, "a whole system of differences involved in language is implied in the same deconstruction" (*SP*, p. 52). What does such a deconstruction then consist of, what does it accomplish, and to what effect is it being carried out? Using the complex representative structure of the sign developed (by referring against Husserl's express intentions to various descriptions of this philosopher) to subvert the notion of an inner expressive discourse that Husserl wanted to be free of all indicative relation, Derrida reprivileges the hitherto derivative notion of the sign. This reprivileging, however, does not go without a total redefining of the notion of the sign itself. Two movements are thus characteristic of deconstruction: a *reversal* of the traditional hierarchy between conceptual oppositions (expression/indication, presence/sign) and a *reinscription* of the newly privileged term. What makes such an operation possible is the fact that all conceptual dyads constitutive of the discourse of philosophy constitute a "dissymmetric, hierarchially ordered space whose closure is transversed by the forces, and worked by the exteriority, that it represses" (*D*, p. 5). But the inferior and derivative term of these nonhomogenous oppositional spaces reprivileged through a reversal of the given hierarchy is not yet the deconstructed term. The newly reprivileged inferior term in the process of deconstruction is, as Derrida says, only the "negative" "and atheistic face (the insufficient but indispensable phase of the reversal)" (*D*, p. 54), "the negative image" of the "radical otherness" (*D*, p. 33). To pause at this negative face of the radical Otherness, at an interminable negative theology, and at a metaphysics of absence is to remain in the immanence of the dyad or system to be deconstructed. The deconstructed term, however, as a result of a reinscription of the negative image of absolute exteriority and Otherness, of what Derrida also names *displacement* or *intervention,* is no longer identical with the inferior term of the initial dyad. The deconstructed term indeed escapes "the specular nature of philosophical reflection, philosophy being incapable of inscribing (comprehending) what is outside it otherwise than through the appropriating assimilation of a negative image" (*D*, p. 33). Although it uses the same name as its negative image, the deconstructed term will never have been given in the conceptual opposition it deconstructs.

Hence, what does deconstruction accomplish? If the sign and its threefold structure of representation is privileged over presence and over the ideal expressive discourse of the silent inner voice, then the medium of presence, representation as *Vorstellung,* becomes dependent on the very possibility of the sign. In other words, ideality is not without the repetitive nature of the sign. Derrida writes: "We thus come—against Husserl's express intention—to make the *Vorstellung* itself, and as such, depend on the possibility of re-presentation *(Vergegenwärtigung).* The presence-of-the-present is derived from repetition and not the reverse" (*SP*, p. 52). The deconstructed term, the reinscription by elimination of the traditional notion of the sign (as derivative of presence), thus coincides with "the primordial structure of repetition" governing the structure of representation and, therefore, "all acts of signification" (*SP*, p. 57), plus those of indicative and expressive communication as well. Thus, "the primordial structure of repetition," "the possibility of repetition in its most general form," serves to account for[42] the *terms* of the initial conceptual dyad and for the *contradictions* and tensions that make the dyad a hierarchy. This primordial structure indeed functions as a sort of *deep structure* underlying the system of differences and oppositions, for which it is not to be mistaken.

Such a structure of originary repetition is "more 'primordial' than what is phenomenologically primordial" (*SP,* p. 67). Since, however, the notion of the primordial is necessarily linked to presence, this structure cannot be called primordial in the traditional sense. Moreover, it manifests a strange kind of temporality. Indeed, since the primordial structure of repetition derives the ideal from repetition, from that which until this point was thought to be derived from presence, it obeys what Derrida terms "the strange structure of the supplement . . .: by delayed reaction, a possibility produces that to which it is said to be added on" (*SP,* p. 89). Thus *accounting* for both presence and absence, the structure of originary repetition as a product of deconstruction represents "a meditation on non-presence—which is not perforce its contrary, or necessarily a meditation on a negative absence, or a theory of non-presence *qua* unconsciousness" (*SP,* p. 63).

Let me recapitulate: By analyzing the ethico-theoretical decision constitutive of philosophy—a decision in favor of the *presence* of the *present* to be achieved in the medium of a silent voice free of all signs and of all indication (and even of imagined words) that purely affect itself—Derrida shows that such an idea of presence has to rest on "the primordial structure of repetition," on a structure which makes something like presence both possible and impossible. Indeed, "without this non-self-identity of the presence called primordial," "how can it be explained that the possibility of reflection and re-presentation belongs by essence to every experience?" Without an originary trace, that is, "a bending-back of a return," and without "the movement of repetition" (*SP,* pp. 67–68) constitutive of the possibility and impossibility of self-affection, how could there even be (and not be) something like self-reflection?

Thus, deconstruction, in this precise case—the deconstructed term of "the primordial structure of repetition," or the trace—"is inconceivable if one begins on the basis of consciousness, that is, presence, or on the basis of its simple contrary, absence or nonconsciousness" (*SP,* p. 88). Or, put another way, deconstruction is an operation which accounts for and simultaneously undoes self-reflection.[43]

In *Speech and Phenomena* Derrida had already remarked that the difference constitutive of the self-presence of the living present reintroduces as a *trace* the impurity of spatial depth, that is to say, a non–identity into self-presence. This trace "is the intimate relation of the living present with its outside, the openness upon exteriority in general, upon the sphere of what is not 'one's own' " (*SP*, p. 86). Moreover, as the *spacing* of self-presence, this trace coincides with the origin of time. And, finally, because sense, as Husserl recognized, is always already engaged in the order of "signification," that is to say, in the "movement" of the trace, the trace is also in the shape of "protowriting *(archi-écriture)* . . . at work at the origin of sense" (*SP*, pp. 85–86).

The *primordial structure of the arche-trace* with its three functions is that which determines the scope and significance of deconstruction. This threefold structure simultaneously accounts for the possibility (and impossibility) of the self-presence of the present, of time, and of sense. Deconstruction aims at nothing less than producing such a primordial threefold structure that can account for the exteriority constitutive of three fundamental and interrelated topoi of Western Metaphysics: presence, time, and sense. Since Western Metaphysics conceives of these three concepts or ideas as generating themselves in a movement of unmediated auto-affection, the primordial structure of the arche-trace assumes the role of reinscribing them back into the nonreflexive and nonpresent exteriority of the absolute Other of the arche-trace. Indeed, philosophy, already against its will and unknown to it, could never avoid linking presence and self-reflexivity to an irreducible non–presence which has a constitutive value. In order to show how the arche-trace with its three-fold structure assumes this function of both engendering and reinscribing presence, time, and sense, let me now turn to analyzing the "theoretical matrix" outlined in the first part of *Of Grammatology.*

Of Grammatology examines the possibility of a "science" of writing in a historical epoch that, first, determines as language the totality of its problematic horizon, while already pointing at the limits of that horizon, that is to say, at its Other, at writing. It is thus an epoch in which, second, science as *episteme,* while still determined by the idea of *logos* as *phone* and presence, paradoxically opens itself more and more to nonphonetic forms of writing. Third, this epoch, moreover, is characterized by a challenge to the traditional idea of the book as something that refers to a natural totality by what is profoundly alien to it: writing and the text. These are for Derrida the signs through which the *Other* of science as *episteme,* of language and of the book as a natural totality, empirically comes into manifestation—*empirically,* that is to say, through an effect of specular reflection still inscribed in philosophy. As the negative image only of a radical Otherness, writing and the text are what *can appear* and become visible of this invisible radical Otherness. And *as such,* that is, as text and writing, this Otherness will remain the object of a phenomenology, of a phenomenology of writing, for instance. A grammatology, however, would reach out for that radical Otherness beyond writing and the text, which are nothing but the negative faces under which it can appear, that is to say, become present *as such.* Indeed, in *Of Grammatology,* Derrida clearly stresses that what grammatology (a "science" that while rein-scribing all the concepts on which sciences rest can no longer be called a science) designates as trace or arche-trace "will never be merged with a phenomenology of writing" (*OG,* p. 68).

Thus, after the deconstruction of the conceptual dyad of presence and the sign in *Speech and Phenomena, Of Grammatology* deconstructs the opposition between speech and writing. But before dealing with this deconstruction itself, it is imperative to consider its preliminaries.

Deconstruction does not operate from an empirically present outside of philosophy since that outside is only the outside *of* philosophy. Decon-struction does not proceed from a phenomenologically existing exteri-ority (like literature, for instance) that would claim to represent the truth of philosophy, because that truth is only the truth *of* philosophy itself. In order to undermine the heritage to which concepts belong, *all* the inher-ited concepts have, on the contrary, to be mobilized. They are all indis-pensable. Here is what Derrida says:

> The movements of deconstruction do not destroy structures from the out-side. They are not possible and effective, nor can they take accurate aim, except by inhabiting those structures. Inhabiting them in a *certain way,* because one always inhabits, and all the more when one does not suspect it. Operating necessarily from the inside, borrowing them structurally, that is to say without being able to isolate their elements and atoms. (*OG,* p. 24)

Consequently to prevent the danger of a regression, before decon-structing one has "at first . . . [to demonstrate] the systematic and his-torical solidarity of the concepts and gestures of thought that one often believes can be innocently separated" (*OG,* pp. 13–14). It is, of course, impossible here to describe exhaustively, as does *Of Grammatology,* the field of forces constituting the conceptual dyad of speech and writing. Let me then only recall that the privilege of speech over writing in Western Metaphysics is founded on the idea that speech as logos is the logos of Being. What makes speech in the Western tradition the medium par excellence of Being (as logos) is the "fact" that in a language of words "the voice *is heard* . . . closest to the self as the absolute effacement of the signifier: pure auto-affection that necessarily has the form of time and which does not borrow from outside itself, in the world or in 'reality,' any accessory signifier, any substance of expression foreign to its own spontaneity. It is the unique experience of the signified producing itself spontaneously, from within the self, and nevertheless, as signified concept, in the element of ideality or universality. The unworldly character of this substance of expression is constitutive of this ideality" (*OG,* p. 20). Compared with speech as *phone,* with this self-effacing signifier that raises the voice to the universal medium of signification, all other signifiers necessarily appear as being exterior, non-proper, sensible, and derivative. Writing, moreover, being understood as the graphic signifier of the verbal signifier that signifies the signified (that, in the last instance, is always what Derrida calls the transcendental signified), is doubly exterior to the sense. It has solely a technical and representative function. Compared with the self-affecting logos in self-effacing speech, with a signification, consequently, that takes place without any obstructing and obscuring signifier, all sensible signs, and writing in particular, are necessarily inferior and secondary. This is the relation between speech and writing in the discourse of philosophy from Plato[44] to Husserl. There are only a few exceptions where the hierarchy is reversed, as in the case of the Leibnitzian characteristic violently criticized by Hegel.

The deconstruction of this opposition takes place in the second chapter (entitled "Linguistics and Grammatology") of Part One of *Of Grammatology.* It is preceded by a critique of linguistics for deriving its claim to scientificity from its *phonological* foundations, thus for reiterating the classical opposition between speech and writing to the benefit of the articulated unities "of sound and sense within the phonie" (*OG,* p. 29). Therefore, it is only by overthrowing linguistics that it becomes possible to develop a "science" such as grammatology. Yet, as Derrida points out, this overthrow is already being carried out by linguistics itself. After a meticulous analysis of Saussure's attempt to exorcise writing at the moment he promotes linguistics—"the modern science of the logos" (*OG,* p. 34)—to scientific heights, Derrida writes: "It is when he is not expressly dealing with writing, when he feels he has closed the parentheses on that subject, that Saussure opens the field of a general gram-

matology which would not only no longer be excluded from general
linguistics, but would dominate it and contain it . . . Then something
which was never spoken and which is nothing other than writing itself
as the origin of language writes itself within Saussure's discourse" (*OG*,
pp. 43–44). With this the traditional opposition of speech and writing
ceases to be clear–cut. It becomes blurred in Saussure's writing. Thus,
when he asserts that the inner system of language is independent of the
phonic character of the linguistic sign, it becomes apparent "why the
violence of writing does not *befall* an innocent language" (*OG*, p. 37).
Indeed, how could writing represent speech without an originary violence already at work in speech itself? But it is especially Saussure's
famous thesis of the arbitrariness of the sign that completely blurs the
traditional opposition of speech and writing. Saussure excluded writing
from language and chased it to its outer fringes because he considered it
to be only an exterior reflection of the reality of language, that is, nothing
but an image, a representation or a figuration. The thesis of arbitrariness,
according to Derrida, "successfully accounts for a conventional relationship between the phoneme and the grapheme . . . [and] by the same
token it forbids that the latter be an 'image' of the former" (*OG*, p. 45).
But without a natural relation between speech and writing (as is true of
the symbol, which, for that reason, is excluded from linguistics), writing
cannot be chased from speech.

This blurring of the distinctions of the conceptual dyad, speech and
writing, a blurring brought about by a play on the incompatible strata of
Saussure's *Course,* leads then to the operation of deconstruction. It reads
as follows:

> Now we must think that writing is at the same time more exterior to
> speech, not being its "image" or its "symbol," and more interior to speech,
> which is already in itself a writing. Even before it is linked to incision,
> engraving, drawing, or the letter, to a signifier referring in general to a
> signifier signified by it, the concept of the graphie . . . implies the frame-
> work [instance] of the instituted trace, as the possibility common to all
> systems of signification. (*OG*, p. 46)

Implicitly, Derrida has reversed the hierarchy and *displaced* the newly
privileged term: writing. This displacement and reinscription rests on the
notion of the *instituted trace.* Since writing coincides in this context with
the concept of the trace or, more precisely, the arche-trace, it will be
necessary to distinguish what this concept implies in order to understand
what this deconstruction is able to account for.

First, it has to be remarked that the deconstructed term—the *instituted trace*—entails a detachment of "these two concepts from the classical discourse, from which they obviously are borrowed" (*OG*, p. 46). Generally speaking, a trace represents a *present* mark of an *absent* (presence). But this is not what the *instituted* trace or the arche-trace is about. The notion of an institution, by contrast, refers in general to a cultural and historical instauration. The trace, in its colloquial sense, is instituted this way, but not the *instituted trace*. What then is the arche-trace or the *instituted trace* if it is neither a trace in the colloquial sense nor simply instituted? The arche-trace, on the contrary, is the movement which produces the difference of absence and presence constitutive of the colloquial sense of trace as well as the difference of nature and culture constitutive of the idea of institution. To understand this, let us unravel the major functions of the *instituted trace*. Derrida writes: "The general structure of the unmotivated trace connects within the same possibility, and they cannot be separated except by abstraction, the structure of the relationship with the other, the moment of temporalization, and language as writing" (*OG*, p. 47). At the risk of oversimplifying, it is nevertheless necessary to separate these *three* possibilities characterizing the general structure of the *instituted trace* (or arche-trace, or arche-writing).

1. The arche-trace as the origin of all relation to an Other

The arche-trace is "the irreducible absence" (that is, an absence that is not the absence of a presence) or "the completely other" that announces itself *as such* within all structures of reference as the present (mark or trace) of an *absent* (presence). This manifestation of the absolute Other as such (that is to say, its appearing within what is not it, its becoming present, tangible, visible), consequently, coincides with its occultation. "When the other announces itself as such, it presents itself in the dissimulation of itself" (*OG*, p. 47). What becomes present of the absolute Other, through "the dissimulation of its 'as such' " (*OG*, p. 47), is but a *present* mark that retains it as Other in the same and refers to it as an *absence*. Thus, the arche-trace, actively manifesting itself as such in the dissimulation of itself, engenders the *difference* of sign and referent, of presence and absence. It opens up the possibility of all relation to an Other, of all relation to an exteriority, in short, the structure of reference in general. If this constitution, through announcing and dissimulation, can be viewed as an *active* synthesis, the fact that the *absence* of the irreducible Other is constitutive of the *presence* in which it appears as such makes it equally a *passive* synthesis.

To conclude: the empirical trace or mark "where the relation with the other is marked" (*OG,* p. 47), or the sign which always stands for an absent presence, depends on (and becomes possible only through) the arche-trace as "the completely other" that precedes all particular relations to an Other.

2. *The arche-trace as the origin of temporality*

As the origin of the experience of space and time, the fabric of the arche-trace "permits the difference between space and time to be artic-ulated, to appear as such, in the unity of an experience" (*OG,* pp. 65–66). The arche-trace as "an absolute past" (a past that is not a past presence or a present-past), as an irreducible "always-already-there," also opens up "the difference between the sensory appearing *(apparaissant)* and its lived appearing *(apparaître),"* between appearance and appearing (*OG,* p. 66). In other words: the absolute past announcing itself as such through its own occultation appears as *time.* The "*dead time* within the presence of the living present, within the general form of all presence" (*OG,* p. 68), within the sensory appearing of time without which no such appearing is possible, however, is *space* as the lived appearing of time. Indeed, without spacing, no such experience as time, as the presence of the present, is conceivable.[45]

Consequently, this spacing of time (passive synthesis) and this appearing *as such* of the absolute past as time (active synthesis) accounts for the origin of temporalization (of time *and* space). For Saussure this means that the arche-trace represents the possibility of signification, which is always dependent on articulation.

3. *The arche-trace as the origin of language and sense*

While trying to define the order of language (langue) in its independ-ence from the phonic nature of language, Saussure compares this inner system of language to writing. Speech "draws from this stock of writing, noted or not, that language is" (*OG,* p. 53). But "before being or not being 'noted,' 'represented,' 'figured,' in a *'graphie,'* the linguistic sign implies an originary writing" (*OG,* p. 53). Yet how is language, on the one hand, and notation, on the other, founded on the general possibility of the arche-trace as arche-writing?

The originary writing or the arche-trace is not to be mistaken for writing in the narrow sense as it appears in the given opposition of speech and writing. Neither is it to be identified with the stock of writing from which speech draws its possibility. The arche-trace or arche-writing is the condition of possibility of these differences. Arche-writing, which

unlike speech and writing in the colloquial sense has no sensible existence,[46] by announcing itself *as such,* thus by simultaneously dissimulating
itself, engenders *speech* as haunted by what it is not: the system of differences that Saussure compared to *writing.* This active synthesis of speech
and writing (in a truly phenomenological sense) by the very movement
of the arche-trace does not exclude a passive synthesis as well.

Indeed, through what Derrida calls "the being-imprinted of the
imprint," which differs from the imprint as much as the being-heard of
speech is different from the sound-heard, the arche-trace is passively
constitutive of speech. Derrida develops this passive synthesis of speech
when reflecting on Saussure's reduction—a reduction not unlike a phenomenological reduction—constitutive of the very object of structural
linguistics: the object of structural linguistics, actually, is not the real
material and physical sound, the sound-heard, but its acoustic image, the
being-heard of the sound.[47] Defending Saussure's notion of "psychic
image" against Jakobson's objection of mentalism, and preserving the
Husserlian distinction "between the appearing sound and the appearing
of the sound in order to escape the worst and the most prevalent confusions," Derrida stresses that Saussure's linguistics, whose object is the
internal system of language, that is to say, a system independent of the
phonic nature of language, is not to be mistaken for "a mundane science
. . . [for] a psycho-physic-phonetics." On the contrary, this investigation
into the non-mundane region of the "psychic image" (an image that is
not another natural reality) and into the being-heard of the sound leads
to a definition of the *form* of language as a system of differences constitutive of each particular speech-act. Yet this specific space of differential
features passively constituting speech *"is already a trace"* (*OG,* pp. 64–65).
For this system of differences is only the negative face, the face through
which the arche-trace appears as one term of an opposition that it engenders as a whole.

It having been shown how the arche-trace (or the instituted trace, arche-
writing, or differance) as an "irreducible arche-synthesis [opens] in one
and the same possibility, temporalization as well as relationship with the
other and language" (*OG,* p. 60), it becomes possible to present a necessarily provisional and reductive draft of the theoretical matrix of deconstruction (see the table on page 48). On its horizontal axis, this matrix
displays the arche-trace's active and passive synthesis of presence, time,
and speech (while all three, traditionally, are thought to engender

The Theoretical Matrix of Deconstruction

ARCHE-TRACE			as the condition of possibility of metaphysical dyads			
as originary synthesis	the origin of all relation to the OTHER	Active	manifests itself *as such* as	PRESENCE	of an	ABSENCE
		Passive	is, as	ABSENCE	constitutive of	PRESENCE
	the origin of TEMPORALITY	Active	manifests itself as the experience of	TIME	through the dead time of	SPACE
		Passive	is, as	SPACE	constitutive of	TIME
	the origin of LANGUAGE	Active	manifests itself *as such* as	SPEECH	as a priori	WRITTEN
		Passive	is, as	WRITING	the form of	SPEECH

themselves through auto-affection and self-reflection) as well as of their canonical derivatives: absence, space, and writing. The vertical axis of this matrix inscribes the structural possibilities simultaneously realized by the arche-trace. The matrix is consequently a layout of the various levels simultaneously to be observed in a deconstruction. Yet, since for didactic reasons this originary synthesis had to be broken down in its successive moments so as to clarify the scope of deconstruction, its matrix is also an inadmissible simplification. The notion of the arche-trace (and all of its nonsynonymical substitutions: arche-writing, differance, and so forth) refers to an order which resists (and *accounts for*) the founding conceptual oppositions of philosophy. Thus, most of the concepts used to describe the movement of the arche-trace are inappropriate. Originary constitution, active and passive synthesis, genetic and structural production are still terms that belong to metaphysics in general and to transcendental phenomenology in particular. Consequently, using them to account for a constitution of presence, time, and language—a constitution that reveals the self-referential term present in the dyad not only to represent *as such* its absolute Other, but also to necessarily depend on the negative image of that Other—can only be strategic. Actually, this synthesis is neither passive nor active; it is a "middle voice that expresses a certain intransitiveness" (*SP,* p. 93) and that remains undecided. For the same reason, the notion of structure is to be rejected, as well as its opposite (the genetic point of view).

Although deconstruction investigates the conditions of possibility of the *conceptual systems* of philosophy, it is to be mistaken neither for a quest for the transcendental conditions of possibility of knowledge (Kant) nor for a new version of Husserl's transcendental philosophy.[48] Since the transcendental question in Derrida represents at first a precaution against falling back into a naive objectivism, or an even worse empiricism, it is a strategic question. Regarding the notion of the arche-trace, Derrida writes:

> The trace is not only the disappearance of origin—within the discourse that we sustain and according to the path that we follow it means that the origin did not even disappear, that it was never constituted except recip-rocally by a nonorigin, the trace, which thus becomes the origin of the origin. From then on, to wrench the concept of the trace from the classical scheme, which would derive it from an originary nontrace and which would make of it an empirical mark, one must indeed speak of an originary trace or arche-trace. Yet we know that the concept destroys its name and that, if all begins with the trace, there is above all no originary trace. We must then *situate,* as a simple *moment of the discourse,* the phenomenological reduction and the Husserlian reference to a transcendental experience. (*OG,* p. 61)

These remarks having been made, a few of deconstruction's prerequisites and prior conditions can finally be underlined. If deconstruction and the production of a particular deconstructed term such as the arche-trace, a notion that comes to account for a series of interrelated metaphysical pairs of oppositions, cannot simply be reduced to the questions of tran-scendental phenomenology, neither can they be said simply to have broken with these questions. Deconstruction, consequently, presupposes the scholarly knowledge of transcendental phenomenology in order to distinguish and not "confuse very different levels, paths and styles" (*OG*, p. 62). It is imperative to be able to rigorously separate what in deconstruction corresponds to the regions of natural experience and what to the transcendental experience in order to understand how this operation leads to the production of an irreducible nonphenomenal that can no longer be explained in terms of a phenomenological reduction and a transcendental phenomenology. In the final analysis, deconstruction is an operation that accounts for the conceptual difference between factual or regional experience and transcendental experience.[49] It is precisely from paying little or no attention to these distinctions that notions like trace, writing, supplement, and so on, could as easily find their way into a regional science such as literary criticism, where they could serve to denote either existing and apprehensible marks or, at best, what Husserl would call *reell* (as opposed to *real* and *ideal*) traits characterizing differential systems and the phenomenological notion of writing.

This leads then to another problem. The matrix of deconstruction shows how the arche-trace through an active and passive synthesis engenders presence, time, and speech on the one hand, and on the other, absence, space, and writing. Consequently, showing how time, speech, and presence (or, the word, the logos, God) are always already broached and contaminated by their Other is not yet deconstruction. Such an operation does not lead a single step outside metaphysics. It is, as Derrida says, "nothing more than a new motif of 'return to finitude,' of 'God's death' " and so forth, and consequently is nothing more than negative theology, negative dialectics, and negative specularity (*OG*, p. 68). Deconstruction begins only where the difference of a term such as presence, for instance, and its other, absence, is accounted for from an absolute Other. Or, to put it differently, deconstruction begins when a concept that designates a real, empirically apprehensible experience and the concept of its "ideal" and phenomenal opposite that vouches for a transcendental experience are explained by means of an irreducible nonphenomenal structure that accounts for the difference under examination.

A further confusion also stems from an insensivity to philosophical distinctions. It concerns the "status" of the deconstructed term. The spacing as well as the order of the differential traits represents the origin of signification (of language and of sense, in general). Yet, in spite of their general invisibility and nonpresence they are still phenomenal and represent only the negative image of the absolute Other. Thus pointing

out blanks, pauses, punctuations, intervals, and so on, that is to say, neg-
atives without which there is no signification, or in short, establishing
the textuality of a discourse, is not yet deconstruction. Deconstruction
aims at something that can never become present "as such," and that
without concealing itself can only appear *as such*. The *text* as a deconstructed term will never be identical to the visual features of the black-
on-blacks[50] or to the generally unperceived (but structurally present)
intervals and differences that form signification.[51]

This brings us back to Lyotard's use of the notion of deconstruction.
Since *Discours, figure* demonstrates at least two different kinds of deconstruction, the question that appears in what I have developed up to this
point is this: How is this double deconstruction possible, and how are
these two notions interrelated? The first notion of deconstruction is
silently at work in Lyotard's book and coincides with the *stricto sensu*
definition elaborated here. This deconstruction leads to the development, through its various substitutions and levels of the concept, of the
figural as difference. But at the same time, this notion serves as a framework for another use of deconstruction that designates the irruption of
the extra- or nonlinguistic—of the figural—into the differential and
structural order of discourse. Since, however, the figural deconstructs the
linguistic order according to three possible articulations of the figural, it
becomes necessary to distinguish as many as three different kinds of *transgressive deconstructions:* (1) the *figure-image,* which deconstructs "the con-
tour of the silhouette," or the outline of the image; (2) the *figure-form,*
which transgresses the unified form and is "indifferent to the unity of
the whole"; and (3) the *figure-matrix,* which deconstructs the very space
of the phantasmatic matrix and which is "a space that simultaneously
belongs to the space of the text, to the space of the scenario and of the
theatrical scene: writing, geometry, representation, all being deconstructed by their mutual mingling." Lyotard, consequently, calls the last
form of the figural "difference itself."[52] Now, none of these particular
transgressive deconstructions, relative to the particular level of intervention of the figural, can claim priority over the others:

> In each case the presence of the figural is negatively indicated by disorder.
> Yet there is no privileged disorder. One cannot ascertain that the decon-
> struction of a space of figurative representation is less provocative than that
> of "good" abstract forms. The critical force of a work of art derives much
> more from the nature of the deviation *(écart)* on which it rests than of the

level (of figures, here) on which it brings the effects of this deviation to bear.[53]

If the fact that a particular deconstruction reaches "deeper strata of the generation of discourse"[54] cannot hold as a pretext for privileging such a deconstruction, and if, moreover, the very presence of nondiscursive instances in discourse is not yet sufficient to "make the other scene present," then this implies that deconstruction—as we understand it at this point, as a transgression of linguistic discourse, a transgression that, as a regression, affirms what language negates—is linked to the "logic" of desire.

Before continuing, it is important to remark that the denegation *(Verneinung)* that founds language and its deconstruction by an affirmative recess are not symmetrical. One has to be attentive, says Lyotard, to "the impression of a return produced by the prefix re- which clearly indicates that going back and having gone for the first time are not the same since in the meantime one had to come back."[55] This asymmetry and non-specularity of the two movements that give birth to critical poetry derive from the unfulfillment of desire in poetic language. Indeed, if the work of art is said to originate in the phantasmatic matrix that produces images and forms, it also has to represent the nonfulfillment *(inaccomplissement)* of that same matrix, for otherwise the work of art would remain a clinical symptom. Phantasms elaborate scenarios for the sole purpose of fulfilling the desire. For that reason a transgression of the linguistic space by phantasms will remain caught in the form this transgression takes. Yet this form, since it is the form of the phantasm, is also, as a necessarily bad form, "the at least potential *transgression of the form.*"[56] It is the death-drive as a re-gressive compulsion that in the work of art comes to prevent the form of deconstructive regression from becoming an identity and a unity mirroring the good form of communicative language. The deconstructive recess, by transgressing its own form, thus prevents the desire from fixing and fulfilling itself in a particular scenerio. In this way, desire is prompted into becoming a critical instance and thereby achieves the dissymmetry of the deconstructive recess and the order of language that it transgresses.

Poetic language then—a language where desire remains unfulfilled, alive, where the constitutive and destitutive moments do not mirror or reflect each other—is, so to speak, a "superficial" or "surface" *scene* of deseizure and dispropriation *(désaisissement)* of both phantasms and the order of language. But because poetic language, as Lyotard understands it, represents a language that under the impact of the death-drive restores difference and dissymmetry by hampering desire's fulfillment, and that undermines the philosophical and pathological specularity and reflexivity in a work of art, it therefore shows the figural at work as difference. Hence, two remarks, at least:

1. With the idea of the nonfulfillment of deconstructive transgression, Lyotard makes all particular transgressions of the linguistic order work at the production of the figural as difference and, thus, circles back to a *stricto sensu* definition of deconstruction. Only if a transgression is prevented from becoming the fulfillment of a desire, and consequently the negative specular image of what is transgressed, can one start speaking of deconstruction.

2. If poetic language as critical language represents a sort of "surface" scene (and not a *structure,* for Lyotard, from his premises, has to reject that term) where the reflexive opposition is transformed into heterogeneous difference, then it is to be understood as the scene whence all the particular and necessarily symptomatic transgressions of the differential order of language can be accounted for. It represents a scene which as soon as one turns one's back to it[57] gives birth to critical theory and theoretical discourse in general with its understanding of literariness as self-reflexivity.

Undoubtedly a theory that identifies deconstruction with self-reflexivity was, and to some extent still is, in the present state of critical consciousness, a better instrument for freeing the mind of traditional approaches than what necessarily would be understood as an out-and-out nihilism likely to paralyze the mental faculties of almost everyone. If, however, such an approach reveals its philosophical implications by straining the notion of self-reflexivity, the confusion between self-reflexivity and deconstruction can become fruitful. Indeed, a rigorous application of the idea of self-reflexivity leads to the elevation of thought *(Erhebung des Gedankens)* and the work of the concept *(Arbeit des Begriff)* that deconstruction measures swords with. It is thus not surprising that Paul de Man, who in his early work equates deconstruction with the self-reflexivity of the text, not only keeps identifying deconstruction with the generally more American methodology of self-reflexivity, but also abstains—with some irony, no doubt—from calling his more recent readings deconstructive.

In this context, de Man's discussion of Derrida's interpretation of

Rousseau in *Of Grammatology* is of particular interest. In "The Rhetoric of Blindness: Jacques Derrida's Reading of Rousseau," de Man recognizes that "Derrida's work is one of the places where the future possibility of literary criticism is being decided."[58] Yet, to become fruitful to literary criticism, Derrida's work has first to be submitted to a critique by literary criticism itself. This is why "The Rhetoric of Blindness" reproaches Derrida's reading of Rousseau—a reading that leads to the development of the notion of "a structure of supplementarity" that has to account for the numerous "contradictions" of Rousseau's discourse, which de Man neglects to mention in his review—as being nothing but "Derrida's story of Rousseau."[59] This story is a bad story opposed to the good story of Rousseau. But why is Derrida's story a bad one? In the process of determining Rousseau's place in the history of Western thought, Derrida is said to "substitute Rousseau's interpreters for the author himself," and thus while "the established tradition of Rousseau criticism . . . stands in dire need of deconstruction . . . instead of having Rousseau deconstruct his critics, we have Derrida deconstructing a pseudo-Rousseau by means of insights that could have been gained from the 'real' Rousseau." But this distinction between the good and the bad story must be dependent on de Man's own story, which reads as follows: "there is no need to deconstruct Rousseau" himself. De Man's story is indeed a function of his understanding of deconstruction as supplying the reflexive moment to the inevitable blindness of critical texts, as well as of his notion of literariness as the text's self-reflexivity. For, being a literary text, Rousseau's "text has no blind spots: it accounts at all moments for its own theoretical mode."[60] In an attempt to bypass the deceitful academic distinction between an author's consciousness and unconsciousness, de Man, indeed, attributes a self-awareness and a self-control to literary language itself. Of Rousseau's language, he writes: "The key to the status of Rousseau's language . . . can only be found in the knowledge that this language, as language, conveys about itself, thereby asserting the priority of the category of language over that of presence—which is precisely Derrida's thesis."[61] Deconstruction as self-reflection would consequently be grounded in the self-consciousness of the text. Self-consciousness, however, is only the modern mode of presence being understood as subjectivity. Indeed, de Man attributes a series of cognitive functions to the text: "The text . . . accounts for its own mode of writing, it states at the same time the necessity of making this statement itself in an indirect, figural way that knows it will be misunderstood by being taken literally.

Accounting for the 'rhetoricity' of its own mode, the text also postulates the necessity of its own misreading. It knows and asserts that it will be misunderstood." If de Man calls " 'literary,' in the full sense of the term, any text that implicitly or explicitly signifies its own rhetorical mode and prefigures its own misunderstanding as the correlative of its rhetorical nature, that is, of its 'rhetoricity,' " then literariness, writing, and the text are understood according to the model of a conscious subjectivity, that is, of a self-reflexive presence.[62] Consequently, it comes as a surprise when de Man still claims that it is precisely this self-reflexivity of the literary text[63] that preserves it from metaphysics: "Rousseau escapes from the logocentric fallacy precisely to the extent that his language *is literary*."[64] Thus, deconstruction and self-reflexivity are for de Man the same. Such a conclusion becomes inevitable when literariness, textuality, and writing are being thought in terms of self-consciousness. But *writing,* a notion which has, as the result of a deconstruction, an irreducible nonphenomenal meaning, deconstructs and disrupts all reflexivity. Derrida writes:

> Constituting and dislocating it at the same time, writing is other than the subject, in whatever sense the latter is understood. Writing can never be thought under the category of the subject; however it is modified, however it is endowed with consciousness or unconsciousness, it will refer, by the entire thread of its history, to the substantiality of a presence unperturbed by accidents, or to the identity of the selfsame *(propre)* in the presence of self-relationship. (*OG,* pp. 68–69)

If deconstruction has been developed by Derrida (and Lyotard, as well) to account for the contradictions inherent in the conversion of reflection, it is precisely because deconstruction and self-reflection are not identical. Moreover, the ideas of self-reflection, specularity, self-referentiality, and so on, are essentially metaphysical and belong to logocentrism. Deconstruction, in contrast, by showing how the two asymmetrical moments of self-reflection are engendered by either a "deep" *structure* or a "surface" *scene,* opens a breach in the ideological closure of self-reflection.

In "Rhetoric of Persuasion (Nietzsche)," de Man further develops his understanding of the self-reflexivity of the text and, consequently, of literariness. As had already been suggested in *Blindness and Insight,* the text's self-deconstructing movement is here said to rest essentially on its tropological level. In this manner, de Man distinguishes a variety of deconstructions based on the metaphor, the metonymy, the synecdoche, the metalepsis, and so forth. At close sight all these particular deconstructions appear either to be operations of immanent criticism or to reveal the ways in which a text refers to itself. They relate propositions of the text to their implicit presuppositions, they indicate the necessity of all discourse to criticize itself in the language of what it criticizes, and so on. Yet, of these different operations which were shown above to precede deconstruction properly speaking, de Man says that they represent "moments in the deconstructive process" by means of which the "rhetoric becomes the ground for the furthest-reaching dialectical speculations conceivable to the mind."[65] Is the presupposed autonomy and self-reflexivity of the text, its literariness as well, related to the life and self-becoming of the Hegelian concept *(Begriff)?* As the following passage proves, de Man's notion of literature derives only negatively from Hegel's dialectics and is conceived on the model of negative dialectics:[66] "a text . . . allows for two incompatible, mutually self-destructive points of view."[67] This negative specularity, which undoubtedly corresponds to certain reflexive strata of the text, does not account for the global situation of a text. Already, in "Action and Identity in Nietzsche," de Man had allowed for a speculation about the whole of the text that is not identical to its (reflexive) totality, when he wrote: "Moreover, the reversal from denial to assertion implicit in deconstructive discourse never reaches the symmetrical counterpart of what it denies . . . The negative thrust of the deconstruction remains unimpaired; after Nietzsche (and indeed, after any 'text'), we can no longer hope ever 'to know' in peace."[68] Paradoxically, it is de Man's unflagging investigation into tropology and rhetorics that undermines the possibility of knowledge by putting into question the metaphysical integrity of the text as constituted by cognitive rhetorics. Consider, for instance, "Excuses *(Confessions),*" where de Man undertakes a "deconstruction of the figural dimension" of the text, that is, of its cognitive tropes, its reflexive metaphors that stand for the totality of the text and produce the illusion of "specular symmetry." This deconstruction, which "is a process that takes place independently of any desire," which is "not unconscious but mechanical, systematic in its performance but arbitrary in its principle, like a grammar," opens up what de Man terms "the absolute randomness of language, prior to any figuration or meaning."[69] This prefigurative dimension of the text—its limit as de Man shows in his reading of Shelley's *Triumph of Life*[70]—"never allowed to exist as such," where language or fiction "stands free of any signification," this moment of its *positing* becomes tangible through a figure such as the anacoluthon or the parabasis.[71] Both reveal disruptions and sudden discontinuities between codes. As such, this dimension of the prefigural is akin to the performative rhetoric of a text, which the cognitive rhetoric can never hope to dominate. Indeed, the process of the text's own production figures in the text only as a disruption of the cognitive rhetoric's attempt to account for it through reflection. It is precisely this dissymmetry, "this disjunction of the performative from the cognitive,"[72] which, in "Excuses *(Confessions),*" vouches for a practice of decontruction which no longer rests on the idea of the text's self-reflexivity. De Man, despite the weight of the philosophical tradition that stands behind this notion, calls this practice irony.

While in "Excuses *(Confessions)*" he accounts for the inability of cognitive rhetoric to exhaust and dominate the text's performative function (in which cognitive rhetoric, moreover, appears to be inscribed), in "The Epistemology of Metaphor" de Man undertakes a deconstruction of the metaphor of the subject as the totalizing instance of the text. De Man here shows that the impossibility of controlling tropes, an impossibility due to an "asymmetry of the binary model that opposes the figural to the proper meaning of the figure,"[73] implies an inextricable entanglement of the self-reflecting subject with a narrative. The subject, as well as his cognitive function in the text, is, consequently, neither outside the signifier's play nor outside the *positing* of the text. This, of course, calls then for a concept of text that goes beyond its narrowly regional conception and its reduction to a self-reflexive and self-deconstructive totality.

Yet, such a notion of the text, as well as the *literally* deconstructive practice it presupposes, proceeds from the border of the text. This outside of the text, an outside that does not coincide with naive empirical or objective reality and whose exclusion does not necessarily imply the postulate of an ideal immanence of the text or the incessant reconstitution of a self-referentiality of writing (*D,* p. 35), is in fact *inside* the text and is what limits the text's abysmal specularity. This infinite, as well as the finitude of the text's signification, finds its limits in the non-reflexive margins of the text.

2

The Law of Tradition

ONE WAY OF CELEBRATING deconstructive thought is especially delusive: aggrandizing its achievement debilitates it; idealizing its operations flattens it and renders it indifferent. Such ambivalent celebration takes place when Derrida's thought is said to be radical and dissident to such a degree that all attempts to situate it in, or with respect to, the history of philosophical thought would amount to defusing its alterity and explosive potential. Although Derrida himself might occasionally have encouraged the historical contextualization of his own enterprise, those who find him "interesting" on the condition that his work is ever so singular—in total defiance of classical philosophical thought—would argue against him that the general thrust of his work does not warrant such an approach. To localize Derrida within the history of philosophy— apart from reestablishing a variety of philosophemes previously deconstructed, such as the assumption of philosophy's internal homogeneity, and of its history, as a continuum for the development of its idea—would be to ascribe a position to him in which his thought is conventionalized and ossified. Obviously, all effort to describe unfinished research in terms of the tradition of philosophical thought, and in particular a kind of research such as Derrida's, which by its very nature (that is, for structural reasons) must remain incomplete, runs the risk of solidifying not merely the precariousness, instability, or hesitation vital to work in progress, but, more significantly, what at the heart of the Derridean project articulates itself as the thought of something that for essential reasons must remain incomplete, ultimately undecidable, and that does not let itself be fully saturated by a context. But these are not the grounds on which Derrida's radicality is commonly asserted. Rather the singularity, or irreducibility, of deconstruction, is seen to be rooted in either its witless disrespect for, or its *critical* letting-go of, the whole tradition of philosophical thinking. In the following, I shall attend to some of the presuppositions that come with such an evaluation of a thinker's achievement. Indeed, what are the evidences that remain unquestioned, and hence intact, behind the claim that deconstruction has exceeded once and for all philosophy's traditional evidences?

To characterize a thinker's work as breaking with the entire tradition is a quite traditional mode of thought. Moreover, such a break with tradition and traditionalism is in the best tradition of *philosophical* thought. The rupture in question is a function of the singularity, uniqueness, and spontaneity of a position that without prejudice or bias—independent of tradition-bound everyday truth; of the truth of traditions that have grown on a national soil; and, finally, of the truths of a calcified tradition of philosophizing itself—invents itself in a new beginning. Since Aristotle conceived of the beginning of philosophy in wonder—the *Grundstimmung* of philosophical thought, as Heidegger calls it—philosophy requires that it always be reenacted as if for the first time. A radical break with the tradition and its limits—an *epoche* in Cartesian or Husserlian terms—secures the freshness of the beginning of a thinking that lives up to the initial pathos of the philosophical *thaumazein*. Such a break with the tradition is constitutive of the genuine tradition of philosophical inquiry. It is not possible to philosophize in a true fashion without desiring to disregard, neglect, ignore, overcome, dismantle, leave behind the whole tradition. This fundamental exigency of an always-new start assures the essential radicality to which philosophy as philosophy must aspire. Thus, to describe a thinker's work as completely breaking with the tradition, and as escaping historical and historiographical characterization, is a sure way to situate that thinker in the tradition of genuine philosophical thought, that is, as a repetition of the inaugural first time of philosophical wonder.

The epitome of philosophical radicality is reached when the break in question is construed as one with philosophy as a whole, in short, when the rupture with tradition is linked with the topos of the end of philosophy. Indeed, not only is this theme of the end, or death, of philosophy a powerful, most venerable philosophical topos, but it also, and always, heralds the beginning of a new, more radical philosophy. The eschatological discourse belongs in an intrinsic manner to the philosophical program of an essential rejuvenation of thinking. The very claim that Derrida's texts would announce the end of philosophy, irreversibly break with the history of philosophical ideas, and undermine all possibility of localizing his thought within, or with regard to the course of, the history of philosophy, therefore, does nothing but reactivate one of the most crucial self-determinations of philosophy since its inception. Appreciation of his work in terms of a radical departure from the history of classical philosophizing, espouses the philosophical dream of a pure difference in thought and with it the equally philosophical desire for the self-foundation of thinking.

Yet to assign radicality to a thinker's work on the basis that it leaves the tradition behind does not merely reenact the program of the tradition; in addition, the difference that this work is believed to make becomes meaningful only in relation to what is said to have been overcome. Clearly, the very freshness of any irruption of philosophical thinking engages the arising philosophy in an interminable war with its predecessors. If the new beginning, the radically different position that surpasses all previous efforts of philosophy, philosophy included, is to be truly radical—indeed, not just any new beginning will do; arbitrary beginnings will have to be discarded—this new other beginning will have to enter into an exchange or debate with all, or at least some, major figures of the tradition. Otherwise, the significance of the new beginning cannot be attested; its (universal) relevance cannot be demonstrated. The very dream of a first time forces radical thought, and the thought of radicality, to enter into an inescapable agreement with the ideas and philosophical procedures that have been handed down. Without them, the pretention to novelty and otherness cannot be upheld.

As a corollary, it follows that any "serious" attempt to "argue" for the radicality of Derrida's break with the tradition, and hence for the impossibility of positioning his thought in the philosophical continuum, will require sustained negotiations with the tradition and the established conventions of philosophical thought. An inevitable conventionalization is the result, consequently, of any such effort to ascertain the absolute otherness of Derrida's work. If such a claim is sustained through demonstration and argumentation, it will succeed in establishing Derrida's thought as a new beginning *in* philosophy, that is, as a reenactment and pure manifestation of philosophy itself. This is a question not of a possible risk, but of an unavoidable necessity and of an irreducible complicity with the tradition that comes with the demonstration of the *originality* and absolute *radicality* of a thinking that would swerve away from the tradition.

After everything that Derrida has developed with respect to the concept of history as a metaphysical concept—in particular in *Edmund Husserl's "Origin of Geometry": An Introduction (O)*—it would seem impossible to bring the code of tradition to bear on any analysis of his thought. Together with a statement such as the following from *Memoires: For Paul de Man,* that "we can no longer propose a tableau or a history of deconstruction," Derrida's assertions about history would indeed seem to confirm the previously mentioned assumption that deconstructive discourses are so radical and so new that all historical and genealogical views and periodizations of them are per se excluded. But if the deconstructive discourses have indeed "sufficiently questioned, among other things, the classical assurances of history, the genealogical narrative, and periodizations of all sorts," as Derrida ascertains in that same text,[1] and if, hence, "it is no longer possible to *use* seriously the words of tradition," this does not imply that they must not be *mentioned* at all with respect to deconstruction.[2] The speech-act distinction between use and mention, however, is insufficient to capture the manner in which the necessity of having recourse to the philosophical concepts of the tradition, at least as crossed-out concepts, is still to be maintained and affirmed, even though they are set aside by deconstruction.[3] Rather than effacing all possible reference to the tradition, deconstructive work on the tradition irrevocably *reaffirms*—albeit not without multiple warnings—continued referral to the tradition and its code.

After all, deconstruction does not defy the tradition in the name of an otherworldly thought, so infinitely novel that it would escape all inscription. But a difficulty seems to arise from the fact that deconstruction is not *one* unequivocally identifiable thought. In contradistinction to the one single thought that is, according to Heidegger, proper to genuine philosophies, deconstruction, unlike the thinking of Being, for example, is not the unifying unthought of the tradition as a whole. What, consequently, can its relation to the tradition be, if as an interrogation of that tradition it does not have the unity of a more originary origin? How can it be said to reaffirm referral to the tradition if it is neither a unique thought nor once and for all determinable as to its essence? Deconstruction is precisely a questioning of the assurances of an univocally identifiable thought, itself included. Rather than describing it as one thought, one must speak of deconstruction in the plural, not only because it would each time be singular (and hence infinite and incommensurable), but, especially, because deconstruction cannot be reduced to one way, or one method.[4] This, of course, does not mean that, positively, there would

be many deconstructions—and even less, were this the case, that they
would be of equal pertinence—it means that in *itself* deconstruction is
manifold. Hence, it has no *itself*. From this it follows with necessity that
no context, whether textual or historical, could ever hope to situate and
decide upon deconstruction. It is consequently aberrant to expect that
such a plural thought could (and should) relativize itself with respect to
traditions that have been kept alive within the cultural horizon of
Western thought. Such a demand can only arise if, as is the case with
Habermas for instance, one confounds the Derridean project with what
amounts indeed to a philosophical trend among the traditions that have
become reflective within our cultural horizon, namely the project of
extending the sovereignty of rhetoric over logic, or of pursuing a systematic aestheticization of philosophy. If the Derridean project could be
identified in terms of such positions, then his thinking would let itself
be relativized against the history of philosophy. It would thus seem difficult to claim that a thought that does not let itself be reduced to a
theme, position, or method could still be required to entertain a relation—a necessary one, moreover—to the tradition.

Although, strictly speaking, deconstruction can no longer be situated
within a history of ideas and the continuum of philosophical thought on
which such a history rests—deconstruction is, indeed, a questioning of
the possibility of such a history—it is not without relation to the whole
of the tradition, the tradition *as a whole*. More precisely, deconstruction
continues to relate to what constitutes the tradition *as* tradition. Although
thinkers such as Derrida—and this is true of Heidegger as well—no
longer simply busy themselves with furthering the venerable canon of
philosophical problems, thus giving some the impression that they are
indulging in mere "literature," or "freeplay," their work remains connected to what specifically makes up the philosophical tradition, namely,
the striving for universality. It is a relation to tradition as an overcoming
of traditionalisms, as an approach to what can be established about things
that is valid for all cultures, languages, peoples, histories, and that thus is
capable of openness to an Other *as such*. This is not to contend that the
intellectual endeavors of philosophers such as Heidegger and Derrida
would simply continue the universalist project constitutive of the
Western tradition of philosophical thinking. It is merely to say, at first,
that their endeavors make sense only with respect to that heritage of the
tradition.

Yet before making this point in greater detail, let me first briefly estab-

lish that Heidegger and Derrida indeed conceive of their enterprise as
determined by the demand for universality. For Heidegger, the philosophical destruction of the "sclerotic tradition" of thinking Being[5]—of
ancient ontology—is, as a *philosophical* destruction, situated in a historical
tradition of thinking that begins with Greek thought, which arises from
(and against) the nationalistic and traditionalistic boundaries of Greece as
a singular nation and people, and which is the most intrinsically fundamental trait of our Western and European tradition.[6] Thanks to their
language, the Greeks were capable of transcending, for the first time,
Heidegger holds, national custom and tradition, and of bracing themselves for being in its totality *(das Seiende im Ganzen)*. The question of
Being is the reenactment of that initial beholding of something universal.
In spite of the sharp critique leveled, in particular in *Edmund Husserl's
"Origin of Geometry": An Introduction,* against the connection of the universalist project of philosophizing to the spiritual unity of the European
Occident, or the West, Derrida's work is aimed at exhibiting structures
of the greatest generality—"universal structures"[7]—that pertain under
all circumstances, unconditionally—that is, that are not only valid for
the thinking (and speech-acts) of all different peoples, but even "valid
beyond the marks and society called 'human.' "[8] Although both Heidegger and Derrida are up against the tradition of metaphysics, their
debate with that tradition yields to the demand for universality. It is this
demand that for Heidegger links his destruction to the tradition that
begins with Greek thought. Although Derrida can no longer make a
claim for continuity in the Heideggerian sense—owing to his critique
of the notions of the West, of Europe, but also of any *Ur-Vater* at the
origin of philosophy—it remains true that his thinking has a universalist
bent; and in that, it is philosophical. Although the complex relation that
both Heidegger and Derrida maintain with the tradition's fundamental
exigency of universality—which is also the minimal condition under
which Otherness as Otherness can be thought—no longer lends itself to
placing them *within,* or even *at the end* of, that tradition, this relation
assures the "historical" and "philosophical" pertinence of their thought.
More important, this complex relation secures the "intelligibility" of
their intellectual enterprise. Although deconstruction, (and to some
extent Heideggerian destruction) is structurally undecidable, it is not for
that matter undeterminable. The deconstructive discourses are absolutely
detached from the tradition and absolutely absolved from themselves so
as to escape strict identification, but the tradition, insofar as it is that of

universality and relation to an Other in general, leaves the mark on them that ensures their adherence to that heritage. This minimal mark of attachment under the absolute break with the tradition, this limitation in tearing themselves free, prevents these discourses from becoming indeterminate. And since the attachment in question is to the demand for universality, it not only prevents these discourses from slipping into the idiosyncratic and unintelligible, but also secures the very level of their intervention and, if one still could say so, the universal relevance of their contribution. I would contend that the main task in dealing with the writings of these thinkers is if not to focus directly on what they propose as to the structures of intelligibility and universality, then at least to refer every possible discussion of particular issues in these thinkers' work to their debate with the elementary rules of a tradition that seeks to raise itself above the empirical (geographical, biological, racial, mythical, nationalistic, traditionalist, historical, and so on) conditions of its emergence. Such an approach, however, in order to be intelligible and credible itself, needs to actualize figures of the tradition so that the tradition will appear in what constitutes it in its greatest generality. To do so is not to engage necessarily in conventional history writing, or in the attempt to localize a position for a thinker such as Derrida; and if such actualizing of the tradition takes, at times, a tripartite shape, this is not, for that matter, necessarily a dialectical unfolding of ideas. What such seemingly historiographical developments seek to achieve is to determine a particular dense nexus of the minimal rules of intelligibility and universality that constitute the tradition from which, and against which, the Derridean moves can be shown to be pertinent, and to "make a point" of sorts.

The following remarks on the kinds of relation to the tradition that can be found in Husserl and Heidegger are not intended to sketch out a genealogy of the type of relation that I shall decipher in Derrida's work to what his thought breaks away from. Indeed, as should become clear from what I shall say about Derrida's "relation without relation," to use a formulation from Maurice Blanchot that Derrida makes frequent use of, to the tradition, that relation is a far cry from what one usually calls a "position," a "stand," or a "platform." And yet what Derrida elaborates, and what he achieves in however oblique a fashion, with regard to philosophy and its complex relation to its own tradition, is intelligible only if one can demonstrate the points of continued contact with the tradition in a project that, indeed, speaks of something other than that of which the tradition speaks, and that also speaks about it in ways different from those the tradition has handed down to us.

I open these remarks with a discussion of the dedication of *Being and Time* to Husserl. This dedication, which Heidegger, in a rather sinister move, later agreed to delete in order to get his work republished in 1938, reads as follows:

Dedicated to
EDMUND HUSSERL
in friendship and admiration
Todtnauberg in Baden, Black Forest
8 April 1926

Recalling his years of friendship with Heidegger, Karl Jaspers, in *Philosophische Autobiographie,* appears to be completely mystified as to what might have motivated his friend to dedicate *Being and Time* to his teacher. For Jaspers, his younger friend's gesture can only be an act of hypocrisy, since both of them had agreed on the necessity of maintaining a common front against the philosophy of the university establishment. At one point, Jaspers evokes a scene during which he expressed to Heidegger his surprise that Heidegger "had quoted professors as if his problems were not entirely different from theirs." He notes that "the dedication of Heidegger's first book to Rickert, the second to Husserl suggested an affiliation with people of whom he had previously spoken with contempt. And that in [so dedicating them] he would have pretended to belong in a traditional manner to a world against which both had taken a stand."[9] Jaspers, indeed, could not envision resistance to professorial philosophy and the academic establishment other than through an opposition "expressive of an impulse of existence," to quote his own words.[10] This kind of rejection of professorial and professionalized philosophizing elicited the following objections by Heidegger, as Jaspers recalls. "In contrast, you are traditional in your factual philosophy."[11] What Heidegger points out here is a clear double bind: any existential opposition against the philosophy establishment is paid for by a naiveté regarding actual philosophizing. In Heidegger's eyes, Jaspers is traditional in the very philosophical way in which he seeks to break away from the tradition. Rather than inaugurating a new beginning by espousing a radical cancellation of the tradition, the existential opposition to it uncritically and unthinkingly reinstalls that tradition in the factual way the opposition is carried out. If, indeed, not one single step forward can be made in philosophy without support from the tradition, then any attempt such as Jaspers' to repeal academic philosophy merely marks time.

Heidegger's dedication of *Being and Time* to Husserl undoubtedly emphasizes the need to think within the context of the tradition. Yet to recognize this need does not necessarily entail the entertainment of traditional modes of relating to the tradition in question. Heidegger by no means held what he terms "little Moritz's," that is, a simpleton's, notion of philosophy, the notion of one "who believes that out of five authors you can make a sixth . . . just by thinking them to the end."[12] Nor does he think within the tradition to rethink already posed traditional problems. As is made clear from the outset of *Being and Time,* to think within the space of the tradition does not mean letting oneself be told by what has already been thought what sort of objects one ought to choose to think about. Tradition in the sense of the canon of the questions that were handed down not only deprives the thinker of his "own leadership in questioning and choosing," but also papers over what it transmits by "barring access to those original 'wellsprings' out of which the traditional categories and concepts were in part genuinely drawn."[13] Yet, if to think within the tradition cannot mean to pick up and think through to an end what has already been thought—the traditional canon of so-called philosophical problems—what then is one to understand by the contention that one cannot help thinking within the sphere of tradition? In *Identity and Difference,* Heidegger goes as far as to write: "Whatever and however we may try to think, we think within the sphere *(Spielraum)* of tradition."[14] Indeed, to think within the tradition implies thinking back into what *Being and Time* had called the "original 'wellsprings' out of which the traditional categories and concepts," were drawn, an operation that is possible only through a *destruction* of the tradition in view of its "productive appropriation."[15] Such destruction, in which thought bends backward—it brushes the tradition the wrong way—to what constitutes the traditionality of the West, which, in however complex ways, lent itself to the tradition(s) of Western metaphysics, that is, to the thought of universality in its Platonic-Christian version—is, says Heidegger, "to be carried out along the *guidelines of the question of Being,"* and is "possible solely within such a formulation."[16] In other words, for Heidegger, to think *within* the tradition can only mean to *think back* to the origin of the tradition, to what has always remained unasked throughout the history of thinking in the tradition, and with respect to which the actual tradition of thinking can be defined as an obscuring of that unthought. But not only is reaching back to the unthought of the tradition the very means by which that tradition is made intelligible in the first place, it also says something about the nature of thought itself. The destruction of the tradition makes sense only if it is carried out along the guidelines of the question of Being, Heidegger says. What this implies is that the unthought to be discovered is the question of Being, that is, the question concerning the difference between Being and beings, in short, the difference that makes all the difference. Thinking for Heidegger, indeed, is ultimately the thinking of Being, that is, of the difference that opens up the possibility of relating to beings *as* beings in the first place. All other modes of thought, the modes that characterize the tradition—modes that explore the relations between beings, as well as between beings and their transcendent cause—are dependent on the forgotten question of Being. As such, that question represents the forgotten nature of thought itself; all handed-down types of thinking can be defined and be made intelligible when related to the unthought in question. In short, to think within the tradition means to break down the types of problems and modes of inquiry passed on, in order to uncover the withdrawn opening from which these problems and ways of questioning gain their significance. Such an attack on the traditional modes of thinking—characteristic not only of professional and professionalized philosophy, but also of the extra- or anti- university establishment, which has never failed to submit to the norms of academic discourse—aims also at making another beginning. The new beginning that the destruction of the tradition seeks to inaugurate is not, however, one altogether heterogenous with the tradition or one easily at home with, say, repressed foundations of a homegrown brand of thinking. Heidegger avoids both extremes on the spectrum of empiricism by attempting another beginning *of* the tradition. With this other beginning, what constitutes the tradition as tradition is allowed to unfold and to develop its potential. In contradistinction to the dream of a radically heterogenous beginning—that is, the dream of an absolute Other—and the celebration of merely ethnic, racial, and nationalistic differences, Heidegger's gesture of reaching through the tradition of Western thought toward that opening question of Being, of which the whole Western tradition is nothing but the after-image, secures this new beginning's pertinence and significance, if not its universality. By furthering the development of the hidden matrix of what traditionally is called thinking in Occidental Europe or the West in general—that is, the tradition of metaphysical (and that includes empiricist) thinking—the thinking of Being, or thinking *as* thinking, prevents philosophy, now no longer a discipline with a tradition, from closing itself, *in principle, at least,* to other, or non-Western, thinking.

To exemplify this necessity of thought to think back through the tradition to the very aperture of meaning itself, of which the Western tradition of philosophical thinking is the forgetful acknowledgment, I shall briefly discuss Heidegger's initially surprising contention, in *Introduction to Metaphysics,* that in asking the fundamental metaphysical question concerning beings in general, the totality of beings, the Being of beings, one is not as free, or *ungebunden* (unattached, independent, unbound), as one may wish to believe. "In asking this question we stand in a tradition," Heidegger notes. Therefore, one must ask the question not in its abridged form, say, "Why are there beings?" but in its full original wording: "Why are there beings rather than nothing?" Heidegger writes: "Ever since the question about beings began, the question about non-being, about nothing, has gone side by side with it. And not only outwardly, in the manner of a byproduct. Rather, the question about nothing has been asked with the same breadth, depth, and originality as the question about beings." Yet, if the question is to be asked in "strict observance of the original tradition regarding the meaning of the fundamental question," this is not so simply because of this tradition's dignified status.[17] Let us see what happens if the question is asked in the abridged version. If the question is worded "Why are there beings?" one starts off from beings, from the evidence that they are, and are given to us, aiming at the ground, or cause, of their being. In short, one asks a question that in essence is not different from the mode of questioning practiced in everyday life, which inquires into relations between already constituted things. Thus, the question "Why are there beings?" looks for an answer that in nature is not different from the question that looks for the vine-pest—this is Heidegger's example—as the cause for a vine disease in the vineyard. In asking, "Why are there beings?" "tacitly we are asking after another and higher kind of being," God, or the Big Bang.[18] But if this is so, then we are not asking the fundamental metaphysical question, the one that is concerned with the totality of what is, the Being of beings. By cutting the question free from its traditional wording—from the addendum "rather than nothing," an addendum that prevents one from taking the fact that beings are at face value, as an unquestioned evidence—not only does one ask a question that ultimately makes no difference, but, more seriously, one annihilates what Heidegger calls the question's "original power" as a question. This is its power to hold open the thought of Being as the Being of beings, and to thematize the difference within which beings and their causes can become meaningful in the first place. Faithfulness to the original wording of the fundamental question of metaphysics is the very condition under which the Western tradition of metaphysics can be transcended toward its forgotten beginning—the forgetting of which represents the advent of the specifically Western idea of universality and relation to an Other—toward the possibility of a new beginning grounded on a more universal universality than that of Western thought.

This brings me back to Jaspers' indignation regarding Heidegger's dedication of *Being and Time* to Husserl. Although Heidegger's admiration for Husserl was restricted to *The Logical Investigations,* as one knows, this acknowledgement is still highly significant. The faithfulness and continuing relation to the tradition that it expresses is not so much an acknowledgment of influence, or dependence, on a master, as it is of the importance of tradition itself, that is, of what has been thought, and of what thus remains to be thought as the unthought of the tradition of philosophical thinking. Indeed, in order to transcend the tradition and move toward the question of Being, of which this tradition as a whole is the systematic occultation, Heidegger needed, as Otto Pöggeler puts it, "a teacher who once again reactualized the specific project of the tradition as a whole" *(der die Tradition noch einmal als eigenen Entwurf ausführte).*[19] This teacher, through whom Heidegger maintained the connection with the tradition, namely, Husserl, was indeed the philosopher who aimed at re-inaugurating the originary project of Western thought in its entirety. Only a philosopher for whom the utmost philosophical urgency consisted in a total repetition of the project of Western philosophical thought—Gérard Granel, in *Traditionis Traditio,* calls him "Husserl, the Greek,"[20]—could provide the necessary connection with the tradition in a way that would also allow the questioning of the very limits of that tradition in a new universalist perspective.

Such a reenactment of the tradition as a whole becomes manifest in Husserl's concern with science or *episteme* whose doxacritical thrust opens up a world of universal pertinence, beyond specific cultures and histories. From *Logical Investigations* (in particular its fourth investigation) and the first pages of *Philosophy as a Rigorous Science,* where Husserl defines his own project as an attempt at a universal science, to the later work—the *Vienna Lecture* and *The Crisis of European Sciences and Transcendental Phenomenology*—where such a science is shown to continue the Greek foundation of philosophy, Husserl's phenomenology clearly spells out the fundamental, if not minimal, conditions of a tradition that unlike all culturally bound traditions is a tradition in a unique sense: it passes on an attitude and a world-view that is determined by its universality. In the following brief outline of Husserl's position on the tradition of universality, I shall limit myself to the texts of the *Vienna Lecture* and *The Crisis*.

In Part I of *The Crisis*, Husserl determines this particular work's aim— but retrospectively that of the entirety of his previous writings as well— as the "attempt to strike through the crust of the externalized 'historical facts' of philosophical history" in order to "inquire back into what was originally and always sought in philosophy, what was continually sought by all philosophers and philosophies that have communicated with one another historically."[21] What this inquiry shall exhibit is "an absolute idea," the idea of a "universal science, a science of the universe, of the all-encompassing unity of all that is."[22] Both the *Vienna Lecture* and *The Crisis* argue that European humanity bears this idea within itself, and that this very idea distinguishes Europe from all "merely . . . empirical anthropological type[s] like 'China' or 'India.' "[23] This idea, which is "a remarkable teleology, inborn, as it were, only in our Europe . . . is quite intimately involved with the outbreak or irruption of philosophy and its branches, the sciences, in the ancient Greek spirit."[24] In the first, original establishment of philosophy in Greece—an establishment that is indeed an "irruption," a "breakthrough," of "a *new sort of attitude* of individuals toward their surrounding world," in that it is characterized by a reorientation, an *Umstellung* of the original *Einstellung*[25]—philosophy "conceives of and takes as its task the exalted idea of universal knowledge concerning the totality of what is."[26] With this change in attitude, Greek mankind leaves its finite and factual humanity behind, and raises itself to a "mankind with infinite tasks," to "humanity struggling to understand itself."[27] Because Greek humanity, by virtue of a conception of the world "unfettered by myth and the whole tradition," and "absolutely free from prejudice," free in short from all contingencies whether racial, biological, national, or historical, is "the first breakthrough to what is essential to humanity as such, its *entelechy*," Greek humanity and European humanity, to which that universal thinking gives its momentum, are not "merely factual, historical delusion[s], the accidental acquisition of merely one among many other civilizations and histories," Husserl concludes.[28] Of course the fact that Europe or the West has not lived up to its most innate telos is not a counter-argument to Husserl's demonstration that Europe—the "concept of Europe"—is constituted by the telos of a universal science and a humanity with a "universal ("cosmological") life-interest in the essentially new form of a purely 'theoretical' attitude."[29] The counter-argument in question is itself based on this idea and telos. Yet, in spite of Europe's falling short of fulfilling this telos, it is a telos that at least according to its originary conception does not seek to *level* all cultural differences in the name of a unitary culture; rather it is, as Klaus Held has shown, constituted by "a respect for the manifold of these ways of appearing."[30] Indeed, the very universal thrust of the theoretical attitude allows it to be open to Otherness, to other cultures and histories. Openness to Otherness, the very ability and readiness to allow for Otherness as such, presupposes philosophy in the sense of a universal science, a science of all that is, and a science which for Husserl is linked to the origin of the concept of Europe in Greek thought. Although such a conception breaks with all finite traditions, it itself is at the heart of the *philosophical* tradition—tradition having acquired a new meaning and a style different from the style of handing down customs, habits, and modes of thought grounded in circumspective behavior, and so on.[31] As Husserl notes at the beginning of *The Crisis,* this ideal of a universal science is one that must be carried out only in accordance with its own principles, not by taking it "over blindly from the tradition"; it "must grow out of independent inquiry and criticism."[32]

In short, the dedication of *Being and Time* is not primarily an acknowledgment of influence, or of professorial authority. In *What Is Called Thinking?* Heidegger notes: "A thinker is not beholden to a thinker— rather, when he is thinking, he holds on to what is to be thought, to Being. Only insofar as he holds on to Being can he be open to the influx of the thoughts which thinkers before him have thought. This is why it remains the exclusive privilege of the greatest thinkers to let themselves be influenced."[33] In the context of *What Is Called Thinking?* Heidegger is referring to the relation of Nietzsche to Aristotle, but what Heidegger ascertains here can as well be applied to his own relation to Husserl.[34] To conclude, then, Heidegger's acknowledgment of the importance of Husserl for *Being and Time* establishes a relation to Husserl as the one who, in *Logical Investigations* in particular, had attempted to realize, once again, the full idea of the early Greek philosophical endeavors. It is a relation that shows Heidegger engaging the very telos that Husserl claimed was constitutive of the tradition of a kind of thinking that would transcend all traditions and traditionalisms. But this proximity to Husserl, to the tradition as a whole, to what unifies the tradition—the telos of a universal cognition of all that is—allows Heidegger, without simply affirming or negating it, to question the idea at the very heart of the tradition itself. Husserl's colossal effort to reenact the very essence of the European tradition of thought makes it possible for Heidegger to construe this thought as being the negative, so to speak, of a forgotten thought to which the tradition as tradition bars access. The idea of a universal cognition by which the tradition of European thought comes to being, through which something like a *tradition* of universal philosophizing becomes possible in the first place, is itself the form that the forgetting of Being has taken throughout the history of Western thought. Heidegger, consequently, rather than trying to repeat, as Husserl did, the project of early Greek thought, seeks to retrieve an origin that could only come into view after the unifying project at the heart of the Western tradition of thought had been made fully explicit. This other origin of the origin of the tradition is an origin that in being forgotten made something like tradition possible. It itself, however, is beyond tradition. More precisely, this other origin of what inaugurated the tradition of universalist thought—the question of Being—though lacking for essential reasons a tradition of its own, underwrites the whole history of metaphysical thinking. Therefore, the thinking of Being, of the difference between Being and beings, remains of necessity firmly connected to the tradition that it deconstructs.

Heidegger has argued, moreover, in particular in his essays on technology, that in spite of its negativity, the tradition of universalist thought is the *only* way in which Being and its history occur. The *tradition,* animated by the telos of a universalist cognition in which humanity as such comes to its self-understanding, is merely the other side of the coin which shows the mark of the *history* of Being. The other beginning *(der andere Anfang)* of which Heidegger speaks in the preface to *Being and Time,* must thus be a beginning of a different (if not greater) universality than that which has been sought in the metaphysical and theological principles of Western thought. But, no matter how much more fundamental, more originary, this other universality of Being may be, it manifests itself only under the figure of the universality aimed at through the tradition, never as such, never purely. As Heidegger has time and again emphasized, it cannot be a question of shaking off the tradition, if the goal is to think the other beginning, but of appropriating the tradition primordially. The project of elaborating on the underpinnings of universalist thought—a project that continues and breaks with this telos of Western thought—involves both support from, but also a tension vis-à-vis, the tradition, as Heidegger's talk about "Auseinandersetzung" makes clear.[35] The thought of Being, the thought of the other beginning, does not merely presuppose that one "know the tradition. We must know more—i.e., our knowledge must be stricter and more binding—than all the epochs before us, even the most revolutionary," Heidegger writes.[36] Rather than relinquishing the tradition, the thinking of Being binds itself to the tradition more rigorously than ever. This binding is the condition under which the thought of Being and of a universality other than metaphysical universality can still continue the demand for universality that comes with the originary breakthrough of philosophy of which Husserl spoke, but which, according to Heidegger, became lost in the metaphysical tradition of universality, even though Heidegger may be reticent to use the term "universality." The ties to the tradition are required as well to secure that what is thus established about a universality greater than metaphysical universality is indeed of universal pertinence. The thinking of Being is only another name for the relation of thinking to the tradition, not, however, in the sense of a constituted telos that would unify Western cultural concerns, but to what precisely has been obscured by the West's universalist self-conception. The thinking of Being, by contrast, is the thinking relation to "that depth from out of which [each time in a novel fashion] the essential always comes to man and comes back to man," in short, to the *thaumazein* that represents the Greek breakthrough.[37] Relation to the tradition comes thus to mean *responsibility* for, and *response* to, the originary questioning of Being.

In the aftermath of Husserl's reactivation of the very project of the tradition as a whole, and Heidegger's attempt to reawaken the question of Being, that is, the wonder that Being *is* (rather than is not) the tradition's unifying unthought, what remains to be thought? What can thinking mean, and what, if any, universally pertinent moves remain for it to engage in when with Husserl and Heidegger all possible essential and active relations to the tradition of thought seem to have come to their (logical) completion? And if Husserl's and Heidegger's philosophies reflect, respectively, on the tradition of universality and on universality's "universal" unthought conditions, what can thought still claim to be able to establish with respect to the universal, and in terms of its own legitimation? I will not broach these questions frontally, because I suspect that the continuity, stagnation, or possible discontinuity that such questioning implies is itself put into question by post-Heideggerian thought, and in particular by Derrida. Yet, since thinking cannot be determined in its specificity without historically localizing it with regard to the tradition of thought that it responds to, and with which it is engaged in a process of *Auseinandersetzung,* the danger of disciplining such thought by aligning it with figures from which it is shown to break away, and thus to remain in a certain continuity with what elaborated itself through those figures, is perhaps minimized (without any definite hope of neutralizing the danger in question, since such neutralizing would also amount to a neutralization of the thought under discussion) in a mode of approach to Derrida's thought and its negotiations with the tradition that is less direct than the more global characterizations that I have given of Husserl and Heidegger. I will limit myself to a brief discussion of one particular problem in Derrida in order to argue for a certain lateral, oblique displacement of the essential relations of thought, tradition, and universality. This is to argue neither for simple continuity nor for simple rupture, but for a different relation of thought to the tradition, neither inside nor outside, and for which the measure ultimately has to be found in the thought of displacement itself.

If I choose to talk here of *differance,* I do so because some have argued—most recently Jean-Luc Marion—that differance would be the result of a generalization of the ontological difference, and that it would remain caught within the horizon of the Heideggerian conception of Being. Since I will deal at length with this argument in Chapter 3, I will limit myself here to recalling that the major objection that must be made against such a contention is that the ontological difference is not a genus. In the introduction to *Being and Time,* Heidegger cautions against taking Being for something that could be generalized: "As a fundamental theme of philosophy Being is no sort of genus of beings; yet it pertains to every being. Its 'universality' must be sought in a higher sphere . . . The transcendence of the Being of Dasein is a distinctive one since in it lies the possibility and necessity of the most radical individuation."[38] Whatever differance may be, it cannot result from a generalization of the ontological difference. Another approach would be to claim that Heidegger has prepared in advance the thinking of differance—which, says Derrida, "in a certain and very strange way [is] 'older' than the ontological difference or than the truth of Being" (*M*, p. 22)—in that in *Identity and Difference*, for instance, he would have recognized the inherent limits of thinking difference as difference in the language of metaphysics. Thus, a straight line of descent could be shown between Heidegger's thought of difference as difference and differance. Let me briefly examine that argument.

Indeed, in his search for an instance "older" than the ontological difference, Derrida could be seen to follow up on Heidegger's acknowledgment that meditation on difference as difference takes place "in the language of the tradition" and yields "to the key words of metaphysics, Being and beings." Yet to conceive the difference in terms of these guiding words is not to think it *as such,* but merely to represent and metaphysically name it. The thinking of difference, Heidegger notes, "directs our thinking [precisely] to the realm which the key words of metaphysics—Being and beings, the ground and what is grounded—are no longer adequate to utter. For what these words name, what the manner of thinking that is guided by them represents, originates as that which differs by virtue of the difference. The origin of difference can no longer be thought of within the scope of metaphysics."[39] The ontological difference, consequently, is not Heidegger's last word on difference. Yet in his attempt to seek to determine difference as difference, independent of all categorial determinations of Being, the name of Being included, Heidegger admittedly remains only on the way to the essential origin of difference as such.[40] It is, of course, no accident, and certainly no shortcoming of Heidegger's philosophical venture, that he does not properly name or conceptualize difference as such. Since it is the difference from which all differents originate, no concept or name can be adequate to it. Difference as difference conceals itself under all its possible concepts or names. Moreover, when he rejects Being as a name for difference, Heidegger concedes that difference as such is indeed *without any "as such."* It has nothing proper to it, except that unrelentingly it differs, and retreats from what *in propria persona* is advanced about it.

Such a difference that differs from *itself* in that it withdraws from all the conceptual and ontological differents that originate from it has, at first glance, all the allures of "differance." In addition, Derrida makes frequent reference to Heidegger when discussing differance, and this seems further to suggest that differance is nothing but the outcome of the program that Heidegger set up for thinking in *Identity and Difference*. Yet, difference as difference is (only) the essential origin of difference, and, moreover, of difference thought of in binary terms. Yet difference as a letting come forth and simultaneous withdrawal of the Dif-ference *(Unter-Schied)* in the differents themselves—in concepts that are opposed in a bipolar way—is only one of the several meanings and kinds of difference that enter what I have called the non-originary arche-structure of differance. When one takes difference *as* difference, as well as the ontological difference, as just one difference among others, the philo-sophical dignity and the unifying prospect of the question of difference is thoroughly displaced (though not, for that matter, rendered irrelevant). But even more important, in order to tie Heidegger's meditation on the ontological difference and on difference as such into differance, Derrida had to refine, in a formal and technical manner, and in a way not to be found in Heidegger, the minimal traits that characterize its structure as one of a (self-)differing and (self-)deferring difference. What of Heideg-ger's notion of difference as such becomes woven into the multifaceted construct of differance, is only this minimal structural arrangement, and it is woven into differance as one element in the more complex and more universal structure of differance. Rather than following directly from Heidegger's meditation on difference as difference, differance dis-places the genealogical and filial lines as well as the unifying potential of any fathering concept, in the interest of gathering the essential traits of a plurality of concepts of difference. Differance, in short—and this could be said, with due consideration, of all other Derridean infrastructures— gathers together in a knot traits from heterogeneous filiations. But that knot of differance does not unify, and thus does not provide a foundation for, what becomes tied together. Differance does not father the various fathering concepts of difference that it interlaces by their main traits in a nonunitary arche-synthesis. Indeed, from what we have seen about dif-ferance, any such arrangement must defer to and differ from a knot in its most economical torsion. In sum, then, differance is neither a result, an offspring, or a child of one particular notion of difference through generalization, nor the completed or even radicalized fulfillment of the task Heidegger had set out for thinking.

To conclude, I shall draw only a few possible conclusions from what I have said about differance—about the gesture of thought that charac-terizes it—and, moreover, I shall do so in only a very schematic fashion. First of all, with Derrida the homogeneity of the tradition assumed by both Husserl and Heidegger becomes a point of contention. Although Derrida has time and again described the project of Western metaphysics as one that seeks to think full presence, this statement does not serve to totalize the entire tradition. On several occasions, he has reminded us of the fact that there is not *one* metaphysics, not *a* metaphysics that would be one, thoroughly united and in continuity with itself. What Derrida means by this is not merely that in addition to metaphysics there would be a number of counter-traditions to the dominant tradition, such as, for instance, the materialist counter-philosophies that according to Ernst Bloch have always accompanied, in more or less public fashion, the philosophical establishment. "There is not one metaphysics," by contrast, refers to the structural limits of the presumed unity of metaphysics, and thus also to the kind of unity that any philosophy can have that claims to be part of it (or to stand in opposition to it). Derrida writes: "The *unity* of metaphysics or of 'the sequence called "Western metaphysics," ' belongs to *a representation,* to a self-representation of something that, therefore, can be called *the* metaphysics only in accordance with the name that this thing gives itself, and according to the form of circular closure that it wishes to give itself."[41] Yet, if it is *ultimately* impossible to bring the whole tradition as such into view, as Husserl did, defining its unifying telos as the idea of a universal science, and a science of the universe, it is also *ultimately* impossible to establish a more fundamental essence of it—the forgotten, yet unifying question of Being. Such reluctance to take the totalizing self-characterization of philosophy by Husserl and Heidegger for granted in no way characterizes deconstruction as a critique. Derrida's questioning of Husserl's and Heidegger's gestures is not to be equated with the self-criticism of philosophy—with metaphysics's dialogue with itself and its regular critical interrogation of its own foundations—which belongs to the tradition of philosophical thinking itself. Derrida does not disagree with Husserl's contention that the telos of Western thought is and should be universality, and with Heidegger's contention that there is a sphere of universality higher than the telos of a universal science, namely, the question of Being. The question, rather, is how purely this necessary telos of universality, or of the question of Being, can be met, but not because the complexity of what is to be unified would be far too great or, even worse, because there would be something radically, or absolutely, incommensurate with the demand for universality. The question that Derrida poses is one regarding the inner, structural limits of this very demand—the inevitable reference to (and hence structurally necessary inclusion of) the non-Western in the very idea of universality, or the singularity of the Other that all universality must continuously presuppose if it is to make sense at all. Deconstruction is not a challenge to the need to unify, or to universalize. Rather its own intelligibility hinges on the demand for universality, and culminates in deconstruction's interpretation of universal structures, which takes into account singularities without reducing them to the status of examples or cases.

Yet, if for structural reasons the unification of the tradition encounters limits, and pluralizes itself on this basis, all relation to the "whole" of the tradition will be thoroughly affected by the limits in question. Philosophical thought, rather than being able to follow, to master, to engage in patricidal writing about a master name or problem, sees itself confronted with a host of fathers, with a plurality of equi-primordial issues on one given level of thought, or connected to one specific topic. With this, thought acquires an irreducible plurality in itself. But it is thought *in the mode of universalizing thought,* and of the universal's unthought, that pluralizes itself. It is thus not a return to empiricism, or the nonphilosophical altogether, but an opening out to a pluralization, dissemination, or manifolding within the universal or within the *Unter-Schied.* It is an opening out by thought to a quasi-transcendental *Othering* (due to the universal structures that happen to limit the classical universalist demands) in the tradition of universalizing thought and its fundamental questioning, that displaces (without overturning) the unifying privileges of universalizing and fundamental questioning. Such thinking, which allows pluralization within itself, although it does not rescind thought's universalizing thrust, brings a certain uncertainty, a negative certainty, to bear on the universal medium of thought. It is the negative certainty that it is for essential reasons impossible to establish *what,* in the end, rules the exchanges between the universal and the disseminating Othering.

But let me return to the question of genealogical localization. Although Derrida has claimed it to be indispensable, for instance, to place oneself within the opening of Heidegger's questions, he has also been very critical on many occasions of Heidegger's philosophical idiom. But even this criticism, including Derrida's "disseminative gesture," is made, at least to a certain degree, in Heideggerian language. Undoubtedly, the same can be said of almost all Derrida's writings: they draw on the very resources—critically or constructively—of the texts that become the object of a Derridean *Auseinandersetzung.* Yet, precisely because of this intimate interlinkage of Derrida's thought with the texts in which he intervenes, the question arises as to the relation of his thought to that of the thinkers he discusses, of what is proper to him and to the others.

Reviewing Derrida's treatment of the question of Being, John Caputo has argued that one of the effects of using Heideggerian language to debate the question of Being is to produce "an altered reading of Heidegger which shows that the dissemination and delimitation of the truth of Being has already taken place in Heidegger's text."[42] Caputo does not mean to say that Derrida has reinterpreted Heidegger in a more fundamental manner, showing that there was always more to him than previously believed, or that Derrida has developed his own thought by disguising it, so to speak, in Heideggerian language. Rather what he suggests is that in this practice of drawing on Heideggerian resources to delimit the question of Being, Heidegger and Derrida, as specific philosophical voices, figures, or authorities, dissolve and can no longer simply be held apart. In the to-and-fro of the debate in which Derrida's statements, on the one hand, let themselves be conducted and carried by Heidegger's text, but on the other hand, claim precedence, it becomes impossible to establish strictly what is properly Heidegger's or what is Derrida's own. Indeed, just as the hyphenated *aletheia* is no longer a historical name by which the Greeks are privileged, but, as Caputo puts it, a name "that points to that process by which Being and truth are granted without privilege, to us as well as to the Greeks, to the Greeks as well as to everybody else,"[43] so the thought of differance—the enabling and disabling structure of all thinking, the thinking of Being and the thinking of differance included—cannot strictly speaking be said to be Derrida's proper, or to be the result of a generalizing extrapolation from Heidegger's thought on difference. In a discourse such as the one under consideration, the traditional distinction between the universalist pretense of philosophy and the fact that this universalizing thrust is articulated each time in a singular and personal style becomes blurred as well. This distinction becomes foregrounded by a "region" of universality "before" the difference drawn between what has been called universality hitherto and a singularity traditionally understood as the case to be subsumed under the universal rule, or to serve as an example of it.[44] Yet, as my analysis of differance has made clear, I hope, it is also possible—up to a point at least—and hence, necessary to establish what in the thought of differance belongs to Heidegger and what does not. Still, this possibility—and more generally, the possibility if not of continuing, then of opening up, delimiting, or reinscribing the thinking of a thinker—is in a certain way secondary, compared with what is set forth—on its own terms, in its own right, if one can still use those terms—under the title "differance." What has been said about differance as a cluster of traits proper to a variety of concepts of difference should be sufficient evidence as to its philosophical novelty. Yet, although the thought of differance is intelligible only with respect to the tradition, or at least to certain figures of the classical philosophical heritage, and what constitutes it as such, the novelty of differance is not simply rooted in a reactualization or repetition of the constituting event of philosophy. Undoubtedly, Husserl's program of a reactivation and fulfillment of the telos underlying the Western tradition, or Heidegger's repetition of the inaugural question of Being, admits to an essential singularity of the unique event of philosophy itself: the first time of the event tacitly implies iterability if it is to be reactivated or repeated. Differance is first and foremost a response to this singularity rather than to the telos or the unthought of the Western tradition that philosophy must reactivate in a novel fashion each time as if for the first time. But in thus focusing on the singularity without which no handing down of a telos, or no repetition of the unthought, could take place, differance reflects the law of that singularity as well. Although differance is an elaboration of a constitutive singularity *of* the tradition, and hence is intelligible only with a view to what has been bequeathed to philosophical thought, the thinking of differance combines with a singularity so irreducible that this thinking cannot any longer be said to reenact, or critically rework, the tradition. Its novelty is not akin to the irruption of the *thaumazein* or the repetition of this breakthrough event at the origin of the tradition. It is due to the incalculable, or infinite, conditions of the *irrupting event* of the event itself, to which this thinking is a response.

Now let me, at this point, recall Heidegger's claim that thinkers are never dependent on other thinkers. They respond only to what is to be thought, Being, the ultimate subject matter of thinking. Yet, for Heidegger, the thought, and the unthought to which a thinker responds in his *Auseinandersetzung* with the work of a predecessor or contemporary thinker, is the one thought, or unthought, that unifies these thinkers' thoughts. Even if *one* does not imply totality here, the one thought in question gathers, brings together in an event that could be called a becoming unified (an *infinite* unification) of the entirety of a thinker's work. It is to this one thought or unthought in the work of a thinker that another thinker responds in a relation that is a relation of responsibility for taking and carrying on the question of Being. But what if the oneness of thinking, the unifying question of thought, enters into a con-

figuration with other "thoughts" with the result of displacing the unifying privilege of the thought of Being? What happens when the silent
voice in which Being is heard, and with which thinking as response to
Being begins, rings in concert with other voices? Something of this kind
takes place in the thinking of differance. In the thought of differance,
the thinker no longer responds to one thought, to the unifying thought,
or unthought, that gathers the whole tradition around the forgotten
question of the ontological difference. In such a thought a multiple relation not to the tradition or its unthought alone but to a host of other,
and even heterogeneous concepts of difference occurs that comes to
delimit and to disseminate (without suspending it altogether) the unifying
gesture of the thinking of Being. In a relation of thinking as exemplified
by differance, philosophical thinking no longer relates to a tradition, but
rather relates to traditions, or more precisely to the multiple limiting
instances that restrict the master concepts at the heart of those concepts
that serve to think the essence of tradition. But with a thought such as
differance, thinking is also barely thinking anymore, if thinking is, in a
Husserlian sense, a relating to the telos of universality or, in the Heideggerian sense, a responsive relation to the question of Being. Thinking,
with differance, becomes a response to multiple heterogeneities and
entails a responsibility to establish their commerce with the dominating
concepts. Thinking here extends beyond its unifying concepts and gestures. Finally, such thinking without relinquishing universality as the
telos of Western thought, or Heidegger's attempt to conceive of a
thought of universality more originary than that characteristic of the
European Occident of Platonic and Christian inspiration, opens the concept of universality, not so much by expanding it through space and time
as by exploring the conditions of possibility of this incontrovertible
demand of thinking—conditions that, as limits, also spell out the ultimate
boundaries of this exigency without which thinking would not be
thinking.

3

The Eclipse of Difference

WERE ONE TO WRITE a general philosophical history of the concept of difference, one might be tempted to view it as the history of the progressive emancipation of difference from identity. Beginning with the Parmenidean conception of pure identity, of Being free of all difference, such a history would document the movement of difference from its position, in Plato, as one pole of a dialectical structure to its acquisition of the dominant role in the constitution of identity, or the Absolute, in German Idealism. The correctness of a history of this kind would seem further to be demonstrated by the fact that in contemporary literary criticism—in a certain trend at least—"difference" has become the key term. Indeed, not only does the criticism in question seem to confirm and validate the history of such an emancipation, but in this light, it positions itself as the culminating moment of this particular view of history. Difference here reigns supreme. A quick glance at recent book titles reveals the term not only apposed to everything, but in everything. It is said of anything and everything, indiscriminately, manifesting a determination that, as a practice, criticism ought to make a difference too. If at the dawn of philosophical thinking difference scarcely left the shadow of identity, identity now barely shows its face, and, with its departure from the scene, this brand of criticism would seem perhaps to have liberated itself not only from the exigency in Western thought to think of difference and identity in relation to each other, but also from the thought that difference exists only within identity, the One, the whole— whether or not the concept of difference has been taken up in the concept of the unity of all that is.

Still, this criticism does not represent a homogeneous body of utter-

82

ances and gestures, and whatever claims it may make need to be examined individually. Clearly, they are not all of equal thrust or importance. I propose the following rough classification of the critical discourses on difference. A first kind of such criticism uses the term as an incantation, in the vain hope of appearing different. This criticism has transformed the Kierkegaardian claim that to exist means to be different into the maxim that being different is requisite in order to make it in the profession. A second type is based on the assumption that difference is an elementary and original form of the *real* itself. This variety of criticism, centered on issues ranging from gender difference to differences of race, draws on empirical understanding and appreciation of difference. Combined with a thorough familiarity with the field and competence in the discipline that corresponds to it, such criticism can, of course, yield invaluable insights into sociological, political, psychological, and physiological differences. The third, and final, sort of discourse on difference sounds a more philosophical note. It is a criticism that aims at demonstrating—through reading both literary and philosophical texts—that philosophical difference is undecidable, that is, that discrete distinctions, including the difference between philosophy and literature itself, cannot be upheld. By multiplying distinctions and differences, this approach to literary and philosophical texts aims at showing that the infinite duplication and multiplication that emerges from its readings escapes the mastery of philosophy. It is on this last kind of criticism that I wish to focus my attention, in particular, on its place in the history alluded to, and especially on the nature of the concept of difference that it puts to work.

But, before beginning, I wish to recall Giorgio Vattimo's criticism in *Les Aventures de la différence* of what he terms "the thought of difference" in contemporary French philosophy.[1] Although Vattimo's target is the doctrine of difference in Gilles Deleuze and Jacques Derrida, he approaches this doctrine primarily through the works of the latter's disciples, in particular Bernard Pautrat, Jean-Michel Rey, and Sarah Kofman. As a result, Deleuze and Derrida are portrayed as having developed a theory of difference according to which difference is repressed and forgotten by Western thought. As a follow-up to Heidegger's meditation on the ontological difference, and as a return to Nietzsche's rememoration of an originary difference under the figure of Dionysos, this theory, aimed at bringing difference back, rendering it present again, would demonstrate a way of stepping out of and beyond metaphysics. In what certainly amounts to a caricature of Derrida's thought, Vattimo claims that for Derrida the forgotten difference is of the order of "the signified, the Platonic idea, the *ontos on* of the whole of metaphysics," since "man's discourse unfolds only within difference whether he forgets it and takes it as a natural frame, or repeats it all over again in poetic discourse."[2] In the case of Deleuze, Vattimo holds, difference is of the order of a universalized Platonic simulacrum free of all structures, models, and referents, thus annulling, in its endless duplication, the very possibility of distinguishing and establishing hierarchies between differences.[3] By repeating difference in a parodistic rewriting of metaphysics, through which full presence is to be restored to the forgotten difference, Derrida and Deleuze uphold a relation of conscious remembering of difference, thus revealing their roots in a metaphysics of subjectivity and self-consciousness. And Vattimo concludes that the only difference this parodistic duplication of metaphysics inherent in the thought of difference—a duplication, he contends, that remains eminently contemplative in a Spinozist sense—can make is to harden and solidify the metaphysical concept of difference itself. Further, rather than making a difference with respect to the whole of metaphysics, the thought of difference "dissolves difference," since it tends "to cover up and forget the different possible ways of problematizing difference."[4]

I will return later to Vattimo's reasons for so describing the thought of difference in the writings of Derrida. At this point, however, I wish to linger on Vattimo's arguments against the so-called radicality of what he construed as "the thought of difference," precisely because they seem to apply as well to the third type of literary criticism, which, in North America, seeks to debunk philosophical difference and hierarchies between concepts in the name of a generalized difference, and practice of difference. Indeed, it is a criticism that, while failing to question the metaphysical notion of difference itself, is based on its mere repetition and multiplication. By merely reenacting, even if infinitely, philosophical difference in the rewriting and duplicating of the philosophical text in parodistic fashion, instead of delving into the nature of the concept of difference itself, this criticism only contributes to a further stiffening of the classical concept of difference. It might well be a criticism that unknowingly, and despite its shocking looks, plays into the hands of what is most traditional in philosophical thought. What this practice unearths as philosophy's Other, what according to it cannot be mastered by philosophy—a plethora of differences—is what always already falls under philosophy's jurisdiction. Above all, this sort of criticism only confirms philosophy in its belief that there is no outside to it, since mere multi-plication and abyssal infinitization of difference do not represent any essential threat.

Moreover, a rewriting of the philosophical text intended to exhibit and render conscious the play of difference that supposedly grounds it is possible only from a position of consciousness. Such a praxis of difference is also eminently self-reflexive. Further, the vertiginous and highly vir-tuoso performance through which such self-reflexivity takes shape, and in which, rather than being put into question, the elemental binarism of philosophical difference becomes overpotentiated, reveals this criticism's indebtedness to the metaphysics of subjectivity and to the ideal, if not the ideology, of subjective mastery.

What are the implications of the foregoing assessment of the third kind of critical discourse on difference? The most immediate conclusion is that this discourse does not break with traditional philosophical thought, and especially not with its concept of difference. If this is the case, this third form of criticism might not have achieved the emanci-pation of difference from identity, or the goal of bringing the history of this emancipation to a definite end. Yet before arguing that the discourse in question and its practice of difference remain, in spite of the profuse production of differences, intimately connected with identity—indeed, to such a degree that to describe this discourse as a reading centered on difference is at best one-sided—it must be asked whether difference can ever be severed from identity, and thus, whether a history of a successful emancipation of one from the other is at all thinkable. First, the history of philosophical thought shows that such emancipation was always only partial. What takes place from Parmenides to Hegel, and beyond, is a relative liberation in which difference, rather than being effaced in the face of identity, is shown to have its only meaningful place within iden-tity, and to play a constitutive role in the becoming effective of identity, whose priority nonetheless remains unrivaled. But apart from the factual history of philosophy, there are essential reasons that prevent the severing of difference from identity. By abolishing the difference between differ-ence and identity, philosophy would slip back into the nonphilosophical, in short, into a kind of empiricism, in which the power of the manifold and spurious infinity prevail, and where the difference that thinking makes—the thought of identity—has not yet emerged. That the bond between identity and difference is an essential bond, and is constitutive of what difference means in philosophy, becomes evident in any careful analysis of the various articulations of difference to be found in the history of philosophical thinking. Still, Aristotle's notion of difference *(diaphora)*, more precisely of *differentia specifica,* stands out as a privileged vantage point for my purposes, since this concept became the metaphysically relevant concept of difference for the history of Western philosophical thought. Since Aristotle's theory on difference is far from being clear and coherent, such a discussion ought to take the form of a learned and thoughtful debate with the relevant passages in the *Metaphysics, Topics,* and *Posterior Analytics.* For my purposes, however, the following exposition must suffice.[5]

Let me recall that *differentia specifica* is only one among several kinds of difference. Indeed, the term *diaphora* is much broader than simply (logical) difference. As the following passage from the *Metaphysics* demonstrates, it first signifies the "being other of things": "Things are said to be 'different' when they are other *(hetera),* but are in some respect the 'same': other not merely numerically, but formally or generically or analogically. To be different things must be generically other, or contraries, or other in their very being."[6] From the start it must be noted that only that which, although other, is also in some respect the same can be called different. The difference of species belonging to one and the same genus, *differentia specifica,* is just one mode of being other in the above sense. But *differentia specifica* is also *the* metaphysically privileged determination of being other, indeed, the determination that alone merits being called "difference." It alone provides *essential* difference, compared with which the other types of difference, although based on sameness, are of limited bearing, because their origin is ontic. This is, in particular, the case of what is *properly* predicated of things, that is, of the characteristic peculiar to a peculiar thing. The proper *(idion, proprium),* though always characteristic of a given thing, or species, and hence effectively contributing to its distinction, is a function of the thing's or species' relation to other things or species. It is not *kath'auto,* having only empirical necessity. The proper, as a characteristic peculiar to a peculiar thing, is neither a general characteristic nor a combination of general characteristics. Some differences, by contrast, although they rest also on the defining character of sameness, and thus qualify as genuine differences under Aristotle's definition, measured against the specific difference, seem barely to merit the title. One of them, the difference between species that no longer meet in a univocal concept, but meet only in an analogical one (such as quantity or quality), a difference which Thomas Aquinas designates *diversitas,* according to Aristotle, can no longer properly be called difference. What then is *differentia specifica?* What sets it so radically apart from all other modes of difference, and thus establishes its essentiality, is its pertinence to the category of the genus.

Aristotle's general definition of *diaphora,* or difference, shows that difference requires that what is said to be different must in one respect be the same *(to auto ti onta).* As soon as such sameness is no longer guaranteed, as in the case of simple diversity, one can no longer rigorously speak of difference. Yet the specific, or logical, difference that permits the distinction of one species from another is a difference operative *within* the genus (and not, as in the case of the proper, within species, that is, among already constituted things). The genus is what is common to all species, yet not in the sense of one independent essence shared by all the species, but as that within which difference creates the species. Through difference the genus becomes realized as species. *Differentia* is thus, as Silvian Nacht-Eladi remarks, "the genus itself in activity . . . Differentia and genus are one thing."[7] In conclusion, if difference, in the sense of *differentia specifica,* is the genus itself in activity, in its capacity of becoming different "on each occasion that it is realized in a different species,"[8] then the genus, the generic, the general is that which assures the sameness of difference, and of the different. If according to Aristotle the *differentia* is the essence of the thing or species, it is thus because it is the realized genus itself, shared differently in all the things or species of a *genus proximum.* In spite of being a singular way of being genus, the *differentia specifica,* because it is difference in genus, also has a generality that sets it apart from the character peculiar to a thing. Moreover, being genus in activity, *differentia specifica* as the essence of a thing or species—as its definition—is *kath'auto,* the result not of a semantic-differential relation to other things or species, but, as Josef Simon remarks, of *"relation of the thing itself,* which therefore cancels itself out as relation. The 'specific' difference is to signify the essence itself and not to contain any demarcation of the essence."[9] In summary then, difference as specific difference presupposes the sameness of genus within which alone it is meaningful. It is as difference within genus that the concept of the *differentia specifica* is the essential philosophical concept of difference, a concept in which difference is intimately linked with identity.[10]

Yet if difference cannot properly be thought without a common milieu, an identity, a *genus proximum* in which it takes place, what happens to this requirement in a criticism which, in its readings, intensifies and proliferates difference? If the requirement in question no longer applies, this "difference" might no longer coincide with the philosophical concept of difference. It would perhaps be of the order of what, following Aristotle, we can barely call difference anymore. In that case, however, all the operations of this criticism remain extrinsic, and without any bearing on the philosophical concept of difference. Assuming, on the contrary, as I do here, that in effect the criticism in question continues to put classical difference to work, what kind of identity could such criticism presuppose, and knowingly or unknowingly promote, under the guise of an unlimited plurification of difference? Indeed, if Vattimo is correct in claiming that the thought of difference, as he understands it, merely solidifies and stiffens the metaphysical concept of difference, then the criticism I am considering, which is aimed at debunking philosophical difference, must, paradoxically, and at least surreptitiously foster some unity, identity, or totality in the practice of "making (a) difference." Although such critical multiplication of difference may seem to invite nihilism and subversion, nothing could be less true. Indeed, as I have already suggested, multiplication of differences is only one aspect of the practice of critical reading. It also proceeds by forcing difference into line, and to the subsequent reciprocal annihilation of all differences, to the self-cancellation of any position via its opposite, different Other. Yet as Derrida has noted, annulment and equalization of what is in the mode of *pro* and *contra* is a "free shot which aims . . . to collect its interest" ("C'est le coup pour rien, qui ne se tente d'ailleurs jamais sans intérêt").[11] The interest in question is an interest in eliminating, through reciprocal equaling out of differences, difference itself. Critical readings know only one kind of difference. According to this very restricted concept holding all difference to be identical, difference is determined by a relation of inversion and reversal, of opposition, understood as a relation of equalizing canceling of terms standing against each other. This generic relation of a homogeneous kind of difference is generalized, which means that difference itself becomes annulled in an equally homogeneous whole of the differents. This whole—the end product of critical readings of this kind—is the tightly woven knit of the crisscrossed relations of inversion that string the differences together. From the outset, it has been what has made the differences the same, not merely "in some respect," but in all respects. Rather than the emancipation of difference from identity, difference eclipses itself in this criticism and becomes a genus, the genus of difference, rather than difference in genus, replacing, as it were, Parmenidean Being with the identity of difference. Instead of a radical break with philosophical difference, this criticism, all differences considered, repeats the former's major features, yet in a manner that impedes the possibility of questioning philosophical difference's presuppositions and limitations. Such blockage of an inquiry into the metaphysical concept of difference is, indeed, what allows this criticism to be characterized as a parodistic rewriting of metaphysics.

By contrast, Heidegger's thought of the ontological difference is an investigation into the very presuppositions of the philosophical concept of difference. I recall that Vattimo charged French contemporary thinkers with forgetting the very source of inspiration from which they drew their "thought of difference," namely, Heidegger's meditation on the onto-logical difference. Whether this is a correct assessment remains to be seen. Yet, compared with the parodistic rewriting of metaphysical difference in the third kind of criticism discussed, Heidegger's elaboration of dif-ference is fundamental and radical. It amounts to a foregrounding of the classical concept of difference in a difference more originary, in that it conceptualizes that from which differents come into a relation of standing against one another. It is a thinking of difference on this side of all the possible modes that difference as relation can assume, the relation of inversion or reversal included. This is a concept of difference that not only is philosophically more fundamental than the ones evoked hereto, but that *truly* makes a difference. It is a *radical* difference, indeed, radical in all the senses of the word: it is marked by considerable departure from the usual or traditional meaning of the term; it is basic and fundamental, growing from, or proceeding from, a root which it constitutes itself. What then is the difference that Heidegger calls the difference between Being and beings, the ontico-ontological difference, ontological differ-ence, or, in his later works, simply "Dif-ference"?

From its beginning in Greece, Western philosophical thinking has systematically unfolded in the space provided by what Heidegger calls "the *one* basic differentiation" ("*die* ursprüngliche Scheidung"), the dif-ference between Being and beings.[12] This difference is, as Heidegger puts it in *Identity and Difference,* "the ground plan in the structure of the essence of metaphysics."[13] Indeed, the difference between the twofold meaning of *to on,* as *ta onta* or *to einai,* is the matrix from which Western thought springs. Yet, from the beginning, Western thought has also con-ceived of Being only from the perspective of beings, and with respect to them alone, understanding Being, consequently, as only another, however excellent or superior, being or existent. In thus representing Being, and with it the difference between Being and beings, "in respect of what differs in the difference, and without heeding the difference as difference,"[14] Western thought has covered up the founding difference—not only the difference which allows for the Being *of* beings, but the difference in which the possibility of philosophical thought is rooted as well. Because of this consistent interpretation of Being in terms of beings (as *ousia*), Western thought, according to Heidegger, has been from the start onto-theo-logy, metaphysics, in short.

Yet, if it is true that Being is nothing but the Being *of* beings, it is also true that, as such, it must be radically different from beings themselves, even from the universe of beings, from being in totality. Above all, Being cannot possess ontic qualifications, and chiefly among them, being in the sense of existence, presence, presence-at-hand *(Vorhandenheit)*. As Heidegger notes, the distinction between Being and beings is not "merely a distinction of the intellect (ens rationis)."[15] As a matter of fact, the ontological difference is a distinction in neither the usual nor the philosophical sense of the word. It is not fabricated by our understanding, and hence of the order of understanding's activity of representation, but a distinction made by what Heidegger calls *thinking*. It is not even a distinction in a strict sense. More precisely, the difference between Being and beings is not a difference based on *distinction*. In other words, it is radically different from the philosophical concept of difference.

Even though *differentia specifica* characterizes a thing or a species as a relation determined in itself, hence as a relation that is almost not one anymore, the definition of the essence of a thing or species presupposes its distinction from other essences, or definitions. As distinction, however, the *differentia specifica*—difference *per genus et differentiam*—is rooted in relations between things or species. But relations, whether they occur between real things (ontic beings) or things of thought (universal concepts such as individuals, species, or genera), presuppose that these things are not only already determined things, or concepts, but that they *are* to begin with. Moreover, difference as distinction finds the "between" for the beings to be distinguished by already between them. It is a given that they already occupy. Difference as distinction, or difference as relation in such a given *between,* and between things already constituted, however, is something which our representing has added to the things or species under consideration. It is, as Heidegger writes in *Identity and Difference,* "something made up by our understanding."[16] Finally, since relation presupposes the existence of what is different, the difference added by understanding to things or species is *ultimately* ontic in origin.

From the foregoing it ought to be clear that the philosophical concept of difference does not account for the "between" in which one finds that things and species in their difference are already present. Consequently, the question arises: "Where does the 'between' come from, into which the difference is, so to speak, to be inserted?"[17] The difference that this "between" makes is necessarily more fundamental than all philosophical (logical) or commonplace distinction. Since this difference is presupposed by all difference as distinction and relation, it must be "older" than distinction and relation. To circle back, then, to the difference between Being and beings, let me note that if this difference were a distinction, it would also apply to a region in which one "finds that Being and beings in their difference are already there."[18] Yet Being is not there in the same way as beings are. If beings are what *is,* Being refers to the being (in a verbal sense) of beings, to what gives being. The difference between Being and beings is the difference between Being as the horizon whose opening makes it possible for beings to appear within it, and beings as those things which appear and come to stand within that horizon itself (including the manifold relations and differences that go with them). It is a difference between dissimilars, in other words. The difference between Being and beings, the ontico–ontological difference, is therefore the (ontological) difference which *Being itself* makes and in which difference as relation (between existent things, or between them and the non-homogeneity of what metaphysics calls reality, the One, God, being, and so on), that is, difference between things or concepts, can come to the fore, difference according to what Jean-Luc Marion has termed "the 'vulgar concept' of difference."[19] The ontological difference is no distinction at all; it is not a difference *between* Being *and* beings, it is what lets beings into the between of their manifold differences. The ontological difference which comes specifically into view as soon as Being is thought in its difference from beings, and beings in their difference from Being, is thus the "Dif-ference *(Unter-Schied)*" that opens the "between" for the difference between Being and beings as well.

To bring this unheard-of difference into view, properly and on its own terms, yet not, as Habermas contends, as "Being, as distinguished from beings by way of hypostatization,"[20] but as the Being *of* beings, is the primary task of thinking. The subject matter of thinking is Being in its difference from the beings whose Being it is, in short, "difference *as* difference," difference as the difference of Being and beings, difference as such *difference*.[21] This then, is the point where the excellence of the question of Being, that is, of difference *as* difference, becomes apparent. It is also the moment at which it ought to be obvious that the difference Heidegger attempts to think neither originates in the philosophical concept of difference as distinction nor extends that concept by metaphysically hardening it in a manner similar to that designated by Vattimo as "the thought of difference." As the "ground" of all difference based on relation and distinction, difference *as* difference not only is in a position of anteriority to difference, but also differs in nature from the vulgar concept of difference. It is incommensurable with vulgar, consequently with philosophical, difference as well.

By elaborating in the following what sort of "experience" in thinking inaugurates Heidegger's meditation on the ontological difference, I hope to render this privileged status even more telling. Heidegger's concept of the ontological difference derives from his elaborations on man's relation to what is—to man's existence in the world, as well as to beings in the world. As he notes in *The Essence of Reasons,* whatever shape the human being's relations between him and beings take, they presuppose that the human being (or, for that matter, *Dasein*) has always already surpassed beings in a totality, and in totality.[22] Only on condition that the whole of what is has been surpassed can any distinguishing and deciding occur within the realm of beings. Seen in the light of beings, all relation to them, say their representation, is always already above and beyond them. "The representation of what is, judged from what is, is always beyond what is—*meta.*"[23] In the human being's relation to beings, beings thus become equivocal *(zweideutig)* and twofold *(zwiefältig).* They not only are represented as beings, but faced in their Being as well. What this means is that all of the human being's relations to beings, himself and the human Others included, are grounded in the possibility of the essence of *Dasein* that Heidegger calls *transcendence.* Whether or not the human being is aware of it, he has transcended himself, as well as the totality of what is, in the thought of the Being of what is. Consequently, the breaking up or out of the ontological difference is rooted in *Dasein*'s surpassing, in the transcendence that characterizes it in essence. As *"a basic constitutive feature of Dasein that happens prior to all behavior,"* transcendence occurs in the form of the rift between Being and beings. This rift of the ontological difference is the possibility of *"the* ability [of the human being] to differentiate," and to distinguish. It is an ability, Heidegger remarks, "in which the Ontological Difference becomes fact-ical."[24] In sum then, the thought of the ontological difference follows from the insight that all relational differentiation between beings pre-supposes prior to it that beings be experienced in their Being, and in what is present in its presencing *(Anwesen)*. The thought of the ontolog-ical difference is thus rooted in an experience *with* common or philo-sophical difference, which in essence is of another order than both empir-ical difference and what has been abstracted from it. The thought of the ontological difference as grounded in *Dasein's* transcendence of beings toward their Being is *thinking at its most elemental* in that it provides the very "between" for common and philosophical difference, or distinction, that is, for common and philosophical thinking. Articulating the recog-nition that the human being is always already turned away from what is toward its Being, the ontological difference is also the *most elemental philosophical thought*. Finally, with the exploration of this elemental thought of difference, there begins *philosophy as discipline,* or metaphysics, as thinking in which the difference that thought makes—the thought of Being—is forgotten. The unmistakable privilege of the ontological dif-ference thus becomes evident. It is the recognition of the difference that thinking makes with respect to what is, the immediate, or the universe of beings. The ontological difference articulates the rift instigated by thinking as thinking in what is by transcending it toward its Being. The ontological difference is a function of thinking's most elemental char-acteristics. As a consequence, Jean-Luc Marion's contention in *God without Being* that "to think outside of ontological difference eventually condemns one to be no longer able to think at all"[25] comes as no surprise.

If thinking at its most fundamental is the thinking of the difference that thinking makes, of the thought of Being that surpasses beings, one cannot but agree with Vattimo's verdict on "the thought of difference." Instead of indulging in a self-reflective parodistic repetition of the play of metaphysical difference—a repetition and a play oblivious to the very opening of Being that permits its restricted, however infinite, or abyssal economy—it is more important for one to take up again Heidegger's meditation on the ontological difference intent on deepening the thought of this difference itself.[26] Needless to say, if the fate of thinking as thinking depends on the elemental thought of the ontological differ-ence, it is of capital necessity and urgency not only to further expand on that thought, but to reawaken it to begin with. Indeed, as Heidegger has pointed out, this thought, because it is so elemental and simple, is always prone to an inevitable degeneration. It is always exposed to the possibility of slipping into triviality, even of emptying itself of all content. Such covering up of the question of Being, or of the ontological difference, is not accidental, but is, as *Being and Time* asserts, grounded in the very nature of the discovered.[27] It stems from the fact that the ontological difference is the opening difference for all other distinctions, whose very appearance pushes the originary difference from which they arise into oblivion. This is already sufficient reason to keep the question alive. Still, the question has suffered a recent decline in interest among those who busy themselves with difference and differences—the French thinkers of difference according to Vattimo and, or rather, I would contend, certain North American critics. Yet, in addition this particular unconcern with the ontological difference—an unconcern that fosters the multiplication and hardening of metaphysical difference—another, very different indifference to ontological difference has taken hold in certain trends of contemporary thinking, with entirely different implications. When I say "indifference" in this case, I do not mean a mere lack of general concern or engagement, a neglect based on naiveté, ignorance, or personal taste. On the contrary, it is a deliberate indifference, one that is fully aware of the ontological difference's status for thought as such, one that is not only conscious of the consequences of disinterest, but even wills them. Of the thinkers whose work is actively engaged in such disinterest I name a few: Emmanuel Levinas, Jean-Luc Marion, Paul de Man, and, in a certain way to be elucidated hereafter, also Jacques Derrida. In what is to follow, I will concern myself with such an indifference to the ontological difference in two diametrically opposed positions, those of Marion and Derrida, which divide along a line that separates theology from philosophy. I choose to discuss the question of the indifference to the fundamental difference in the writings of both thinkers, not only to show that such indifference lends itself to different styles of thought and diametrically opposite intentions, but to demonstrate that a certain indifference to that difference, rather than fostering a petrification of metaphysical difference, as is the case with the criticism and practice of difference, opens an entirely new vista on, and field of research about, difference *itself*.

For Marion, the "relation" of communion between the human being and God is a relation of absolute asymmetry, in which the Other, the God-Father, is absolutely inaccessible to man, the son. For this negative theologian, God is Other to the point of having no being anymore—

God without Being is the title of one of his books—and hence, unlike beings, God is no longer subject to the opening event of Being, the last and ultimate form of idolatry. The human being's "relation" to this invisible Other, beyond all possible appropriation, is no longer a relation of difference, and, consequently, is no relation at all. One of the poles of the "relation" remains, indeed, in total indeterminacy; all that takes place within it is exclusively attributable to God. It is a gift. Borrowing the term from Urs von Balthasar and Levinas, Marion conceives of the nonrelational communion between man and God as *distance*. "Distance implies an irreducible gap, specifically, disappropriation. By definition, it totally separates the terms that, precisely for this reason, can play through in their sending and return," Marion writes.[28] In the irreducible gap that totally sets the two distant poles apart, God, without being, and thus free from the "tyranny" of Being, "dissolves the link that links Him to our thinking." As the ab-solute, "he is freed of all relation, thus also of all thinkable relation by which He would be linked to an absurd other than Him."[29] And yet, in a paradox of faith, this absence of relation is conceived of as the possibility for a communion between the human being and God that becomes more intimate as God becomes more undefinable.

For the problem that I seek to address here, it is important to remark that compared with the "difference" that the ab-solute God makes with respect to the human beings and the world, everything else, ontic difference first and foremost, fades into utter indifference. But more than this, ontic difference's most fundamental distinction, "the fundamental ontic difference between what is and what is not[,] becomes indifferent—for everything becomes indifferent before the difference that God marks with the world," Marion claims. Commenting on Romans 4:17, where God is said to give life to the dead and to call the nonbeings as beings, Marion argues that faced with the call of God, the intra-worldly difference, between the dead and the living, is not destroyed, but rather is superseded by indifference, since "nonbeings are revealed as beings only by virtue of the call of God."[30] But God's indifference to the fundamental ontic difference can also manifest itself the other way around. From an exegesis of a Pauline text, 1 Corinthians 1:28, where it is written that "God chose the ignoble things of the world and the contemptible things, and also the non-beings, in order to annul the beings—in order that no flesh should glorify itself before God," Marion concludes that "that which is can be, for God, as if it were not: the fact of being a being—and of remaining such, for it is not a question here of destruction, but of annulment—in no way insures against nothing; just as nonbeing, once chosen, is discovered as if it were, so being, once annulled, is discovered as if it were not."[31]

But in light of the difference that God marks with the world, not only does ontic difference become indifferent, but the most radical of all differences—the ontological difference—veers into insignificance as well. In a difficult and compact exigesis of 1 Corinthians 1:26–29, Marion argues that that text also "outwits Being by setting being in motion as if it were not bent to the fold of Being."[32] What transpires through Marion's analysis of this Pauline text is that in "the world" the decision to attribute being to something "depends neither on the categories of a philosophical discourse nor on Being deploying itself in ontological difference, but on instances separated by the limit between 'the world' and the 'call' of the God who gives life." Indeed, "the world" extends being to something by distorting beingness, and with it ontological difference. The reason for this is that " 'the world' in its funding does not belong to the domain of ontological difference or of the fold Being/being."[33] It is from the start dazzled from the outside by the invisible light of God, and all its attribution of beingness to itself and to worldly things is a function of "the world's" attempt to become its own foundation, to be founded on itself, against God. Marion remarks: "Before the difference between beings, before the conjunction of beings to Being, before the fold of ontological difference, the 'world' holds the discourse of the acquisition of funds—to glorify itself before God." This distortion of beingness by "the world" is, according to Marion, the funding that the philosophical discourse on Being dissimulates. Yet, "the world's" judgment of what is and what is not, a judgment made in the intention to forge itself, and in which "Being [is led] astray outside of the path of Being, to the point of outwitting the Being in beings, of disarticulating ontological difference,"[34] is repealed by God, not by refuting it, or by destroying it, but by opposing to it the glory of Christ, which makes the world's self-glorification pale into insignificance. Rather than being what permits the world to found itself, with Christ, being is attributed to that which, in the eyes of "the world" does not appear, namely, to "that which believes in the call" of God.[35] God's abrogation and inversion of the judgment of the world does not ontically destroy it. Nor does His attribution of being to the believers, inverting "the world's" self-forging attribution of being to itself, proceed on the basis of Being. Marion concludes: "A line, along which the 'world' divides into beings and nonbeings that on which it wants to found itself, crosses another line, along which the call reestablishes beings and nonbeings in the measure of their faith. The crossing of these two lines decidedly distorts the play of being by withdrawing it from Being, by undoing being from the rule of Being. This crossing traces a cross over ontological difference, a cross that abolishes it without deconstructing it, exceeds it without overcoming it, annuls it without annihilating it, distorts it without contesting its right. In the same way that a window opens the view to an immense space that it nevertheless measures by a crossbar, this crossing opens ontological difference to a differing that renders it indifferent only by excess and that places it in reserve only in that it preserves it from an entirely different dilemma."[36] In a gesture of deliberate and calculated theological distortion of Heidegger's notion of the *Es gibt,* Marion calls this play radically foreign to that of Being, a *gift* of the distant God. Whereas the self-funding attribution by "the world" of beingness to itself also precedes the correct philosophical discourse on the ontological difference as the latter's hidden ground, the divine gift of beingness is radically anterior to that difference. Not only does it annul this difference by its sheer indifference to it, but the gift of God frees beings from the tyranny of Being. Marion remarks: "The gift liberates Being/being through the very indifference by which it affects it. The gift, in liberating Being/being, in liberating being from Being, is itself finally liberated from the ontological difference—not only the sending, not only the distortion, but the freeing of the first instance, charity."[37] In conclusion, then, "all of ontological difference . . . find[s] itself reinscribed in the field of creation: the *creatum,* while remaining neutral, would go beyond the strict domain of the *ens (creatum)* to comprehend as well, though in a different capacity, Being taken as *'neutrale tantum.'*"[38]

Marion sees the gaze of boredom as it has found exemplary literary expression in Valéry's *Monsieur Teste* as a first step toward seeing the indifference with which a faith in a God defined in terms of *agape* regards the ontological difference. The gaze of boredom, he claims in an analysis that implicitly, but also critically draws on Heidegger's interpretation of this existential mood, is, indeed, an attitude in which all idols become disqualified and rejected for what they are, namely, idols of the visible (yet without boredom's being already in possession of what Marion calls the icon of the invisible). In conformity with Heidegger's claim that "genuine boredom," "profound boredom," "removes all things and

men and oneself along with it into a remarkable indifference," and that
in it "everything about us seems so hopelessly commonplace that we no
longer care whether anything is or is not,"[39] boredom is indifferent primarily to what is, to beings, its own being included. "It abandons, so far
as to abandon itself, with neither love nor hate, through pure indifference," Marion writes,[40] and he adds, "Before the fact that being is,
boredom does not budge, does not see, does not respond. Boredom does
not suffer any exception to its crepuscular gaze, and the being purely
there forms no exception. No idol before boredom, not even the unsur-
passable spectacle of a given being. But, as nothing more essential than
given being . . . can ever appear, boredom will never manifest itself more
absolutely than in its uninterest for the given being. Boredom, which
lends no interest to given being itself, and undoes itself from that which
gives given being: Being, which here sets in motion ontological difference, in the open."[41] In conclusion, then, to boredom, nothing,
including the ontological difference, makes any difference anymore.

Although boredom is only a preliminary step toward theological indifference to difference, not yet that indifference itself, Marion's analysis of
it permits us to situate and to evaluate such indifference from a philosophical point of view. But before trying to do so, let me emphasize that
Marion does not naively strike the most fundamental difference with
indifference. He is aware of the philosophical implications and pitfalls.
That such is the case becomes evident when he notes that to conceive
of "a being that no longer refers to Being . . . but to another instance,
in relation to which another difference is freed, a difference more essential to being than ontological difference itself,"[42] "does not coincide . . .
with the metaphysical lack to think ontological difference; for to think
within ontological difference without thinking that difference itself, following the example of metaphysics, obviously implies that one still thinks
from it."[43] Marion's attempt at "a game *without* ontological difference"[44]
seeks to avoid both the dangers of metaphysical thinking and empiricism,
which he knows to stand in an irreducible complicity with the first. He
aims at a dismissal of Being that would, indeed, free beings from their
"dependence" on Being, thus shielding beings and the differences
between them from referring to Being. By dismissing that through which
beings are—Being—and by thus determining them without recourse to
Being, Marion hopes to set beings free for another and, as he puts it,
more essential difference, the difference with God. Such a theological
difference, according to Marion, would fall prey neither to metaphysical

naiveté nor to theological empiricism.[45] With this I return to the question of the philosophical implications of such indifference.

It follows from boredom's indifference to everything, including the ontological difference, that in this state of mind one is no longer affected by provocations of any sort, and least of all by essential provocations. As Marion holds, boredom is blind, lucidly blind, "blinded by its very lucidity."[46] It is blind in particular to all "amazement, stupor, bedazzlement, which alone allow the silent 'voice' of Being to make itself heard."[47] Yet if boredom is blind in a lucid way to wonder, to the *thaumazein,* that is, the amazement at the fact *that* beings are, "the wonder of wonder," as Heidegger refers to it,[48] boredom deliberately closes itself to the very possibility of the thinking of Being, the thought of the difference that Being makes with respect to beings, in other words, to the possibility of philosophical thinking. In short, boredom's indifference is also, and primarily, indifference to thinking. In its indifference it thus shares the theological indifference to difference. As Marion acknowledges, to think outside the ontological difference is to be no longer able to think at all. But, he adds, "to be no longer able to think, when it is a question of God, indicates neither absurdity nor impropriety, as soon as God himself, in order to be thought, must be thought as 'id quo majus cogitari nequit,' in other words, as that which surpasses, detours, and distracts all thought, even nonrepresentational."[49] Still, Marion's theological indifference to the ontological difference does not spring from blind and simple faith. Furthermore, this non-ontotheological theology—a theology that dispenses, as the ultimate in idolatry, with the notion that God has being—that conceives of itself as a non-ontic science, thus refuting Heidegger's contention in "Phenomenology and Theology" that theology is of ontic origin, abandons neither thought in general nor the thought of the ontological difference. Quite the opposite is the case, since for Marion the ontological difference is, indeed, "a *negative* propaedeutic of the unthinkable thought of God," that is, of a difference before which even the ontological difference must blend into indifference.[50] Thinking, especially thinking at its most extreme, that is, as the philosophical thinking of Being and the ontological difference, is the necessary springboard for a thinking of the Ab-solute that in return will strike the thought that has negatively led up to it with total indifference. In *L'Idole et la distance,* Marion refers to such a thinking of God as a "thinking *without postulates.*"[51]

According to Marion, a twofold indifference also dominates Derrida's thought of differance: an indifference of differance to all (ontic) differences between differences and an indifference to the ontological difference, in that the latter is made to be a particular case of the general differing of differance.[52] Before I confront this assertion and with it Marion's contention that in spite of its indifference to the ontological difference, differance remains trapped within its horizon, let me remark on the claim that in the light of differance all ontic differences lose their specificity. Obviously, a satisfactory refutation of this claim would require a thorough determination of the "status" of differance. For the moment, I refer only to the empirical evidence that Derrida's work, like that of the so-called postmoderns, is characterized by an unmistakable sensitivity to differences, to the difference, even the heterogeneity, between them. As Hegel noted in *Philosophy of Right,* ontic differences— "the infinite variety of circumstance," the "endless material and its organization"—are not of philosophical concern. Since philosophy is philosophy, its "attitude to this infinite multitude of topics should of course be most liberal" (*PR,* p. 11), he writes. A similar liberalism is obvious in all of Derrida's writings, not because ontic differences are insignificant for the business of philosophy, but rather because, with the thought of differance, the sensitive philosophical distinction between the ontic and the ontological is shown to remain, in its very irreducibility, "indebted" to ontic difference. The recognition of an encrypted referral of philosophy to ontic difference, to its plural and even incommensurable nature, fosters a liberalism of a different kind. But what of the claim that Derrida is indifferent to ontological difference. To respond, let me first elaborate, however briefly, on Derrida's treatment of this Heideggerian concept.

In the essay "Differance," Derrida claimed that "*differance,* in a certain and very strange way, [is] 'older' than the ontological difference or than the truth of Being" (*M,* p. 22).[53] Whatever perplexity such assertion may provoke, whether because of the quite correct assessment that, indeed, nothing can be more *radical* than Being, or because of the uninformed opinion that the search for something older (in a very strange way) would merely confirm the competition among philosophers looking for deeper and deeper grounds, two things need to be mentioned. First, something "older," and older in a very strange way, clearly indicates that what is to be thought with differance no longer partakes in the philosophical genealogy of the term *older,* from, for example, its conception in mythical theology as what "is most honorable," namely, "Ocean and Tethys as the parents of becoming and water as that by which the gods swore," to Thales' understanding of the ground and origin of the world as the older principle,[54] to Heidegger's originary, that is, ontological understanding of the anteriority of Being *(früher, die Frühe des Seins)*. Second, the need to think a difference "older" than the ontological difference is prescribed by Heidegger himself. This is clear, as I shall try to demonstrate hereafter, from the whole thrust of Heidegger's argument in *Identity and Difference*. Yet, as will also be seen, Heidegger follows up on this presciption in only a very limited way. One might object that Heidegger's notion of Appropriation *(Ereignis)* makes good on his own demand. But Appropriation, though perhaps "older" than the ontological difference, does not conceive, *in terms of difference,* of a difference "anterior" to the ontological difference. As he has said, "from the perspective of Appropriation it [even] becomes necessary to free thinking from the ontological difference."[55] The need to thus eliminate the conceptuality of difference, including ontological difference, from the thinking of Appropriation originates in the different nature of the later Heidegger's "categories" of thinking. They are, Ute Guzzoni remarks, "of an onticity and a concreteness which implies a wholly new kind of generality—a generality not of superordination and subordination, but of juxtaposition, relation *(Bezug),* constellation."[56] In contrast to Heidegger's relinquishing of the notion of difference, I wish to show that differance (in a very strange way) follows up on Heidegger's call in *Identity and Difference,* and rather than abandoning the traditional conceptuality of difference, saves it as a legitimate conceptual construct and problematic, susceptible to still another turn, and one very different from what the unifying, harmonizing constellation of Appropriation is meant to achieve.

In *Identity and Difference,* Heidegger sets out to bring the subject matter of thinking—Being as difference—into focus so that difference *as* difference comes into view. In following difference as such "to its essential origin *(Wesensherkunft),*" Heidegger seeks to think Being "in terms of the difference," "Being as well as beings . . . *by virtue of the difference,*" from which they appear.[57] But since such a meditation on difference *as* difference takes place, unvariably, "in the language of tradition," and yields "to the key words of metaphysics, Being and beings," difference *as* difference becomes—"tentatively and unavoidably"—determined *as* the difference of Being and beings.[58] In other words, although Heidegger wishes to think difference *as* such, difference *as* difference, his meditation characterizes the plane in which the differing occurs in terms of what arises from it. Difference *as* difference, ineluctably, turns out *as* the difference between Being and beings. Although difference as the between, as *Unter-Schied,* is "only" the aperture for the bipolar Being/beings grid (and all subsequent binary schemes), and not binary itself (at least not in a simple fashion), the power of tradition and the inescapable key words of metaphysics compel thinking to conceive it in bipolar terms. Heidegger is thus forced to admit that his thinking remains only on the way to the essential origin of difference as such.[59] But, at the same time, the necessity of thinking difference beyond ontological difference has been established in all clarity, and is described as a task that can no longer be achieved within the horizon of metaphysics.[60]

It is important to realize that all Heidegger's attempts on the way to thinking difference as such in *Identity and Difference* remain caught within the predicament outlined here. Indeed, his major move in that work, thinking difference as such as the differentiation of coming-over *(Über-kommnis)* and arrival *(Ankunft),* proceeds from a step back into the more essential characteristics of the ontological difference, and in no way escapes the binary grid of metaphysics. Starting from the insight that Being *is* beings (*is* being understood transitively), Heidegger restates the difference of Being and beings as a difference between what transits (without leaving its own place) and what arrives in the unconcealed in which it is sheltered (although the unconcealed is not there without what arrives). Heidegger writes: "Being transits [that], comes unconcealingly over [that] which arrives as something of itself unconcealed only by that coming-over." Or, "Being shows itself as the unconcealing coming-over *(Überkommnis),*" whereas "beings as such appear in the manner of the arrival that keeps itself concealed in unconcealedness." As a result of this reformulation of Being and beings, the difference between both, the between in which the differentiation occurs, becomes recast as the occurring of "the being apart, and the being toward each other *(Aus- und Zueinander),* of overcoming and arrival." Whereas difference holds open the space in which Being and beings relate to each other in their difference from each other, this aperture itself, the *Unter-Schied,* is categorized as a "space" of *auseinander-zueinander,* of "away from and toward each other." Difference, then, is the "dif-fering *(Austrag)* of the two [and not just any two, but of Being and being in a more fundamental interpretation]," that thus enter a "relation" of differing from and being held toward each other, a "relation" that for its part does not escape the figure "two" either.[61]

Yet, although the attempt to think difference *as* difference, free from all categorical determinations of Being, the name Being included, "fails" or, more precisely, remains on the way, the task itself continues to exist. Even though Heidegger recognizes that the ontological difference, or Being, is ultimately an obstacle to thinking difference as such, this in no way means that he would have rid himself entirely, with the notion of Appropriation, of the question of difference. It is certainly the case, as Vattimo has asserted, that the history of the metaphysics of Being coincides with the history of difference. Yet, the decline of Being, in Heidegger's later work, does not for that matter signify a decline of the *problematics* of difference. Heidegger's emphasis on difference as such in *Identity and Difference* must suffice as evidence here. Indeed, the thought of difference as such is not an ambiguous or dubious gesture on Heidegger's part, one endowing difference with a structural consistency or a metaphysical stability akin to the Platonic *ontos on,* shielded as it were from the event-character of Being, as Vattimo holds.[62] Heidegger's efforts to free the thought of difference from Being are precisely intended to prevent such a thing from happening. Indeed, difference as such lacks the quality not only of Being, but of propriety as well, and to such an extent that no *as such* is appropriate to it. To think it remains therefore an infinite task.

Older, earlier, than the ontological difference, then, is difference as such, or dif-ference *(Unter-Schied).* It is a difference that can only be thought in terms of what originates from the difference, never as such. Indeed, difference as such incessantly and invariably comes forth *as* ontological difference (and, subsequently, *as* vulgar difference) only to withdraw in such coming forth. The difference older than ontological difference is thus to be characterized as a dif-fering into two (Being and beings, first and foremost) in which unconcealment is necessarily covered up *as such.* It is a dif-fering that, although not of the order of the binary, cannot but take the shape of difference. To think it *as such*—on this side of metaphysical language—is precisely to think it as the inevitable, if not fated, differing into two.[63]

With this I circle back to Marion's contention that différance is indifferent to the ontological difference.[64] If différance, as Derrida holds, is "older" than the ontological difference, moreover, older "in a very strange way," différance is, undoubtedly, indifferent to the primacy and excellence of the ontological difference, including difference as such, difference as difference, from which the ontological difference originates.

Indeed, as Marion clearly apprehends it, Derrida's indifference to the ontological difference manifests itself in his taking it, in spite of all its philosophical priority, as just one kind of difference among others, as it were.[65] Differance brings ontological difference into conjunction with a number of other concepts of difference, differentiation, differing, deferring, and so forth. Still, this kind of indifference to the question of Being, and to the Heideggerian concept of difference *as* difference, implies no abatement of the necessity and urgency of that question. Nothing can replace it, nor can it come to stand propaedeutically for something else. The indifference of differance is thus of a nature entirely different from that of the distant God. If Derrida could characterize differance as "older," in a very strange sense, this does not mean that differance is an older, or earlier, ground *of* the ontological difference or, for that matter, of the other kind of differences clustered together in its quasi-synthetic arrangement. Indeed, differance recognizes an irreducible difference between differences, a difference finally antithetical to the notion of a ground, even if that ground were, impossibly difference *as such*. Differance is a cluster of a number of concepts of difference. But each one of these concepts enters differance by one or several structural features of differing, dif-fering, deferring, differentiating, and so on, which constitute differance as a grid of traits on which each (the fundamental and originary ontological difference, as well as the difference as such that dif-fers into it) draws in order to be the incommensurable concept of difference that it is. From each sort of difference, differance takes up a trait of differing, that is, the *minimal, and iterable, trait of identity,* that characterizes this difference in its very heterogeneity. Rather than dismissing identity (and the inner necessity that links identity and difference), rather than generalizing difference, which, as *Glas* acknowledges, would result in a general homogeneization (*G,* p. 199), differance articulates the minimally identical traits of all particular.kinds of differing, taking, moreover, the incommensurability between differences into account. And yet, such concern with the identical does not, therefore, confer structural stability, and even less the status of an *ontos on,* upon differance. Given that the minimally identical traits of differing that it knots together are ultimately incommensurable, differing, dif-fering, and deferring, differance as an infrastructure can never close upon itself. Not only is it structurally open, but it differs from and defers itself.

As the quasi-synthetic arrangement of traits distributed among a variety of concepts of difference, differance inscribes all those concepts that are based on differential duality, as well as difference as such, which inevitably dif-fers into the ontological difference. Differance, consequently, must also be understood as the attempt to foreground not only difference as binary opposition, but, more important, difference as binary, polar, dual, to begin with.[66] Differance itself, therefore, cannot any longer be of the order of the dual, and follows paths of thought that are generally blocked by twoness. The elemental arrangement of the differing, dif-fering, deferring traits of differance aims at tying the becoming dual of difference or rather the becoming (metaphysical) difference of difference, to traits in excess, and in a relation of dissymetry, to difference as dual, or to the necessity with which difference develops into duality (and, subsequently, opposition). Not only does differance not entail the generalization of difference, not only is it not a structure akin to the Platonic *ontos on,* it resists, as their foreground, all binary codes and binary formalization.

Contrary to Marion's assertion, differance does not remain within the horizon of the question of Being. By weaving the ontological difference's characteristic traits into the quasi-synthetic arrangement of differance, the question of Being loses none of its radicality. Rather, as the most radical, hence, different kind of difference, it submits itself with a special urgency to being questioned in the light of a differing to which it itself must bend. The indifference to the ontological difference that such inscription entails does not, however, stem from an indifference to thinking. Indeed, only by developing and further refining, in a formal manner, as it were, the minimal traits that constitute the ontological difference, difference as such, and the relation between both, could the Heideggerian problematic of Being and of the "between" be tied into the cluster of traits of difference that is differance. In addition, the very gesture of drawing the constitutive differing traits of a manifold of (incommensurable kinds of) differences into one formation is an eminently philosophical gesture. It is the attempt, as it were, to account for the fact that difference is said differently, *diaphora pollakos legetai.* In Derrida's thinking, one that conceives of itself as philosophical in a non-ontotheological sense, thought is not abandoned, not even in a propaedeutic fashion, as was the case in Marion's negative theology. Although the silent voice in which Being is heard is divested of authority in that the ontological difference is tied by one of its characteristic traits into the quasi-synthesis of differance, thinking is not therefore annulled. By being shown to be linked by one of its main traits to a cluster of differences, philosophical thought as the thinking of Being encounters an essential, because structural, limit. However, this limit also opens up new possibilities for thought, possibilities foreclosed not only by the metaphysical definition of thinking as the thinking of Being, but also by Heidegger's restriction of the essence of thinking to the thinking of Being. If, indeed, one can, in the case of Derrida, speak of an indifference to the ontological difference, it is an indifference to difference as the capital unifying and opening "ground" for all differences (between beings, and between themselves). By tying this capital difference—the ontological difference, but also difference *as* difference—to a cluster of lateral differences such as differance, thought encounters the very limit of its limitlessness.

4

Answering for Reason

THE PHILOSOPHICAL DEMAND that reason be rendered (that an explanation or a reasoned account be given), and that this be done by answering *to* the principle of reason, is, undoubtedly, coextensive with the philosophical project from the outset. And this responsibility that philosophy incurs as philosophy also has a history of its own. From Aristotle to Leibniz, the principle of reason to which philosophical accounting must yield requires, in conformity with the Aristotelian metaphysical conception by which philosophy becomes directed toward exhibiting primary roots and principles, that effects be explained by their causes. As a principle, however, this demand that reason be rendered does not become formulated until the seventeenth century. But, more important, Leibniz's statement of the principle of reason does not simply represent a mere codification of what two millennia of philosophizing had just presupposed. Leibniz's explicit casting of the principle of reason is also the beginning of a new type of reason in the West—modern, scientific reason—as well as a new type of answering to this sort of reason, namely, rational thinking or rationality. Some have intimated that postmodernism, with its critique of reason, withdraws altogether from this (rational) history of philosophical responsibility. Postmodernism, it has been said, proclaims the death not only of modern reason, of rationality, but of reason in general. Its critique of reason has been accused of surrendering the very demand that reason be rendered. And thus it would seem that postmodernism revokes the Western heritage, as well as its project, for the benefit of the West's absolute Other, its opposite—irrationality.

Even before one takes stock of the epistemological value of a concept such as postmodernism, one must ask: Why has the postmodern questioning of rationality and reason been construed so hastily as irrationalism? What makes the defenders of classical or modern reason conclude that this questioning is itself a critique, a rejection of reason altogether? What threat causes these shrill screams to keep one's hands off reason to revert so easily (in the name of reason) to obscurantism and irrationalism—precisely what the postmodernist questioning of reason becomes accused of? It is this that reveals the intimate link that exists between rationalism and irrationalism. Undoubtedly, much of what is sold today as postmodern—particularly on the art scene—exploits the label "postmodern" for the purposes of what is now a profitable eclecticism, nostalgia, or even mere sentimentality. But it is not primarily postmodern aesthetics—the aesthetics succeeding the specifically modernist trends in art and literature beginning at the turn of the century—that is the true target of the champions of reason. In conformity with the conceptual history of "modernity," according to which "modernity" stretches from Cartesian rationalism to rationalism's climax in the European Enlightenment, postmodernism has come to mean, for the defenders of reason, the period of philosophical thinking following Kant. The criticism to which reason and rationality becomes subjected from then on is, for these defenders of reason, nothing less than a call for a return to the irrational. Although it cannot be denied that at times this critique has given way to irrationalism, such a thoroughgoing condemnation of the philosophical efforts since Kant is not only theoretically but historically wrong. The question why the indictment of the postmodern critique of reason is so precipitate thus becomes all the more urgent. Undoubtedly, there are different reasons for this fast and furious response, reasons that range from sheer incomprehensibility to moral indignation.

In what follows I shall concentrate on another reason, one that is, by rights, more elemental than those already referred to, since it touches upon a certain limit of thinking, that is, a limit of philosophical thought. Indeed, the most striking aspect of all the literature that criticizes the so-called postmodern attack on reason is the failure to make a basic, if not absolutely elementary, philosophical distinction regarding the principle of reason. Even if it is granted (but are things that easy?) that some of the criticism of reason has turned irrational, it must still be said that it has also been an attempt to bring reason—especially in its modern, techno-scientific form—before the tribunal of reason itself. What has been called "postmodernity," that is, philosophical thought after Kant, demands of reason that reason be rendered. Yet if such is indeed the case, it is not the end of the history of the principle of reason. By asking for reason's credentials, this critique inaugurates another phase in the history of reason. The distinction that I have been referring to is thus that between answering *to* the principle of reason and answering *for* it. To disregard this capital difference amounts to a refusal of a question about reason itself that, at first glance, is in full continuity with the traditional demand of reason to render reason. It is, indeed, in order not to have to ask this question that the defenders of reason—the defenders, that is, of a version of reason that more often than not has already been severely truncated in an attempt at desubstantializing reason, and that, as is the case with Jürgen Habermas, has been reduced to mere formal and procedural rationality[1]—reject wholesale the postmodernist interrogation of reason as simple irrationalism.

To ask for the credentials of reason does indeed have some disturbing implications. Although answering *for* reason is a direct consequence of reason's demand to account for all claims made, to answer *for* the call and claims of reason itself is, primarily, an act different from answering to the principle of reason. In asking what grounds this principle, which itself is a principle of grounding, one engages in a sort of thinking which inevitably obeys a different logic than that called upon by the principle of reason. Nonetheless, it does not simply disobey the principle of reason and thereby veer toward irrationalism. As Derrida has put it,

> to answer *for* the principle of reason . . . , to answer *for* this call, to raise questions about the origin or ground of this principle of foundation *(Der Satz vom Grund),* is not simply to obey it or to respond *in the face of* this principle. We do not listen in the same way when we are responding to a summons as when we are questioning its meaning, its origin, its possibility, its goal, its limits. Are we obeying the principle of reason when we ask what grounds this principle which is itself a principle of grounding? We are not—which does not mean that we are disobeying it, either.[2]

If this type of inquiry into the very credentials of reason—an investigation that, following the call of reason, must be made of all its versions, whether substantialist or merely formal, ahistorical or temporal, *Zweckrationalität* or *Wertrationalität*—appears irrational to the champions of reason, it does so, indeed, because this inquiry's "logic" does not, for principal reasons, fully comply with the demands of reason. It does so, moreover, also because this type of inquiry is no longer classifiable as a *critique*. Yet this is not due to its abandoning of the rational standards of criticism. The goal of answering for reason is not to further divide reason into what constitutes it and what does not, into what does or does not serve it, or to decide on the transcendental conditions of reason's proper and (epistemologically and ethically) successful powers. Nor is it simply a critique (in the name of an Other of reason that would be more plentiful, more just) of reason's alleged shortcomings with respect to the singular, the marginal, the exotic, and so on—a critique, that is, of its so-called repressive character. To engage in such an inquiry—in spite of the fact that such inquiry into the ground of the principle of reason is not critique and thus not assimilable to either reason or non-reason—as an extreme consequence of the principle of reason itself is clearly an act that, because it breaks the rules of reasoning for *principal* reasons (as an inquiry into the grounds of the principle itself), is also, in a complex manner, in compliance with reason. Hence, Derrida's question as to "who is more faithful to reason's call, who hears it with a keener ear, who better sees the difference, the one who offers questions in return and tries to think through the possibility of that summons, or the one who does not want to hear any question about the reason of reason?"[3] In order to sketch an answer to this question I turn to Habermas' scathing criticism of what he conceives of as an all-out abrogation of reason and rationality in postmodernity.

Modernity and rationality are interconnected in a conceptually compulsory manner in that the two notions stand in an intrinsic and internal relation to each other. According to Habermas, therefore, postmodernism, as a farewell to modernity and its discourse as a whole, would of necessity represent a departure from rationality. Postmodernism, he has argued, is in pursuit of an "immemorial" anarchism, which, after Nietzsche, characterizes the Other of reason in essentially two forms—forgotten Being (Martin Heidegger) and ecstatic sovereignty (Georges Bataille). Such an approach, which claims the status of an esoteric, specialized knowledge *(Sonderwissen)* that is beyond discursive thinking and critical authority, would culminate in the business of deconstruction, a mode of thinking disconnected from all serious scientific analysis. This mode of thinking, moreover, can only result in an empty and formalistic incantation of undetermined authority. Deconstructive thinking, according to Habermas, does not merely dismiss peremptorily the objection of pragmatic inconsistency; it makes such an objection altogether irrelevant by collapsing the distinction between literature and philosophy. Habermas remarks: "If, following Derrida's recommendation, philosophical thinking were to be relieved of the duty of solving problems and shifted over to the function of literary criticism, it would be robbed not merely of its seriousness, but of its productivity."[4] From a perspective such as Habermas', it thus makes sense to launch an investigation of the philosophical relation between postmodernism and rationality. But the outcome of such an investigation is exclusively polemical. In the history sketched out in *The Philosophical Discourse of Modernity*—a history characterized in terms of a play of reciprocal outdoing or outbidding *(Überbietung),* in which one thinker tries to outwit his predecessor with increasing radicality until all the means of the paradigm that they are simultaneously criticizing and drawing on are exhausted, and which would thus be subjectivist history, subjectivism being nothing else but this obsession to outdo through inversion and radicalization the thinking of one's precursors—Habermas has nothing positive to say about the criticism to which reason has been subjected from the left Hegelians on to Martin Heidegger, Theodor W. Adorno, Jacques Derrida, and Michel Foucault. Habermas does, admittedly, seek to return to the level of the critique of reason inaugurated by Kant, and "the trace of communicative reason" to be found in the early Hegel.[5] His modest attempt, he claims, is capable, as he repeatedly stresses, of bringing about nothing less than a change of paradigm. Yet practically nothing in the history of thinking he outlines can be put to any use in his own attempt to undercut *(unterbieten)* this history of criticism. In a curious disregard of the practice of determined negation which he advocates so forcefully when it comes to criticizing others, Habermas concludes that postmodernity and rationality are simply incommensurable.

At no point does Habermas question the epistemological value of the buzzword *postmodern.* Born in North America, this term, as Todd Gitlin has argued, "extrapolates the long-established eclectic logic of American culture" and its "vulgarized pluralism."[6] Since its importation to Europe, this term has taken on as many meanings as the words "modernism" or "modernity" can possibly assume. To the architects, it means post-functionalist, anti-Bauhaus architecture; to the literary critics, post-Joycean writing; to the philosophers, the end of the project of the European Enlightenment; and to the theologians, something else still. Instead of being a picture puzzle *(Vexierbild),* as Albrecht Wellmer has suggested, the term postmodernism is a ragbag concept.[7] Moreover, Habermas also seems to subscribe uncritically to what the prefix *post* of postmodernism suggests—a definite end or overcoming of a period, with its mode of thinking and political attitudes, as well as the beginning of a new era that, because it is new, must be improved. Yet, if postmodernity is constituted by the before-mentioned reciprocal outdoing or outbidding of one thinker by another, postmodernity is, at best, only another phase of modernism. Modernism, for Habermas, represents the program of emancipation (from a liberal perspective) as it has crystallized most recently in the historical period of the European Enlightenment. It is characterized by conceptions of development, innovation, and, especially, overcoming and going beyond, as well as by the idea of a strict, serial linkage of the ensuing transgressions. This period, which stands under the sign of the *novum,* is dominated, as Gianni Vattimo has remarked, by the idea that "the history of thought is a progressive 'enlightenment' which develops through an ever more complete appropriation and reappropriation of its own 'foundations.' "[8] Yet these are also the categories that sustain Habermas' conception of postmodernism's relinquishing of the program of the Enlightenment through a history of successive, and increasingly radical, outdoings. Much more could be said about the history of postmodernism as outlined by Habermas. I present only this, which points to the questionable explicatory value of the notion of postmodernism, namely, that the idea of a definite end of a historical project, of a reappropriation and recuperation of the Other of Reason at the end of history, is itself modern in nature.

Indeed, as Wellmer has pointed out, the notion of postmodernism, in addition to designating the end of the project of the European Enlightenment and, thus, the end of Greek or Occidental civilization, can also be construed as outlining "the contours of a radicalized modernity, of a self-enlightened Enlightenment, of a post-rational concept of reason."[9] Such an understanding—although developing within the same conceptual and categorial parameters as those that inform Habermas' definition of the postmodern as a total sell-out of Enlightenment ideas and their concept of reason—conceives of the postmodern as a process headed in the direction of a more encompassing concept of reason. This is what, ultimately, makes it possible for Wellmer to speak of the notion of "postmodernism" as a picture puzzle. Such a concept of reason would be more radical because it would have opened itself to all its Others, that is, to all those respective Others within reason that the different types of the criticism of reason have brought into view. Wellmer distinguishes three such different Others: the uncontrolled libidinal forces that a psychological destruction of reason shows to inhabit it (Freud); the social powers constitutive of reason according to a critique of reason as instrumental or as identity-fostering (Adorno); and finally, the systems of signification or of life-forms that, according to a linguistic destruction of reason, precede it on all accounts (Wittgenstein, and even Heidegger). Whether these three Others of reason are truly the essential Others that the postmodern critique of reason has exhibited is not my concern here. What is at issue is whether these Others must truly undermine, once and for all, the privilege of reason. Indeed, as Wellmer has convincingly argued, rather than leading to a total destruction of reason, these various thematizations of the Other of reason can serve to conceive of reason in a new and, I would add, more comprehensive manner. They invite us, so to speak, to sublate or integrate. Thus the disillusionment produced by the insight into the libidinal powers in the background of reason can have the power to strengthen the rationality of the subject by making it capable of living with its own limits; understanding of the social power and authority at the heart of conceptual thought and the logic of identity, as well as of conceptual thought's alienating tendencies, can be forged into an instrument by means of which the concept is overcome by the concept itself; and, finally, the insight that untruth occurs because of specific blockages in language can lead to the attempt to draw on resources within language to counter these linguistic restrictions, and thus to bring truth into its own. In other words, rather than destroying reason, the different critiques of reason, however trenchant, can be made subservient, Wellmer argues, to a new self-appropriation of reason. These critiques give reason another chance, so to speak. Indeed, the challenge of the postmodern thematizations of the Others of reason to reason itself—which is the central experience of the death of reason—is cathartic, to say the least. It leads to a concept of reason far more radical, and far more ambitious, as far as the power of reason's reappropriation of its limits is concerned.

Yet, for Habermas, the whole history of philosophy's interrogation of reason since Hegel contains not one positive contribution to the question of reason. Habermas' abstract negation of the whole tradition of the modern questioning of reason becomes epitomized precisely in this rejection of the idea of a comprehensive notion of reason. This is clearly directed toward Karl-Otto Apel's confidence that the different forms of the criticism of rationality—including even what he construes as the most complete neglect of the rational criterion of pragmatic consistency in

French post-structuralism's effort to decenter the subject—are themselves rooted in "a more comprehensive form of rationality."[10] By
resorting to the old (Kantian) distinction between intellect *(Verstand)* and
reason *(Vernunft)*, Apel does indeed seek to understand the different
sorts of criticisms which have been directed against reason in the framework of the tradition of a philosophical self-limitation and self-differentiation of reason. The various types of this criticism would thus be
fully justified, since they would be aimed against making absolute,
abstractly isolated, and hence deficient forms of intellectual rationality
(Verstandes-Rationalität). Rather than imply a *parti pris* for irrationality,
such criticism of reason would consequently be rational, according to
Apel. For, apart from the fact that it could not be developed without at
least a tacit recognition of philosophical discursive rationality, such a
criticism of reason would represent a matter of reason itself.

Habermas' rationale for refusing to give any serious credit to the tradition he is reviewing is that its criticism of subject-centered reason is
self-defeating. It defeats itself, moreover, because, rather than subject
such a notion of reason to an immanent critique, it radicalizes that criticism. That is, it displays a criticism that opens an attack on the (rational)
roots of criticism itself. By challenging the very foundation of criticism,
such a criticism of reason has, for Habermas, become total and self-
referential *(selbstbezüglich)*. Furthermore, he notes that such a totalizing
self-referential putting-into-question of reason becomes entangled in the
classical aporias or paradoxes of the philosophy of subjectivity, because
it must have recourse to the very tools of subject-centered reason to
debunk its authority. Even a radical criticism of reason which would seek
to avoid the paradox of self-referentiality by reverting to the realm of
rhetoric—as a Derrida alienated in de Man's sense would do—would
not escape it, because the merely inverted (subjectivist) foundationalism
of such an attempt not only would fall prey to the weaknesses of the
criticism of metaphysics all over again, but also would represent an ultimate dulling of "the sword of the critique of reason itself."[11] Such entanglement in the paradoxes of self-referentiality is inevitable, Habermas
contends, if we continue to fight, as do Heidegger, Adorno, and Derrida,
the " 'strong' concepts of theory, truth and system," that is, the universal
status that philosophy once claimed for the answers to its universal questions. Yet reason, according to Habermas, is not bound to hold on to
"these goals of metaphysics classically pursued from Parmenides to
Hegel." Since Hegel, moreover, these traditional philosophical issues no

longer exist. It would therefore be superfluous for any criticism of reason "to grasp the roots at such a depth that it could scarcely avoid the paradoxes of self-referentiality."[12]

It is not my concern here to show that Habermas does not do justice to the philosophers he discusses in his book. Therefore, I want to shift the terrain of the discussion. First, I wish to claim that the postmodern interrogation of reason which has triggered a renewed interest in the question of rationality in philosophy is not exhausted by the rediscovery of the irrational, whether as a boundary problem of rational cognition or as what calls the foundation of Western culture into question. From the Greek mathematicians who discovered the irrational as a limit of rationality, through the moment when the irrational becomes a philosophical problem proper—that is, when philosophy puts the subject in the very center of its concerns (and the irrational becomes thus determined as a region inaccessible to human cognition)—the irrational has been the unavoidable counter-concept of rationality.[13] It is precisely this conceptual machinery that is called into question in certain of the works that are labeled postmodern. If Jean-François Lyotard can claim that postmodernism corresponds to the occurrence of a "major shift in the notion of reason," and thus in the very nature of what we understand by knowledge, he can do so, indeed, because of what he believes to be the role of paralogism in contemporary thought, whether scientific or artistic.[14]

However, before I discuss Lyotard's *Postmodern Condition,* it must be recalled that, since its publication in 1979, Lyotard has expressed misgivings about his own endorsement of the term "postmodern." He writes: "As you know, I made use of the word 'postmodern': it was but a provocative way to put the struggle in the foreground of the field of knowledge." Lyotard, who makes this qualification in light of "what is called postmodernity or postmodernism on the market place of today's ideologies" and the current eclecticism in the arts, especially denounces in such qualifying statements the diachronical periodization of history that the prefix *post* expresses as a thoroughly "modern obsession." He notes as well that "the postmodern attitude is still implied in the modern one insofar as modernity presupposes a compulsion to get out of itself and to resolve itself, therefore, into something else, into a final equilibrium," be it utopian or political, and that "in this sense postmodernity is a promise with which modernity is pregnant definitely and endlessly."[15]

Let me then first recall that, according to Lyotard, one ought to conceive of the postmodern as constituted primarily by a crisis of narratives, more precisely of the grand narratives, such as the speculative narrative or the narrative of emancipation, whose function it had been to unify or to legitimize both knowledge and social practice. As a result, this postmodern incredulity toward metanarratives, and the subsequent recasting of the function of legitimation, leads to an explosion of mini-narratives or language games which profoundly affect the status of knowledge and the idea of reason. Lyotard exemplifies this transformation of knowledge by referring to the language games of science and its new practices of validation. He argues that science and, in particular, scientific research and argumentation put all its stakes in working on proofs, rather than being driven by a quest for performance. Yet what this means is that the pragmatics of science is essentially geared toward "searching for and 'inventing' counter-examples, in other words, the unintelligible; supporting an argument means looking for a 'paradox' and legitimating it with new rules in the games of reasoning."[16] Indeed, the major characteristic of modern science, according to Lyotard, is that it "emphasizes the invention of new 'moves' *('coups' nouveaux)* and even new rules for language games."[17] This notion of "moves," which is quite decisive for what Lyotard claims to be going on in contemporary science, describes the agonistic dimension of knowledge formation. Scientific knowledge becomes plural and its languages become manifold to such an extent indeed that science, while playing its own game, not only is incapable of legitimating other language games, but "is above all incapable of legitimating itself, as speculation assumed it could."[18] But, as Lyotard insists, this does not mean that the question of legitimation becomes obsolete altogether. On the contrary, the most "striking feature of postmodern scientific knowledge is that the discourse on the rules that validate it is (explicitly) immanent to it." "For," he adds, "it is not philosophy that asks this question of science, but science that asks it of itself." But such inclusion "within scientific discourse [of] the discourse on the validation of statements held to be laws" gives rise, of course, "to 'paradoxes' that are taken extremely seriously and to 'limitations' on the scope of knowledge that are, in fact, changes in its nature."[19] As a result, rather than have a universal metalanguage that would legitimize and systematize all pieces of knowledge, the myriad of new moves is accompanied by another myriad of newly invented rules for the arguments advanced. Lyotard characterizes the shift in the notion of reason as follows: "The principle of a universal metalanguage is replaced by the principle of a plurality of formal and axiomatic systems capable of arguing the truth of denotative statements; these systems are described by a metalanguage that is universal but not consistent. What used to pass as paradox, and even paralogism, in the knowledge of classical and modern science can, in certain of these systems, acquire a new force of conviction and win the acceptance of the community of experts."[20] But these formal characteristics do not suffice to explain the postmodern understanding of knowledge and reason. As Lyotard tries to show, modern science is thematically geared toward new objects as well, in particular toward singularities and incommensurabilities. Lyotard concludes that what one learns from this research "is that the continuous differentiable function is losing its preeminence as a paradigm of knowledge and prediction. Postmodern science—by concerning itself with such things as undecidables, the limits of precise control, conflicts characterized by incomplete information, *'fracta,'* catastrophes, and pragmatic paradoxes—is theorizing its own evolution as discontinuous, catastrophic, nonrectifiable, and paradoxical. It is changing the meaning of the word *knowledge,* while expressing how such a change can take place. It is producing not the known, but the unknown."[21] What thus seems to distinguish postmodern reason from classical or modern reason is its irreducible plurality and its willingness to sustain it. As Lyotard insinuates at the beginning of *The Postmodern Condition,* postmodern knowledge "refines our sensitivity to differences and reinforces our ability to tolerate the incommensurable."[22]

What this brief account of Lyotard's analysis of the shift in the notion of reason in postmodern science indicates is that postmodernity is not a farewell to reason altogether, but a shift toward the reason of the plural, the indeterminate, the random, the irregular, the formless, the paralogistic. It is with respect to these that the unified, the lawful, the regular, and so on, are shown to be derivative formations. What this account also shows is that the concern with rationality in our time is perhaps more than just an attempt by philosophy to react retrospectively to discussions and events that did not take place within its core. Herbert Schnädelbach has argued—and I follow his lead—that if rationality is thematized today by philosophy, it is so because philosophy seeks, by means of a detour, to reappropriate a traditional, if not hereditary, theme in a transformed shape. Indeed, although the concepts of rationality and reason have the same linguistic origin, they clearly are not substitutes for each other. Whereas rationality suggests solid scientific seriousness, reason is open to the suspicion of mentalism and metaphysical obscurantism. But reason in modern philosophy was never merely one faculty of consciousness among others. As Schnädelbach has argued, from Descartes to Kant and Hegel, "the philosophy of reason appears with the claim to secure the self-foundation of philosophy by reverting to the very reason of the philosophizing subject."[23] Let me add that if we look at reason in philosophy from antiquity on, reason, *logos,* appears as that which is constituted by the *logon didonai,* that is, by the giving of a reasoned account in which the philosophizing subject publicly accounts for itself as well. The concern with rationality and, in particular, with what happens to it in the advanced sciences is thus an attempt to reach beyond a notion of rationality defined by logical consistency to what Charles Taylor has called the "richer" concept of rationality and, ultimately, to philosophy itself.[24] What is striven for here, however, is not a philosophy as it was before rationality superseded reason, but a philosophy in a transformed shape.

Nonetheless, it is questionable whether Lyotard's account of the transformation of reason within postmodernity allows such a philosophy to come to light in its most consequential and uncompromising form. Indeed, Lyotard's description of the new paradigm of reason sounds very much like an inversion of the old or modern one. The categories that he uses to pinpoint postmodern reason are the binary opposites of the traditional objects and values of reason. Discontinuity, undecidability, instability, and dissension cannot avoid drawing their very meaning from the horizon and telos of continuity, decidability, stability, and consensus. Lyotard's emphasis on paralogism and paradox as the postmodern forms of legitimation—that is, on those operations of thought which Habermas abhors to such a degree that he appears unable to confront them in *The Philosophical Discourse of Modernity*—makes sense only with respect to the standards of logical and articulated argumentation. Let us therefore consider the following: If the postmodern transformation of the idea of reason consisted only in such value inversions and the subsequent dependency of what Lyotard calls "islands of determinism"[25] on these inverted values, it would be hard to understand all the fuss made over the so-called resurgence of irrationalism. Indeed, a perhaps much more decisive transformation of thought is in the offing, one which has much greater implications but which at the same time is also much less flashy than the usual value inversions.

It may well be that our epoch, more than any other before, is distinguished by conflicting ways of inquiring into reason, or by thinking about thinking. Some of these ways represent attempts to return to and reappropriate in a modernist fashion elements of the emancipatory Enlightenment concept of reason; others try to show, in a postmodern vein, that reason is irreducibly plural; while yet others, as has been seen, opt for a more encompassing concept of reason in a dialectico-hermeneutical fashion that would reconcile the different critiques to which reason has been subjected. Yet all these different ways of rethinking reason, as a formal procedure of consensus formation, as the agonistic and paralogical play of knowledge production, or as the elaborate self-differentiation of reason through self-criticism, presuppose, each in a different manner, the older concept (or concepts) of reason. The type of criticism to which reason becomes submitted here is, in every case, a function of the constitutive meanings of *logos, ratio, Vernunft*. The formalistic reduction of reason to rules of argumentation, the pluralization of these rules, and the unifying reappropriation of these plural language games do not merely call upon one another to form a complementary whole. The whole which they make up, in spite of their seemingly conflicting stands, is just as derivative of what since the Greeks one has understood as reason. Yet, it *happens* that, in what is called the postmodern challenge to reason, another type of debate with reason has begun to take place. This is a debate that presupposes, in the same way as does each of the various critiques of reason just mentioned, the older concept or concepts of reason, but in a clearly different way. On the one hand, this debate assumes that whatever the "new" meanings are that reason has acquired, these meanings are in continuity with the implications of the older concepts of reason. On the other hand, this debate with reason takes, in a more decisive manner, *all* the implications and exigencies of the concept of reason (formal, substantialist, in terms of content) that it takes to be ultimately indissociable, and affirms them in what is no longer a critique, but an attempt to establish whence reason in this strong sense comes into its own.

As Vattimo has argued in *The End of Modernity,* in the course of referring to Nietzsche, and to Heidegger in particular, there is, indeed, an interrogation of reason in postmodernity that if it sounds the death knell of modernity does so, precisely, because it does not conceive of its inquiry into reason as an overcoming, or outbidding. If the notion of postmodernity has, perhaps, found its most refined expression in Vattimo's work, it has done so because it shows that this sort of interrogation of reason no longer yields to the modernist logic of overcoming or surpassing with the aim of producing novelty. Yet, since this type of inquiry does not follow the modernist's predicament, the knell it sounds is barely perceptible. As a matter of fact, it is not a knell to begin with. Rather than aiming at an *Überwindung,* such an inquiry aims at a *Verwindung* of reason. For Vattimo, the Heideggerian concept of *Verwindung* signifies a "going beyond that that is both an acceptance and deepening." Yet it is not, for that matter, a dialectical surpassing that would take up again what had been left behind in order to further develop it. Drawing on the lexical significations of the German word, Vattimo points out that in a *Verwindung* one gets over something (in the sense of recovering), one commits oneself (in the sense of a resignation) to something that puts itself into one's hands. And since *Verwindung* has as well (though marginally) the sense of distortion, Vattimo defines it as a transformation of something "which is not foreseen by [this something's] . . . own essence, and yet is connected to it."[26] A *Verwindung* of reason, therefore, does not lead to something other, something new (the Other of reason, for instance). All a *Verwindung* does is to twist reason (or metaphysics, according to Vattimo) toward an inessential possibility that nonetheless is its own, and without which, I add, reason would not be reason. Rather than producing an Other of reason, such a *Verwindung* of reason is the sole trace of the tension toward an Other that inhabits reason as a possibility, and as a chance. Since this tension toward an Other is not one of reason's *essential* possibilities, and since it is only (the *trace* of) a *tension* toward an Other, and not an Other itself, a *Verwindung* of reason can never be, in principle, a reappropriating return. Of the foundationalist gesture characteristic of modernity (and of the whole of Western thought as well), such a postmodern interrogation of reason would thus keep only the tension toward something that is not yet reappropriable as an origin in a strict sense, and that could not be thematized as a "thing" either.

Such an investigation as just described is not, by rights, a critical inquiry or a metarational interrogation of reason. It is not of the order of (still yet) another question added to all the questions put to reason, that would, at least provisionally, conclude the questioning process. The difference that such an interrogation makes is of another sort than that of the critical question, and, consequently, this difference is (almost) invisible. It is invisible, first, because this type of interrogation is not subjectable to the watchword *inversion.* No overturning of existing priorities is sought here. And, *mutatis mutandis,* no attempt is made in such an investigation at *returning to,* say, an Other of reason that would be its true foundation. It is in particular not a revision of all those inversions of priorities that the Kantian revolution undertook and, thus, not a return to the nonrational. In bringing forth a tension toward an Other in reason, the postmodern interrogation opens up reason to an inessential and non-reappropriable origin. With this it also engages in a gesture of thinking that cannot be captured by the philosophical gesture of foundation. As a result, all the traditional relations of subsumption and subordination, of the singular and the universal, lose their hold on the operation in question. While not altogether escaping these relations and traditional gestures of thinking, the postmodern interrogation of reason also engages in gestures that are no longer simply under the jurisdiction of philosophy. In this case as well, the philosophical watchwords fall short of identifying these gestures. From what has been established up to this point, it should be clear that the postmodern transformation of thinking that I referred to above is not a transformation that could be conceived of in terms of an inversion of foundational values. It is not of the order of a (reappropriating) return to an Other (of reason). Because of this, such a transformation, although much more incisive than the readily categorizable value inversions, is also less flashy, less obtrusive. What I was referring to is what I perceive to be the thrust of the thinking of Derrida, whom Habermas deigns to call a *nicht argumentationsfreudiger Philosoph,* that is, a philosopher with little enthusiasm for argumentation.[27] Derrida, however, would certainly resist any association with the concept of postmodernism, and for reasons not unlike those which made Heidegger refuse all identification of thinking with passing fads. Derrida's thinking is not motivated by the restricted attempt to overcome a particular historical formation of thought such as modernity. It does not even use modernity as a pretext to call into question some of the more fundamental issues regarding the whole of Western thinking. From the outset, the thrust of Derrida's thinking has been aimed at the most elemental general structures of thinking that underlie all transformations of thought, whether modern or postmodern. For this very reason, it is itself neither modern nor postmodern. Yet, if I nonetheless decide to discuss Derrida's thinking in this context, I do so not simply because Habermas has reserved a very noticeable place for Derrida in his review of the postmodern debate with subject-centered reason. I do so because Derrida himself has, on more than one occasion, spoken of his research as being concerned with the origin of reason, logic, and thinking. But, as we shall see, such a concern with origins does not mean, as Habermas believes, that the origins of reasons which Derrida reveals would consist of "contrasting concepts contrasting with *(Kontrastbegriffe)* reason . . . resistant to any attempts at rational incorporation."[28] Indeed, what appear in Derrida to be the origins of reason are not of the order of what Habermas understands as the Other of reason.

Let me right away remark the following: Any attempt that explores the origins of reason, logic, and thinking cannot make an unconditional use of what it seeks to explain and account for. If it did, that is, if it obeyed without restriction the principle of reason in attempting to answer *for* reason, and if it made something of the order that is to be explained underlie that which is in question, we would, in Plato's words, be treated like children to whom one is telling stories *(muthon tina diegeisthae).*[29] The origins of reason, logic, and thinking must be expatiated upon in a way of their own. This is an elementary philosophical rule, philosophy's first step, so to speak, which therefore very easily sinks into oblivion.[30] Yet it is a rule operative on all levels of philosophical thought. Take, for instance, modern formal logic! Although there are some who believe this to be not only the one, single, scientific logic, but the one, single, philosophical discipline worthy of the name, modern formal logic is in itself unable to account for the assumptions that it presupposes precisely to the extent that it conceives of itself as a formal discipline applicable to almost any subject matter. These assumptions entail the distinction between form and content, as well as the applicability of the one to the other and all that applicability implies in the first place. These are questions that can be posed and decided only by a type of discourse other than that of scientific logic. Such a meta-logical discourse, though not escaping the constraints of logical rigorousness, cannot simply yield to it. If it did, it would fail to explain the assumptions on which the formalism of formal logic is based. Therefore, such a meta-logical discourse—in short, ontology, metaphysics, or simply *philosophy*—has *necessarily* those qualifications of metaphysical obscurity or poetic confusions that the logicians never tire of denouncing as unscientific. Yet what is true with respect to the traditional disciplines of thinking is all the more true where philosophy engages in an inquiry concerning the legitimizing titles of thinking itself. Any *philosophical* inquiry into the origins of thinking, of reason and logic, cannot, if it is to be *philosophical,* describe these origins in the categories constitutive of what these origins make possible. The investigation of what is prior to thinking, reason, and logic must, therefore, follow complex strategies and engage in calculated conceptual games which are not entirely reasonable and logical compared with the standards that these origins are to render intelligible. This explains also why the origins of reason, logic, and thinking are not to be determined as the Other of reason, the opposite of reason, the irrational. These are categories of reason which designate, as Derrida puts it, "an opacity within the system of rationality" (*OG,* p. 259). In *Of Grammatology,* Derrida decides to determine the origin of reason as "nonrational as the origin of reason must be." That this "non" is not to be understood as a negation in a logical sense is obvious from Derrida's discussion, in the same work, of the "rationality" of such an origin. Rationality here does not mean conformity to reason, for Derrida notes that the word in question should "perhaps be abandoned," since what governs these origins of reason "no longer issues from a logos" (*OG,* p. 10). This is indeed an excellent example of a calculated inconsistency and contradictoriness that becomes unavoidable—and for compelling philosophical reasons—if the "reason" of reason is to be interrogated. But what this example also suggests is that for Derrida such inconsistency, or paradox, is not a value in itself. It is a function of a language game aimed at determining the origin of reason according to standards and requirements that are intrinsically philosophical.

The nonrational origins of reason do not stand in a relation of Otherness to reason precisely because they are "prior" to the logic of oppositional differentiation and hierarchization that characterizes reason. As nonrational *origins* they are (in traditional terms) the essence of reason that is heterogeneous to reason, but is not, for that matter, reason's Other. Moreover, they "precede," by virtue of their nature as the origins of reason, the rational distinction ("which they render possible") of the same and the Other, and cannot, consequently, be the Other of reason. And even if it will be necessary hereafter to complicate the nature of their relation to reason, these origins will continue to escape binary schematization. Yet because these nonrational origins of reason are not reason's Other, they are not reappropriable by reason. Reason cannot return to them in order to found itself anew, thereby incorporating and sublating a fundamental unthought in what henceforth would be a more comprehensive and richer concept of reason. These origins, as we shall see, are *limits* in a strict sense *within* which reason can unfold both historically and systematically. They are these things which most intimately belong to reason (as its conditions of possibility) as well as those which reason can *never possess* (and thus they are its conditions of impossibility).

To reason *as* reason, whether formal or dialectical, these limits to which it stands in such intimate relation *must* remain foreign, or, more precisely, imperceptible. As far as reason is concerned, they do not exist and cannot, therefore, become its Other.

What is more, these nonrational origins of reason, which are "not yet logic but the origin of logic" (*G,* p. 242), "the pre-logical possibilities of logic,"[31] cannot be origins in a strict sense. The ground of the ground, as Heidegger has shown, cannot be another deeper, more excellent ground. Likewise, the "reason" of reason, the origin of reason, cannot be said to be a more profound origin. But, in spite of this similarity, there is a world of difference between what Heidegger circumscribes as the ground of the ground, and what Derrida designates as the origin of reason or, more simply, as the origin of the origin. For Heidegger the ground of the ground is Being—that is, Being as the opening, clearing, or lighting *(Lichtung)* of beings and, hence, of the grounding relation that can only be thought between beings—but the nonrational origin of reason is not to be conceived in phenomenological terms as an essential opening, a lighting or clearing, for appearing. The nonrational origin of reason thematized by Derrida does not stand in a necessary relation to reason, as the Heideggerian ground of the ground does to what is called ground in philosophical thinking. As Derrida argues in *Of Grammatology,* the origin of reason is something that adds itself to reason; it is a supple-ment to reason, something exterior, nonnecessary to reason, but also that without which reason could not be what it is. These nonrational origins of reason are of the order of unheard-of trivialities. They are trivialities in the sense that Husserl gives to this term in *Logical Investigations;* they are of the order of what Heidegger calls the simple and are therefore that much more difficult to think. But the origins of reason to which Derrida points do not have the Husserlian characteristic of being essential forms and laws (of meaning) or the unitary character of Heideggerian *Einfachheit* and *Einfalt.* They are simply not subsumable within rationality. This is not because reason is powerless to think its nonrational origin, but, rather, because reason would not be what it is if it did. As Derrida puts it, reason "is constituted by that lack of power. It is the principle of identity" (*OG,* p. 149). In the present space, I cannot do more than gesture toward supplementarity, arche-trace, differance, iterability, and the re-mark, and toward the rich contexts in which Derrida develops these notions as articulating the limits whence reason comes into its own. These origins of reason are incommensurate with reason, yet not as the

Other of reason, but as the structures against which reason stands out as that which precisely has no Other, no exterior, except that which it lets unfold from within itself.

From everything that I have established until now, it should already be obvious that such a nonnecessary and nonessential relation between the origins of reason and reason itself does not allow one to speak of this relation, as Habermas does, as one of an "anonymous, history-making productivity."[32] Habermas must, of course, make this mistake, just as he must misinterpret Heidegger's notion of Being as a counter-force.[33] Otherwise, he could not write the history of the criticism of reason in terms of a history that never escapes "the foundationalist tenacity of the philosophy of the subject" in spite of all attempts to overthrow it by inverting foundationalism.[34] Yet Being is not a force, just as the nonrational origins of reason do not "produce." Only reason produces, but its production is not without the non-originary structures at the origin of reason. Because of this nonnecessary and nonessential (yet not, for that matter, accidental or contingent, but rather, inevitable) dependency of reason on its origins, they are not principles, conditions of possibility, or "radical" foundations either. For all these rest precisely on the origins in question. Hence, one cannot use the philosophical language of grounding, constituting, or opening to conceptualize the relation between the non-originary origins of reason and reason itself. These difficulties have misled Habermas into concluding that, "if the other of reason is more than just the irrational or the unknown—namely, the *incommensurable,* which cannot be touched by reason except at the cost of an explosion of the rational subject—then there is no possibility of a theory that reaches beyond the horizon of what is accessible to reason and thematizes, let alone analyzes, the interaction of reason with a transcendent source of power."[35] From what I have said thus far it should be evident that the terms in which Habermas formulates the problem do not pertain to what is under discussion here—the origin of reason is neither transcendent or originary nor a power. Moreover, if theory, thematization, and analysis are understood in the sense in which they have always been understood, that is, as thinking from and toward a whole, then no theory could ultimately thematize and analyze these non-originary structures of reason. Yet, as has already been indicated, these origins have a certain "rationality" about them which can be brought into view, and which, within the parameters of a very calculated language game, can be articulated with rather great precision. What I call here "rationality" is certainly not of the order of reason, but it is not without ties to it. What "rationality" refers to in this context is, first and foremost, the minimal intelligibility of these non-originary structures of reason. Although they can be said to be undecidable, these structures are not indeterminate for that matter. They have indeed a highly determined organization which the language games in question can describe in the strictest possible manner. Undoubtedly, there are no established conventions with which to comprehend these games, because these games involve a displacement of conventions. Yet it is precisely from these displacements that these language games draw their own intelligibility.[36] The same can be said of the relation that the nonnecessary origins of reason entertain with reason. But, undoubtedly, another task remains, the task of discussing the "status" of these nonnecessary origins of reason with respect to and within the philosophical disciplines that traditionally have served to thematize questions of origins, principles, or conditions. The aim of such discussion is to contribute further to the strictest possible determination of these structures through a problematization of the traditional disciplinary framing of questions regarding ultimate grounds. Indeed, the institutional, discursive, and technical settings of elaborations on grounds or conditions of possibility represent strictly determined frames that are constitutive of the intelligibility (and scope) of the subject matter under discussion. Yet to elaborate on the non-originary origins of reason within the boundaries of the traditional disciplines of philosophy would serve not only to transform these disciplines in depth (with the result that it might no longer be as *simple* to distinguish between them, and to classify them according to their traditional order), but also to thematize the disciplinary norms of intelligibility with respect to these non-originary grounds of reason. The displacement of these norms that these latter "grounds" presuppose is itself a function of their own minimal intelligibility. It thereby contributes to rendering them as precise as possible. One would in this regard have to follow up on Derrida's suggestion, in *Of Grammatology,* to develop a new transcendental aesthetics even if, as he notes, this could no longer be an *aesthetics* in either a Kantian or a Husserlian sense. And, I would add, one ought to develop a new doctrine of the categories in order to come to grips with these non-originary structures of reason, although these structures are not forms of judgment, strictly speaking, or, for that matter, quantifiable, that is, totalizable intelligible entities.

To conclude, let me return to Habermas' contention that the postmodern critics of rationality confuse the universalist questions that philosophy continues to honor with the claims that it traditionally has made about the status of its answers to these questions. In this context, Habermas distinguishes questions regarding the rationality of utterances and the conditions of their range as examples of such universalist questions. Although philosophy still understands itself as the guardian of rationality, and thus requests that all responses to universalist questions mirror themselves in the grammatical forms of universal utterances, philosophy must, he adds, also "reckon upon the trivial *possibility* that they will be revised tomorrow or someplace else."[37] Hence his plea for utterances with weak status claims. This trivial possibility that all utterances regarding universalist problems can be subject to revision is indeed for Habermas a trivial matter, and thus requires only a pragmatic response in terms of fallibilism. Yet if this possibility can *always* happen to a strong utterance, then this is a necessary possibility that has to be accounted for in a manner that may affect the universalist questioning of philosophy itself. Habermas sees no theoretical problem in answering universalist questions in spite of the truth claims made, as opposed to the status that philosophy has claimed with respect to these truths. But if the trivial possibility Habermas refers to is a necessary one, then everything that the criticism of rationality from Heidegger and Adorno to Derrida has, according to Habermas, directed against the strong concepts of theory, truth, and system will also weigh against the weak claim of utterances regarding their irrefutability. More important, Habermas has significantly even fewer problems with the question in general, with the question's questioning form, a form that is invariably universal in thrust. What if precisely that form was at stake in certain of the philosophical writings that have been labeled "postmodern"? This form is at issue, not in order to give in to irrationalist modes of coping with philosophical issues, but, rather, to conceive of what in the *logos* is prior to its questioning form. Obviously, this something cannot be arraigned by a question; it cannot be thought if thinking, in its very essence, is constituted by the form of the question. Still, as I suggested, within the limits of a certain very calculated language game, thinking's pre-questioning forms can also find their articulation. Needless to say, within the discourse of philosophy, that is, within that thinking that the nonquestion "makes possible," any "thematization" of what is prior to the question must inevitably appear (to someone like Habermas, at least) as nonanalytical and stylistic criticism.[38] Yet if rationality is the issue today, is it so merely to spirit away the alleged lack of philosophical argumentation and discursive consistency? Is it not the issue, rather, because thinking has discovered a new sort of finitude which requires not the abandonment of the traditional forms and claims that constituted it, but their displacement within operations of thought whose calculated economy obeys a "rationality" of its own? To pose the question of rationality with regard to the postmodern is then, perhaps, to recover a sort of thinking which, although it presupposes a displacement of all the essential forms constitutive of thought in the tradition of thinking, is more of the order of the philosophies concerned with the "richer" concept of reason and is thus in greater proximity to the traditional exigencies of thinking, both thematic and methodological, than all the celebrations of rationality, whether grounded in reflexive consciousness or in pragmatic consensus formation.

5

Structural Infinity

THE LIMITS OF totalization, if judged by classical criteria, are usually attributed to the infinite richness of the field to be mastered, as well as to the finitude of the empirical subject breathlessly slaving away in the futile attempt to cover that field. Yet, in *Writing and Difference,* Derrida contends that "nontotalization can also be determined in another way: no longer from the standpoint of a concept of finitude as relegation to the empirical, but from the standpoint of the concept of *play*" (*WD,* p. 289). Play, understood here as infinite substitutability, is said to characterize the field of language. In *Of Grammatology* one can read that the play of representation that constitutes language is one of infinite reflection, of an "infinite reference *(renvoi)*" from one thing to another, from one mirror to another, from mirror to thing or image (*OG,* p. 36). This play of language is a play in which the infinitely multiplied elements designate themselves "*en abyme*—to employ the current phrase," as Derrida adds (*OG,* p. 163). No longer suspended at a center, a source, an origin, this play escapes the horizon of truth. More precisely, it is distinguished by what Derrida has called "the stairway or escalade of truth, one truth about another, one truth *on* (top of) another, one above or below the other, each step more or less true than truth."[1] It is a play which, because of its infinite substitutions, also characterizes the text—what Derrida calls the general text. The text, notes Derrida, is an "interminable network" (*D,* p. 205). It extends "far out of sight *(à perte de vue),*" and cannot be brought to a stop (*D,* p. 203). Without boundaries, it describes itself without end, and encloses and fits inside itself an infinite number of other texts. Analyzing a text thus inevitably becomes an infinite task, an endless investigation, one for which one would require an "infinite amount of time" (see *D,* pp. 204–205, 237).

129

I could further multiply and accumulate these references in Derrida's writings to the infinite, the endless, the interminable, all of which can be construed as aborting all possible totalization of a field such as language, or of that of the text. But the list of references to the infinite that I have already given, this repeated recourse to the notion of the infinite, the endless, the interminable in itself outlines the contours of the problem that I want to discuss. If the two forms of nontotalization that have been evoked—nontotalization in a classical sense and nontotalization owing to the play character of a field—are forms that contest what Derrida, in *Of Grammatology,* has called the thought of "positive infinity" (which, beginning with Plato culminates via Spinoza in Hegel's theology of the absolute concept as logos) (*OG,* p. 71), then the following question becomes unavoidable: Is the second type of nontotalization at all different from the first type, which points to essentially empirical reasons—the semantic vastness of the field, the finitude of a human glance—to prove the impossibility of totalization, and is the second type subject, as is the first, to Hegel's verdict—but not Hegel's alone, to infinitist metaphysics' verdict in general—on spurious infinity *(das schlechte Unendliche)?* The question is crucial. For even if one may no longer find convincing Hegel's speculative solution of the problem of the full totalization of what according to its concept must lend itself to such an operation—the Concept itself, or Reason—Hegel's arguments against spurious infinity remain perfectly valid. They remain relevant because the relegation of spurious infinity to the empirical discredits it as a tool of philosophical analysis. Spurious infinity disregards the fundamental difference—*difference itself*—between what is given and the given *as thought.*[2]

As a first step in inquiring into the similarity or difference between spurious infinity and the form of nontotalization that results from the play character of a field, it is certainly in order to recall what Hegel understood by genuine infinity, and to enumerate the most important reasons why he so severely condemned spurious infinity.

For obvious reasons, I cannot develop here the concept of infinity within Hegel's work as a whole. For the history of this concept in Hegel's thought, at least for the segment of it that stretches from Hegel's theological writings at Frankfurt to the second outline of a system at Jena, one can refer to Manfred Baum's exemplary essay in *Hegel-Studien.*[3] Here it will suffice to follow the development in *Science of Logic* of Hegel's thoughts about infinity. Of course, it is necessary to bear in mind that this development takes place within the *sphere of being,* and that distinctions are made in that sphere between quantitative and qualitative infinity. But although the major characteristics of the concept of infinity are outlined in the lowlier sphere of being, this concept is in fact and in truth at home "in the domain of the Notion, of the absolute reflection-into-self out of the finite, in the region of free infinitude and truth" (*SL,* p. 673). Indeed, that lowlier sphere of being does not yet know the true and full concept of infinity. It engenders only an abstract notion of genuine infinity, a notion which is in continuous danger of being annulled by spurious infinity.

Now, it must be recalled that Hegel's distinction between genuine and spurious infinity is not at all a specifically Hegelian idea. In *Science of Logic,* Hegel seems to have explicit recourse only to Spinoza, who rejected that conception of the infinite which represents it as an amount or series which is not completed (and contrasted it as "the *infinite of imagination*" to "the infinite as self-relation," "the infinite of thought, or *infinitum actu*") (*SL,* p. 250). But Spinoza's distinguishing of two infinites itself goes back to Aristotle's demarcation in the *Physics,* Book IV, of *potential* infinity—the infinity that appears in number series as infinite divisibility and as the possibility of infinite addition—from *actual* infinity. What this distinction implies is that one must not mistake the affirmation that a multitude of things can be increased *ad libitum* with the contention that the multitude so formed exists as a completed whole, as a totality. Although Aristotle himself termed actual infinity a self-contradictory concept, he did not simply endorse potential infinity, the infinity of imagination, which Spinoza held "to stop short at quantum as such," and not to "reflect on the qualitative relation which constitutes the ground of the existing incommensurability" (*SL,* p. 251). What Aristotle had already tried to emphasize in his refutations of Antisthene's assertion that each proposition to be demonstrated would entail another proposition to be demonstrated, is that all argumentation based on the potential infinite ignores the true nature of thought. Yet as a concept of thought, true infinity is an ultimate limit within which particularities become determinable, and cannot, for that reason, be transcended. As a universal of thought, the concept of the infinite, although transcending all particular things, cannot itself have a beyond. On the contrary, it is itself the beyond of all particular things within which these things are situated, and thus, in this contrast to the infinite diversity of particular beings, the true object of thought. With this (essentially) Hegelian interpretation of

the relation for Aristotle between potential and actual infinity, the stakes
of the present debate should be manifest. It is a debate on the proper
object of philosophy, and, consequently, on philosophy itself. This will
become clearer as I now proceed to determine, in as succinct a manner
as possible, what Hegel means by genuine or true infinity.

On the lowlier level of the logic of being in which Hegel sets forth
his notion of a true infinity, it names only a higher, a further-determined
form of becoming. Instead of being and nothingness, as at the beginning
of *Science of Logic,* becoming's new determinations are those of the infinite
and the finite, that is, of the spurious infinite as an abstract beyond, on
the one hand, and of the finite as negation fixed in itself, on the other.
In other words, true infinity must be an infinite "which embraces both
itself and finitude—and is therefore the infinite in a different sense from
that in which the finite is regarded as separated and set apart from the
infinite" (*SL,* p. 144). Hegel warns us not to mistake the "true Notion
of the infinite and its *absolute* unity" for "a *tempering,* a *reciprocal restricting*
or a *mixing;* such a superficial conception of the relationship leaves it
indefinite and nebulous and can satisfy only a Notion-less way of
thinking" (*SL,* pp. 112–113). The true infinite cannot, he insists, "be
expressed in the *formula* . . . of a *unity* of the finite and infinite," because
"*unity* is abstract, inert-self-sameness, and the moments are similarly only
in the form of inert, simply affirmative being" (*SL,* p. 148). As already
indicated, the true infinite's nature is to be a higher form of becoming,
and thus to represent "the consummated return into self, the relation of
itself to itself," in short, *being,* not being as indeterminate, abstract being
in its opposition to the nothing, but being already as determinate being,
being present before us. Indeed, compared with the image of the progress
to infinity that is the straight line, and that true infinity comprises within
itself, "the image of the true infinity, bent back into itself, becomes the
circle, the line which has reached itself, which is closed and wholly
present, without *beginning* and *end*" (*SL,* p. 149).

To understand why the true infinite is not a mere static unity of both
the spurious infinite and the finite, it would, of course, be necessary to
retrace in detail the dialectic that plays in the alternating determination
(*Wechselbestimmung*) of the finite and infinite, and that allows the infinite
in general, as at first indeterminate self-relation, to evolve at all, and that,
precisely, with the help of that alternating determination, allows it to
evolve toward affirmative infinity, that is, toward a more developed concept of the infinite. Since in determining hereafter the nature of spurious

infinity some of Hegel's arguments as to why spurious infinity is only another form of the finite (and, conversely, as to why the finite can also be viewed as itself something infinite) will have to be mentioned, the movement of mediation that distinguishes true infinity must not be further explained at this point. Notwithstanding the fact that this development of the concept of true infinity is still fully entangled in the logic of being, and that it has not yet been raised to the region of free infinitude, one can already assess its capital importance.

The reason that the intellect "is so antagonistic to the unity of the finite and infinite is simply that it presupposes the limitation and the finite, as well as the in-itself, as perpetuated." It overlooks the movement of negation that takes place between both the finite and spurious infinity, and thus remains ignorant of the complete and self-closing movement that actuates both determinations, and that brings it about that what arises from that movement is the same as that from which it began, except that it is the result of a process, and fully developed. As already noted, the true infinite must be a unity that embraces itself—itself under the form of spurious infinity and its reflexive opposite, the finite—and its Other. The true infinite is necessarily characterized by absolute wholeness, in other words, by a wholeness that is also self-inclusive to the extent that it is not in opposition to that of which it is the totality. "The by-itself negative denomination 'infinitude' is," as Manfred Baum has put it, "the name for that which is in opposition to all opposition, to the extent that it is the Other to all limitation which, in conformity with the proposition 'Omnis determinatio est negatio,' lies in mere determinatedness, and which is still thought in the idea of an objective infinitude standing in opposition to a finite subject."[4] True infinity is a unity that cannot be a unity in counter-position to separation. It is not in opposition, but rather beyond and above all opposition. Including itself and its Other, and comprising within itself opposition and separation, the true infinite is a completed whole which, instead of still being susceptible to further determination, and hence of a determination of determination, contains this process within itself. For that which the infinite embraces—itself and its Other—is, because it is posited, deprived of the power of limiting and restricting. In the true infinite the process of determination can, therefore, be said to be superseded. In this sense, the true infinite, an infinite which is no longer transcendent, but which is only *through* the finite, or *immanent* in the different forms of the finite, is *the* fundamental concept of philosophy—what Hegel called Notion, or Concept—in short, Reason. Because the true infinite is characterized by a unity of opposites that is in opposition to opposition itself, it is a concept that preeminently realizes the concept. It is an infinity that sets its own limits for itself and from within itself. Since it does not need limits from outside itself to become united, outward limitation is immaterial to it. It is, indeed, that which from within transcends all finite things toward their all embracing ground, a ground which, at the same time, receives full determination only by what it contains. To sum up, then, the true infinite expresses in a privileged form philosophy's requirement of wholeness, totality, and unity. It expresses it in a privileged way because, unlike the spurious infinite, it is complete. By including itself and its Other within itself, by being thus in opposition to all opposition, it is a fully determined whole which, because it includes itself, no longer has an outside. It is, therefore, identical with reason as pure thought.

Contrary to true infinity, which is an all-embracing totality—a totality in absolute self-affirmation, and thus no longer dependent on determination by an Other—the spurious infinite is fundamentally incomplete. Right at the beginning of the chapter on infinity in the *Science of Logic*, Hegel remarks: "the main point is to distinguish the genuine Notion of infinity from spurious infinity, the infinite of reason from the infinite of the understanding" (*SL,* p. 137). Although "the word *infinite,* even if used in infinite series, is commonly fancied to be something lofty and exalted," it is, says Hegel, simply "a kind of superstition, the superstition of the understanding" (*SL,* p. 249). It is, as a matter of fact, indicative of a deficiency of thought. In the section entitled "Alternating Determination of the Finite and the Infinite," Hegel demonstrates that spurious infinity, the infinite of series and progress, instead of being something lofty, is in truth a *"finitized* infinite." He argues that this kind of infinity functions as the *limit* only of the finite, and that it remains, therefore, burdened with the opposition to its Other. Indeed, consider the definition of the finite. It is a negation, "a ceasing-to-be in the form of a *relation* to an *other* which begins *outside* it" (*SL,* p. 250). Compared with the true infinite, which is relation to itself and is not dependent on an Other, spurious infinity as the limit of the finite, as that which calls the finite back to its outside, is "only a determinate infinite, an infinite which is itself finite" (*SL,* p. 140). Since this latter infinite is such only in relation to the finite, instead of its being able to free itself from the finite, the finite "reappears *in the infinite itself* as its other, because it is only in its *connection* with its other, the finite, that the infinite is" (*SL,* p. 142).

Spurious infinity has its own limits in what it stands over against. It is a *finite infinite,* or one among two finites which oppose each other within true infinity's encompassing embrace.

Yet, with the interplay between the finite and spurious infinity, understanding already possesses the idea of the inner unity at the foundation of its distinctions. But this idea remains concealed from it. Incapable of bringing together what it has before itself—the opposition of the finite and the infinite on the one hand, the unity that this opposition presupposes on the other—understanding presses the *relative* determinations of the finite and the infinite "to the point of opposition, with the result that although they are in an inseparable unity, each is credited with a self-subsistent determinate being over against the other." Although the infinite is given, it becomes transcended again insofar as it appears only as the other of the finite, and hence as finite itself. As a consequence, a new limit must be posited, but with the same result of a subsequent return to the finite, and so forth, endlessly. This progress to infinity is accepted by understanding "as something ultimate beyond which thought does not go but, having got as far as this 'and so on to infinity,' has usually reached its goal." But this progress to infinity, argues Hegel, instead of being a real advance, is not only is a "perpetual repetition of one and the same content, one and the same tedious *alternation* of this finite and infinite," in short, an impotence of the negative, but is an unresolved contradiction as well. The limit of the finite becomes transcended by the spurious infinite in an abstract manner only. It remains "incomplete because *it is not itself transcended*" (*SL,* p. 142). To conclude, spurious infinity is a product of what Hegel calls *"incomplete reflection"* (*SL,* p. 150). It is the result of a reflection that does not know how to bring the thought of opposite extremes and that of unity together. It remains fixed in contradiction.

Yet, as Hegel had already noted in *Faith and Knowledge,* "there is no series or sequence in what is truly spiritual, or in the Idea."[5] The spurious infinite as a result of incomplete reflection, of what Hegel in *Faith and Knowledge* calls simply "reflection" or, with Spinoza, "imagination," is an *empirical* infinite[6]—a *sensuous* infinite, according to the *Phenomenology of Spirit,*[7] a *dead* infinite, to quote the *Lectures on the History of Philosophy.*[8] It is itself a consequence of bad, spurious abstraction. It results from setting the spiritual sphere, the universal, the infinite, in contrast to the sensuous, the particular, the finite, turning, in this manner, the Idea into something finite as well. True philosophy, on the contrary, a philosophy yielding completion, achieves the pure Notion or genuine infinity by transcending reflection's application of categories of the finite to the infinite. Hegel remarks in the *Science of Logic:* "Philosophy needs no such help either from the world of sense or from the products of imagination, or from subordinate spheres in its own peculiar province, for the determinations of such spheres are unfitted for higher spheres and for the whole" (*SL,* p. 325).

To put it differently, where thinking should be *in terms of the Notion* ("wo *begriffen* werden soll"), *Vorstellen,* or ordinary thought that falls back on external determination, has no role to play. An infinite regress or progress as following from the entanglement of understanding and reflection with the sphere of the particular and the limit, and above which they appear to be unable to raise themselves, is unfitting to true infinity as the totality of the Notion.

More generally, beyond this short recapitulation of Hegel's determination of true infinity and beyond his decision not to to take the point of view of the finite as the ultimate standpoint, the idea of true infinity is a philosophical *must.* Metaphysics as it has understood itself since Aristotle cannot content itself with the representation of chains, series, or sequences that would proceed from the infinite and extend toward it. Indeed, such a regress or progress ad infinitum implies indeterminateness and limitlessness, in short, the impossibility of knowing.

Yet, according to Aristotle, all particular beings and things are determined, and hence limited beings or things. They are, consequently, middle things of a whole that has its beginning and end. The movement that links beings or things within such a whole, the movement of their reciprocal determination, instead of being an infinite progress lacking all reality, and with which the possibility of the "good"—things' coming into their own—would vanish for ever, must be circular. It must circularly achieve the final end as it develops from a first cause. This movement is that of the all-embracing essence of everything determinate, and is itself the true object of philosophy as *prote philosophia.* It is what from within transcends everything finite toward its origin, which is also its goal—true infinity.

The verdict of philosophy upon spurious infinity is firm and definite: the concept of spurious infinity remains indebted to ordinary thought—it does not raise itself one inch above the empirical. It does not live up to the most fundamental requirements of thought as completion, unity, totality. The question, then, seems obvious: Does Derrida's philosophy, with its continuous emphasis on the infinite, the endless substitutability of play, the text's infinite reference, the infinite task of interpretation, not fall prey to Hegel's, and *eo ipso,* philosophy-in-general's condemnation of spurious infinity? Is Derrida's philosophy unphilosophical because it would be unable to raise itself to the Notion or Concept—the level of the philosophical in general—and does it remain trapped in the realm of the sensuous, the empirical, the finite, of ordinary thinking? However tempted some may be to hastily answer these questions in the affirmative, to do so would be altogether to miss the point of Derrida' arguments.

Indeed, should one not from the outset have paid attention to the fact that Derrida in *Writing and Difference* refers to one of the two modes of judging the limits of totalization—namely, to the classical mode—as a mode rooted in a concept of finitude as relegation to the empirical? The classical reasons for the impossibility of saturating a field are empirical, and are a function of a finite subject's incapacity to come to grips with a superabundance of meaning. Now, since Derrida demarcates the type of nontotalization from the standpoint of play (or the text) from the classical mode of judging the limits of totalization, and since that mode is clearly associated with the empirical, it should have been evident from the outset that this second (Derridean) type of nontotalization is also demarcated from spurious infinity. But that the infinite substitutability of play as a reason for ultimate nontotalization is not, in spite of all the resemblances, to be construed as a spurious infinite, becomes a certainty when, in "The Double Session," we are told explicitly that if polysemy is infinite, and if it cannot be mastered as such, that is not because of a finite's subject's constitutive inability to master it. And Derrida adds, "not, that is, unless one displaces the philosophical concept of finitude and reconstitutes it according to the law and structure of the text . . . Finitude then becomes infinitude, according to a non-Hegelian identity" (*D*, p. 253).

In sum, if infinite substitutability is an obstacle to ultimate totalization, to a true infinite, the reasons cannot be of the order of a finitude that is tributary to the sensuous, or the empirical. The infinity in question can thus no longer be spurious either. What Derrida invites us to think is, as has already been mentioned, an "infinitude, according to a non-Hegelian identity," an infinity that would be breaching the very possibility of what philosophy requires as philosophy—the thinking of totality, or the Notion as true infinity.

It is undoubtedly correct to note that Derrida has often described this sort of infinity in terms of what André Gide, in his *Journal,* called "mise en abyme," an expression which for many was to become a categorial tool of textual analysis in the aftermath of structuralism.[9] This expression, originally from heraldry, designates a structure in which the whole is represented in miniature in one of its parts by the placement of a small escutcheon in the middle of a larger one, and which thus conveys a sense of spurious infinity. But let us also recall that Derrida referred to the principle of *mise en abyme* in *Of Grammatology* by adding: "to employ the current phrase *(comme on dit si souvent aujourd'hui)*" (G, p. 163). His strongest reservations about this expression, however, are formulated in *The Truth in Painting* and in "Coming into One's Own," from which comes the following passage: "I have never wished to overuse the abyss, nor above all the abyss structure [*mise en abyme*]. I have no strong belief in it, I distrust the confidence that it, at bottom, inspires, and I find it too representational to go far enough, not to *avoid* the very thing into which it pretends to plunge us *(je la crois trop représentative pour aller assez loin, pour ne pas éviter cela même vers quoi elle prétend précipiter)*."

The principle of *mise en abyme* is too representational. It belongs, as does spurious infinity, to the realm of *Vorstellung* and imagination. The confidence that it inspires rests on the continuity between itself and the abyss into which it plunges. It is not the same confidence that Hegel accusingly pointed at when discussing spurious infinity, namely, that understanding perceives the infinite progress or regress as the ultimate, and thus comforting, end of thought. In other words, *mise en abyme* is criticized here—in a criticism no less severe than Hegel's ejection from the province of thought of all help originating in the sensuous world and with the lowlier faculties—as an essentially empirical concept. When Derrida refers to infinity, he must, therefore, mean something else, something which, to continue quoting, has only "a certain appearance of a *mise en abyme,*" only, but which is not literally, a *mise en abyme.*[10]

Now, if the reasons that make totalization impossible do not inhere in spurious infinity, but, rather, with an "infinitude, according to a non-Hegelian identity," what sort of infinity is this supposed to be? What other concept could represent a challenge to genuine infinity without running the risk of being annihilated at once by Hegel's verdict, as is the case with the empirical concept of infinity?

Before even beginning to sketch out a preliminary answer to these questions, let me point out that the essay "The Double Session" (as well as the whole body of Derrida's writing) is engaged in a critique of the philosophical idea of semantic totalization. It is involved in an interrogation of the "dream" of being able to reach a sum total of the meaning-elements of (for example) a text—of establishing the unity of meaning of an ensemble of signs or tokens. Despite linguistics' relatively recent claims to it as an integral part of its analyses, semantic analysis, with its insistence on the study of meaning, reference, and truth, is *the* method of metaphysics as *prote philosophia*. It is *the* method for retracing the ultimate cause, the one unity of meaning which from within transcends all finite things. In the perspective of philosophical thought, the concept of true infinity is not merely a semantic concept among others. It is the semantic concept par excellence, if not the concept of the semantic itself.

But the concept of spurious infinity, with all its intra-philosophical shortcomings is, for that matter, a semantic concept too. The endless continuum that it refers to is one of semes reeling along in an infinite perspective. But also within the horizon, present in its absence, is the hope of achieving a sum total. If the Derridean concept of the infinite is to be distinguished from the concepts of potential and spurious infinity, and it is supposed to radically breach the possibility of totalization of the true infinite, of the semantic in general, it can no longer be of the order of a semantic concept. It must be a nonsemantic concept if it is to achieve at all what it purports to do, and if it is not to fall prey to the philosophical verdict that disposes of spurious infinity. Based on the developments of "The Double Session," one could call Derrida's notion of infinity a *syntactic infinity*, keeping in mind, of course, that the text also sets out to "systematically outwit and undo the opposition between the syntactic and the semantic" (*D*, p. 263). In the following, however, I will analyze this type of infinity in terms of *structural infinity*.

The expression "structural infinity" may strike one as odd considering that the very concept of structure is a metaphysical notion par excellence, akin to *eidos,* form, essence, *Gestalt,* and so on. Let me therefore immediately remark that what is true of the syntactic in Derrida's writing is true as well of the "structural": Derrida's thought is geared at systematically outwitting the opposition between the structural and its various others. But in the same way as the opposition of the syntactic and the semantic becomes undone in the perspective of a more "radical" concept of the syntactic, the opposition between the structural and its others is deconstructed in the construction of a more "originary" structurality, so to speak. As a matter of fact, the notion of the "structural" and the notion of "structural infinity" to be developed here are not merely *formal* concepts. Since these concepts will be exemplified by what Derrida calls "text," I can, from the outset, emphasize that the infinity in question is not to be construed as belonging to the order of form, if, as always, form is determined by its opposite, content. Undoubtedly, the notion of structure may appear to be too static, not sufficiently dynamic, to theorize the sort of infinity that Derrida has developed, and that is, as will be seen, the result of the entrapping machinations due to a certain arrangement of a set of "essential" traits. Another term may, hence, appear more desirable. And yet, an important stratum of Derrida's work—his criticism of structuralism, as well as the simultaneous attempt to continue what he calls "the most legitimate principled exigencies of 'structuralism' " (*P*, p. 28)—makes me want within the present context to retain the terms "structure" and "structural."

Thus, before engaging in a definition of the notion of structural infinity, and before elaborating on its function with respect to the semantic concepts of true infinity, spurious infinity, and finitude, let me first prove that the choice of the term itself—and with this, the level of my argumentation—is not arbitrary.

The asemantic inexhaustibility Derrida aims at, "a certain inexhaustibility which cannot be classed in the categories of richness, intentionality, or a horizon" (*D*, p. 250), and which produces the effect of a "so on without end," is, he argues, a function of "a *structural* necessity that is marked in the text" (*D*, p. 223; emphasis mine). Describing the dissemination of the asemic elements of a text, Derrida points out that they produce "a tropological *structure* that circulates infinitely around itself through the incessant supplement of an extra turn" (*D*, p. 258; emphasis mine). The same emphasis on the structural status of such an infinity can be found as far as the concept of *mise en abyme* is concerned. In *Of Grammatology*, for instance, after having shown that in Rousseau's text "the concept of the supplement and the theory of writing designate textuality itself . . . in an indefinitely multiplied structure—*en abyme*— to employ the current phrase," Derrida adds: "And we shall see that this abyss is not a happy or unhappy accident. An entire theory of the *structural* necessity of the abyss will be gradually constituted in our reading" (*OG*, p. 163; emphasis mine). And in *Spurs* we read, in the context of Derrida's demonstration that even though Heidegger valuates proper-ty *(le propre)* and *Eigentlichkeit*, proper-ty becomes disoriented by an oblique movement which "leads to this proper-ty's *(propre)* abyssal structure": "In such

a *structure,* which is a non-fundamental one, at once superficial and bottomless, still and always 'flat,' the proper-ty *(propre)* is literally sunk."[11]
These references should suffice to substantiate my contention that the
nature of infinity that I am dealing with here is structural, that it can be
thematized in those terms, and that in its very structurality it is in con-
traposition to the semantic. But what these references have also indicated
is the *necessary* nature of this structural infinite's "so on without end,"
and, as Derrida stresses throughout "The Double Session," its poverty
and monotony. Contrary to what Hegel stigmatized as the "tedious alternation" and the *"Einerleiheit"* characteristic of spurious infinity, and
whose status, in light of the richness of the infinity, is empirical (and that
means of contingent facticity), the structural infinite's monotonous repetition possesses all the attributes of necessity. Even before one attempts
to define structural infinity, this qualification of necessity provides a decisive clue as to the conceptual status of this notion. In many ways similar
to spurious infinity, structural infinity, or what is called here by that
name, is different from it because it is a nonsemantic concept and is
distinguished by such necessity. But its characterization as necessary, paradoxically, also shows it to vie with the *aprioriness,* and hence necessity,
of genuine infinity while aiming at the same time at nothing less than
unseating true infinity from its central position. And yet, haven't we
been told that the structure in question, even though necessary, is also a
nonfundamental one? Before further inquiring into this seemingly
strange hovering ambiguity of structural infinity, let me proceed to giving
a more detailed account of it—a definition of sorts—although it will
soon become clear that, strictly speaking, it can as little be defined as it
can be the object of a description. But however compelling the reasons
are that make it impossible to define and to describe it, they are no
obstacle to construing structural infinity's nuclear traits as well as their
specific arrangement, as long as that impossibility is proven to be a function of these nuclear traits' nature and combination.

Any one of the infrastructures developed by Derrida—arche-trace,
differance, supplementarity, iterability, and so on—could serve as the
starting point here. Indeed, for reasons of economy, it would be most
appropriate to take the arche-trace as a point of departure. As the minimal
structure of *reference to Other,* this structure of generalized indication
points incessantly away from itself even when its "own" minimal identity
is in question. The structure of reference to an Other, *necessarily,* deports
itself away from itself, toward the Other—infinitely. But instead of

taking advantage of this more economical and, in addition, rather plain possibility, I choose to deal with another, more complex form of the infrastructures' infinitizing application to *themselves*. I will set forth what Derrida calls in "The Double Session" the "structure of the fold," that is, the structure of the *re-mark*.

With the re-mark, with the structure of the fold which has no "limit other than itself as a mark, margin, or march (threshold, limit, or border)," and which constitutes in depth what Derrida designates under the name of "text," we face a *structure of self-reference* which, instead of producing a coincidence with self, always—and endlessly—gives rise to a supplementary turn. Needless to say, for this reason "the fold is not a form of reflexivity" (*D,* p. 270). Now let me try to formulate the major features of this structure in as condensed a manner as possible. What one has to understand is that the re-mark is not only a replication of the marks, or semes, of the text, but a repetition-toward-themselves of these marks as well, and, consequently, the addition to themselves of a supplementary fold. Marks, semes, states Derrida, are constituted differentially, diacritically. If such is the case, the marks, as they are deployed within the series which they designate as well (as designating all other marks of that same series), designate in addition, or, more generally, must blend into, or take the fold of, the asemic space of production or inscription that unfolds between the terms of the series. In addition, the marks of a text are, therefore, also descriptions/inscriptions *((d)écrit)* of the structure and movement of the texture of the marks. They signify the movement of the very operation of signifying too. Yet, even though each mark, while referring to itself and the other marks of the series, also represents the spaced-out semi-opening *(l'entr'ouverture espacée)* "which relates the different meanings to each other," the valence thus added to the series of the semes is not a supplementary meaning that would come to enrich the series (*D,* p. 252). What is added to the series as it becomes re-marked by the asemic space of diacritical differentiation—in the form of a delegate or representative—is, in truth, a non-sense, something which by right has no meaning, since it is itself the possibility of meaning. This delegate, which in traditional philosophy would be called the transcendental space of possibility, but which because of its asemic nature cannot claim such rank, is always one trope too many or too few with respect to the in-itself meaningful totality of the marks of the series. Conversely, by becoming represented and thus inserted into the series, the space between the marks also re-marks itself incessantly. And since no mark can confer meaning to what has no meaning as the condition itself of meaning, the tropic delegates of the blanks between the marks make the space of inscription disappear. By being represented it withdraws ceaselessly, in this second movement of the re-mark. In short, "as soon as there is something (there) to see (or not to see) having to do with a _mark_ (which is the same word as _margin_ or _march_), whether . . . [the mark] is marked . . . [by other marks in the series] or unmarked, merely demarcated (the _entre,_ the void, the blank, the space, etc.), it re-marks itself, marks itself twice. It folds itself around this strange limit" (_D,_ p. 258). Because of the supplementary marks of the asemic spacing by which the mark re-marks itself, it becomes impossible for the mark to recoil upon itself in self-coincidence. But the complication that arises from the fact that that supplementary mark re-marks the space of inscription is that it becomes structurally impossible ever to bring the space of inscription of the marks to a stop, to capitalize it, and to make it identical with itself. Instead of being made to recoil reflexively into itself, the space of inscription, by becoming re-marked, retreats and withdraws from itself. This is the reason why the non-sense of the spacing "that relates the different meanings to each other . . . and in the process prevents them from ever meeting up with each other cannot be accounted for by any _description_"—not even by phenomenological description, for that matter. Description, claims Derrida, "will always run aground at the edges of this _greater_ or _lesser_ extent of theme which makes it possible that 'there is' a text" (_D,_ pp. 252–253). Because the mark in replication applies to itself its own asemic condition of possibility, which not only exceeds it by its sheer heterogeneity but which is ceaselessly made to disappear by its own re-marking, all hope of ever totalizing the meaning of a series of differentially constituted marks becomes suspended. All such attempts can hope to produce are the "endless multiplication of folds, unfoldings, foldouts, foldures, folders, and manifolds, along with the plies, the ploys, and the multiplications" (_D,_ p. 270). And if this is so, it is clearly for structural reasons. It is because of the very particular arrangement of the traits and movements characterizing the re-mark that a series or system of differentially constituted semes cannot be totalized.

If it is impossible to effect a sum total of the meaning of a series of such marks or semes, then the reason for this is not that this series would be exceeded by some infinite richness of content. If something forbids us to seek an overall and totalizing meaning of a text—_a_ meaning in short—of a series or system of marks, if it is also useless to let oneself become entangled in a text's interminable network of references, this is so precisely because the limit to semantic totalization is of a kind other than that of spurious infinity. This limit is that of the re-mark. Itself re-marked inside the text under the structural form of the process of endless cross-referencing, it is a limit that comes about "through the angle and the intersection of a re-mark that folds the text back upon itself without any possibility of its fitting back over or into itself" (*D*, p. 251). It is the limit of the *syntax* of that fold. Syntax means here the arrangement, combination, and intimate connection of all the nuclear traits of the re-mark. The set of referential vectors the re-mark is henceforth woven of, as well as the nature of what that woven texture is made of—a weaving and fabric thoroughly different from the kingly weaving process and its organic that web Plato speaks of—distinguishes the re-mark as a truly structural agency. It is an agency whose *symploke* is not unitary, not one, and not one of homogeneous material. The manner in which its elements are tied into one another prevents it from lending itself to a harmoniously equilibrated whole. Since this non-closure springs primarily from the arrangement of its referential vectors, structural reasons impede its coinciding with itself.

Let me return at this point to the question of the *mise en abyme*, which I had left in abeyance. The space of inscription of the marks through which they must affect themselves, and which also folds itself back, evading for structural and necessary reasons all possible phenomenologization, ceaselessly recedes. It recoils into an abyss. Derrida writes:

> In the recoiling of the blank upon the blank, the blank colors itself, becomes—for itself, of itself, affecting itself ad infinitum—its own color-less, even more invisible, ground. Not that it is out of reach, like the phenomenological horizon of perception, but that, in the act of inscribing itself on itself indefinitely, mark upon mark, it multiplies and complicates its text, a text within a text, a margin in a mark, the one indefinitely repeated within the other: an abyss (*D*, p. 265)

Having established in the preceding pages that the abyss structure, contrary to a *mise en abyme*, is one of structural necessity, I can now further refine the specific nature of its "ontological status." As I have shown, Derrida rejected *mise en abyme* because of the confidence it inspires, and because it is too representational. By pursuing the implications of this critique of the empiricist nature of the *mise en abyme* principle, I may be able to explain more precisely what until now has been called structural infinity.

It is certainly appropriate to mention here Derrida's critique, in "White Mythology," of Nietzsche's putting into *abyme* a particular metaphor (that of the hive) "in order to figure the metaphoricity of the concept, the metaphor of the metaphor, the metaphor of metaphoric productivity itself." What Derrida objects to in such a "generalization of metaphoricity by putting into *abyme* one determined metaphor" is that such a procedure "is possible only if one takes the risk of a continuity between metaphor and the concept." The result of such a procedure is "an empirical reduction of knowledge and a fantastic ideology of truth" (*M,* pp. 262–263). The question of metaphoricity is not of immediate concern here, but I must underscore that as an overly representational, here metaphoric, concept, the *mise en abyme* inevitably produces a continuity, similar to the one between concept and metaphor resulting from Nietzsche's operation, between the chasm and what the *mise en abyme* pretends to ruin by infinitely reflecting it. When such a continuity is achieved, the radical difference between both is missed, in all senses of this word. Such continuity is revelatory of the empirical essence of the operation of the *mise en abyme* because it is oblivious of philosophical difference in general, of *the difference philosophy makes,* as well as, in this particular case, of the difference between ground and what is grounded. Indeed, the putting into *abyme* does "not *avoid* the very thing into which it pretends to plunge us." It disregards the difference. Therefore, Derrida could, in *The Truth in Painting,* insist that

> like all *production,* that of the abyss came to saturate what it hollows out. It's enough to say: abyss and satire of the abyss. The feast, the "feast of thought" *(Fest des Denkens),* which engages upon the *Kreisgang,* in the *pas de cercle:* What does it feed on *(de quoi jouit-elle)?* Opening and simultaneously filling the abyss. Accomplishing: *den Kreisgang vollziehen.* Interrogate the comic effect of this. One never misses it if the abyss is never sufficient, if it must remain—undecided—between the bottom-less and the bottom of the bottom. The *operation* of the *mise en abyme* always occupies itself (activity, busy position, mastery of the subject) with somewhere filling up, full of abyss, filling up the abyss.[12]

The *mise en abyme* saturates what it hollows out. It does so by not avoiding the abyss into which it pretends to plunge what is to be ruined, thus neglecting philosophically fundamental differences, differences that consitute the philosophical. The principle of putting into *abyme*—which reappropriates the abyss in the same way as does that sort of thought which stops short at the edge of the abyss, Hegelian *Aufhebung* with its concept of true infinity—is one that in its mere empiricity is entirely derivative from the infinite sublation of the chasm. The *mise en abyme,* then, is for Derrida, as for Hegel, marked by philosophical naiveté: it is empirical, oblivious of difference; it obliterates differences.

And yet, does not the *mise en abyme,* or spurious infinity, however derivative from true infinity, also regularly come to threaten it? Although genuine infinity is by right infinitely different from spurious infinity, does it not also methodically make it collapse from within? Genuine and spurious infinity are, in spite of their radical difference, or rather because of it, interlocked. Although one is derivative from the other, neither exists without the other. An economy of relations, and of mutual dependencies, regulates their intra-philosophical play. With this insight into their interdependence in the philosophical discourse, a new philosophical task arises that Derrida formulates as follows: "to establish laws of reappropriation, to formalize rules that constrain the logic of the abyss and shuttle between the economic *and* the non-economic, sublation *and* fall, the abyssal operation that strives necessarily for sublation *and* within which collapse is repeatedly produced." This clearly outlines the task of deconstruction insofar as the difference between true and spurious infinity is concerned. Deconstruction cannot consist of precipitating into the abyss, or of eliminating the difference between the abyss and what is plunged into it. Its task is, on the contrary, to establish rules by which *mise en abyme,* or spurious infinity, is subjected to speculation, although they regularly breach speculative thought from within, as well as the rules which cause genuine infinity to remain interlocked with its opposite in the *text* of philosophy. The elaboration of this economy, which in traditional terms would amount to the thinking of the essence of the abyss, or the abyss *in general,* consists here, rather, in the thinking of the *general abysmal.* Such thinking takes place, not by plunging oneself—romantically—into the abyss, but on the contrary, by saving "oneself from falling into the bottomless depths by weaving and folding back the cloth to infinity, textual art of the reprise, multiplication of patches within patches."[13] In short, by constructing what I have termed the structural infinite. This is the law that rules the interplay within the philosophical text between spurious infinity and true infinity, a law respectful of their radical difference, but capable also of formalizing these differents' interdependence as, precisely, differents. In thinking the economy of the abyss, deconstructive thought does without the abyss.

As the law that regulates spurious and genuine infinity's modes of the reappropriation of the abyss, the general abysmal, or structural infinity, has no place within philosophical discourse and its problematical horizon. On the contrary, it regulates the relation of the philosophical concept of true totality to what from within that totality—that is, from inside philosophy—appears as its outside, finite infinity. But if this is so, then it also becomes understandable why structural infinity is in so many ways similar to spurious infinity. In addition to being within philosophical discourse the Other of true infinity, spurious infinity is, indeed, also the representative, the delegate, the ghost, as Derrida would say, of that other sort of outside that is the law that regulates philosophy's inner play— structural infinity. As the tropic substitute for structural infinity—an infinity that makes it impossible for true infinity ever to recoil into its own totality—spurious infinity inevitably draws upon itself the condemnation of philosophy. One of the decisive similarities between structural and spurious infinity is that neither simply destroys the true infinite. In the same way as spurious infinity challenges genuine infinity from within while being at the same time at its service, the structural infinite accounts for the possibility of what it also comes to restrict. As a matter of fact, the infinitist play of the structural infinite prescribes, as Derrida formulates it in "The Double Session," "the structural site" of such a "theological trap" as is the genuine infinite, the trap that consists of thinking the structural infinite with a capital "I" (*D,* p. 258). What the instance of structural infinity achieves is not simply to throw genuine infinity into the abyss. Its function is to account for a trap such as that of true infinity, of totality, of the Notion, by exhibiting its structurally necessary limits. I cite again:

> The supplementary "blank" does not intervene only in the polysemous series of "white things," but also *between* the semes of *any* series and *between all* the semantic series in general. It therefore prevents any semantic seriality from being constituted, from being simply opened or closed. Not that it acts as an obstacle: it is again the blank that actually liberates the effect that a series exists; in marking itself out, it *makes us take* agglomerates for substances. (*D,* pp. 253–254)

Let me draw some conclusions about the general status of the structural infinite. As I have shown, it is of the order of a necessary, and not empirical, law that constitutes genuine infinity *in its relations* to spurious infinity. It opens up the possibility of genuine infinity, of the dream of totalization, but in such a manner that it remains essentially limited by its indelible reference to its Other. Structural infinity accounts for the possibility of such a theological trap while simultaneously tracing the impossibility of ultimate totalization in the same conditions that open up such a possibility. Let me recall at this point that Derrida called for a displacement of the philosophical concept of finitude, and for the necessity of elaborating an infinitude according to a non-Hegelian identity. As has been shown, structural infinity is infinite, although it is not subjected, regulated, by the empirical, as is the case with spurious infinity. In addition, it is infinite in a necessary manner, which contributes to radically distinguishing it from spurious infinity, and to bringing it into the vicinity of true infinity.

But if it is infinite in a necessary manner, it is so also because it is finite, "finitude" being taken here in a different sense. Indeed, without summoning Derrida's persistent criticism of the finite, it should be clear by now that the infinitude of this structural infinite hinges on the finitude of the field subjected to infinite substitutions. In "Dissemination" we read: "In the dial's *finite* apparatus, the polysemous phase of dissemination reproduces itself indefinitely" (*D,* p. 351; emphasis mine). The finite field of the play, or text, is the result of a limited *symploke* of its major characterizing traits. Yet they are arranged in such a manner that in bypassing an organizing center, they are capable of infinite substitutability. The law of the play is structural, that is, a law of limited arrangements of the traits which, lacking a totalizing center, give rise to the necessary (on these conditions) possibility of infinite substitutions. Structural infinity, then, is a law that establishes a necessity for a possibility— infinite substitutability that hinges exclusively on finite reasons. And such possibility is all the philosopher has to account for.

But such a play that ultimately prohibits totalization is also, as "Dissemination" insists, no more finite than infinite. These terms are no longer adequate for such a structural law as the general abysmal, which has been constructed by means of a passage through these terms in order to account for their interplay in the field of philosophy. In *Speech and Phenomena,* Derrida, after having written that "the *infinite* difference is *finite,*" adds the following lines, which should be applied to the notion of structural infinity as developed here as well: "It can therefore no longer be conceived within the opposition of finiteness and infinity, absence and presence, negation and affirmation" (*SP,* p. 102). Structural infinity is, indeed, a notion that serves to account for both the difference and the commerce of infinity and finitude in the discourse of philosophy, and it is, therefore, unquestioningly of a different order from both.

6

God, for Example

WHETHER DEFINED as a positive infinity or supreme being unfolding itself in pure and full presence, or as Other to the point of transgressing being, God is an entity with which man is said to stand in a certain relation. In this relation man enters into communication with God either as a presence or as an absence, according to the modes of knowledge or veneration. Although Derrida's texts directly broach neither the question of God nor man's relations to God, these questions make themselves felt in a contextual, oblique manner through Derrida's more explicit investigations into the relations and the commerce between different, seemingly exclusive types of discourses. The question concerning God and man's relations to the Divine in a network of discursive (and historical) interlacings, dispatches, and referrals is embedded in Derrida's texts, and this implicit and pervasive encounter with the question of God motivates and legitimates an explicit focus on what Derrida's texts imply about the question of God, more precisely, of what it could mean to *think* God, for example. Indeed, overlooking the contextual frames in which reference to theological issues is made in Derrida's texts leads one either to mistake Derrida's developments on this subject as belonging in style and content to negative theology (as did Mikel Dufrenne in "Pour une philosophie non théologique," a text added in 1973 to the second edition of *Le Poétique,* an accusation that has been recently repeated by Gianni Vattimo in *Les Aventures de la différence*) or else to claim (as does Jean-Luc Marion in *L'Idole et la distance*) that Derrida altogether eliminates the theological question.[1] Failing to heed the frame of Derrida's argument concerning the notion of God foils every attempt at determining the point to which the treatment of the question of God is supposed to lead.

Indeed, as I proceed, it will become clear that the notion of God is essentially (in all the senses of this word) intertwined for Derrida with a variety of threads, traces, marks, or indicants. What, then, are the contexts of Derrida's discussions of the notion of God?

I take the essays "Violence and Metaphysics," "On a Newly Arisen Apocalyptic Tone in Philosophy," and "How to Avoid Speaking: Denials" as the major texts in which Derrida addresses questions of theology.[2] "Violence and Metaphysics," where Derrida discusses Levinas' concept of an "ultimate relation" (beyond relation) to the absolutely Other, is framed by a debate regarding the relations between the Greek *logos* (philosophy, in short) and Jewish thought, that is, a theology about God as absolutely Other. More precisely, it investigates the economy of relations—the dialogue and the war—between the discourse of philosophy and that of the prophets as two ways of dealing with the question of the Other. As Derrida notes toward the end of the essay, non-philosophy, that is, thought's inclination before the Other, is capable of profoundly shaking the discourse of philosophy and thus of awakening the Greek *logos* to its origin as well as to its death—to its Other, that is. Judaic thought, by contrast, cannot escape the necessity "to reawaken the Greek in the autistic syntax of . . . [its] own dream," thus jeopardizing the intended immediacy of its nonconceptual relation to the Other (*WD*, p. 152). But it is also the case, as Derrida remarks, that "in having proffered the *epekeina tes ousias,* in having recognized from its second word (for example, in the *Sophist*) that alterity had to circulate at the origin of meaning, in welcoming alterity in general into the heart of the logos, the Greek thought of Being forever has protected itself against every absolutely *surprising* convocation" (*WD*, p. 153). "Violence and Metaphysics" is, in essence, an attempt to determine the necessity that compels each of these conceptions of the Other to communicate, to enter into a dialogical exchange, and to wage war against each other. It is against this backdrop of a reflection on the commerce between two very different modes of relating, a reflection that ultimately seeks to establish the *law* of that exchange, that the question of God, as broached in that essay, must be read. This question then appears to primarily concern the mutual challenge between philosophy and its discourse on the Other in general and the attempt to face God in a nonconceptual manner.

Derrida's analysis, in "On a Newly Arisen Apocalyptic Tone," of Kant's attack on Johann Schlosser's (and, in the last resort, Friedrich Heinrich Jacobi's) neo-Platonic mysticism, that is, of two opposing types

of philosophizing—that of the true philosophers and that of the mysta-
gogues—and of Kant's proposed truce, hints at "some *inadmissible*,"
"excluded middle," which, as a "transcendental structure," organizes the
exchanges between the two discourses in conflict and requires them continually to refer to each other in their opposition. It is only with respect
to this "transcendental structure" that the question of the apocalyptic
tone raised in the essay makes sense.[3]

"How to Avoid Speaking: Denials," Derrida's first "explicit" con-
frontation of the accusation of negative theology, is a text that seeks to
elucidate what happens between, on the one hand, a specifically Greek
experience of an Otherness that escapes all dialectical, analogical, and
participationist appropriation by philosophy—the Platonic thought of
the *khora*—and, on the other, the *via negativa* in its Christian form. Here,
again, all specific discussions of a theological nature are to be seen as
embedded in an attempt to understand "what happens in terms of structures and relations" between those two very different views or experiences of the Other.[4] The analysis of this exchange requires a third paradigm, one that is neither Greek nor Christian, namely, the apophatic
movements of Jewish and Arab thought. Yet, Derrida chooses to focus
on Heidegger, more precisely, on what in Heidegger could resemble, in
an exemplary fashion, the "most questioning legacy, both the audacious
and most liberated repetition of the traditions that I have just evoked."[5]
It is in the context of this discussion of Heidegger's thought that Derrida
tries to formulate the law regulating the exchange between the Greek
experience and negative theology, as the law of the becoming theological
of philosophical discourse.

In short, all the specifically theological issues raised by Derrida in the
context of these three essays are part of an overall concern with establishing the economy and the law of exchange that regulate the relations
between different types of discourse on the relation to the Other. The
issue, however, is not simply to relate the question of God, and man's
relation to such an entity, to the genus of a philosophically higher concept of the relation to an Other, such as the concept of the Other in
general, but rather to relate them to structures of reference in which all
discourses on the Other are always already caught, and which they continue to engender. To link God in this manner to a network of quasi-
transcendental structures of referral also implies that, for Derrida, the
possibility of God is not exhausted by the Heideggerian thought of Being
as the opening through which God can come to the fore as a supreme

being. In what follows, I will be concerned with this attempt by Derrida to reach back through the question of Being and its opening function for a supreme being, toward a series of traits that are older, so to speak, than the ontico-ontological difference, as well as with the implications that such a movement of thought represents for thought itself.

As is well known, Heidegger has, time and again, clearly distinguished between Being (the Being of beings) and God as a supreme being. If being is, indeed, as the whole of the metaphysical tradition asserts, the primary and most fundamental characteristic of God—if one presupposes that God is—then the possibility of God, and of theology as well, implies a fore-understanding of the being God of God, and ultimately the thinking of the truth of Being. God can come into existence or become meaningful and understandable as divine only on the condition that Being has cleared the lighting for God's appearance. As long as God is, the anteriority of Being to God is inevitable since he must be endowed with being. As an ever so excellent being, as first in the order of beings, God then necessarily yields to ontic rather than ontological determinations. Most attempts to strip God of the predicate of being or existence, like negative theology, conceive Him as partaking in a mode of being or essence that is more elevated than being and essence. Therefore, negative theology and its attempt to conceive the divine supra-essentiality *(hyperousios),* a being above or beyond being, remain phases or moments of positive onto-theology. Yet what about an enterprise, like Jean-Luc Marion's, that seeks to determine God without being (*God without Being* is the title of one of his books)? After having rightly criticized metaphysics' idolatry with respect to God—to put it in Kantian terms: after having demonstrated that to conceive of God as the all-comprehensive entity *(Inbegriff)* of everything real, and as a ground (however necessary that may be from a practical point of view) in an analogy to free will, is idolatrous because such an approach does not detach all empirical threads *(empirische Fäden)* from the supra-sensible notion of God[6]—Marion contends that the question of Being and of the ontico-ontological difference commits a new and final idolatry by proclaiming the anteriority of the truth of Being to the essentially ontic question of God, because "anteriority" is an empirical relation.[7] (Whether or not Being is "prior" to God will be discussed later.) Yet, does such freeing of the notion of God from what Marion sees as the last metaphysical subjection of God to the meaning of Being truly achieve an adequate encounter with God as absolutely Other? Such liberation of God from Being might, indeed, not only not lead to an end of ontic projections of the absolute Other, especially if God is determined as Father, seen, as He was by Marion, within the trinitary scheme, but might even increase the danger of anthropologization. Indeed, as Jean-Luc Nancy has put it, proposing a notion of God based on the concept of charity *(agape),* and of man's relation to God as one that is to be thought in terms of *distance,* risks sacrificing the specificity of God. All that one says about God can immediately be said about anything else, "about 'event,' about 'love,' about 'poetry' and so on and so forth."[8] Brutally put, God is not God if, even as *absconditus,* He cannot be said to somehow exist: in short, if He does altogether escape the truth of Being. In spite of its explicit intentions, even a non-onto-theological theology as radical as Marion's seems to verify this. Perhaps God is a necessarily idolatrous notion.

Within the theoretical space of onto-theology, God's supremacy as a being is based on His role as an efficient ground for all beings as defined by their need for a foundation. God is here the anterior, prior entity, linked as a founding ground to the beings grounded in Him and by Him. The possibility of a relation of an existent transcendent ground to what it grounds is itself to be conceived of in foundational terms, namely, through foundation's self reflecting in God's own self-grounding. Only as *causa sui,* that is, as the folding of the act of foundation upon itself, can God assume the distinguishing function of an efficient ground for what is. *Causa sui,* as *causa prima,* is thus, for Heidegger, God's name in philosophy.[9] Because God must be posited as existing as an absolute and universal grounding efficiency, His difference from and relation to what He grounds remains a distinction and relationship between beings. God, in contradistinction to Being, must hence be apprehended, if not *per genus,* at least *per differentiam,* and His relation to what He grounds (as well as of beings to Him as their ultimate cause) is to be understood precisely as a *relation,* that is, as a mode of belonging and referring that makes sense only among existents. The same is true as well of all the attributes that characterize the relation of a ground, principle, or *arche* to what they make possible, create, engender, and so forth, that is, such traits as anteriority, priority, dignity, domination, power, and so forth. All these attributes reveal the ontic conditionality of the transcendent cause to the extent that they describe orders between two determined things or beings.

For Heidegger, thinking, qua thinking, is always and necessarily the thinking of Being—more precisely of Being in its difference from beings, or, as he puts it in *Identity and Difference,* difference *as* difference.[10] From the perspective of the thought of Being, that is, from thought as such, whatever His anteriority and superiority may be, God is inevitably of the order of what is, a being among beings. For the meditation on Being as Being in its difference from beings, a difference that is constitutive of thought as such to the extent that this difference secures the opening space for what is, as well as for all the relations that can possibly take place between beings, the question of God is not properly of the order of thought in an eminent sense. Indeed, in his essay of 1927 entitled "Phenomenology and Theology" Heidegger contends that theology as a science of faith is a positive science and, therefore, for fundamental reasons, closer to chemistry and mathematics than to philosophy.[11] But, more important, one ought to refer to Heidegger's contention that philosophy, as *prima philosophia,* has been from the start a *theology,*[12] that is, a discourse on that being par excellence which, as *causa sui,* is the ultimate ground of all beings, and that, as such a discourse, it has been oblivious to thought as such. Indeed, to think the "relation" of the transcendental to what is in terms of a grounding relation is to remain caught in the ontic realm, in its manifold relations between things, and ultimately not to think at all. Accounting for the existence of what is by making it dependent on an existing cause necessarily obscures the question of the meaning of Being. Still the ontico-ontological difference, difference *as* difference, remains the element, the dimension of thought as such.

If Being, or difference as such, is the very Opening for all beings, God included, as well as for all the possible relations between beings, and between beings and the infinite positivity, then Being, because it is not a supreme or absolute being or ground, does not stand in a relation to beings. Since Being is only the Being *of* beings and nothing else, nothing, indeed, outside of beings, there is not even, as Derrida remarks, "a *distinction* in the usual sense of the word between Being and existent" (*WD,* p. 138). For the same reason, beings have no relation to Being, since Being is nothing else than that beings are. To think Being in its difference from beings is indeed not to distinguish it from beings and then to calculate the relations that might exist between them. Therefore, to think Being as the Opening of all beings and of God cannot mean to establish an anteriority of Being to beings and God, or to substitute Being for God, or even to ground God in Being. (Thought, as Heidegger understands it, as the thinking of Being and difference, is indeed not relational.) In which way, then, is God linked to Being, if He does not relate to it as its foundation? Although the metaphysical God is different from Being to the extent that He is an existent, He *is,* in the onto-theological tradition of thinking, the destinal figure of Being as Difference. From the perspective of the thinking of Being, to think God is to think Him *as* the figure of the unthought of Being. In this context, let me quote a footnote in Derrida's essay "Violence and Metaphysics:"

> The Thought of Being is what permits us to say, without naiveté, reduction, or blasphemy, "God, for example." That is, to *think* God as what he is without making him an object. This is what Levinas, here in agreement with all the most classical infinitist metaphysics, would judge to be impossible, absurd, or purely verbal: how to think what one says when one proposes the expression, *God*—or *the infinite*—*for example?* But the notion of examplariness would, undoubtedly, offer more than one piece of resistance to this objection. (*WD,* p. 138)

Indeed, and without yet beginning to draw on some of the resources offered by the notion of examplariness, the thinking of Being, precisely because it does not substitute Being for God, can think God as the example par excellence of a mode of thought oblivious to difference. God *as* the metaphysical name for Being is primarily an excellent example of the unthought. But more important, since God as an existent yields, as can be seen, to ontic conditionality, or to put it differently, since God in onto-theological theology is always represented in an idolatrous manner, the thinking of God, as well as the relation of man to Him, is analogical and schematic by nature: God is always an example (perhaps, ultimately, of himself). Now since this analogical transfer, by which a continuity between God as the supreme being and all other beings becomes established, is itself of the order of the relations that characterize the ontic realm, the thought of Being is that pre-conceptual, pre-relational, pre-analogical thought that by thinking God, for example, lets God be what He is, an example of the unthought Being and of unthought thought.

Because the ontico-ontological difference provides the opening for the meaning of a being such as God, it, according to Marion, "does, indeed, acknowledge 'God,' but exclusively under the idolatrous figure that onto-theology provides of Him, namely, the condition of being."[13] Marion recognizes that since the ontico-ontological difference is "*almost* indispensable to all thought," and since it is impossible, or at least extremely difficult, to think outside the ontological difference, the question of Being cannot simply be neutralized.[14] Indeed, the impossibility in which the thought of Being finds itself, of thinking God as such, qualifies that thought "as a *negative* propaedeutic of the unthinkable thought of God," in other words, as a propaedeutic of that non-onto-theological theology that Marion proposes, where God is freed of Being, and beings as well are liberated from this last and final idolatry.[15] Derrida, in contrast, by "neutralizing" Being in the thought of differance, which Marion understands as a generalization of the ontico-ontological difference, not only would jeopardize the negative propaedeutical character of Heidegger's philosophy for a theology that seeks to liberate itself from thought in order to come into a relation to God that is no longer relational by eliminating all thought of God, but also would consign thought to remaining caught up in the ontico-ontological difference. Marion writes: "One does not leave the ontological difference by putting it into question . . . One remains all the more inscribed within the ontological difference as one traverses it and pulls it in all directions."[16]

Let me then try, in as succinct a manner as possible, to recall one more time Derrida's treatment of the ontico-ontological difference. On several occasions Derrida has questioned the absolute originariness of that difference, despite Heidegger's insistence, in *Identity and Difference,* on the non-phenomenologizable nature of Difference—the Difference in question cannot appear *as such,* be named *as such,* represented *as such.* But, adds Derrida, precisely because it is impossible to properly name Difference, even the name "ontico-ontological difference" cannot, despite its decisiveness, succeed. Derrida writes in "Ousia and grammé": "the determinations which name difference always come from the metaphysical order. This holds not only for the determination of difference as the difference between presence and the present *(Anwesen/Anwesendes),* but also for the determination of difference as the difference between Being and beings" (*M,* pp. 66–67). The notions of beings and Being, ontic and ontological, "ontico-ontological," "are, in an originary style, *derivative* with regard to difference," and ultimately because they belong essentially to the history of onto-theology, that is, "to the system functioning as the effacing of difference," they are forgetful of Difference itself (*OG,* p. 23). Derrida recognizes that it is inevitable for thought to pass through the determination of Difference in terms of the difference between Being and beings, but precisely because this determination is also a metaphysical appropriation, pretending to say properly what Difference is, it is necessary as well to again erase that determination. In

"Ousia and grammé," he notes that there may be a difference that "is older than Being itself. There may be a difference still more unthought than the difference between Being and beings" (*M*, p. 67). This difference, a difference that comes into view as soon as one becomes aware of the fact that "within the decisive concept of the ontico-ontological difference, *all is not to be thought in one go (tout n'est pas à penser d'un seul trait),*" this difference beyond Being and beings, is what Derrida has called the arche-trace or differance (*OG*, p. 23). These concepts do not imply a generalization of the ontico-ontological difference; they follow from a meditation on Heidegger's contention that Difference cannot be named *as such,* and hence cannot, in the last resort, be determined as the difference between Being and beings. Arche-trace and differance are notions, not names or concepts, that refer to a Difference which, for structural reasons, erases its essentialization or phenomenologization: the arche-trace must be thought of as a quasi-originary structure of referral—the trace of a trace (without the anteriority of a present referent)—whereas differance represents the thought of a difference that ceaselessly differs from and defers (itself). Both notions follow, in a certain way, from Derrida's reflections on Heidegger's claim, in "The Anaximander Fragment," that the difference that is forgotten from early on, the difference between Being and beings, is itself a trace. Heidegger speaks in this connection of *die frühe Spur des Unterschieds,* the early trace of (the) distinction.[17] The arche-trace and differance formalize, so to speak, this assertion and elaborate on the minimal traits that a thought, such as that of difference, as a trace before all determination, must necessarily imply.

In short, then, differance is not a generalization of the ontico-ontological difference but rather the generalization of a set of traits to which this difference yields in spite of its recognized superiority to all regional differences (and in this sense, Marion's accusation that differance establishes an indifference and lack of privilege between constituted differences misses the point). These traits are linked to its self-effacement as difference in the revelation of what is indeed distinguished, what is present and presencing, and, ultimately, Being and beings. What is generalized in the notion of differance is a structure of self-deferral, of a ceaseless deferral of difference *in propria persona,* a structure whose thinking is required to account not only for all regional differences, but also for the ontico-ontological difference, not to speak of the difference between the ontic and the ontico-ontological difference. If all thinking must necessarily be the thinking of Being, provided thought is not to remain enclosed in the determined existent and thus cut off from Being and limited to thinking nothing, then the thinking of differance, rather than replaying the ontico-ontological difference, transcends it, and with it, the thinking of Being, or thought *itself*.

Although the two parties to the distinction—what is present and presencing—reveal themselves from early on, they do not do so, Heidegger notes in "The Anaximander Fragment," "*as* distinguished. Rather, even the early trace of the distinction is obliterated when presencing appears as something present and finds itself in the position of being the highest being present."[18] The highest being present, excellent being, or God, obliterates the early trace of difference, precisely by virtue of being present. As a full presence, an immobile and unfading substance, God neutralizes all anteriority and exteriority by making the trace derivative to Himself. In Him, the trace and difference are reappropriated and retrieved in parousia. The full presence of God, of Him who says, "I am He who is," does not suffer any reference to Other than Himself, lest that Other be derived from Him. As non-trace and absolute origin, God, then, is the origin of all traces, which are secondary compared with the plenitude of presence He enjoys. Derrida concludes:

> The subordination of the trace to the full presence summed up in the logos
> . . . [such is the gesture] required by an onto-theology determining the
> archeological and eschatological meaning of being as presence, as parousia,
> as life without differance: another name for death, historical metonymy
> where God's name holds death in check. That is why, if this movement
> begins its era in the form of Platonism, it ends in infinitist metaphysics.
> Only infinite being can reduce the difference in presence. In that sense,
> the name of God, at least as it is pronounced within classical rationalism,
> is the name of indifference itself. (*OG*, p. 71)

But such a concept of God, like that of God as the absolute Other, as Derrida recalls in "Violence and Metaphysics," is subject to those "classical difficulties of language" always encountered by the philosophical discourse when it is solicited to think the absolute Other as infinitely present to Himself (*WD*, pp. 115–116). In the essay in question, Derrida objects to Levinas not only that the attempt to think either the positive infinity of God and/or his irreducible alterity encounters insurmountable obstacles in philosophical discourse, but that to tie both together in the concept of the infinitely Other presents an even more unsolvable crux. If the positive infinite has to rely on a negative term (in-finite) through "the negation of (finite) spatial exteriority," this positivity is perhaps not positively infinite, but finite (*WD*, p. 114). If the "infinitely Other" can be what it is only if it is Other, that is, other *than*—and indeed, "the other is always relative, is stated *pros heteron*," as the Stranger knew in the *Sophist*—the Other "is no longer absolved of a relation to" another ego and, therefore, "no longer infinitely, absolutely other" (*WD*, pp. 126–127). Hence, "the other cannot be what it is, infinitely other, except in finitude and mortality (mine *and* his)," Derrida notes (*WD*, pp. 114–115). In short, since it is impossible to separate infinity and alterity from negativity, from death in the last resort, a positive infinity and absolute alterity called God must compromise with such negativity. Taking this conclusion a step further, Derrida writes that to *exclude* death from God or positive Presence means "the exclusion of every particular *determination*. And it means that God is *nothing* (determined), is not life, because he is *everything,* and therefore is at once All and Nothing, Life and Death. Which means that God is or appears, is *named,* within the difference between All and Nothing, Life and Death. Within difference, and at bottom as Difference itself" (*WD*, pp. 115–116). These objections to the possibility of thinking full presence, positive infinity, and absolute alterity are, of course, questions of language: questions that philosophical discourse necessarily encounters to the extent that, in language, it tries to think, for example, God. (See also in this context Derrida's remark, in *Speech and Phenomena,* that as a linguistic statement " 'I am who I am' is the admission of a mortal" (*SP*, p. 54).)

Of course, against these difficulties one can always mobilize the resources of negative theology, which knows that it speaks a language that necessarily fails because it is inferior to *logos* as God's understanding, if one is not to draw the skeptical conclusion that God is a mere fiction (*WD*, p. 116). Neither Heidegger nor Derrida, however, chooses either of these options. For Heidegger, as can be seen, the God of the philosophers, that is, the producing ground of the *causa sui,* is the destinal figure in which the forgetting of Being is enacted in onto-theology. But what about Derrida? In "Violence and Metaphysics," after citing Levinas' statement that we are "in the Trace of God," Derrida remarks that this proposition "risks incompatibility with every allusion to the 'very presence of God.' A proposition readily converted into atheism: and if God was an *effect of the trace?* If the idea of divine presence (life, existence, parousia, etc.), if the name of God was but the movement of erasure of the trace in presence? Here it is a question of knowing whether the trace permits us to think presence in its system, or whether the reverse order is the true one. It is doubtless the *true order*. But it is indeed the *order of truth* which is in question" (*WD*, p. 108). Like Heidegger, Derrida makes room for God, so to speak. Rather than drawing the skeptical conclusion that because of the classical difficulties encountered by the concept of God it must be abandoned, the concept or name of God becomes exemplary not of the historical destiny of Being, but of something that articulates itself into the linguistic difficulties referred to. God, or what Derrida calls in *Dissemination* the "theological trap," is the dream of an absolute erasure of the trace, that is, of the inevitable negativity and endless referral to Other that all attempts to think a positive infinity and full presence must meet, and of making the trace subservient to full presence (*D*, p. 258). But this exemplary function of the name of God also demonstrates, in an exemplary fashion, that the dream of full presence is not possible without the trace. For what is the trace but the minimal reference to an Other without which no God can come into His own, and which, on this account, always makes God differ from Himself? In this sense God is necessarily the effect of the trace, of a structure that retains the Other as Other in the full plenitude of a self-present entity. Yet since a trace is only a trace if it is erasable—a nonerasable trace would be a "Son of God," according to Derrida (*WD*, p. 230)—it harbors in a structural fashion the possibility and site of its occultation and oblivion by the idea of God. As a necessary possibility, necessary because structurally always possible, "the theological trap" is thus an inevitable, if not a necessary trap. It is not an illusion that could simply be disposed of. I quote from *Of Grammatology:* "The 'theological' is a determined moment in the total movement of the trace" (*OG*, p. 47). Without the possibility of its effacement in the name of God, the trace could not be more "originary" than God.

There are thus obvious limits to a demystification in the style of the Enlightenment of an idea such as God. Derrida, I believe, would reiterate, in the case of God, what he has said about the apocalyptic tone, namely, that its "demystification must be led as far as possible, and the task is not modest. It is interminable, because no one can exhaust the overdeterminations and the indetermination of the apocalyptic stratagems."[19] In the same way, the theological strategies are endless, because they can always achieve their ends even by renouncing all ends. A good and recent example of such a strategy is Marion's reinterpretation of the Nietzschean notion of the death of God as the death of the last idol of God. But as

Derrida has done in "On a Newly Arisen Apocalyptic Tone," it is important to distinguish the limits encountered by such a demystification from
those that distinguish a deconstruction: the latter are "(perhaps) more
essential."[20] From what we have seen, to make God an effect of the trace
is to conceive of the "theological trap" as a determined moment in the
total movement of the trace: more precisely, as a function of the structural
possibility of effacement that characterizes it. Yet this is not the only limit
that a deconstructive attempt to come to grips with the notion of God
must face. For the moment, however, I return to Derrida's statement
that God might be or is an effect of the trace.

To say that God is the effect of the trace means that God *as* God is
dependent on a structure of referral that, as such, ceaselessly refers to an
Other, away from itself, so as to have itself no *as such*. Since all reference
to self, all full self-presence, cannot do without such a structure of referral
and demarcation if it is to be what it is—a self-consciousness, a *causa sui,*
a positive self-present infinity—the trace, and differance for that matter,
are transcendental structures of sorts, quasi-transcendental structures, as
I shall call them. Of this quasi-transcendental structure, God is the *exemplary* revelation. As the absolutely Other, God is the *self-presentation* of
the structure of the trace, that is, of "the divisible *envoi* [dispatch, referral,
and so on] for which there is no self-presentation nor assured destination."[21] But this exemplary revelation is also the most violent occultation
of the trace, since all self-presentation can only come into its own by
forgetting the trace of the referral to the Other and the difference within
the self without which no self would be possible, especially if it is the
self-presentation of the quasi-transcendental structure of the trace (itself).
God is also exemplary in his revelation of the trace because he is the *One*
absolute Other, compared with the plural characteristics of the trace.
Indeed, if the trace is a structure of referral to Other (in general), its
referrals refer to other referrals without decidable destination, the latter
remaining unsaturated. If God is said to be the effect of the trace, then
this also implies that His possibility is dependent on a structurally infinite
network of referrals that comes to only an illusion of a halt when it
represents itself, reveals itself, in exemplary fashion, as the One example.

If asked to compare Derrida's debate with the notion of God with
Husserl's statement of the priority of the subjective a priori over God,
or with Heidegger's notion of deity which, as a pre-comprehension of
the being-God of God, also precedes all relation to God, what would
one have to say? One would, obviously, have to elucidate the ways in

which the trace is at the origin of meaning, and of the meaning-relation to an ego in general. (Here I refer the reader to the first part of *Of Grammatology*.) Yet, I will not engage here in an elaboration of this difficult question. I choose rather to make a remark, and a remark only, on how Derrida's treatment of the trace of God compares with Heidegger's declarations concerning God as the destinal figure of the obliteration of Being in the history of metaphysics. Let me advance the following formula: If God, for Heidegger, is the destinal figure in which the transcendens pure and simple, Being in other words, retreats, a retreat through which the history of Being begins, God, for Derrida, is the result of an always possible, henceforth necessary, effacement of a quasi-transcendental structure that, as a structure of "thought," is older than the thinking of Being. God is the exemplary effacement not only of the ontico-ontological difference but of the difference between that originary difference and the ontic difference as well. Or, to venture another formula: God's name is the exemplary presentation, and hence oblivion, of a transcendental difference that allows for no name, the name of Being included.

Because the trace, or differance, has been determined by Derrida as being *neither* a name *nor* a concept, *neither* sensible *nor* intelligible, *not more* in time *than* in space, and so on, Dufrenne, despite Derrida's repeated assertion that these notions "block every relationship to theology" (*P*, p. 40), and in particular that they are irreducible to negative theology, has charged Derrida with negative theology and with resuscitating the dead positive God of philosophy under the forms of the trace and differance. Derrida has admitted, in the essay "Differance," for instance, that the style of his approach often resembles the *via negativa* of negative theology, "occasionally even to the point of being indistinguishable from negative theology" (*M*, p. 6). Yet paying no attention to what amounts to an admonition on Derrida's part, Dufrenne interprets Derrida's (and Blanchot's) attempt to reach back to "an ultra or an arche," in order to break with logocentrism, as theological in intent since all positing of a beyond, and all experience of a transcendence, would by definition be religious; and although this beyond is, as Dufrenne recognizes, situated on the far side of the intelligible and the intuitable, the mere fact that it becomes narrowed down by means of the *via negativa* shows that it is, indeed, of the order of negative theology. Dufrenne rightly remarks that "if one reaches back to an ultra-transcendental, one must explain how it functions as a condition of possibility." But rather than looking for the answer to that question in Derrida's text, Dufrenne hastens to the conclusion that if God is the effect of a trace, the trace must "produce this effect"; with the trace "a non-presence becomes productive"; "there is no creation *ex nihilo,* but a creative *nihil,* a determining indeterminant," he contends. In short, the trace, according to Dufrenne, "engenders" God and presence, and must therefore be "a sort of fore-God, not the negation of God, but a negative God *(un Dieu en négatif)*."[22] But just as little as Being substitutes for God does the trace replace the divine. Furthermore, the trace, in the same way as Being, does not *relate,* does not stand in a *relation,* to God. In the same way as Being is the Being of beings and of God, the trace is the trace *of* God. This implies, as well, that the trace or differance must not be understood as a cause that would produce or engender what is traditionally called an effect. The trace does not create. All these activities are, as can be seen, ontic relations: that is, relations pure and simple. Since God is an effect of the trace, and the trace is *nothing* apart from being the trace *of* God, no relation enters the difference between God and the trace. Now, to determine what happens between a quasi-transcendental structure such as the trace and what it is the structure of is undoubtedly one of the most difficult problems that Derrida's thought poses for us. It stems not only from the fact that the trace or differance is not technically a condition of possibility, though without it no God would come into existence, but also from the fact that, as the retained trace of the *relation* of Other in God, it is a condition of impossibility for a God who can only be the one who He is if He disregards this possibilizing structure of the trace. Paradoxically put, the trace (though this is true as well of all other infrastructures), constituting through self-effacement, structurally allows for the possibility of its being disregarded, neglected, rejected, overlooked, and so on. It is a condition of possibility that inscribes the possibility of *not* being *valid,* of its exception. This retreating condition of possibility and impossibility, although it is nothing apart from being the trace of God, is neither God Himself, who is the trace's self-representation, nor nothing in the sense of a *nihil negativum.* It is a well-defined structure of referral (to Other) and, hence, of deferral (of self) that is presupposed (but not *aufgehoben*) by all self-identity, whether that of a singular being or of God. As a matter of fact, what represents perhaps the best refutation of a suspicion such as negative theology is that the trace is not something indefinite, undetermined, or ineffable. On the contrary, it is a rather well-articulated construct whose undecidability follows from clearly determinable structural features.

So much for my discussion of the confusion of the thought of the trace with the *absconditus* of negative theology. Derrida, in "How to Avoid Speaking: Denials," has tackled the question of negative theology in no uncertain terms. Undoubtedly, it would be most interesting to discuss here in its totality Derrida's multi-leveled treatment of negative theology, and especially his affirmation that any discourse, the deconstructionist discourse included, can *always* become theological, in a becoming whose law is elucidated in an analysis of the logico-grammatical structure of the type of discourse that proceeds through negative attribution. Of that analysis, however, I will mention only a very short segment, and that, moreover, in only a very schematic manner. As part of that analysis, Derrida distinguishes between two movements and two tropologies concerning the negative in Plato's texts. The first concerns the status of the idea of the good *(idea tou agathou)* as situated beyond being, presence, or essence, *epekeina tes ousias*. Without being itself, the good, from beyond all that is, is said to give birth to being, presence, and essence. There thus seems to be a clear discontinuity between that beyond and what it engenders. But this negativity, instead of being established apophatically according to the logic of the neither/nor, proceeds from a *hyperbolization* of what the idea of the good is supposed to transgress and make possible. Here, in the case of the good, the determination of the beyond obeys a logic of the *hyper,* that is, of transgression through excess—a logic that anticipates the hyper-essentialisms of all Christian apophases. Such negative determination through hyperbolization of the excellent prevents the latter from becoming foreign to what it exceeds. By maintaining a more or less homogenous, homologous, and analogical relation between being and the beyond of being, that which exceeds being becomes capable of accounting for what is. In short, though beyond being, and apparently suffering no longer any ontological predicates, the good *epekeina tes ousias* remains comparable to what it exceeds and does not interrupt this analogical continuity.[23]

The second movement and tropology concerning the negative occurs in Plato's treatment in the *Timaeus* of the notion of *khora* and its status beyond the limit. Derrida argues that with respect to this absolutely irreducible beyond of a "space" from which all intelligible paradigms, all types and schemes take their origin, Plato mobilizes two concurring languages. The first proceeds by multiplying negations, but its neither/nor logic rapidly turns into an and/and logic through which the thought of *khora* becomes reappropriated by the Platonic ontology and dialectic at the very moment Plato speaks of it *as if* it were a mixture of the two negated determinations. From here on, the *khora* can be interpreted according to its traditional modes, *as* the mother, the nurse, the engendering receptacle of the universe. Rather than being treated hyperbolically, the negative is subjected here to an anachronistic treatment: properties of things are transferred to it that are posterior to it in time and space. In conclusion, it can be said that this mode of language on the beyond, or third genre, yields as well to those schemes of analogy that establish continuity between what ought, in principle, to be in radical disjunction. Like the *idea tou agathou*, the *khora* is subjected to an analogical transfer through which this beyond is tied into what it must ultimately transcend, the ontic and the ontological.[24]

Yet, the other language in Plato's text on the *khora* marks the irreducibility of the space staked out by the *khora*, by insinuating that it is something that no dialectic, no scheme of participation, and, ultimately, no analogy can hope to link up with any philosopheme whatsoever. Here, the neither/nor cannot any longer be transformed into an and/and. No figure, no turn of speech, can account for it, because the *khora* is the space that itself inscribes and makes possible all turns. It repels all anthropomorphic and theomorphic schemes.

> Radically nonhuman and atheological, one cannot even say that it *gives* place *(donne lieu)* or that *there is* the *khora*. The *es gibt*, thus translated, too vividly announces or recalls the dispensation of God, of man, or even that of the Being of which certain texts by Heidegger speak *(es gibt Sein)*. *Khora* is not even that *(ça)*, the *es* or *id* of giving, before all subjectivity. It does not give place as one would give something, whatever it may be; it neither creates nor produces anything, not even an event insofar as it takes place. It gives no order and makes no promise. It is radically ahistorical, because nothing happens through it and nothing happens to it. Plato insists on its necessary indifference; to receive all and allow itself to be marked or affected by what is inscribed in it, the *khora* must remain without form and without proper determination. But if it is amorphous *(amorphon; Timaeus, 50d)*, this signifies neither lack nor privation. *Khora* is nothing positive or negative. It is impassive, but it is neither passive nor active.[25]

Since it is radically *an-analogical*, the only way to speak of the *khora* is to call it always by its name, *khora*, a name that certainly is not a proper name.[26]

In "How to Avoid Speaking: Denials," Derrida continues this analysis, asking what takes place between an experience such as the *khora*, on the one hand, and, on the other, the *via negativa* in its Christian form: that is, between "the wholly-other who is neither transcendent, absolutely distanced, nor immanent and close,"[27] and the apophasis toward the excellent in negative theology. Rather than following Derrida's text in his elaborations on prayer—an analysis directed against Marion's contention that prayer is a pre- or non-predicative mode of speech (the only one appropriate to speak of God, to God), and against which Derrida objects that prayer's inclusion of praise and celebration maintains an irreducible relation to the logical function of attribution, and hence of predication, and thus fosters an analogical understanding in negative theology of the absolute Other as well—I choose to return to what happens between the thought of the *khora* as absolutely an-analogical and that type of language that tries to reappropriate it by certain turns of speech. Indeed, it seems to me that the analogical transfer of metaphoric properties to the *khora* is not only a paradigm not only of what takes place between the experience of the *khora* and the *via negativa* of the Christian sort, but of what we have seen happens between the thought of the trace and the concept of God as well. What is the self-presentation of the trace, its exemplary revelation *as* God, if it is not the result of a projection of ontic distinctions and relations onto something whose double genitival "relationship" to God transcends that of possessor or source? But, because of this "relationship," the trace of God is also *only* the retained mark of the Other in the self-constituted full presence of a positive infinity. Like the *khora,* the trace is an-analogical, but as the minimal structure of relation to, it also harbors the possibility of analogization. As the trace of *God,* the trace allows for its own analogization in God's self-presentation. God, then, is exemplary in His revelation of a quasi-transcendental structure precisely to the extent that He is the analogy of it. God's exemplarity would, thus, be the result of his analogization of the possibility of relation to the Other.

Before risking a final, and I hope happier, but obviously provisional, formulation of the question regarding God and the trace—what I am trying to come to grips with here lends itself to, and invites, an interminable analysis, not because of its depth, unfathomableness, or whatever, but because it escapes, by its very nature, all subsumption under standard categories of thought (a hint at the limits of deconstruction to which I will return in a moment)—let me briefly return to the notion of God's exemplarity.

The thought of Being, Heidegger insists in *Identity and Difference,* cannot render Being more distinct by an example *(Beispiel)* since there is nowhere in the realm of beings an example for the essence of Being.[28] But, according to Derrida, the thought of Being would make it possible to think *God, for example,* and to do so without reduction, naiveté, or blasphemy. As I have tried to show, this is possible only if God exemplifies, is exemplary of Being. But an example serves also to guide more securely the eidetic attention, the *Wesensblick* directed upon Being as such, as Heidegger remarks in *An Introduction to Metaphysics* and in *Identity and Difference,* and does so in spite of the fact that "it remains questionable whether an individual being can ever be regarded as an example of being."[29] God, therefore, is perhaps the exemplary example both of the impossibility of exemplifying Being and of the need to do so in order to guide the *Wesensblick.* To think God, for example, is to think of him *as* an example, or a case, an exemplary one, of a universal figure such as Being. (This is indeed what happens in an essay such as Heidegger's "The Onto-theological Constitution of Metaphysics.") The question, then, would be: What is the law that calls for this impossible and yet inevitable exchange between Being and its examples, God included. Derrida's elaborations on the trace of God perhaps give us a hint. Indeed, if God is the exemplary self-presentation of an an-analogical structure such as the trace, God is the trace of a structure that constitutes the possibility not only of analogization, but perhaps of exemplification as well. The first analogization of the an-analogical structure of the trace is also the first *example* (of analogization)—God, for example—an example that cannot by right be rendered more distinct through any example. Let me, then, cast the thought of the trace of God into the following formula: this thought means that God is the self-presentation as *primum exemplum* of the non-exemplifiable structure that constitutes the structure of the example.

This, then, is the point where we can return to the question of the limits that a deconstruction of the notion of God must necessarily encounter: the trace—plural, multi-leveled, even when in the singular— as the relation to the Other that opens up the scene for God to come onto the scene as its primary self-presentation and exemplification cannot *as such* be objectified and thematized, or subjected to given categories of thought. All talk about it, including the demonstration of the function of the trace in terms of philosophical discourse, runs the risk of essentially deforming it. This deformation, ultimately, consists of the becoming theological of the philosophical discourse on the trace. It is a deformation that is always possible and yet, from what has been established up to

now, inevitable: the trace of God, after all, is the trace that not only
"precedes" Him but also calls upon Him for the impossible task of exemplifying it.

A final remark on how this thought of the trace compares with Heidegger's thinking of Being might be appropriate at this point. It differs
from the thinking of the ontico-ontological difference not only in that
the latter appears already as a metaphysical determination of *die frühe Spur,*
but in that it makes it possible to account for the necessity Heidegger
himself feels to speak of trees (as in *An Introduction to Metaphysics*) or apples
and pears *(Identity and Difference)* when confronting the task of saying
what Being *is*. The thought of the trace (of differance, supplementarity,
and so on) sets forth the law, if you will, which calls for the analogization
and exemplification of that which by right refuses all such treatment. It
is a law which accounts for the fact that the philosophical demonstration
of that law can always, and easily, turn into theology in which it represents itself as the law-giving God.

At the beginning of this essay I said that all of Derrida's major discussions of theology take place as investigations into the exchange and dialogue between several types of discourses on the Other. To conclude,
let me try to say something about what such an approach implies for
philosophical thought itself. Toward the end of his essay on Levinas in
Writing and Difference, Derrida notes that the true—that is, philosophical—name for thought's inclination to the Other, for the renunciation
of the concept, the a priori and transcendental horizons of language in
front of God, is *empiricism*. Theology, for Derrida, is thus not only empirical as science, as it is for Heidegger when he defines it as the positive
science not of God, but of Christianity. It is empirical as well where it
concerns itself with God as its object to the extent precisely that it dreams
"the *dream* of a purely *heterological* thought," of "a *pure* thought of *pure*
difference" (*WD*, p. 151). (Vice versa, all such dream *in* the philosophical
discourse is the dream of the nonphilosophical and turns into theology.)
Although Derrida recognizes the complicity between metaphysics and
empiricism, and hence the reason why the nonphilosophical can indeed
come to resolutely challenge it, his emphasis on the fact that philosophy
has from its beginning armed itself against such a threat by making alterity
circulate at the origin of meaning shows a clear commitment, it seems
to me, to philosophical thought as opposed to pure heterological thought
such as theology. But what can it mean for philosophical thought if by
foregrounding the thought of Being, and of ontological difference, in

the thought of the trace, thought as the thought of Being becomes deplaced? If, as Marion remarks, to "think outside of ontological difference eventually condemns one to be no longer able to think at all," or to engage in something that can no longer be called "thinking"—a possibility that he cheerfully takes upon himself when it comes to God as the one who "surpasses, detours, and distracts all thought"—do we then have to conclude that Derrida's thought, like that of Levinas, and of Marion, has become theological?[30] Undoubtedly, to inquire into a difference older than Being, into a trace *of* Being, a trace of which Being would be a trace, is no longer to philosophize and to think, strictly speaking. It is an inquiry geared toward elucidating what happens in philosophy to the thought of the absolutely Other: the temptation, or the danger, if you will, to theologize it is always imminent. The investigation of the trace or of differance is aimed at showing how thought can always become non-thought. Although this demonstration encounters the difficulties and limits that I have pointed to, in style, *ductus,* and intent, it is certainly closer to philosophy than to theology.

7

Strictly Bonded

P H I L O S O P H I C A L   T H O U G H T, according to Hegel in *Philosophy of Right,* is the activity of absorbing in *(aufheben)* or elevating to universality what is merely immediate and particular. To attain such purification of the object of thought it is necessary that the "mind be trained against capricious fancies, and that these be destroyed and overcome to leave the way clear for rational thinking" (*PR,* p. 260). Such training or formation *(Bildung)* of the mind against everything arbitrary—a formation through which the mind becomes capable of identically repeating itself—represents the production in thought of a *second nature,* a spiritual nature of the mind, in short, of what Hegel calls "habit" *(Gewohnheit),* a formation through which the spiritual becomes habitual to man (*PR,* pp. 108–109, 260). Habit, which, as Hegel notes, can also kill a man, is at the same time the dividing line of reason. Considering the condescending treatment that habit generally receives, Hegel's claim may seem surprising. Yet the positive role that he imputes to habit and habit-formation as far as thinking is concerned, however original, springs from the recognition that from Aristotle to Hume habit has been an ontological-gnoseological concept. Hegel, after acknowledging that the definition of the concept of habit poses significant difficulties, proceeds to situate and determine it in the third part of his *Encyclopedia,* entitled *The Philosophy of Spirit,* Section I, "The Subjective Spirit." The proper setting for "habit" is indeed that moment in the development of subjective spirit when the feeling soul, whose self has been disunited to the point of madness, overcomes the inner contradiction of the spirit by achieving a Being-for- and with-itself. "This Being-with-self *(Beisichselbersein)* we call it habit," Hegel notes.[1] Habit allows the soul to become a self as an "in itself simple relation of ideality to itself," that is, as a formal or abstract universality. Habit achieves such abstract universal Being of the soul by reducing the particularity and contingency of feelings to "merely existing determinations of itself."[2] In thus reducing feelings to determinations by means of which it takes possession of what formerly affected it indiscriminately, the soul becomes free of their affective power, and hence free for itself. In habit, Hegel remarks, the soul "takes the immediate and singular content by which it became affected, into itself, and *inhabits* it *(sich in . . . ihn eingewohnt),* and it does so to such a degree that it moves around in it in freedom." Hence, man no longer relates to "a *contingent* and *singular* sensation, representation, desire, etc., but *to himself,* to a *universal mode* of acting that has been posited by himself and that has become *proper* to him, and which makes up his individuality. Therefore he appears free."[3] Habit in this sense is determined by Hegel as "the mechanism of the feeling of self," and is compared to memory *(Gedächtnis),* that is, the mechanism of intelligence. By means of this mechanism, based on *repetition* and *exercise,* the soul opens itself to the activity associated with the consciousness of spirit.

Although the proper setting for habit is thus in subjective spirit, at the very juncture between feeling and real soul, "the form of habit comprises all sorts and all stages of the activity of spirit," Hegel continues.[4] Indeed, since the very mechanical nature of habit—a characterization that has earned it the name of *a second nature*—shows habit still to be unfree (however much its immediacy is the result of a *positing* by the soul), there arises the need to free habit and its idealizing function from the form of Being that it has in subjective spirit.[5] In addition, "the universal to which the soul relates in habit is merely . . . *abstract universality* produced by reflection through the *repetition of a manifold of singularities.*"[6] The mechanical, automatic function of habit, whose emancipatory role Hegel demonstrated for subjective spirit (and consequently justified, in contradistinction to the usual contempt in which it is held), becomes fully denaturalized only in pure thought. Hegel writes: "Entirely free *thinking,* thinking that takes place in the pure element of itself, needs habit and speed *(Geläufigkeit)* as well. It needs this form of *immediacy* by means of which it is unhindered and penetrated propriety of my *singular self.* I *exist* only as thinking I for myself through such habit."[7] Habit, indeed, by reducing sensation of one's corporeality, allows the thinking subject to freely devote himself to pure thought, and he does so all the better as he develops habit (as it is operative in the realm of thinking) under the form of *Erinnerung* and *Gedächtnis*. For such pure thinking, the universal to which it relates, rather than being the abstract universality of the feeling soul, has become "the *concrete universal* that determines itself."[8] But with this it also becomes obvious that habit is not limited to being a constitutive ingredient of thinking in the order of subjective spirit, but extends to thinking in its objective form as well. A *certain* form of habit must continue to secure the Being-with-itself of pure, absolute thinking, of a thinking that is its own subject, and that eliminates any interferences.

Habit, then, by means of which all capricious ideas become successfully eliminated from thinking, is what makes it possible for thinking to raise itself to the universal. Routine, to return to *The Philosophy of Right,* allows thinking to take the freeway of the rational, "the high road where every one travels, where no one is conspicuous *(sich auszeichnet)*" (*PR,* p. 230). But this habit, which is constitutive of philosophical thought, is also what makes philosophical thought profoundly ethical *(sittlich).* Indeed, in what amounts to a reappropriation of Aristotle's evaluation of the ethical role of habits, Hegel determines habit in paragraph 151 as the very mode of appearance of ethicity, as that through which the spirit is alive and present as a world (*PR,* pp. 108–109). Moreover, what is true of ethical life is true of philosophical thinking as well. Just as marriage (the first moment of the first moment that is the family in ethical life) cannot primarily be based on love, on what Hegel calls "the transient, fickle, and purely subjective aspects of love" (*PR,* p. 262), so philosophical thought cannot be based on the merely singular and contingent. Similar to marriage, by which "the sensuous moment, the one proper to physical life," becomes transformed into "something only consequential and accidental, belonging to the external embodiment of the ethical bond" (*PR,* p. 113), with the effect that it turns into "something wholly conditioned," philosophical thought must destroy natural immediacy, show it to be a consequence, and thus endow it with "intellectual and ethical significance" (*PR,* p. 114). Philosophical thinking must indeed deprive the natural, the immediate, and even the capricious, of their incidental and autonomous character by showing them to be results—interior or exterior—of the concepts' self-development. One might perhaps wish to object here that if thinking achieves the universality without which it could not be thinking only on the basis of a reduction, it can hardly be called ethical. But the reduction in question raises the singular and the capricious to a minimum of ideality which allows for its identical repetition. Although paradoxically such minimal identity is achieved through a reduction, the universalization in question is the very condition that makes recognition of the singular possible. Without this universalizing reduction it is indeed impossible to do justice to the capricious or singular. Moreover, since such a reduction shows the contingent and the singular to be "something only consequential and accidental," it fosters significance by putting previously isolated, autonomous entities or proprieties into logical relation, creating logical dependence and derivation among them. Such an operation of interrelating by thinking is ethical as well, in that it produces a spiritual bond between elements which until then were separated.

I recall here that in habit the immediate and singularized content that previously affected the soul so as to disunite it has been fully taken into the soul's ideality, and to such a degree that the soul fully *inhabits* it *(eingewohnt)*. In relating in the mode of habit to its determinations, the soul, says Hegel in the *Encyclopedia,* becomes increasingly *at home (heimischer)* in its exteriorizations. It acquires an ever greater *familiarity (Vertrautheit)* with them (*PR,* p. 191). The reduction through habit is indeed a taking possession of the immediate and singularized, by which this content becomes stripped of any previous otherness. It is recognized as such, for the first time, and as the Hegelian text insinuates, according to modes of relation that characterize the law of the home, of the *oikos*.

That habit-formation and habitual practice, whether in ethical life proper or in philosophical thought, are constitutive of their ethicity, is emphasized as well through the qualifications of familiarity and homeliness. Indeed, what may look like a mere play on words, Hegel's juxtaposition of *Gewohnheit* (habit) and *Wohnung* (habitation) in paragraph 151, is based on the original meaning of the Greek notion of *ethos*. He writes: "Custom *(Sitte)*—*ethos*—the Ancients did not know anything about conscience—. . . *habit,* custom *(Gebrauch)*—(primarily habitation in Herodotus) convention of men—custom *(Sitte)*—from domicile *(Sitz)*?"[9] Yet although this play on words is grounded in a most venerable tradition, according to which the original meaning of *ethos* is dwelling, or customary domicile, whence its meaning of "traditional mode of acting, talking, and behaving," there are more essential reasons for Hegel's linkage of habit to habitation, and for the analogical treatment of thinking and ethical life. Early in *Philosophy of Right,* Hegel recalls that the free will, whose embodiment in an existent is what right is, is genuinely a will and free only as *thinking* intelligence. Hegel writes: "This self-consciousness which apprehends itself through thinking as essentially human, and thereby frees itself from the contingent and the false, is the principle of right, morality, and ethical life" (*PR*, p. 30). But the sphere of right, and within it the particular phase of ethical life, is, indeed, only one phase in thinking's essential raising of itself to its essential habit, a habit that will ensure thinking's essential ethicity in that in it, through it, as it, thinking is (close) by itself *(bei sich)*, at home with itself.

Yet, as *Philosophy of Right* suggests, habitation—dwelling—is dwelling together in a family. And although the family is only the first moment of the system of ethical life, its analysis yields knowledge that will illuminate not only the nature of the sphere of ethical life in general, but that of philosophical thinking as well, that is, of the whole of Hegelian thought. This is, indeed, what Jacques Derrida has set out to do in the left-hand column of *Glas*. But before entering into a discussion of Derrida's analysis of the scope and limits of the topic of the family in Hegel's writings, let me first, since I am concerned here with the question of philosophical or speculative thinking, try to define what sort of linkage it is that family and ethical life achieve in a paradigmatic fashion. To answer this question, I will have to focus on a notion in Hegel that is not a concept strictly speaking, yet not for that matter a metaphor either. Whereas the mode of relating that constitutes the sphere of abstract right is that of property, *Eigentum,* which "as abstractly self-related actuality," "contentless and simple relation of itself to itself" (*PR*, p. 37), and should be translated as something like "properness," the sphere of morality is characterized by relation properly speaking, what Hegel terms *Verhältnis,* and which he has dealt with in great detail on various occasions, in particular in the *Greater Logic*. But the notion of *bond, Band* in German, which describes the particular mode of relating and of linkage in the family, and in the ethical sphere as a whole—the state, not the family, Hegel notes, is the "absolute bond"[10]—is never, to my knowledge, explicitly thematized. Yet Hegel makes abundant use of it in the sections on the family both in *Philosophy of Right,* and in the corresponding sections of the *Encyclopedia*. I might also add that "bond" is a notion which is not mentioned in any of the existing dictionaries or indexes of Hegel's writings.

Although Hegel relies on the notion of the bond to conceive of the ethical unity, and in particular that of the family, this does not mean that the notion in question would appear in that context alone. But if Hegel does refer, in the two spheres that precede ethical life, to various bonds, he does so only to add immediately that these connections, these bonds, are only exterior, "*external* conjunctions whose bond of connection is neither life nor the concept." Connections of this sort are, as Hegel notes, the business of the Understanding (*PR*, p. 47). At best such bonds pertain to the "universality of the freedom of personality,"[11] that is, the being bound for itself *(für sich gebunden)*[12] in abstract law of the individual, who, as Hegel puts it in a handwritten note, "can decide or not decide to acquire possession, or to engage in contract, since he is not bound to do so." He continues: "In the sphere of morality I bind myself, and I find myself, am bound."[13] But the bonds of morality are not yet true bonds. As Hegel shows in his discussion of ironic subjectivity—whose absolute self-complacency can become the bond and substance of a community of sorts—the moral bond is, if not a parody or perversion, at best a mere anticipation of the true bond. The true bond is, indeed, the truth of the Being-for-itself of personality, and of the bonds rooted in relation that characterize the sphere of morality. In the bond, both have been sublated and elevated. Let me then try to determine with as much accuracy as possible what a bond is.

Bonds, *Bänder,* strictly speaking, are only those elements that serve to secure unity and cohesion in the ethical world. In the preface to *Philosophy of Right,* Hegel already refers to "the bonds of the ethical world" in this sense (*PR*, p. 9). The ethical world, however, is like the having-become-actual of the concept of freedom in the existing world and like the nature of self-consciousness, a substantial order, that is, according to Hegel's understanding of "substance," an order in which the objective is filled with subjectivity, or where the object has the form and existence of subjectivity. Now, what constitute the substantiality of the ethical world are precisely its bonds. They are by right, so to speak, the substance *(das Substantielle).* The bonds are the substance of the ethical, first, because in them, and through them, this world has its subsistence *(Bestehen).* Hegel speaks in this context of the bonds that give "men, with all their deed and destiny, coherence and subsistence" (*PR*, p. 100). They are *actual* bonds that, as Hegel puts it in a handwritten note, actually exist, persist for themselves *(für sich bestehend).*[14] However, the bonds of the ethical world are substantial bonds not only because they constitute an enduring substratum, but also because they are endowed with the "actual living soul *(Lebendigkeit)* of self-consciousness" (*PR*, p. 106). The bonds of the substantial order are bonds that know themselves, so to speak, in that they are objects of knowledge in and for actual self-consciousness.[15] In short, bonds "*are*—'are' in the highest sense of self-subsistent being," as "an absolute authority and power infinitely more firmly established than the being of nature." But they are not, for that matter, "something alien to the subject. On the contrary, his spirit bears witness to them as to its own essence, the essence in which he has a feeling of his selfhood, and in which he lives as in his own element which is not distinguished from himself" (*PR*, p. 105).

These substantial bonds, Hegel notes, are no longer relations, properly speaking. In the addendum to paragraph 147 he refers to the ethical order as an "absence of relation," a *verhältnislose Identität,* that is, a relationless identity.[16] He also qualifies these bonds as "substantial relations."[17] If bonds constitute a relationless identity, they do so because the bonded is not of the order of personality, and especially not of the order of the moral subject, but rather of the order of the individual which has liberated himself toward its substantial freedom, thus becoming a "link in the chain of social connections" (*PR*, p. 124). Whereas the sphere of abstract right gives rise to relations that remain exterior to the fundamental relation of self-possession and possession of property, and whereas in the sphere of moral law the subject relates to abstract values merely according to the mode of *sollen,* in the ethical sphere the laws are truly binding. They are binding because they have their existence in me: "Ich bin das Dasein, verbindlich," Hegel remarks.[18] Because of this absence of an essential difference between the individual and the laws of the ethical world, the bonding of ethical life is not to be thought of any more in terms of relations. This is, as Hegel remarks several times, what makes it so difficult for the intellect to come to grips with the ethical, substantial bond.

Bonds, paradoxically, are unintelligible to the understanding because they are too subtle, and impossible to dissect. They resist the separating power of the intellect, because in principle, at least, they are in themselves *(an sich)* indissoluble. It is this quality of indissolubleness that causes Hegel to call the bonds sacred: "—*ethical*—*divine* bond," Hegel writes.[19] In an extensive note in the margin of paragraph 132 of his own copy of *Philosophy of Right,* we read: "What is the sacred?—that which holds men together, and were it only as lightly as does the rush in the wreath *(wie die Binse den Kranz)*—what the most sacred?—what for all eternity makes the minds united and unified *(einig und einiger)*—actual substantial bond—in which that self-isolating subjectivity which I want to preserve for myself, has perished and is absolutely satisfied—so infinitely powerful in itself that I myself am wholly in it."[20]

If the sacred, the sacrosanct, is "the embodiment of the absolute concept or of self-conscious freedom" (*PR,* p. 33), "the *identity* of subjective knowing and willing with the true good" (*PR,* p. 91), then the bond that it forms, the actual and substantial bond, is not only a light bond, holding the bonded lightly together, but one as well in which the bonding is of such a nature that the intertwined rush-like individuals remain distinct while at the same time forming a wreath in which no distinction between elements, between beginnings and ends, is possible any more. The manner in which the rushes are bound together lifts their isolation into something which is not a composite of elements, but a unity of the individuals intertwined in the wreath and the wreath itself. Such a bond is possible only in the ethical sphere, in which human beings have become individuals who *as* individuals (in contradistinction to their former determinations as personalities and moral subjects) are distinct from one another within a whole that is of their own willed making, and that thus knows itself in and through the individuals. It is this which permits Hegel to insinuate that the bond also binds itself into the unity that it fosters among its elements. Only such a bond, in which a unity is achieved between bonded individuals and the bonding bond—the wreath—is strictly speaking a bond, because it alone can achieve inwardness.

But what about the (incredible) lightness of the substantial bond? Its lightness, which is that of its spiritual nature, and which therefore should not be taken lightly, originates in this bond's dependence on the linguistic sign. This is most evident in the case of marriage, but, as Hegel recalls, it was already the case with stipulation in a contract. In paragraph 164, Hegel argues that the "ethical bond of marriage," its "knot, is tied and made ethical only after this ceremony [in which both parties declare their consent to enter the ethical bond of marriage], whereby through the use of signs, i.e. of language (the most mental embodiment of mind . . .), the substantial thing in the marriage is brought completely into being" (*PR,* p. 113). Here as elsewhere, the substantial bond is rooted "in language—which is binding for the will"—as Hegel puts it in a note in the margin.[21] Language, "the most worthy medium for the expression of our mental ideas *(Vorstellung),*" is what constitutes the ethical bond as something that has to be "held before the mind," represented, through the "particular determinate existence" of linguistic symbols (*PR,* p. 60). Linguistic formality, as it occurs during marriage ceremonies, ensures, indeed, that what is enacted in marriage not only has validity, but is recognized as such by others. Hegel notes: "Formality is essential because what is inherently right must also be posited as right" (*PR,* p. 273). In addition, this linguistic declaration in front of the family and the community, through which the (marital) bond becomes enacted, implies that the ethicity of the spiritual unity that it represents "consists in the parties' consciousness of this unity as their substantive aim," that is, as the relegation of "physical passion . . . to the level of a physical moment, destined to vanish in its very satisfaction" (*PR,* p. 112). In other words, the substantial bond of marriage is what it is only if it soars above the contingency of passion and the transience of a particular caprice.

A bond, in the strict sense of the word, presupposes such restriction of the contingent, the particular, the immediate, the natural, and their transformation into moments that *as* moments are not separate from what they know as their whole, which becomes posited by them. Yet, although language as a medium of formality is thus required in the ethical sphere not only of the family, but of civil society, and especially of the state, it is not certain whether the lightness of the bond of philosophical thinking also necessarily calls for a positing by means of linguistic signs. Language, Hegel says elsewhere, is the very medium of universality. Yet the question remains whether for the self-thinking of the Concept in Absolute thought, *actual* linguistic articulation is indeed required, or whether instead it is sufficient for thinking to conceive of the possibility of articulation in order to weave itself into the lightest of all bonds. After all, since language, for Hegel, is only a presenting exteriorization, based on natural signs, language must raise itself to the Concept, and deny itself in this manner as a system of natural signs. The telos of language is its own *Concept* of language, universal language.

Bonds, understood in a substantial sense, are as much a part of ethical life as of philosophical thinking, insofar as the latter is rooted in habit and in profound familiarity with spirit. It is not without interest to mention here that what Hegel refers to as the rushes intertwined into a wreath, his metaphor for illustrating how thinking bonds are wrought, also has the meaning in German of truism or triviality. In one idiomatic expression at least, in *Binsenwahrheit, Binse* has this meaning, and designates self-evident though banal truth. The bonds of philosophical thinking, although far from trivial, are indeed something in which thought is always already at home, in which it is with itself, in the family. As such, philosophical thought has nothing conspicuous about it. Even if philosophical thought as *noesis noeseos* thinks itself, and weaves itself into itself, such activity of the spirit, as a familiar activity, one in which thinking is truly at home, does not obtrude because of its excellence or of its seemingly highflown gestures. There is nothing flashy about thinking; it has the dullness of the marital bond, if you wish, but in that dullness it also reveals its substantive aims.

Derrida, in *Glas,* seems to be in agreement with this Hegelian conception of thinking, and of the binding power of its bonds. Indeed, in what some, curiously enough, have labeled Derrida's first text that is more playful than philosophical (and that would thus signify, as Richard Rorty has recently remarked, a departure from thinking's universalist claims to merely private fantasizing), one sees Derrida agree with Hegel's demand for universality, and the habitual reduction that it is based on, and agree to such a degree that it would make even the most zealous of Hegelians (if they deigned to read *Glas*) blush with envy for such seemingly unreserved faithfulness. But it is indeed a faithfulness that Hegelians cannot match, precisely because it is not Hegelian (in the historical sense). It is a faithfulness to the enterprise of thinking. Derrida's admiration in *Glas* for the Hegelian bond—for speculative thought—is apparently unconditional. The left-hand column of *Glas* is a monument honoring the force of Hegelian thought, its power to do justice, through idealization, reduction, limiting restriction, or mise à mort, to abolish everything inside or outside the system. Such celebration and admiration, however, does not preclude a tireless interrogation of certain limits of the bonds of thinking and their intrinsic ethicity. Apart from attempting to decipher the "very twisted form, so difficult to grasp," of the Hegelian system's structure (G, p. 121), the monumental column that *Glas* erects in honor of philosophical thought will also represent a sort of intervention in it. Such intervention, however, is not what has come to be known as an "unraveling" or "undoing" of the Hegelian bond. Indeed, "the critical displacement (supposing that is rigorously possible)" will not be as dramatic or flashy as what is practiced or stigmatized in academia under the name of "deconstruction." Strictly speaking, the bond of thinking cannot be undone—it is truth itself, and truth, as Derrida has said, *must be (Il faut la vérité)*. It *must* be, as we shall see, because it cannot not *be.* It is a question not of overcoming thinking's universalist bent and its idealizing reduction, but of reading thinking against the backdrop of certain necessary possibilities from which it comes into its own, but which it also must remain unable to think if it is to remain thinking.

Derrida's active interpretation, faithful to the letter of the Hegelian text, will in its very repetition of Hegel's writings and intentions "reveal" a certain exterior, a margin to the bond of thinking. It is an interpretation that presses another exteriority toward the center of the question, one that would not correspond to the Hegelian concept of exteriority (*G,* p. 6). In addition, by exposing Hegelian philosophical thought to the necessary possibility (necessary because always possible) of recontextualization—by facing it with the Genet column erected on the right side of *Glas*—this thought acquires additional, if not deviant, meanings that are not accounted for by philosophical thought without for that matter having been excluded explicitly or implicitly through reduction. The law that establishes the minimal identity of what, through iteration and recontextualization, changes from proper meaning to aberrant meanings would make up the margin I just referred to. This margin could be termed the margin of the bond—in German, *die Bande des Bandes,* the bond of the bond, the margin by which the bond is bound. In German, as well as in French, *bande, Band* means not only shackle, chain, fetter, more generally string, band, tie, but also barrier, edge, margin, border, frame. *Die Bande,* the dictionary tells us, has been borrowed (in the eighteenth century) from the French *bande,* whose proper meaning is "bond, bondage," which itself originates from the West Germanic *binda,* and belongs to the family *binden* in New High German. Apart from the displacement through repetition that it may be able to inflict upon the Hegelian notion of bond, bond as margin is here at first only a convenient term to problematize a certain margin of the bond of thinking, a margin that for essential reasons remains a nondialectical outside of the wreath of thinking. Yet, I will not thematize this margin by exploring the effects that a recontextualization of Hegel's philosophical language suffers from its exposure to the literary column of Genet, or by exploring what the very iterability of Hegel's system holds in terms of deviancies. I shall restrict myself to the thematic level of the Hegel column, and show how Derrida, by exposing in a step-by-step fashion the power of Hegelian thought as far as all *its* others are concerned, is led to formulate a limit of the bonds of thinking that is no longer simply *its* limit.[22]

Yet I cannot follow Derrida through all the different steps by which he shows philosophical thought to be capable of appropriating, and doing justice to, ever and ever more refined opposites of the system. I must limit myself to a restricted protocol of some of the major arguments in which Derrida celebrates the power of Hegelian thought.

But first a word, in very general terms, on the Hegel column of *Glas.*

In the largely expository left-hand column, whose commentary and narrative is only rarely broken by inset passages of texts, and into whose
smooth surfaces only a few judas holes dig pockets, Derrida has set out
to think *Aufhebung,* and in particular the mode of linkage, interrelatedness, connectedness that it implies. His guiding thesis throughout this
attempt is that although the family is only the first (natural) moment of
Sittlichkeit and, in the same way as the latter, a relieving naturalization, a
determined representation of spirit, it is possible "to make a problematic
pertinence within the whole field appear in the family" (G, p. 16).
Undoubtedly, the spirit's general at-home-with-itself is not the mind's
feeling of its own unity ("seine sich *empfindende* Einheit") in the family as
the immediate substantiality of the mind, but since there is nonetheless
a representative relation between both, the question arises as to the necessity and scope of the relation. To what extent, then, Derrida asks, is the
bond of thinking a family bond? But, he says, to ask such a question not
only is not a critique of Hegel, it is not even a question put to his texts
that would attempt to *think* the family bond, as well as the bond of
thinking, the spiritual bond par exellence, if thinking means here what
it has always meant in the history of thinking, namely, "what forms the
question in general . . . what imposes the question's questioning form,
the copulation question/response." Derrida will not ask: *What is* the
family bond, or *what is* the wreath of thinking? Such questions have "an
ontological, that is, dialectical, 'destination' " (G, p. 191), and, indeed,
as *Glas* will show, presuppose the being in place of the bond. "We are
not going to ask ourselves here *what is* this operation [of *Aufhebung*]?
Since the ontological question . . . unfolds itself here only according to
the process *(processus)* and structure of *Aufhebung,* confounds itself with
the absolute of the *Aufhebung,* one can no longer ask: *what is* the *Aufhebung?*" Derrida writes (G, p. 34). Rather than asking questions, Derrida
will take what he calls a "bastard path" through Hegel's texts, a path
"that will have to feign to follow naturally the circle of the family, in
order to enter it, or parcel it out *(partager),* or partake *(partager)* of it as
one takes part in a community, holy communion, the last supper scene,
or part *(partager)* it as one does by dissociating" (G, p. 6). Such an
approach, by displacing "the very literalness of the question's statement"
(G, p. 20), aims at something that, in the force of the Hegelian system
he is going to celebrate, "does not let itself be *thought* or even arraigned
(arraisonner) by a question" (G, p. 191).

Derrida will thus concern himself with the pervasiveness of the prob-

lematic of the family through Hegel's system and thinking, with thinking's embeddedness in the family problematic, with how to think outside
or apart from the family if thinking is always already a family question.
These questions become posed in *Glas* in the context of a debate with
very different critical approaches to Hegel's text, approaches which cover
the whole range from traditional philological criticism to what resembles
contemporary "deconstructive" criticism. In his discussion of these various "methodological temptations" (*G,* p. 20) to critically disband the
Hegelian bond, Derrida argues that, "measured by the power of the
greater logic" (*G,* p. 224), all these attempts fail. Among them, psychoanalysis, especially in its Lacanian form, and Left Hegelian criticism of
Hegel (Feuerbach and Marx) as well, figure prominently in *Glas.* Neither
one nor the other, Derrida shows, can hope to dislodge the speculative
bond. The unconscious, rather than being able to unsettle Hegelian
thought, is shown to be structurally necessary for the system (see, for
instance, *G,* pp. 177ff.), and Marxist criticism of Hegelian thought, by
reproducing within itself the very logic of what it seeks to dismantle, is
shown to be itself an idealist gesticulation (see, for example, *G,* p. 201).
Yet, for what is to follow, I limit myself to discussing only those critical
operations on Hegel's corpus in *Glas* which have in one way or another
been used in contemporary readings and "deconstructive criticism" of
Hegel.

The first methodological temptation that Derrida chooses to take up,
with respect to the question of the family in Hegel's writing, is that of
philological criticism. It consists in reading the texts from the *Encyclopedia*
and *Philosophy of Right* on the family in the perspective of Hegel's early
analyses of Christianity and the Christian family. Yet such a genetic
reading, according to which the early texts would represent the matrix
of the later system, is in no way a critical intervention in the system,
since the teleological thrust on which it is based is precisely one of the
issues elaborated in Hegel's writings on the Christian family. The "question of the bearing *(démarche),* the teleology or not of the reading . . .
finds itself *already* posed, within the 'younger' elaborations, precisely as
an ontological question, a question of the ontological. It is the question
of the *Wesen* (essence) and of the copula *is* as a question, the relation or
name of father-to-son. To know for example whether the 'later' texts
can be treated as the descendant and akin consequence, filiation, the
product, the son of the youthful elaborations that would be the system's
paternal seed; to know whether the second, following, consequent or

consecutive texts are or are not the same, the development of the same text, this question is posed in advance, reflected in advance in the analysis of Christianity," Derrida writes (*G,* pp. 55–56). Indeed, the question of such an anticipating reading, in which the early texts would represent the matrix of the final system, is posed in the youthful texts in terms of the unity of the Father and Son, of the Father's presence in the Son— in short, in terms of the question of the copula *is.* The Last Supper scene, that is, the family scene in which the conciliation and unification of the Father and Son are asserted, sets the truth for the question of ontology. The space of ontology—and no ontology is strictly speaking possible according to Hegel, before or outside the Gospels—thus becomes insep- arable from the familial. What this means, is that in the spirit of Chris- tianity, "unification, conciliation *(Vereinigung),* and being *(Sein)* have the same sense, are equivalent in their signification *(gleichbedeutend).* And in every proposition *(Satz),* the binding, agglutinating, ligamentary position of the copula *(Bindewort) is* conciliates the subject and the predicate, laces one around the other, entwines one around the other, to form one single being *(Sein)*" (*G,* p. 56). As a result of this determination of the copula as a filial relation, and of the filial relation as a finite relation that "*is* as the passage to the infinite" (*G,* p. 29), the philological procedure that would explain the accomplished system from its seeds in the early writ- ings on Christianity is a function of the speculative identity that these same writings stipulate, with respect to the Father-Son relation, and to the question of the copula in general. Such an approach, whose very possibility is dependent on the Christian idea of an identity of unification and Being, has thus no critical bearing on the system whatsoever.

This early Hegelian determination of the copula as a filial relation, which causes the philosophical attempt to explain (or reduce) the accom- plished system's construction in terms of family structures, to remain caught itself in this very structure, has still further implications. Derrida alludes to them when he writes, "The bond announced between the question of the copula and the question of the family also bears this consequence: if one tries to articulate an apparently 'regional' (sociolog- ical, psychological, economico-political, linguistic) problematic of the family onto an ontological problematic, the place that we have just now recognized cannot be gotten around," this being precisely that place developed by the early Hegel, and in which "the ontological (the pos- sibility of *Wesen, Sein, Urteilen*) no longer lets itself be unglued or decap- itated from the family. And par exellence from the question of the father-to-son . . ." (*G*, pp. 56–57). The very spirit of the Christian family precludes the critical possibility of ever raising a regional determination of the family against its ontological determination, not only because the first is dependent for its own meaning on the latter, but also because ultimately both are one and the same. Hegel insinuates, indeed, that only in Christianity is it possible to know what a family is, in other words, that only if one knows "the absolute sense of the absolute family, the family's being-family," is it possible to know "what one believes one knows familiarly of the family" (*G*, p. 219). In the following, I will be concerned with only one such attempt to critically try to explain (or reduce) the philosophical and speculative understanding of "family" by referring it back to some regional determination of the family. I will be concerned with its linguistic, rhetorical, or figural determination.

If, indeed, as Derrida contends, the whole of the Hegelian system must be understood as a family business, what then is the linguistic status of "family"? Is it a figure, a trope, a symbol, or what? Is it nothing but a trope? Can the family discourse in the constitution of Hegel's absolute onto-logic "be relegated to the subordinate regions of a rhetoric" (*G*, p. 94), whether in the critical hope of purging the absolute discourse of all regional ascendancy, or in order to show that such rhetorical contamination is rigorously inescapable? Derrida argues here that rhetoric, rather than falling outside speculative thought, belongs intrinsically to the system itself, and to the very content that unfolds within it. The passage from the initial developments on the subject matter of the family to its all-pervasive presence in the final system, and from the determination of the family as the first still-natural sphere of *Sittlichkeit* to the Holy Family of Religion, and the latter's subsequent sublation in the absolute knowing, indeed sets to work, as *Glas* demonstrates, "an ontotheological theory of the figure, an ontotheological rhetoric and semiotic that belong by full right to the very content of the discourse" (*G*, p. 34). Since all regional determination of rhetoric is dependent for its meaning on this onto-theological rhetoric, rhetoric can in no way serve to unnerve or undo the logic of speculative thought.

In his reading of Hegel's text "The Spirit of Christianity," Derrida argues that within Hegel's thinking it is impossible to "rigorously distinguish between a finite family and an infinite family. The human family is not *something other* than the divine family. Man's father-to-son relation is not *something other* than God's father-to-son relation. Since these two relations are not distinguishable, above all not opposed, one cannot pretend to see in one the figure or metaphor of the other. One would not know how to compare one to the other, how to feign knowing what can be one term of the comparison before the other" (*G,* p. 64). The question of the figure is a very fleeting one, since, according to Hegel, one cannot know outside of Christianity, that is, outside of the concept of the Holy Family, what a family is. But if this is so, then the classical distinction at the basis of semiotics and rhetoric, the distinction between the proper and the figural, the sign and the signified, becomes blurred, to say the least. The traditional modes of conceiving the relation between semiotic's and rhetoric's constitutive terms thus need to be rethought. As Hegel argues in "The Spirit of Christianity," the ligament between the sign and the designated is still an objective bond *(objectives Band),* something that remains outside them in a third term. Yet in an act of communion, that is, in a family act, the bond becomes spiritual, and hence the third term disappears, and with it what it previously linked: a signifier and a signified, proper and figural meaning. With the sublation of the sign in Christianity, then, all questions of comparison or allegory are eliminated. What holds, what bonds that which is no longer a figure and a reality properly speaking, is of such a nature that within it "diversity falls *(fällt diese Verschiedenheit weg)* and with it the very possibility of a comparison, of an equation" (*G,* p. 68). In the face of the speculative bond that gathers together in one and on the same plane the Father and the Son, the infinite and the finite—in which therefore no partitioning can take place, although it must presuppose the possibility of division, and which consequently is the unity of unity and separation—all critical gestures, which by nature are based on a divide, on a separation, either flounder or find themselves drawn upward, because their spiritual ana-logues in the speculative bond are what secure the meaning of that which seems to escape the latter's structure. If, indeed, the bond is "the ligament of the ligament and the nonligament in which life in the same stroke *(du même coup)* bands and unbands itself erect *(se bande et se débande)*" (*G,* p. 83), any attempt to unband or disband, if not insignificant from the start, amounts to nothing less than weaving the dialectics that it seeks to unravel.

But not only does the bond of thinking eliminate the possibility of choosing between what is proper and what is figural, between a signifier and a signified, a choice in which a rhetorical criticism would have to be rooted; it also makes a textual reading, or a criticism based on such a reading, impossible. As Derrida notes, "Hegel takes into account the textual fact, but also the necessity of relieving it" (*G*, p. 76). Indeed, from the conceptual perspective that is Hegel's, "what is a difference of style or rhythm, verily of narrative space?" (*G*, p. 43). These differences based on "the factuality of the narratives, *récits (Erzählungen),* the variations concerning places, times, circumstances change nothing in the conceptual intent," Derrida recalls (*G*, pp. 61–62). Indeed, "the concept reduces the difference to nothing" (*G*, p. 43). To attend to such differences in the text is either not to read Hegel, to read him badly, or merely to content oneself with reading him. He who is just content to read will see in the Hegelian text "only formal contradictions, but if the reader, on the contrary, knows how to read (no longer just being content to read), matters will go completely otherwise" (*G*, p. 76). When reading becomes a spiritual activity, a living contradiction is no longer "a formal effect of philosophical discourse, but the essence of the relief" (*G*, p. 148). Opposition and contradiction, rather than interrupting the speculative circulation of the bond, are what permit it. Derrida concludes: "Thus the Hegelian system commands that it be read as a book of life. The categories of reading must first bend to that" (*G*, p. 83). Once the formal differences in a textual order are relieved in the reader's spirit, one can no longer intervene in the system and the bond of thinking, however furiously or desperately one tries.[23]

Considering to what degree thinking thus seems to be successfully entrenched in its constituting habit, what could make the Hegelian bond tremble at all? That Derrida's analysis of the familial moment is geared to producing a displacement of sorts, a disimplication of the system's structure and development, has been emphasized from the outset. Yet all the methodological temptations reviewed up to this point do, where they do not simply fail, confirm the system's coiling upon itself. Moreover, such a displacement of the family moment cannot rely on the family's and marriage's self-dissolution or self-destruction, and on all the categories that such self-destruction implies. Family, Hegel notes in *Philosophy of Right,* is merely an ideal moment, "whose true ground is the state, although it is from . . . [it] that the state springs" (*PR,* p. 155). In the dialectical process that leads from the family to the state, the dissolution of the family (as a first, still immediate, and natural form of *Sittlichkeit*) is a structural necessity. Civil society is the first to "tear the individual from his family ties, [and to] estrange the members of the family from one another." Whereas the family is grounded in bonds that are of the order of feeling (and hence still natural bonds), civil society, by destroying these bonds, shapes itself as a "universal family" (*PR,* p. 148), before both the sensible and the universal family become superseded in the state. Within this frame, Hegel distinguishes a variety of forms of dissolution or destruction that happen to the substantial bond of the family: natural dissolution through the death of the parents; ethical dissolution through the education of the children; contingent dissolution owing to the inner limitations of its members; necessary dissolution stemming from the fact that as the first natural unity of *Sittlichkeit* the family depends entirely on feeling and must therefore be sublated by the state, which is not only indissoluble merely in itself but absolutely indissoluble. Such modes of dissolution are dialectical dissolutions, and because of that, reassuring. If Derrida is then to challenge the family bond, and through this bond, the whole of the Hegelian system, he cannot do so for reasons to be qualified as necessary, contingent, or capricious. All of these are of the order of negativity, and can consequently be internalized—with nothing of them remaining—in the speculative weaving of the bond. All these different modes of destruction are destructions inherent in the process.

At the beginning of *Glas* Derrida declares that he is interested in "what always remains irresoluble, impracticable, nonnormal, or nonnormalizable" in Hegel's exposition of the family moment (*G,* p. 5) and, let us add, in the habitual gesture of philosophical thinking. Among the many instances in which Derrida detects such difficult, seemingly contradictory, developments on the family in Hegel's corpus, I shall focus only, and very briefly, on Hegel's treatment of the figure of the sister, in particular on Antigone.

After an elaboration of the undoubtedly paradoxical status that Hegel attributes to the sister-brother relation, which he characterizes as an asexual relation, as a relation into which no desire enters, and which thus seems to be the only exception in the Hegelian universe of two consciousnesses relating to each other without waging war, Derrida passes on to an analysis of Hegel's fascination with Antigone. It is a fascination with a sister who escapes the Hegelian logic of femininity (which sees the essence of the woman in her becoming a wife or mother) by remaining "an eternal sister taking away with her her womanly, wifely desire." Dead before ever being able to get married, this sister never becomes citizen, wife, or mother. But in spite of the exigencies of Hegelian philosophy, Hegel, in *Aesthetics,* as Derrida notes, "finds this very good, very appeasing." Hence the following question: "Unique example in the system: a recognition that is not natural and yet that passes through no conflict, no injury, no rape; absolute uniqueness, yet universal and without natural singularity, without immediacy; symmetrical relation that needs no reconciliation to appease itself, that does not know the horizon of war, the infinite wound, contradiction, negativity. Is that the inconceivable? What the greater logic cannot assimilate?" (*G*, p. 150). In other words, is Antigone an impossible figure, a figure "inadmissible in the system," an unclassable instant or instance that would escape the ringlike unfolding of thought steeped in philosophical habit? Is it here that the bond of thinking encounters an outer limit that it cannot swallow, a leftover, a remainder that it cannot digest? Yet this figure, which by rights ought to be so singular as to preclude any possibility of relation, fascinates Hegel. Derrida, consequently, is led to wonder whether "what cannot be assimilated, the absolute indigestible," played, nonetheless, "a fundamental role in the system," fundamental precisely because of its *absolute* indigestibility (*G*, p. 151). Fundamental, as well, in that its role as an element *excluded* from the system endows it with the quasi-transcendental function of assuring "the system's space of possibility. The transcendental has always been, strictly, a transcategorial, what could be received, formed, terminated in none of the categories intrinsic to the system. The system's vomit" (*G*, p. 162). What would be strictly inassimilable because it exceeds the system on all accounts—absolutely— fascinates the absolute knowledge, paralyzes it, interrupts its life, cuts off its breath; and yet it also, and this comes down to the same thing, Derrida remarks, supports "it from outside or underneath a crypt. Crypt—one would have said, of the transcendental or the repressed, of the unthought or the excluded—that organizes the ground to which it does not belong. What speculative dialectics means (to say) is that the crypt can still be incorporated into the system" (*G*, p. 166). What absolutely falls outside the system thus acquires a transcategorial, quasi-transcendental function, and that is a function rooted in, or with respect to, the thinking bond. Instead of becoming something that would challenge the system pure and simple because it cannot be received by it, the absolutely excluded must be understood as that ex-position whence the system's annulations fold into one another so as to achieve thinking's being-with-itself.

   Once again the system seems to have operated successfully. The structure of thinking—of strict thought, thought in the strictest sense—seems to have no exterior limit if this limit can always be shown—and Hegel imposes this rule of thought—to be the limit *of* thinking. If exteriority,

and in particular absolute exteriority, as was the case with the unbeliev-
able and powerful liaison without desire between Antigone and her
brother[24]—an "immense impossible desire that could not live" (*G*,
p. 166)—if this is the system's exteriority, *its* outside, then it obeys the
logic of opposition and is, strictly, a function of the Hegelian proper—
"*In seinem Anderen*. The 'its other' is the very syntagm of the Hegelian
proper," Derrida recalls (*G*, p. 83).

   With respect to this logic no displacement is possible, Derrida remarks,
"without displacing—this word itself must be reinterpreted—what in
the text called Hegelian imposes this rule of reading, say a displacement
that itself escapes the dialectic law and its strict rhythm." And he adds,
"We do not yet seem to be there, and that can no more be done at one
go *(d'un coup)* than by a continuous approach. The event cannot be as
noisy as a bomb, as garish or blazing as some metal held in the fire. Even
were it still an event, here it would be . . . inapparent and marginal" (*G*,
p. 107). If neither a direct punctual strike at the system nor a continuous
unraveling of it proves possible, perhaps an approach that yields to the
rule of detour and strategy (without telos) is capable of a more successful
intervention (if it is still possible to speak of success in this case). From
the very beginning of *Glas*, Derrida has announced that he shall obey
the Hegelian rule throughout this work only at the cost of a detour (*G*,
p. 21). And, indeed, he will proceed "by *à-coups*, fits and starts, jolts, little
successive jerks, while touching, tampering with the borders" of the
Hegelian text, and will do so starting at the first line of the Hegel column
(*G*, p. 5). On this zigzagging course, a variety of issues come into view
in which such marginal displacements of the bonds of thinking seem to
occur. These, as we have seen, are not the result of contradictions or
inassimilable remainders—contradictions are immanent to the process,
and the inassimilable ultimately turns into a transcategorial possibility of
the thinking bond itself. If marginal displacements come to the fore, from
the first page of *Glas* on, in or alongside the power of the Hegelian
system, to whose exposition and celebration I have limited myself up to
this point, they do so because the Hegelian text (not unlike the Freudian
text to which the following citation refers) contains "heterogeneous
statements, not contradictory ones, but of a singular heterogeneity: that
which, for example, relates in a text . . . decidable statements to undecidable statements" (*G*, p. 209; modified translation). The heterogeneity
in question is singular because it does not have the form, "in the ontological hierarchy, of a negativity homogeneous to all the other forms of

negativity." Although "nothing is ever homogeneous in the different ruptures, stances, or saltations of speculative dialectics," the heterogeneity in question perhaps no longer simply lets itself be interned into "the [therefore] *general* (thus homogeneous) heterogeneity of the whole set of the ontological system" (*G*, pp. 198–199). More precisely, the singularity of this heterogeneity, on which the possible displacements or disimplications of the Hegelian bond depend, stems from the impossibility of deciding whether the statements in question belong to the ontological system or to an altogether different order. The singularity of these statements derives from the fact that they can (and will) *always* go both ways, that they are divided in two, and lend themselves to two readings.[25] They are thus not simply other, nor are they simply the same as the decidable statements to which they relate. Such statements, or concepts for that matter, escape the structure of opposition; they are determined outside opposition, and hence are undecidable (*G*, p. 209). But they are potentially capable of decidability, of oppositional determination, and hence of meaning. The heterogeneity of statements or concepts on which possible displacements of the bonds of thinking rest is so singular because they also serve to bring these same bonds into their own. Of these statements or concepts, Derrida writes that "they carry and de-border" the system of meaning, "but they cannot not give birth to it" (*G*, p. 242). The unique example that was Antigone illustrates in paradigmatic fashion what such undecidable concepts are likely to achieve. Although the extreme singularity of Antigone de-borders the system, this same singularity cannot not turn into the transcategorial possibility of the system itself.

But a question remains. It is the question concerning the ability of singularities or exteriorities to *lend themselves* to becoming the foundation, however abyssal, of speculative thought. Radically outside the system, they offer themselves nonetheless in a foundational role. This offer, sacrifice, or gift, by the exterior, without which the system could not come into its own, *remains* at the margin of the system, of the bond. The offer (itself) has no other opposite; it is without counterpart, or benefit. It is thus absolute in quite another sense than the speculative absolute; but this margin outside the system, hence not the system's margin, is potentially capable of being it. An analysis of this gift by marginal exteriority should thus yield some insights into what I have called the bond, or the banding, of the bond.

On the margins of thinking, language inescapably loses its familiar

resonances. Indeed, what is in question at these margins is nothing less
than strict language, the strictures of language obeying the logic of oppositional determination. Yet to thematize the margins of strict thinking
does not necessarily call for loose language, or for a diminishing of precision.

The example in *Glas* of such a gift in the margin that I choose to
discuss is that of the religion of light in Hegel's *Lectures on the Philosophy
of Religion*. If I privilege this example among the many others that punc-
tuate *Glas* from the outset, I do so not only because it explicitly thematizes the absolute gift, but also because, in the Hegel column, it is the
most explicit *thematization* of the margin of the system. Before turning
to the example itself, it is necessary to recall that Derrida turns to an
analysis of the particular moment of the philosophy of light in Hegel's
writings on religion in the context of a discussion of the temptation to
reduce "to a typical, certainly essential, but very determinate phase of
phenomenology" a certain "season disorder" *(mal de saison)* of the absolute knowing that stems from a multiplication of dialectical moments
"that no longer assures it of being able to reappropriate itself in the
trinitarian circle" (*G,* p. 233). It is the temptation to demonstrate that
even the play of the text or of writing can be shown to be an entirely
recuperable "Bacchanalian intoxication" of the spirit from which the
spirit could recover by making it another moment through which it
introduces itself to itself. Derrida's elaborations on the religion of light
thus occur in the context of a debate on the limits of his own celebration
throughout *Glas* of the power of the bonds of thinking. Without
assessing these limits, such demonstration would indeed turn into another
methodological temptation—the temptation of Hegelianism.

The example of the first moment of natural religion—the cult of
light—is not just an example among others. Indeed, this moment, in
contradistinction to all other moments, is characterized by an absence of
figure and representation, and thus already anticipates absolute knowing,
which is said to be absolutely free of all *Vorstellung*. Hegel characterizes
this figure of an absence of figure *(Gestalt der Gestaltlosigkeit)* that distinguishes the cult of light as a light that not only burns everything, but
burns itself as well. Therefore, the all-burning is, according to Hegel, an
essenceless play of light. By destroying itself through all its figures, it
consummates itself, and thus having no self to which to relate itself, it
never accedes to a for-itself. With the all-burning of the cult of light,
neither sense, nor time, nor circle, nor bond has yet begun. But, if such

is the case, how, then, can this first moment of natural religion become a moment in the first place, a moment that would prime the dialectical process? Derrida asks: "If the all-burning destroys up to its letter and its body, how can it guard the trace of itself and breach/broach a history where it preserves itself in losing itself?" (*G,* p. 240). Or, differently put, how is the process, once it has started, capable of reducing pure self-consuming? Yet it is precisely at this juncture where Hegel describes something that seems to radically drop outside the bonds of thinking, something that spends its very self, and that thus seems to lack the minimal requirements of a germ, seed, or semen for developing into something—it is at this juncture that one experiences, as Derrida emphasizes, "the implacable force of sense, of mediation, of the hard-working negative" (*G,* p. 240). Indeed, Hegel argues that the pure fire *must* pass into its opposite. In other words, what is in fact an absolutely irreducible for the infinite concept, something that puts its history out of order, and points to a play that lets itself not be reappropriated by the spirit, *can be what it is,* namely, such an absolute irreducible, *only if it turns into its contrary,* and if it becomes the system's first moment. "In order to be what it is, purity of play, of difference, of consuming destruction, the all-burning must pass into its contrary: guard itself, guard its own movement of loss, appear as what it is in its very disappearance," Derrida notes (*G,* p. 240). To be what it is, the all-burning that drops out of the system, the all-burning must remain by keeping hold of itself. And it will remain what it is precisely by losing itself, by ceasing to be what it is. Yet with this (self-)conserving consummation, by which the all-burning annuls itself in order to be what it is, the annulus is opened, the annulations of history and of the bonds of thinking have been broached. That which disorders the system has turned into the system's first moment. At this point, a remark or two is called for. With the all-burning we have encountered a remainder of the system, a bond of the bond, that, precisely because it does not simply fall through the so-called meshes of the system, cannot simply be retrieved. "Everything that falls (to the tomb) in effect yet comes under *(relève du) Sa,*" Derrida writes (*G,* p. 226). Indeed, what remains, remains as spirit, that is, as raised or erected fallenness (See *G,* pp. 23–24). Yet the remainder, or the margin, that we have encountered with the all-burning is of a different sort. It is a remainder that, while being intimately bound up with the system's bondings, cannot fully be assimilated by it. Derrida, therefore, calls it a remainder that suspends itself, a "suspended remain(s)" (*G,* p. 226). Such a suspended remainder is what puts speculative thought, or the Concept, out of order, without destroying or paralyzing it absolutely (G, p. 233). Indeed, since this remainder can be what it is only if it loses itself as remainder by becoming the first moment of the system, by thus tying itself up with the system, what "jams it [the system] inconceivably" is also what confirms the implacable force of the hard-working negative.

Let us recall here that when Hegel writes that the all-burning *must* turn into its contrary, that is, must "insure its guarding . . . bind itself to itself, strictly," it can do so because this demand is *strictly speaking* in line with the very logic of the all-burning itself. Turning into its opposite by ceasing to be what it is, becoming the first moment of the system by sacrificing itself as the all-burning, is not something that happens to the all-burning from the outside. It is an inner necessity that if the all-burning is to burn all, it must set itself ablaze (and thus be what escapes the system) *and* extinguish itself (and thus become its first moment). "Both processes are inseparable," Derrida writes. "They can be read in any sense, any direction whatever, from right to left or left to right; the relief of one must value *(faire cas)* the other" (G, p. 241).

So what is at stake where one can, so to speak, "regard on both sides of the revolution? . . . This perhaps: the gift, the sacrifice, the putting in play or to fire of all, the holocaust, are under the power of *(en puissance)* ontology" (G, pp. 241–242). What becomes thinkable here is perhaps the gift (itself) "before" it inescapably, and according to its own logic, gives *itself to itself,* "before" it is met by the counter-gift that opens the annulations of the bond of thinking. What becomes thinkable perhaps is the irruptive event of the gift (itself), the limitless expenditure, the lav- ishly giving *before* it has become the gift *itself* that opens the circularity of the bonding exchange. *Perhaps.* The "perhaps" here is not a sign of language's turning imprecise, vague, empirical. On the contrary, the "perhaps" in question points in all rigor to the pre-ontological status of what amounts to a condition of possibility, of sorts, that offers itself to thought here. Although conditions of possibility are generally what are shielded from all "perhapses," the thought of the gift that "*engages* the history of Being but does not belong to it" (G, p. 242) is the thought of something that is not yet, but that cannot not be(come). The "perhaps" articulates rigorously the wavering ontological status of the gift's event.[26] "The gift *is not;* the holocaust *is not,*" Derrida writes, ". . . but as soon as it burns (the blaze is not a being), it must, burning itself, burn its action [*operation*] of burning and begin to be" (G, p. 242).

With fatal necessity, the gift *must* give rise to speculative thought. "The *Taumeln,* the vertigo, the delirium *must* determine itself as for-(it)self and take on a stable subsistence." But although the gift has thus always already opened the exchange, "the gift, the giving of the gift, the pure *cadeau,* does not let itself be thought by the dialectics to which it, however, gives rise" (G, p. 243). As soon as thinking *thinks* the gift—that is, as soon as it asks *what* the donation of the gift *is,* the energy of the gift has already yielded to the constraint of determining itself as for-itself, and has thus fallen prey to the first and elemental ruse of dialectical reason. With the thought of "this movement before the constitution of the *Selbst*" (G, p. 244), to which this movement must inescapably give rise, and which although it is not the *Selbst*'s Other (*das Andere seiner Selbst,* as Hegel puts it), remains fatally entangled in it, Derrida has not laid bare a positive remainder upon which the system would run aground. The pure gift, the pure play of the all-burning, cannot not open up the system's annulations. In a gesture that avoids both the methodological temptation of Hegelianism and the naiveté of establishing in all security a domain that positively would remain unassimilated by the system of speculative thought, Derrida, by contrast, *will already have* dwelled—*in* the Hegel column itself—on the "logic" that organizes the exchange between (speculative) thought and the suspended remainder that cannot not give birth to it. He *will* already *have* speculated on the logic of the contraband that organizes the play of bonding, banding, and disbanding the margins of thinking.

That such is the case becomes evident from what Derrida in *Glas* develops with regard to what I would call the infrastructure of re-strict-ure *(re-stricture)*.[27] I will not try to establish in detail the various elements and implications of this complex structure. To do so, it would be necessary to draw together everything that Derrida unfolds with respect not only to the notions of the strict, constriction, striction, stricture, restriction, re-striction and so on, but to the manifold themes of enclosing in bands, compressed passages, ligaturing, strangulation, contraction, and so forth, as well. For my purposes the following must suffice: the infrastructure of re-strict-ure permits to think the production of the *strict,* that is, that which has been narrowed down and restricted so as to have been bound by itself to itself, and thus to be itself: "what is called spirit, freedom, the ethical, and so on" (G, p. 101). The strict, Derrida argues throughout *Glas,* is the result of constriction *(striction)* or, rather, counter-constriction by which the constricture of natural determination or empir-

ical singularity is radically overcome. This liberating constriction proceeds through "closing up, squeezing, containing, suppressing, sub-
jecting, compressing, repressing, subduing, reducing, forcing,
subjugating, enslaving, hemming in" (G, p. 99). In a movement that
Derrida calls "strict" as well (G, p. 101), what has been subdued, compressed, choked to death is raised to, or erected as, the universality of
the strict. It is in this sense that Derrida's statements (which are largely
extrapolations from certain statements by Hegel) about the spirit, must
be understood: what strictly is the spirit is a raised corpse, a corpse
strapped in bandages, strangulated, from which all singular, natural life
has been torn, and subsequently unbandaged and elevated to universality.
However gruesome and violent such idealizing constriction may sound,
it is a counter-constriction to a first natural constriction. Moreover,
without such structural constriction no operation could take place in
consciousness; "without the suspensive and inhibiting constriction, the
absolute would not manifest itself," Derrida writes (G, p. 106). Indeed,
without such structural compression and choking, not only would the
manifold of empirical singularity remain the ultimate reality, it would
also be impossible to recognize it as such. The absolute minimum of
ideality required to identify it presupposes such constriction. This structure of constriction which owes its ideality "to its own inner limit, to
this contraction, or this strangulation it gives *itself*," and by virtue of
which it "avoids losing itself in abstract indetermination" (G, p. 107), is
absolutely necessary. Without it, there would be no ethical objectivity
in general (G, p. 196). This constriction could only be displaced, Derrida
suggests, by "a displacement that itself escapes the dialectic law and its
strict rhythm" (G, p. 107). But "the counterforces of constriction," especially in the form of the repressed and the unconscious, can still be
thought according to the law of dialectic "as species of general negativity,
forms of *Aufhebung*, conditions of the relief" (G, p. 191). Rather than
challenging the idealizing constriction, such counter-constriction only
contributes to its operation. Another violence, one that would not be of
the order of negativity, would be required if what Derrida calls the
"strict-ure against strict-ure" (G, p. 107), re-stricture or re-
(con)striction, is to succeed.[28] What such re-(con)striction would *be*
cannot easily be said. *Glas* suggests that "the heterogeneity of all the
restrictions, of all the counterforces of constriction" (G, p. 191), may
indeed not simply be definable in terms of negativity. Yet, precisely
because of this, such strict-ure against strict-ure must almost remain
unapparent and marginal. The displacement of such a re-(con)striction

would seem to lack all strictness. Re-strict-ure, however, is, *perhaps,* that trait which all forces and counterforces of constriction (whether dialectical or not) share in one way or another. In that sense, it could be said to function as "a transcategorial or a transcendental of every possible re-(con)striction" (G, p. 191) Derrida holds. With this in mind I now turn to what Derrida establishes about the role of constriction in the irruptive event of the gift.

To analyze the movement before the constitution of the *Selbst* is to bring into view the very constriction by which this movement is turned into a first bonding moment for thought. This movement is that of the pure gift, the sacrifice, or the putting in play or fire, as was seen with the all-burning. Yet, since this gift has always already opened the exchange—ineluctably, to give is to invite reciprocity—the general economy of the pure gift has always already been restricted "into a circulating economy. The contraction, the economic restriction forms the annulus of the selfsame, of the self-return, of reappropriation. The economy restricts itself; the sacrifice sacrifices itself" (G, p. 244). This (con)striction by which the pure gift opens the (impure) sphere of circulation—because it is what makes the order of the selfsame possible—cannot any longer be thought in the terms of what it is responsible for. Derrida writes: "The (con)striction no longer lets itself be circumscribed *(cerner)* as an ontological category, or even, very simply, as a category, even were it a trans-category, a transcendental. The (con)striction—what is useful for thinking the ontological or the transcendental—is then *also* in the position of transcendental trans-category, the transcendental transcendental. All the more because the (con)striction cannot not produce the 'philosophical' effect it produces" (G, p. 244). To think the "logic" of (con)striction, therefore, is to think the "logic" that causes any radical Other of the system to become tied up, in a strict movement, with the system. The "logic" of con(striction) itself, since it is responsible for opening the pure gift to the sphere of the circularity of the selfsame, is also the condition of possibility of the categorial or the transcendental. Although "outside" the categorial and the transcendental, it cannot help being inside—strictly speaking, (con)striction is also always already in the position of a transcendental of the transcendental. In other words, when the investigation of the remainders of speculative thought reaches the level of the conditions of possibility, categories, or transcendentals, these remainders in question—(con)striction itself—turn into a transcategorial of the categorial. Derrida concludes:

> There is no choosing here: each time a discourse *contra* the transcendental

is held, a matrix—the (con)striction itself—constrains the discourse to place the nontranscendental, the outside of the transcendental field, the excluded, in the structuring position. The matrix in question constitutes the excluded as transcendental of the transcendental, as imitation transcendental, transcendental contraband *(contre-bande)*. The contra-band is *not yet* dialectical contradiction. To be sure, the contraband necessarily becomes that, but its not-yet is not-yet the teleological anticipation, which results in it never becoming dialectical contradiction. The contra-band *remains* something other than what, necessarily, it is to become. Such would be the (nondialectical) law of the (dialectical) strict-ure, of the bond, of the ligature, of the garrote, of the *desmos* in general when it comes to clench tightly *(serrer)* in order to make be. Lock *(serrure)* of the dialectical. (G, p. 244)

Within the Hegel column, thus, a contra-band unfolds—in a movement that is neither continuous nor spontaneous—which cannot help becoming a moment, a condition, a transcendental of the bonds of thought, although it remains other than the strict bonds into which it turns itself. Even within the Hegel column itself (not to speak of the play between the two columns of *Glas*), it is not a question of choosing— the philosophical over the nonphilosophical, or the other way around. One will invariably turn into the other. Hence, what remains, perhaps, is the reading in counter-band, the reading that calculates the law of the constraints by which outsides become raised to a structuring position of insides. In the Hegel column of *Glas* this law is called re-strict-ure.

To think the law by which the donating margin becomes subjected is also, and foremost, to think habit (as such), habit as the possibility constitutive of thought. Indeed, what the (con)striction of the pure and marginal gift achieves is nothing less than the destruction and overcoming of the very gift in the margin, of its giving energy, by making it subservient *to itself,* and turning the gift, in this manner, into a for-itself, an identity. Of this (self-identical) gift, the giving margin—the pure donation—will always already have been a consequence, a retrospective *Folge.* The transformation of the donating margin into a content or a result from which margins strictly speaking are derivative is the elemental occurrence of habit as inaugurative of what Hegel calls thinking. In such a determination, indeed, the mad energy of the donation, as Derrida calls it, in other words, the particular, contingent, and absolutely fragile singularity of the irruptive event, is put into the shackles that free this gift for the simple and ideal relation to itself called *habit.*

8

Yes Absolutely

IN HEGEL'S *Phenomenology of Spirit,* the smooth and flawless dialectical run of the Spirit through the various moments that constitute its itinerary comes to a stop while still short of its final fulfillment. This provisional point of closure is the *yes* that, at the end of the section titled "Religion," on the verge of "Absolute Knowing," resounds and bursts forth as spontaneously and unpredictably as any genuine response. Yet this *yes,* reverberating at the crucial transition point between "Spirit" and "Absolute Knowing," is a moment on the Spirit's trajectory. With this *yes,* Spirit says *yes* to itself. It answers its own call for a response to its dialectical progression—for a response that would complete it. Indeed, the *yes* in question is an *affirming* yes. But although this *yes* erupts with all the suddenness and unexpectedness of a genuine response, it coincides with the eruption and surpassing of the idea of the whole or the Absolute, where all the Spirit's elements let go of their antithetical existence. The *yes* of the *Phenomenology* affirms only the totality of that which, up to and including the section titled "Spirit," developed in dialectical oppositions and reversals. It is thus "the reconciling yes" of *ta panta,* which, as is well known, is also released in a burst—the burst of philosophical wonder.[1] And although it shares with the *yes* of genuine response the suddenness of the event, this suddenness itself circles back into that which called for completion, that to which it would genuinely respond. This *yes,* through which the reconciling whole—the absolute identity of all that is in the mode of opposition—imposes itself on religious consciousness, is not yet the full affirmation of absolute knowing itself. Hegel writes:

The Notion of Spirit which had emerged for us as we entered the sphere

199

of religion . . . as the movement in which what is in absolute antithesis
recognizes itself as the same as its opposite, this recognition bursting forth
as the *affirmative (als das Ja)* between these extremes—this Notion is *intuitively apprehended* by the religious consciousness to which the absolute Being
is revealed, and which overcomes the difference between its Self and what
it intuitively apprehends; just as it is Subject, so also it is substance, and
hence it *is* itself Spirit just because and in so far as it is this movement.[2]

As Hegel has argued in his analysis of tragedy in the chapter titled
"Religion in the Form of Art," the very exclusiveness of the two principles or powers of the upper and the nether law that are in conflict in
tragedy results from the ethical substance's actualization in limiting self-
consciousnesses. In the downfall of the two heroes who incarnate this
same substance in particular but opposite ways, both being thus equally
right and wrong, the "unitary being of Zeus *(der einfache Zeus)*" prevails,
the being in whom Apollo and the Erinyes become reconciled.[3] In short,
what bursts forth at the moment when that which is in a relation of
antithetical opposition manifests itself as the same as its opposite is the
idea of the whole as the truth of the finite and antithetical moments.
Yet, this reconciling *yes,* or the Notion of Spirit, is *only* intuitively apprehended in the sphere of religion. Moreover, religious consciousness, or
the ethical, moral, and cultural substance of a people in the mode of self-
consciousness, continues to apprehend its spirit in the form of representation *(Vorstellung)*. Of religious consciousness, Hegel remarks, "This
unity of essence and the Self having been *implicitly* achieved, consciousness, too, still has this *picture-thought (Vorstellung)* of its reconciliation, but
as picture-thought. It obtains satisfaction by *externally* attaching to its pure
negativity the positive meaning of the unity of itself with the essential
Being; its satisfaction thus itself remains burdened with the antithesis of
a beyond."[4] Affirmative reconciliation, the *yes* between the extremes,
will only be fully realized in a sphere beyond representation, that is, in
the figureless sphere of absolute knowing, in which thought itself has
become its own "figure." In absolute knowing, the *yes* that simply burst
forth in the sphere of religion develops into the self-affirming *yes* of the
Notion *(Begriff)*, into an affirmation that is no longer separated from what
is affirmed. Here, in the Notion, the unpredictable and, at the limit,
improbable surge of the *yes* as a response to those moments and movements that are still Other to the Spirit has turned into the affirmative
response of the Spirit to itself. Rather than a response to Other, the
Notion recognizes itself not only in the elements and movements of

the Spirit, but as that movement itself. With this, even the *eruption* of the resounding *yes* toward the end of "Religion," appears in fact to have been anticipated and calculated in advance by the *yes* of the Notion in which all relation to Other has become relation to self in absolute identity. In the absolute *yes* of the Notion, the outburst in all its abruptness and suddeness of the *yes* has become contingent, and hence necessary.

How is one to respond to Hegel's all-inclusive *yes* that, by sublating up to the finite event of its eruption, has also forgone its nature as a response? More precisely, how does one relate to a *yes* that not only is all encompassing but that by virtue of its all-inclusiveness seems no longer in need of responses? More generally, how does one respond to Hegel, whose uniqueness consists in his having attempted to demonstrate that all finitude sublates *itself,* and that the reconciling *yes, the yes* between the extremes, is nothing but the self-sublating suddenness with which each of the extremes erupts into a relation of Otherness to self? Evidently, whatever such a response may prove to be, in order that it be a response—both responsive and responsible—it must respond to the absolute *yes.* Yet, to make such a response, one must first read and hear Hegel to the end—to the eruption of the resounding *yes.* There can be no responsible debate with Hegel without the recognition that all the Hegelian developments take place in view of, and are always already predetermined by, the telos of absolute knowing, or the Notion, that is, by the thought of a figureless and nonrepresentational thinking in which thought can say *yes* to itself in a mode in which even saying is no longer different from what is said. In other words, any genuine response to Hegel must say *yes*—and not in the mode of parrotlike repetitive affirmation—to the call to Other by the speculative *yes* itself, which, as the event of the positive assimilation of all Otherness, addresses itself as a whole to Other. The *yes* of genuine response is, at its most elementary, a *yes* to the very singularity of the Hegelian enterprise, to the call to say *yes* to it in its all-embracing affirmation of self and Other in absolute identity. But such a response, precisely because it is presupposed, requested by the *yes* of Hegel's thought, falls out of its range and power. While the responding *yes* comes to meet the demand for recognition, it necessarily escapes what it thus lets come into its own: the speculative *yes.* Indeed, any genuine response to the Hegelian *yes* implies not only that it be formulated in its most powerful and demanding articulation— that of the end of *Phenomenoloy of Spirit* and the *Greater Logic*—rather than in disembodied or decapitated versions, but also that it resist *corre-*

sponding to the demand and the call of the all-encompassing *yes*. Although the *yes* must stand up to the demand to respond to the speculative yes in all its affirmative power, it must also stand it up. At the very moment that it meets the speculative yes it must fail to keep the appointment. Only thus is it a genuine response.

On the last page of *Glas*—in the Genet column that faces the exposition of Hegel's elaborations on the family—Derrida evokes the Nietzschean moment, or instant of "the vast and boundless . . . Yes *(das ungeheure unbegrenzte Ja),*" from *Zarathoustra* (*G,* p. 291). Although this yes, "common to you and me," appears in a column that accompanies a column largely celebrating the assimilative power of the Hegelian system in the mode of a doubling and contradictory band, or double bind, it does not stand in a simple relation of contradiction to the Hegelian reconciling and speculative *yes*. By contrast, "the vast and boundless . . . Yes" is a *yes* to speculative thought that, at the same time, gives it and its Other the slip. It sneaks away in its response, or, precisely because it is a response in a strict sense, from the affirmative account of all Otherness, *and* from the doubling band in which Genet is largely shown to disband, break up, and reject what Hegel had wrapped up in the tight bands of the speculative bond. In "Ja, ou le faux-bond," an interview given some time after the publication of *Glas,* Derrida remarks: "Beyond the indefatigable contradiction of the *double bind,* an affirmative, innocent, intact, cheerful difference must *in the end (bien)* come to give the slip, escape in one leap, and sign in laughing what it lets happen and pass by in a double band. Standing up the contradiction of the double bind in one blow, and having it suddenly no longer out with the double band. This is what I love, this stand-up *(faux-bond).*" In spite of the ineluctable nature of the double band, "*it is necessary (il faut)*—an altogether other *it is necessary*—that some how the double band not be the last word. Otherwise it all would come to a stop."[5] This affirmative difference is a *yes* that, as the title of the interview suggests, stands up and rebuffs the speculative yes, as well as the inescapable questioning of it that, as its Other, cannot fail to accompany it. Although this *yes* sneaks away from the speculative bond and its negating other, it also affirms it, letting it unfold (from it) in a double procession. This *yes,* then, to Hegel (*and* to what in Hegel, or outside him, fails to fall in line with his yes-saying), is also a *yes* to what Derrida calls "the neither-swallowed-nor-rejected, what remains in the throat as Other, neither-taken-in-nor-expelled."[6] A response that lives up to its concept—and that hence must be responsive to an invitation to respond—can only take its possibility from what in the Other remains open to an Other. This openness—which is the place of the Other—is not the other *of* the speculative *yes*. The latter, as *Glas* shows, is always taken in as that which cannot be taken in, is off the beat, so to speak. The openness from which a response becomes possible— possible only as always unpredictable, incalculable, and improbable—can only be the *faux-bond* in the Other itself, that which in the Other stands up its (his or her) self or identity and gives it the slip. For this openness, a response is responsible, and to it, it responds responsibly. The speculative *yes* permits no yes to itself but a preprogrammed and repetitive *yes* that cannot be the *yes* of a response. What is exluded by the system, what claims to be the excluded Other, the nonidentical, is what it is only in secret harmony, in an inextricable double bind with the system. Blindly it affirms what it negates; surreptitiously it mimics the speculative yes-saying. The *yes* that gives the reconciling *yes* and its Other the slip, and only thus meets the condition under which a genuine response and encounter can take place, is, as I have said, consequently no longer the *yes* of truth. The *faux-bond,* the *yes* that stands the speculative *yes* up, "betrays itself, *it stands itself up,* which means it lacks truth, strays from its truth even so—in betraying itself and becoming after all, in spite of the consciousness or representation of the one who responds or hears, an exact response, punctual and true—it keeps the appointment."[7] At the end of *Glas,* then, an "other end"[8] is affirmed, that of a *yes* which responds to, and is thus different from, the speculative *yes* which it addresses, but which it runs the risk of becoming as it arrives to meet the latter.

The foregoing developments about a responsive and responsible *yes* to Hegelian affirmation synoptically describe the problematic of deconstruction. Although Derrida's writings from *Glas* on cannot *simply* be subsumed under one unifying and univocal title such as "deconstruction," deconstruction and the "operations" characteristic of Derrida's works after *Glas* are *responses* to texts. Deconstruction is "affirmative" in that, in its debate with positions or texts—a debate not rooted in a critical relation—it seeks its legitimate possibility from what in (philosophical or literary) thinking *remains* as an appeal to the Other to respond to thinking's attempt to coil upon itself in a gesture of auto-affective self-positioning. Deconstruction affirms this constitutive relation to outside, this call upon Other, which the most foundationalist, self-comprehensive, and encyclopedic text or thought—any text or thought that successfully includes *its* Other—*must,* for structural reasons, contain within itself. Deconstruction affirms this Necessity which constitutes it, in essence, as a response. But as a response, deconstruction *must,* for equally essential, structural reasons, constantly risk failing to respond, risk becoming a merely acquiescing and repetitive *yes.* It is only by running this risk that deconstruction can be a response. Derrida has pointed to the near-perfect coincidence between deconstruction and Hegelian *Aufhebung:* "it is most similar to it," nearly, almost identical, he writes (*D,* p. 248). Indeed, the very concern with Other in deconstruction (and speculative thougtht) not only exposes deconstruction to the risk of being mistaken for, covered up by, and recovered by speculative dialectics, but also explains why it itself is never safe from the possibility of effectively sliding back into a speculative reappropriation of the Other. If this is so, it is so not merely because in giving a philosophical account of deconstruction Derrida or his interpreters (myself included) may themselves have resorted to Hegelian categories and moves that ultimately fall short of capturing the very "radicality" of deconstruction. In contrast to these empirical considerations, there remains the essential risk of failing to genuinely respond to the call by the Other which renders a genuine response possible at all. Indeed, just as the *place* of the Other in a text or work of thought is nothing but a referential vector, a gesturing, pointing toward and calling upon the Other, which cannot avoid determining itself as for-itself, and hence give itself a self, or identity, so a genuine response, which is at first nothing but a *yes*-saying to the Other as Other, cannot altogether escape the risk of saying *yes* to itself, and hence of opening the annulations of its own identity. Now the very "fact" that a response can always slip into a repetitive *yes* to, in the present case, a philosophy of absolute identity or a self-positioning responding I; or the very "fact" that such a slippage derives from the very possibility of arranging a place for the Other and of responsibly responding to the Other, is, of course, no excuse for overlooking the difference in question. Finally, that deconstruction, on occasion, has all the allures of dialectical thought is no license to identify them. Utterly irresponsive, if not irresponsible, is, however, the claim that the Derridean approach to the Hegelian yes of reconciliation would systematically overlook the Hegelian character of its own way of responding. To level out the difference between the two *yeses* and between each *yes* and *itself* would mean nothing less than to do injustice to *both* Hegel and Derrida.

Rather than opposing it, what deconstruction sets forth in response to the speculative *yes* is thus a *yes* to what in Hegel remains as an address to Other—on whose confirming response the very possibility of closure depends, and which also infinitely transcends it. The speculative, affirmative, reconciling *yes* of Hegelian thought is the yes of absolute knowing, of the Notion or Concept, of absolute identity. From his early writings up to the *Greater Logic,* Hegel has conceived of the unity achieved in the Absolute in terms of "the unity of differentiatedness and non-differentiatedness, or the identity of identity and non-identity." The concept of this unity is to "be regarded as the first, purest, that is, most abstract definition of the absolute," Hegel notes, and will ultimately have to make room for "more specific and richer definitions of it" (*SL,* p. 74). Indeed, the unity achieved in the Absolute as Spirit—the richest and final conceptualization of absolute identity—is a unity in which all external conditions that may have seemed necessary to conceive it show themselves not only to be the instances in which the Absolute is present, in that they sublate *themselves by themselves,* but also to be the Other in which the Absolute *relates to itself.* The Absolute, in relating to Other, consequently, relates to itself. The absolute identity and equality with itself achieved by Spirit is thus that of self-relation and relation to Other, that in which self also relates to itself. As self-consciousness, the Absolute achieves absolute identity, which is also the all-inclusive One or totality.[9]

Considering the fact that "identity" today is a common, if not hackneyed, term used without further qualifications in many contexts, especially in discourses more or less loosely derived from psychoanalysis and sociology, it is necessary at this point briefly to recall the meaning of "identity" in philosophy. The logical and philosophical concept of identity designates the relation in which any object (or any objective realm as well) stands all by itself to itself. Identity, thus linked in elemental fashion to the thought of the singular, is a predicate that serves to distinguish one thing from another of the same kind. Since identity pertains to mere *being itself,* it applies to any object as object, however protean or erratic it may prove to be. Although logical identity, that is, that a thing is identical with itself and implies itself, also takes on in Leibniz's law on indiscernibles a metaphysical or ontological form according to which no two things in the universe are exactly alike and, hence, identical, and thus must differ numerically, the strictly logical definition of identity remained prevalent until the advent of Kant, for whom identity is only a conceptual tool for establishing differences, and not an ontological principle. And yet, as the *Critique of Pure Reason* shows, Kant's insight that the unity characteristic of objectivity must in the last resort be retraceable to the unity that the thinking subject has of itself also reveals a meaning of identity that is formally thoroughly different from the logical identity constitutive of things. This meaning of identity, which applies exclusively to the consciousness of the thinking subject, has motivated idealist philosophers in the wake of Kantian thought to experiment, in Dieter Henrich's words, "first with the subject as principle of identity, and then with the meaning of identity that had been attributed to the subject, even without connection to self-consciousness, thus disregarding the Kantian fundamental distinctions."[10] In question here is Schelling's philosophy of identity. Taking Spinoza as a model, Schelling's philosophy indeed conceives, of the Absolute as the One in which nature and spirit, necessity and freedom, Being and intellectual intuition are identical. Absolute identity, beyond and removed from the problematic of both substance and subject, names here the universe itself. Although it is true that the young Hegel sympathized with Schelling's attempt to transcend in his philosophy of identity the limits of Fichte's subjective idealism, as early as the *Phenomenology of Spirit,* he was already criticizing Fichte's concept of identity and the Absolute for their abstraction. By recasting the Absolute in terms of Spirit, that is, as a relational identity of self-consciousness in which absolute subjectivity and *its* (absolute) Other become unified, Hegel, with his dynamic, processual, and relational concept of absolute identity, makes an elaborate attempt to philosophically realize the idea of the universal One, that is, of a metaphysical and ontological conception of identity, while at the same time avoiding the difficulties of Schelling's monism.

Although Derrida has on several occasions discussed the possibility and the limits of the philosophical and logical concept of identity, most explicitly in *Limited Inc,* the concept of identity deconstructed in "affirmative" response is the Hegelian concept of absolute identity, the *yes* between the extremes of which the *Phenomenology* speaks, and which gains its fullest development in the final chapters of the *Greater Logic.* The concept of identity under deconstruction is a concept that testifies to Hegel's impressive efforts to overcome the difficulties in articulating a philosophical monism freed of both subject and substance, difficulties that have haunted the history of philosophy from Parmenides to Schelling.[11] To correctly comprehend what deconstruction achieves with respect to absolute identity, it is crucial that the latter be understood on its own terms, not as, or mixed with, concepts originating in the sociopsychological and psychoanalytical notions of identity. Bringing the empirical and logically very different concepts of identity that relate specifically to the structure of personality to bear on the analysis of the speculative concept of identity, and on how deconstruction relates to it, produces only utter confusion. In short, without a clear grasp of the Hegelian concept of the absolute identity of Spirit as epistemic self-relation in which self and Other have been successfully reconciled—of Spirit as the Yes between the extremes—all possible assessment of how the deconstructive *yes* relates to the identity of Spirit, of the difference and similarity between deconstruction and speculative dialectic, and especially of the "status" of the deconstructive *yes* itself and hence of the specific kind of heterogenity from which it proceeds, is simply out of the question.

   Yet, in this essay I shall not engage in a systematic elaboration of the speculative concept of identity as it emerges from the last chapter of *Phenomenology* or the final part of *Science of Logic.* All such elaboration presupposes a thorough familiarity with Hegel's speculative criticism— in particular in the *Greater Logic*—of the concept of identity itself. It is to this criticism that I shall limit myself here. Indeed, rather than being Hegel's last word on identity, the explicit thematization of identity in *Science of Logic,* that is, of identity as a reflective determination, is a critical and speculative evaluation of it. It merely paves the way for the considerably richer understanding of it as the absolute identity of Spirit. To mistake Hegel's treatment of identity as a reflective determination for Hegel's positive theory of identity is not only to get his theory of identity wrong, but to misconstrue his entire philosophical enterprise.

   With this, I turn to Hegel's treatment of the question of identity in Book II of *Science of Logic,* entitled "The Doctrine of Essence." In the first section, "Essence as Reflection within Itself," in a chapter titled "Illusory Being," Hegel introduces the notion of identity, and shows it to be coextensive with essence and reflection. Before I embark on an analysis of how identity is to be understood here, some preliminary remarks as to the precise context in which this term is situated are inevitable. Since identity will be defined as a reflective determination, it is especially important to clearly grasp what "reflection" means here. Let me first advance the following: reflection as it appears in *Science of Logic* is no longer the philosophical reflection whose shortcomings Hegel had stigmatized in his earlier work, but a *rectified reflection* which while not yet absolute, or speculative, reflection has been stripped of everything improper to that sphere and is thus a moment on the way to absolute reflection itself. In *Science of Logic,* Hegel has put reflection into its proper place, as it were. To correctly assess the modifications made in reflection so as to assign it a positive, but limited place within the self-knowing Absolute, a word is necessary first on *Science of Logic* itself, on its goal and scope.

Hegel's logic is not based on judgment as the vehicle of truth. For Hegel, formal logic is a dead body compared to which speculative logic represents the living movement of thinking. Hegel's logic is a genuinely philosophical logic in that it explores a field of rationality beyond the logical axioms from which formal logic deduces its logical forms and elements of form. It is an inquiry into the principles of thinking in general and into Thinking as a principle itself, into Thinking as the absolute ground of thought. According to Hegel's logic, this absolute ground is the Notion, or Concept. Hegel writes: "The Notion is the most concrete and richest determination because it is the ground and the *totality* of the preceding determinations, of the categories of being and of the determinations of reflections; these, therefore, are certainly also present in it" (*SL,* p. 617). In the Notion, or the absolute Idea, the idea that has itself for its object, all the possible logical determinations of that one and same Notion—as being, as essence, and finally *as* Notion, that is, as including itself—have been sublated, overcome, and preserved. Since all these determinations of the Notion are figures of thinking, Hegel can claim to have shown how, with the absolute Idea, thinking engenders itself and becomes its own ground, the absolute ground of thinking.

Science of Logic divides into two parts: "The Objective Logic" and "Subjective Logic or the Doctrine of the Notion." But the first part, which contains the development of the categories and the reflective determinations of thinking up to the point where the concept of the Notion begins to impose itself, comprises the two books "The Doctrine of Being" and "The Doctrine of Essence." In contrast to the objective logic discussed in these first two books, the subjective logic represents the true exposition of the logic of the free Notion, or absolute Idea, that is, of logic as a formal ontology. Now, the speculative unfolding of reflection occurs right after the exposition of the doctrine of being, in other words, as part of the developments that ultimately will give rise to the idea of the Notion. The dialectical exposition of the problem of reflection is entirely mediated by its relation to the doctrine of being, and is intelligible only on the basis of the continual cross-references to that preceding realm. But, in addition, it must be read with regard to what will issue from and thus limit the sphere of reflection—the Notion, or the unfolded positive totality of all determinations of thought itself. It is not possible to broach here the difficult question of how exactly the logic of being and the logic of essence (in which reflection is discussed) relate. The following schematic outline of what both parts and both books seek to achieve, and how they relate must suffice. In his treatment of the logic of being, Hegel can be said to have rehearsed the great systems of the metaphysics of being. In this part he discusses the various modes of the sensuous insofar as they are contained in the *logos*. It is an investigation into the meaning of being, or of the immediate, which reinterprets Kant's *transcendental aesthetics,* that is, the aesthetics of objectifying thought and the traditional logic implied by this kind of thinking. The thrust of this whole inquiry is to demonstrate that being, as the immediate and abstract, shows itself *as* something Other, and has its truth in its essence, in something universal presupposing a reflective distance. The logic of essense is the counter-weight to being's self-negation. "The truth of *being* is *essence,*" Hegel notes (*SL,* p. 389). This truth follows upon the negation of the immediate presence of being as being's eternal past: *to ti en einai.* The doctrine of essence, consequently, amounts to a reinterpretation by Hegel of the various historical metaphysics of the intelligible, including Kant's *transcendental analytics*. Yet, this logic of essence is also important as the basis for a speculative critique of the philosophy of understanding, or reflection, in that the concept of essence presupposes precisely the (seemingly) irreducible doubling of the world characteristic of a metaphysics of reflection. Indeed, this metaphysics explains immediate and sensuous being by flanking it with explanation itself, understanding, or essence. A *mundus intelligibilis,* as Saint Augustine termed it, arches up in reflection over and against the phenomenal world, irreconcilably distinct from it. The point that Hegel makes in "Logic of Essence" is that essence, as an internal negation of the whole sphere of being, lacks the stability that it promised. Although the negation by essence of being allows being to turn upon itself—to reflect itself—essence, for its part, fails to reflect itself, and thus to achieve the foothold in itself that would have made the intelligible the deciding truth of being. Essence remains unable to comprehend itself. As a result, the movement characteristic of this part of the *Greater Logic* is bound to reintroduce the immediacy of being. But, since the immediate that is thus reinstituted is the immediacy of the being of essence, it reappears on a higher level. The relapse in question, indeed, opens up the new sphere of the Concept, or Notion. Hegel writes: "The movement of essence is in general the becoming of the Notion" (*SL*, p. 526). The logic of the Notion corresponds to a recast version of Kant's *transcendental dialectics,* since it radically exceeds Kant's limitation of the idea to a merely regulative role. Differently put, the Hegelian Concept or Notion, that is, the major category of the subjective logic, is nothing but the expounded transcendental unity of apperception—the originary unity that Kant had acknowledged as having to accompany all synthesis of the manifold. In this part of the logic, then, Hegel surmounts the reflective dualism of being and essence, being and appearance, that characterized Part I. In the absolute reflection of the Notion, thinking thinks itself. It becomes the all-encompassing totality that leaves reflective dualism behind. This is the end of the process in which substance finally grasps itself as subject. The three parts of this process correspond, as Jean Hyppolite has suggested, to the three moments contained in the German word *Selbstbewusstsein*—being, appearing, self.[12] This process, as it is expounded in the *Science of Logic,* culminates in the self-consciousness of the Notion, or Concept, as the unity of all determinations of thinking.

In this extremely broad and most schematic outline of how the *Science of Logic* is organized, I have made repeated reference to Kant's critical philosophy. Since I will now begin to discuss the notion of reflection which dominates the "Logic of Essence," it must, however, be emphasized that although this second part of Book I corresponds to Kant's transcendental analytics in the same way as the "Logic of Being" corresponds to formal or objective logic, Hegel does not simply rehearse Kant's developments. The two parts of Book I do not merely reproduce the types of reflection characteristic of formal or transcendental logic. In themselves they are indefensible modes of thinking, according to Hegel. Instead, what we encounter in the two parts of Book I are only two different ways of synthetic constitution that are *already* moments *of* true absolute reflection. Indeed, the movement of reflection outlined in the "Logic of Essence" has only a faint resemblance to Kant's corresponding notion. It has already been thoroughly reinterpreted in the perspective of the specular reflexivity of the Notion. It is a kind of reflection that can be called rectified, since its reflective falsifications have been corrected in the perspective of the Absolute; it is thus distinct from philosophical reflection on the one hand and from absolute reflection on the other.[13] In the following, I will limit myself to describing what Hegel calls "the movement of reflection" and what characterizes this notion of reflection itself, leaving aside a detailed discussion of the various phases that reflection must pass through before turning into the specularity of the Notion.

Essence is the main topic of the sometimes rather difficult if not obscure "Logic of Essence." "Essence stands between *being* and *Notion:* it constitutes their mean, and its movement is the *transition* from being into the Notion," Hegel writes (*SL,* p. 391). Essence issues from being. It is a negation brought about not from the outside of being, but by being itself. Hegel holds that essence in "its self-movement is reflection" (*SL,* p. 399). How does Hegel want us to understand this intrinsic relation between essence and reflection? Essence is the negation of being as pure immediacy. For essence, being is secondary and derivative. It is, compared to essence, nothingness, or "illusory being," essenceless being, that is, mere *Schein,* mere semblance. Yet, the non-essence that in the sphere of essence is thus attributed to being shows itself to be essence's own illusory being. "The illusory being . . . is essence's own positing," Hegel remarks (*SL,* p. 393). However, if illusory being is the result of essence's positing itself, then this means that "essence *shines* or *shows within itself.*" This doubling of essence within itself by which it takes on the illusory appearance of being is what Hegel calls *reflection* in the *Greater Logic.* "The showing of this illusory being within essence itself *is reflection,*" he concludes (*SL,* p. 394).

Three aspects of the movement of reflection need to be distinguished: (1) reflection takes place *within* the sphere of essence; (2) it coincides with the establishment of an Other to essence in the sphere of essence itself; and (3) this establishment is nothing but the shining, or showing, of essence in that very sphere. Consequently, essence as reflection is the whole itself, including itself as its own moment. But although the positing in essence's shining within itself of an Other in opposition to self and the self-positing of self are identical movements, reflection, because it opens the difference of the Other in the totality of essence, is also negation. However, this very negativity of reflection that results from the showing-in-itself of essence—a showing supposed to establish the identity of essence—is illusory as well, Hegel holds. In any case, reflection, negativity (or Otherness), and identity are found in profound unison in the sphere in question. This difficult synthesis needs some further clarification.

What remains of being in the sphere of essence—illusory being—"is not the illusory being of an Other, but is illusory being *per se,* the *illusory being of* essence itself," because "*essence* is the reflection of itself within itself," we are told (*SL,* p. 398). The equality of essence with itself is, thus, speculatively speaking, identical with the negativity of essence, since it is the relation to the Other (the nonbeing of being), that is, to essence's illusory being. In the sphere under consideration, reflection of an Other and self-reflection are identical. Hegel writes: "The movement of reflection . . . is the other as the *negation in itself,* which has a being only as self-related negation" (*SL,* p. 399). Indeed, in this sphere—which consists of immediate being's self-negation, in which being returns into itself, and consequently has become essence—the Other to which reflection relates is only an illusory Other, since it is an Other that negates itself as Other. Reflection amounts to a movement in which a relation to an Other is achieved, but this Other is itself characterized by reflection in that it is negation in itself of itself. Therefore, Hegel can claim that reflection is self-related negation, that is, a negation of negation, and can conclude his analysis of the movement of reflection with the following formula: "Consequently, becoming in essence, its reflective movement, is the *movement of nothing to nothing, and so back to itself*" (*SL,* p. 400). But if it is true that reflection in the sphere of essence knows the Other exclusively as the Other of essence, that is, as illusory being, essence is also its own negation because in shining within itself it shows that it has this Other within itself. In Hegel's words, reflection is an "interchange of the negative with itself" (*SL,* p. 400). *Pure* absolute reflection leads only to the very identity of negation with itself. Reflection as pure absolute reflection, or still abstract reflection, is merely "the *illusory being of the one in the other,*" the mere shining of one into the Other (*SL,* p. 622). Hegel notes: "The former, the movement of nothing through nothing back to itself, is the reflection of *itself* in the other; but because the opposition in the reflection has not yet any self-subsistence, the one that reflects is not a positive, nor is the *other* in which it is reflected a negative" (*SL,* p. 445). There is something extremely farcical about reflection. It is a movement incapable of securing any self-subsistence for the terms between which it takes place. The Other that reflection posits negates itself as Other, and thus lacks what must characterize an Other as Other, negativity. By contrast, the essence from which reflection springs achieves at best illusory being. Reflection is a ghostly movement between a bloodless self and an Other reduced to a lifeless husk. In it, no distinction of substance takes place, and hence no movement either, strictly speaking. It is a shadow play between nothing and nothing, in which even the movement from nothing to nothing, on the one hand, and back into itself, on the other, is hardly distinguishible. In this analysis of the sad spectacle of reflection, whose humor escapes only the totally insensitive reader, Hegel has dealt a deathblow to the metaphysics of understanding and reflection. Needless to say, it would of course be terribly wrong to isolate and hypostatize this analysis by conceiving of it as *the* model of Hegelian dialectic and of what Hegel understands by identity. It would mean arresting the development of the Hegelian treatment of both reflection and identity in what, in Hegel's eyes, are the most devastating arguments against these concepts.[14]

Yet, in spite of Hegel's critique of essential reflection, his account of essence and reflection is a dialectical one. Apart from the fact that the shadow play of the ghostly movement between nothings within nothing sets forth only the formal, and hence still empty, moments that will acquire their substantive content only in the logic of the Notion, pure absolute, or abstract, reflection—before all further determination and concretion—*is* the matrix of the logically most elementary idea of a "coincidence with itself *(mit sich selbst zusammengehen)*" and with what it is not (*SL*, p. 400). In one single unity, reflection achieves a coinciding, however illusory, of being-self and Other. It is necessary to recall here that if reflection, by which the essence shines in itself, occurs in the sphere of essence to begin with, it does so because essence is *already* identity. But it is identity in the most elementary way. Indeed, as Hegel puts it, "essence is at first, simple self-relation, pure *identity*" (*SL*, p. 409). It is "pure equality-with-self," "simple identity-with-self," in which "otherness and relation-to-other has vanished" (*SL*, p. 411). Conversely, "identity is, in the first instance, essence itself, not yet a determination of it, reflection in its entirety, not a distinct moment of it" (*SL*, p. 412). "*Essential* identity" is thus "in general the same as essence" (*SL*, pp. 411–412). But this identity of essence, which is reflection in its entirety, achieves its equality-with-self not through "a restoration of itself from another," but through "pure origination from and within itself" (*SL*, p. 411). In other words, essential identity, by knowing no Other and relation-to-Other, is nothing in itself but Otherness sublated, or simple negativity of being-in-itself. But since this identity "contains nothing of its other but only itself, that is, insofar as it is absolute identity with itself," it is also "*in its own self* absolute non-identity," Hegel concludes (*SL*, p. 413). It follows from this that the idea of a coincidence which accomplishes its concept only if it is the coincidence with self and Other must develop further. This happens through the various modes that reflection takes on in the sphere of essence, and that can, in view of the foregoing developments on reflection, be described as an illusory dialectic, but a dialectic notwithstanding of self and Other. This dialectic comes to an end with the emergence from the sphere of essence and reflection, of the ground *(Grund)*. In it, reflection as pure mediation has made room for the real mediation of the ground with itself and thus for an identity in which essence has returned from its nonbeing into positing itself. But ultimately, the dialectic of identity that arises with essential identity only comes *to rest* in the full mediation of self and Other in the Notion. Hegel writes: *"truth is complete only in the unity of identity with difference,* and hence consists only in this unity" (*SL,* p. 414).

One must not lose sight of the fact that the "Logic of Essence," is not merely a debate about reflective thinking as opposed to, and distinct from, the objectifying thinking deliberated throughout the "Logic of Being." Essence is nothing but the "pure, *absolute difference"* (*SL,* p. 413), which is also being sublated in itself. Therefore, essence is tied up from the start with thinking the unity of identity and difference. The "Logic of Essence" comes to a halt, indeed, after the two modes of thinking, of being and essence, have been united in the Notion. Only in the Notion does Hegel believe it possible to achieve both a logically and ontologically satisfactory reconciliation between the relation-to-self and relation-to-Other demanded in the name of reflection.

With the unfolding of the initially abstract notion of absolute reflection, the results of mediation become, of course, more concrete. It now becomes evident that the various specific forms that reflection assumes fail to achieve unity. This failure, constitutive of reflection as analyzed in the realm of essence, thus calls for its sublation in the speculative movements of the Notion by which absolute identity finally comes into its own. This essential failure of identity in the sphere of reflection is a consequence of the reflective mode by which it is supposed to be brought about. The illegitimacy of tearing what Hegel says about identity and its relation to reflection out of its context, and heralding these statements as the final truth of the Hegelian concept of identity, likewise follows. If the increasingly more concrete forms of reflection that Hegel distinguishes fail to establish the sought-for identity, they do so because, *as forms of reflection,* they cannot help giving unequal treatment to what is to be united. Either they subordinate self-relation to Other, or the other way around. What then are the different forms of reflection that Hegel distinguishes in the *Greater Logic?*

Pure absolute reflection differentiates into *positing, external, and determining* reflection. Positing and external reflection stress opposite features in the still abstract notion of reflection examined up to now, making it logically richer. Only in determining reflection does the notion of reflection acquire its full conceptual concretion. Determining reflection, Hegel tells us, is "the completed . . . reflection" (*SL*, p. 406). Since this final mode of reflection pretends to unite what had remained separate in the two previous forms of reflection, it needs to be examined more closely. Determining reflection "is in general the unity of *positing* and *external* reflection" (*SL*, p. 405). If, as Hegel holds, determinatedness is relation to Other, it is essential first to review how positing and external reflection achieve such determinatedness. Indeed, whereas "external reflection, when it determines, posits an other . . . in the place of the sublated being," namely essence, positing reflection "starts from nothing." The determination that it posits "is not put in the place of an other; the positing has no presupposition. But that is why it is not the completed, determining reflection; the determination that it posits is consequently *only* something posited; it is immediate, not as equal to itself, but as negating itself; it has an absolute relation to the return-into-self; it *is* only in reflection-into-self, but it is not this reflection itself" (*SL*, pp. 405–406). In positing reflection, an Other is posited, but since this posited Other relates to itself as sublated Other (it is *only* posited), "the equality of reflection is completely preserved" (*SL*, p. 406). It is as if nothing had happened (except for the putting into place of the formal relations constitutive of reflection-into-self). Now, in determining reflection such determination, by positing reflection, becomes united with external reflection. External reflection, as Hegel has previously shown, starts from something immediately given. It is thus presupposing *(voraussetzende)* reflection. Whatever determinations are posited "by external reflection in the immediate are to that extent external to the latter" (*SL*, p. 403). It stands over against its own starting point. But, says Hegel, a closer consideration reveals that it is "a positing of the immediate, which consequently becomes the negative or the determinate"; hence "this immediate from which it seemed to start as from something alien, *is* only in this its beginning" (*SL*, pp. 403–404). In exterior reflection, the immediate that is presupposed thus becomes determined as the Other of reflection. Therefore, Hegel can conclude: "the externality of reflection over against the immediate is sublated; its positing in which it negates itself, is the union of itself with its negative, with the immediate, and this union is the immediacy of essence itself" (*SL,* p. 404). This return to positing reflection in exterior reflection is thus not a simple return. By being the immanent reflection of the immediate that it at first presupposed, reflection has become determined by this very immediate, whereas the immediate itself has become fully transparent to reflection. In this unity of positing and exterior reflection, the latter has become an "absolute presupposing, that is, the repelling of reflection from itself, or the positing of the determinatedness as *determinatedness of itself"* (*SL,* p. 406). Simply put, in the unity in question, the exteriority of reflection makes reflection coil upon itself, whereas positing becomes determination of reflection by itself. Being posited, in other words, now means being reflectively determined. "Positedness is thus a *determination of reflection"* (*SL,* p. 406), Hegel writes. The relation to Other characteristic of positing has turned into relation to reflectedness-into-self. In determining reflection, reflection is equal to itself. Or differently put, with determinate reflection "essence is determinate essence, or it is *an essentiality"* (*SL,* p. 409). It has persistence, since it is no longer unequal to itself. In determinate reflection, reflection has achieved a unity with itself and its Other which, compared with all previous forms of transitional determination, is stable self-determination.

However, this stability of determining reflection does not last. It disintegrates instantly into the *reflective determinations.* Indeed, although essence is infinite return-into-self, a movement of absolute self-mediation through distinct moments, essence *as* essence can achieve this unity with self in Other only by *shining* "into these its moments which consequently are themselves determinations reflected into themselves" (*SL,* p. 409). Consequently, the essentialities, or reflective determinations, into which determining reflection divides "appear as free essentialities floating in the void without attracting or repelling one another. In them, the determinateness has established and infinitely fixed itself through relation-to-itself" (*SL,* p. 403). The stable essence has thus fallen apart into determinations that have lost all commerce with one another. And Hegel can conclude that in determining reflection, reflection has become exterior to itself, beside itself *(ausser sich gekommene Reflexion).* Indeed, "the equality of essence with itself has perished in the negation, which is the dominant factor," of determining reflection.

Identity is the first of these reflective determinations into which the unity and equality with self and Other diffracts. The others are difference, contradiction, and ground. As a reflective determination, identity marks the fixation of the stability sought by determining reflection into relation-to-self. It thematizes the determinate's bending "back [of] its reflection-into-other into reflection-into-self" (*SL,* p. 407). Essence, reflection-into-self, is the first moment of its shining into itself. As Hegel remarks: "Essence is *at first,* simple self-relation, pure *identity.* This is its determination, but as such it is rather the absence of any determination" (*SL,* p. 409). Identity, consequently, is not only the first moment of essence's reflecting itself into a stable relation to itself and its other; in this sphere, it is merely pure, that is, simple, abstract identity. This is an identity that ultimately is not one since—to refer to Hegel's analysis of the *law of identity*—the reflective movement that constitutes it is "a beginning that hints at something different to which an advance is to be made; but this different something does not materialize . . . the difference is only a vanishing; the movement returns into itself" (*SL,* pp. 415–416). This is further proof, if any is still needed, that what Hegel develops with respect to identity in this part of *Science of Logic* cannot be construed as *the* final word on identity (or on reflection, for that matter). Everything Hegel says about the so-called laws of thinking—in this case, the law of identity—is valid for the concept of identity outlined up to this point: "these laws contain *more* than is *meant* by them, to wit, this opposite, absolute difference itself" (*SL,* p. 416). The concept of identity, indeed, is haunted by absolute inequality, or contradiction per se, and as such is a dialectical concept in anticipation of its fullfilment.

It is not necessary to expand here on Hegel's speculative critique of the four reflective determinations, or essentialities. The thrust of his analysis is to demonstrate that the first three reflective determinations—identity, difference, and contradiction—become sublated by mutually putting their self-subsistant autonomy into question. In brief: The determination of essence as pure *identity* achieves only simple self-relation. It is, therefore, the absence of any determination. Although *difference* is a proper determination of essence, difference either is *diversity,* that is, difference external or indifferent to essence, or operates within identical essence as unmediated *opposition.* In the reflective determination of *contradiction,* the undifferent sides of opposition become mutually relating sides, or moments, of difference. Thus reflected into itself, opposition become contradiction withdraws into its *ground* (*SL,* p. 409). With this, essence has become the *ground* to which all three reflective determinations have returned. Yet, as the last of the reflective determinations, the ground is also sublated determination as such. Hegel writes: "*ground is itself one of the reflected determinations* of essence; but it is the last of them, or rather the meaning of this determination is merely that it is a sublated determination" (*SL*, p. 444). The ground appears as that determination of reflection from which identity, difference, and opposition draw their origin and to which they return. Assuming this function of a ground, the fourth reflective determination signifies the end of reflection. But in the same stroke, all the immanent presuppositions and implications of reflection, which it was unable to realize in its different shapes, come into full view. In Hegel's words: "Ground . . . is real mediation because it contains reflection as sublated reflection; it is essence that, through its non-being, *returns into* and *posits itself.* In accordance with this moment of sublated reflection, the posited receives the determination of *imme-diacy,* of an immediate that, apart from the relation, or its illusory being, is self-identical. This immediate is *being* which has been restored by essence, the non-being of reflection through which essence mediates itself" (*SL*, p. 445).

In the "Logic of Essence," this idea of totality and absolute identity, in which identity and reflection are sublated, starts off with the reflective determination of the ground, which therefore is also the end of deter-mining reflection. But this idea gains full concretion in the notion of Actuality *(Wirklichkeit),* in which the fundamental contradictions of reflection are welded into a successful kind of identity. This last stage in the process of the sublation of reflection and the becoming of the all-encompassing and absolute identity corresponds to the end of objective logic. It makes the transition to the logic of the Notion, the richest category of dialectical thinking. If Hegel speaks of absolute reflection and identity in this final part of the *Greater Logic,* he clearly refers to something for which pure absolute reflection and identity as a reflective determi-nation were at best the blueprint.

Having argued that deconstruction's response to speculative thought is a response to the strong concept of identity, I must now say a word about the deconstructive "operation" on identity itself. First, however, it has to be established, and in no uncertain terms, that deconstruction is not a critique of identity in the name of the nonidentical. Undoubtedly, Derrida has, at times, had recourse to the concept of non-identity to describe the limits of identity. In "Before the Law," for example, he

speaks of the "non-identity in itself" of the sense or destination of a text
such as Kafka's parable, whose "personal identity"—"the identity with
itself of a bequeathed corpus"—passes on nothing but "non-identity
with itself." Yet the identity of Kafka's text that "does not tell or describe
anything but itself as text" is, Derrida charges, achieved not "within an
assured specular reflection of some self-refential transparency—and I
must stress this point—but in the unreadability of the text, if one understands by this the impossibility of acceding to its proper significance and
its possibly inconsistent content, which it jealously keeps back." Not
only, then, is this identity of "Before the Law" not speculatively constituted, but more important for my concerns here, neither is the non-
identity that it is said to pronounce and to pass on of speculative origin.
It shares only the wording with what is called non-identity in speculative
thinking, as well as in the critique of speculative thought. Derrida holds:
"The texts guards itself, maintains itself—like the law, speaking only of
itself, that is to say, of its non-identity with itself *(Il ne parle que de lui-
même, mais alors de sa non-identité à soi)*. It neither arrives nor lets anyone
arrive."[15] If a text such as Kafka's parable "Before the Law" can be said
to close upon itself, it does so in non-identity. But the statement of such
non-identity comes with a conditional clause: *If* the text can be said to
speak only of itself, *then (alors)* it does so at best about its non-identity
with itself. If one uses a language akin to that of speculative thought to
describe what happens in Kafka's parable, that of which this text speaks
when it is said to speak only of itself must then invariably be cast in terms
of non-identity. The reference to non-identity is clearly a tribute paid
to a particular way of phrasing the fact that a text such as Kafka's guards
and maintains itself. The non-identity that a deconstructive reading of a
text such as "Before the Law" points up, however, shares only the name
with the speculative concept of non-identity. Indeed, deconstruction
does not object to the idea of an all-encompassing identity on the basis
that such a concept does not come without remainders. Since all identifying thinking, as well as the thinking of absolute identity, considers
that which is to be identified, or taken up into the all-embracing and
identical whole, from the perspective of identity, such thought, its critics
claim, looks away from what resists identification in what is to be identified. Ineluctable non-identity, they hold, is the remainder that drops
through the otherwise tight nets of identifying, or speculative, thought.

Adorno, from such a position, has opposed Hegelian thought and its
attempt to conceptualize the relation of identity between subject and

object as the identity of identity and non-identity. To counter identifying thought, he has suggested starting by thinking the non-identity of identity and non-identity. Yet, as Ute Guzzoni has convincingly shown, any attempt to think toward a thinking that would no longer be guided by the principle of identity must acknowledge that Adorno's concept of the non-identical is essentially something other than what Hegel designates by that term. Guzzoni remarks: "Although Hegelian dialectic lives, undoubtedly, from the tension between identity and non-identity, identity has never here the meaning of something that is simply in opposition to the identical, precisely because of the tension in question." Indeed, the non-identical in Hegel is a *moment,* and thus lacks any "fundamental heterogeneity with respect to the universal."[16] Non-identity for Hegel is a relational concept whose meaning is determined by *its* Other— identity—and thus it is part of a movement in which dialectically different moments achieve unity. From the outset, the non-identical stands in a relation of opposition to the identical—it is the non-identical *of* the identical—and is viewed as constituted from the start (in the same way as the identical) by the absolute identity toward which it unfolds. Consequently, the non-identical in Hegel (and this is the case with the identical as well) is non-identical only when it is no longer itself, but already beyond itself, that is, tied into the whole of which it is a positive moment. The Hegelian concept of the non-identical, therefore, cannot serve in any way to challenge the speculative conception of absolute identity. Rather than something that falls through the meshes of the Absolute, it is part of the net that itself constitutes the relational whole in question. What follows from this is that the totalizing and unifying thrust of absolute identity cannot be thwarted by any singularity, in particular, by the sensible, or merely brute being before any conceptualization has occurred. Hegel has made this point with all the necessary clarity in his rebuttal of one Mr. Krug, who had challenged transcendental idealism to "deduce each particular cat and dog, as well as Mr. Krug's own pen."[17] In the context of his criticism of Krug, Hegel notes that to object to transcendental idealism because it would neglect "facts" such as "having been born at a very determined time, of dying at a specific time, of receiving daily news through the newspaper about things that happen in the world, and in places where we are not present,"[18] simply shows that Krug has no idea whatsoever of "philosophical construction." He writes: "If Krug had had an inkling, however slight, of the greatness of this task, or of what currently constitutes the prime interest of philosophy, namely to once again put God absolutely at the top of philosophy as the sole ground of everything, as the only *principium essendi* and *cognoscendi,* after He had been put long enough *next* to other finite things, or entirely at the end as a postulate that proceeds from an absolute finitude, how could he have come up with the idea of demanding that philosophy deduce his writing pen?"[19] Apart from the fact that such items as those to which Krug refers are trivial—Hegel challenges Krug to confront, by contrast, the *organization* of a dog or cat, the *life* of a rose, the *individuality* of a Moses or Alexander—they are not even characterized, strictly speaking, by independence, singularity, or finite being. As Hegel's emphasis on thinking the organization, the life, and the individuality of things, animals, or persons demonstrates, singular items have an independent singularity and are philosophically significant only on the basis of what makes them intelligible in the first place. Yet, with this, they are, for Hegel, always already moments of the Absolute as the unity of the intelligible. In short, if anything can make the absolute identity tremble, it is certainly not the non-identical in the Hegelian sense or, as is now to be seen, in the sense that Adorno gives to this term.

For Adorno, "the non-identical negates identity, it is something negative compared to the identical, that is, something that refuses to be identified, and to be taken together with Other in a common unity . . . insofar as it is always more than what it could have in common with Other."[20] In other words, the non-identical in Adorno's sense is never a *moment,* and, as Ute Guzzoni has argued, "Adorno's dialectic is a *dialectic without moments,* as it were, precisely because for him the non-identical is not sublated in the movement of an all-embracing and all penetrating whole"[21] The starting point for his conception of the non-identical lies with the assumption that every object that is encountered, whether in the mode of experience or the mode of conceptualization, encloses a kernel resistant to experience and thought. Guzzoni notes that "for Adorno what is, is there first before an Other—the thinking subject— can direct itself upon it."[22] The non-identical, in Adorno's sense, escapes identifying thought and absolute identification because, in essence, it has an altogether different ontological character, and is heterogeneous to experience, thought, and conceptual arrangement. This remainder would, in principle, have to be distinguished from what Hegel called immediacy, or mere being. The latter does not escape the logic of the Concept; it is, on the contrary, its first moment. As Hegel recalls toward the end of the *Greater Logic,* "at each stage of its further determination

. . . [the universal] raises the entire mass of its preceding content, and by its dialectical advance it not only does not lose anything or leave anything behind, but carries along with it all it has gained, and inwardly enriches and consolidates itself" (*SL,* p. 840). Not only does the idealizing process by which absolute identity enriches itself have no remainder, but to speak of a remainder to the process as a whole is nonsensical, since the Absolute *is* sublated remainder, the remaining totality of all remains. What Adorno calls the non-identical, and which is said to be heterogeneous and incommensurate with the Concept, would have to be radically different from what Hegel terms the immediate, or simple being. Yet such a non-identical, which precedes the speculative logic of identity and non-identity as the heterogenous and incommensurable, is ultimately without relation to the Concept. To the Concept and absolute identity, it is an insignificant non-identical which has no bearing whatsoever on the process through which the Absolute achieves completion in absolute identity. Whereas Hegel's "immediate" (mere being, sensible immediacy) is part of the whole, the nonidentical in Adorno's sense remains outside speculative identity, occupying the place that the latter has assigned to the meaningless.[23] Indeed, in its utter exteriority to absolute identity, the non-identical lacks the negativity of the most minute moment. But by slipping through the so-called meshes of totalizing thought, this non-identity (which is thus clearly understood to be non-relational, and hence of the order of substance) acquires no enabling status, however ephemeral, with respect to such thought. Neither does it make that thought possible by escaping it, nor does it represent the limit of absolute identity. It is, strictly speaking, meaningless. But the meaningless is, as I have said, determined as such by speculative thought. Paradoxically, then, even Adorno's non-identical remains, as the always already anticipated, and hence sublated, remainder of speculative thought.

It would thus seem that the very absence of relation to the Concept robs even Adorno's notion of the non-identical of any (significant) critical thrust. Absolute identity can only be questioned from a "position" which is *neither* inside *nor* outside it, and which entertains a relation to it that is without relation to it at the same time. This is a direct consequence of the relational nature of the speculative Absolute.

The point to be made is that the deconstruction of speculative identity does not consist in opposing a non-identical (either in a Hegelian sense or in one determined by a critique of identifying thought and of the thought of absolute identity) to identity. However, before such a point can be made, a persistent confusion must be addressed: By virtue of its relational nature, nothing of the order of a substantial remainder can, in principle, be held against absolute identity. Only something of the order of the relational could escape the Absolute. Yet, as absolute totality, this relational whole includes all relations, even that to itself. Consequently, for essential reasons, only a *relation without relation* to absolute identity can escape or resist it. As a *response* to absolute identity, that is, to its strongest claim of all-inclusiveness and absolute identity, deconstruction cannot, for equally essential reasons, be confined to exhibiting what absolute identity must exclude or what resists it as remainder, residue, refuse, or rest. Occasionally Derrida has spoken of *rests,* but its italicization or placement between quotation marks is clear indication that the term is not to be taken in its usual sense. Rather than a rigorously identifiable and decidable residue like the Adornean non-identical, the remainder that a deconstruction discerns *in* a speculative totality and identical whole is "a remainder that is both quasi-transcendental and supplementary." Such a remainder is characterized by its *resistance* to a speculative, absolute identity in that it "adds itself to . . . [it] without allowing itself to be added in or totalized," Derrida writes.[24] This remainder, by re-traversing all the moments of the absolute totality, re-marks these moments and hence escapes participation in their organization. It is thus neither of the order of the speculative nor transcendent to it. By virtue of its structure, such a remainder cannot therefore be properly determined. It is neither an identity nor, strictly speaking, something non-identical. As Derrida remarks with respect to *text* as remainder, "dialectical happiness will never account for a text. If there is text, if the hymen constitutes itself as a textual trace, if it always leaves something behind, it is because its undecidability cuts it off from (prevents it from depending on) every— and hence *any*—signified, whether antithetic or synthetic" (*D,* p. 261). A remainder such as the one in question *resists* the meanings of both the identical and the non-identical, and cannot be questioned within their horizon. This undecidability of the remainder with respect to a totality of meaning, or to a speculative totalization as the identity of identity and non-identity, has prompted Derrida to speak of it in terms of remaining *(restance).* Rather than being a positive or negative remainder, the supplementary and quasi-transcendental—hence, undecidable—limit of a speculative totality resists it by *remaining. Remaining* is the structure of that which simultaneously adds itself to and withdraws from a self-iden tical and self-present totalization. As Derrida has noted in *Spurs,* the structure of *remaining* prevents all essential identification: in other words, it escapes the "assured horizon of a hermeneutic question."[25] And: "Such *remaining* is not caught up in any circular trajectory. It knows of no proper itinerary which would lead from its beginning to its end and back again, nor does its movement admit of any center. Because it is structurally liberated from any living meaning, it is always possible that it means nothing at all or that it has no decidable meaning. There is no end to its parodying play with meaning, grafted here and there, beyond any con-textual body of finite code."[26] However, from the undecidability of this structure, discussed by Derrida in *Spurs*—where his example is the Nietz-schean fragment "I have forgotten my umbrella"—and from the impos-sibility of determining it within the horizon of the totality to which it adds itself while subtracting itself from that totality's meaning, it does not follow that all attempts to determine the structural traits of *remaining* should be abandoned. On the contrary, such an effort "must be carried to the furthest lengths possible," Derrida concludes.[27] *The Tain of the Mirror* has investigated and analyzed instances of such *remaining* with respect to the structures that determine their undecidability under the title of infrastructures. Consequently, there is no need to take this issue up again here. Nor is there any reason to demonstrate that infrastructures characterized by *remaining* are not the speculative Other of, and thus within, absolute identity. Infrastructural *remaining* does not stand in a relation of opposition and contradiction to a speculatively identical. Hence, no reflective reappropriation of *remaining as such,* or in general, is possible. Yet, it is always possible that *remaining* be understood in terms of a remainder, initiating the dialectical process of totalization with the opposition of the non-identical to the identical. But what such a becoming "opposite" and "Other" of *remaining* leaves behind is, pre-cisely, *remaining.* I add: this very undecidability of infrastructural *remaining* allows it to play the role of a condition of possibility *and* impossibility for absolute identity. The dialectical non-identical, or Other, can, of course, never acquire such status or position. The non-identical, or the Other, is a moment, and a moment is not a condition of possibility, not to mention impossibility. If the non-identical and Other inaugurate a series of dialectical inversions that ultimately culminates in the identity of identity and non-identity, infrastructural *remaining* is "anterior" to all dialectical reversal or inversion. It is "anterior" to it in that it will always have resisted, successfully or not, becoming a remainder.

Yes as a response to the call upon Other to say *yes* to the speculative *yes* of reconciliation is one such instance of undecidable infrastructural *remaining*. It is a response demanded by the very fact that even the most absolute, that is, self-inclusive, totalization involves, as a performative event, the Other and, hence, the request to say *yes*. Analyzing with respect to Joyce's work what in classical philosophical terminology would be called a "transcendendal condition of all performative dimension," Derrida remarks: "We are in an area which is *not yet* the space where the large questions of the origin of negation, of affirmation or of denegation, can and must be unfolded . . . The *yes* to which we now refer is 'anterior' to all these reversible alternatives, to all these dialectics. They assume it and envelop it."[28] Without this *yes* of the Other to whom the speculative *yes* addresses itself—and with it the entirety of the moments and movements that it comprises—speculative totalization and absolute identity would not get off the ground as an event. Yet this *yes* that the speculative and reconciling *yes* requires is not part of speculative affirmation and negation. It adds itself to all affirmations and negations that the *yes* between the extremes embraces into a whole, yet it resists being added to the organization of the movements of positing and reversal. It is neither inside nor outside in any decidable manner, and, for that very reason, it is not of the order of a non-identical Other *of* the system of identity. As such, it enables the speculative *yes* to *embrace* and reconcile the totality of what is, but it also represents the limit of such affirmation, in that it must necessarily remain excluded from what it makes possible. But, precisely because of its undecidability—of the involved *yes*'s status as neither a moment nor strictly speaking a transcendental, as neither identity nor non-identity, neither self nor Other—this *yes* can always slip, turning into the affirmative *yes* itself or into mere repetitive affirmation of Hegelian reconciliation. Without the possibility of slippage, no response to the call to say *yes* to *yes* is thinkable to begin with. In addition, genuine response to the call to say *yes* to *yes,* and thus to a mode of thinking that is both encyclopedic and self-inclusive, is genuine only if it remains different, even when, by respecting the force of Hegelian thought, the *yes* of response may seem nearly identical to the speculative *yes*.

Unlike Krug's writing pen, whose very insignificance makes it easy prey for dialectical reappropriation, but also unlike all the versions of Hegelian, or Adornean non-identity, which either propel the system of absolute identity forward or entirely fall away from it, the *yes* of response, by answering the call, *remains* and, while enabling the system of identity, resists its own identification by it. The singularity of the *yes* of response is not that of the raw singularity that Krug's writing pen is supposed to exemplify, as opposed to what sort of pen it is, how it is constructed, who fabricated it, and so forth. It is intelligible, but of an intelligibility that includes undecidability. The *yes* of response must be a *yes* that can always be denied. Its singularity is constituted both by the possibility that it might not occur and by the possibility that if it does, its response recedes out of the reach of that to which it consents. These intelligible structural traits of the deconstructive *yes,* all by themselves and alone, explain why and how such a *yes* makes absolute identity tremble. In answering the call to say *yes* to absolute identity, *yes* has, indeed, decon-structed it. In responding to the call, the *yes* of deconstruction opens the space of the Other without whose consent absolute identity as event could not spiral upward, encircling itself and the Other, and re-descend into itself. By the same token, however, an outside of absolute identity has become marked, and *remains*.

9

On Responding Responsibly

THERE IS PERHAPS no theme more demanding than that of "responsibility." Yet this theme, undoubtedly more in demand than ever, has occasioned hasty though well-intended responses that risk erasing, in the name of ethics, the possibility of ethics itself. Indeed, what is in demand is a concept of responsibility on which one could count, that would permit secure, unambiguous decisions in a particular situation, or about a text. This is a prescriptive, normative concept that anticipates and programs response in a calculable manner, by defining responsibility as the mechanical application of a framework of rules that simultaneously relieves the subject of the onus of decision and, hence, of all liability. Yet, a responsible response can come about only if the decision is truly a decision, not a mechanical reaction to, or an effect of, a determinate cause. For a responsible response is only possible outside calculable programs of given ethics. What, then, constitutes responsible responsibility? This is the demanding question of "responsibility." It summons us to speak responsibly about responsibility, which entails that our thought about it must do justice to our inherited concept of responsibility, which regulates our responses to particular situations or texts. But it also means that we must respond to what constitutes the concept of responsibility beyond the forms that the concept has acquired in our tradition, so that the conditions of responsibility not be cast in terms of a given idiom of responsibility. Finally, a responsible treatment of the question of responsibility must itself assume the irreducible uncertainty that comes with all decision in deciding about responsibility's conditions. Consequently, any attempt to address the question of responsibility in a responsible fashion involves at least the following risks. First is the risk of appearing irre-

227

sponsible. Indeed, any adequate response to the given forms of responsibility cannot but show these forms to be inseparable from other forms or concepts (in particular those of intentionality and subjectivity) that serve to fashion, restrict, and limit responsibility, and that thus need to be deconstructed.[1] Second, an inquiry into what properly makes up responsibility, that is, into responsibility's conditions, will inevitably lead to something anethical that, because it does not coincide with a given ethics, will invariably be called anti-ethical.[2] Third, if a responsible treatment of the issue of responsibility does indeed require one to take responsibility for that treatment—for the irreducibly erratic moment in all decision about the nature of what is responsible, for the uneffaceable hesitation that constitutes it, for the inevitable element of chance inherent in a leap toward a conclusion or settlement—all of which are grounded in the structural features of decision, and not in some subjective or existential conditions surrounding it—the risk is that of seeming to move toward ethical arbitrariness. A responsible discourse on responsibility can indeed only assert itself in the mode of a "perhaps." Yet, although usually a disingenuous qualification, a sign of imprecision, the "perhaps" here indicates an essential lack of dogmatic certitude about what, according to its concept, ought to be not only absolutely irreproachable, but also absolutely certain—the conditions of the possibility of responsibility. In this domain nothing is granted, or guaranteed once and for all. Yet, these three risks, and the accompanying incertitude, also define the parameters of responsible decision, of a "necessity" of decision very different from a necessity of norm. To think responsibility calls indeed for an absolutely unprecedented responsibility, one that cannot look back upon given assurances, but that is attentive to and responsive to the structural features of undecidability characteristic of responsibility itself.

Heidegger's concept of responsibility, his understanding of responsibility as responsiveness or respondence, anticipates the responsibility alluded to above. For Heidegger, responsibility is primarily a response to which one commits oneself, or pledges oneself in return. This displacement of the meaning of responsibility achieves, as Reiner Schürmann has shown, a deconstruction of the traditional—that is, metaphysical— conception of responsibility as an accounting before a normative instance or entity. If responsibility means response, then "the debts of accounts and the referent to which it is discharged"[3] become secondary, to say the least. Indeed, what this transmutation brings to the fore—for which etymological justifications such as the term's derivation from the Greek *sponde* (libation, vow) and the Latin *spondere* (to promise, to pledge one-self to) are ultimately inessential—is that responsible thinking or acting is a thinking or acting that answers a call and presupposes a consent, an agreement to engage and bind themselves. In "Nature of Language," Heidegger called this originary acquiescence in responding responsibly a listening that tends toward the *Zusage,* grant, and *Zuspruch,* promise, of language.[4] All response is at first, and in advance, "to this pledge and of this pledge," Derrida writes in *Of Spirit: Heidegger and the Question.* He adds: "It is engaged by it in a responsibility it has not chosen and which assigns it even its liberty. The pledge will have been given before any other event." This Heideggerian thought of an affirmation that precedes all thinking and acting, all question and response, foregrounds the origin of responsibility. Prior to all response to and hence to all responsible thinking and acting in the classical sense, a consent must have taken place to that which addresses itself to us and which subsequently is to be addressed by us. In the aftermath of Heidegger, Derrida has analyzed this "pre-originary pledge *(gage)* which precedes any other engagement in language or action," in terms of the "sometimes wordless word which we name the 'yes.' "[5] In his treatment of "the question of the *yes*" in *Ulysses Gramophone: Deux mots pour Joyce,*[6] Derrida's evocation of Hei-degger's definition in *Being and Time* of *Dasein* as a being called by a call that "comes from afar . . . and which, in a certain way, is not saying anything" (*UL,* p. 273), explicitly acknowledges Heidegger's medita-tions on the origin of responsibility as indeed the constant point of ref-erence. Undoubtedly, the question of the *yes* has been present in Der-rida's work for a long time. Yet focusing on his treatment of the *yes* in *Ulysses Gramophone*—on this pledge before all pledges, this consentment to engage, this acquiescence to a call before all particular responses and codified responsible behavior—makes clear the stakes of Derrida's ongoing discussion of the yes. At stake, indeed, is a displacement of thought's duty and responsibility toward Being, as well as the limitation of its essence to thinking Being. Indeed, for Heidegger, the essence of responsibility is suspended from thinking's call by the One—by what has been assigned as thinking's task since the beginning of Western thought—the essence of Being. Responsibility thus becomes defined by thinking's adequate corresponding to Being. The analyses performed in *Ulysses Gramophone* serve, however, to cut the essentializing link between response and Being, and to prepare for an "increase in responsibility,"[7] one that no longer engages thinking as the thinking of Being alone. But this other responsibility manifests itself as well through the multiplication of the characteristic features of response, implying not only a cluster of traits of addresses and responses, but also a cluster of heterogeneous yeses.

Yet before beginning a discussion of Derrida's texts on Joyce, let me recall some of his statements about *Glas* that appeared in two consecutive interviews published in 1976 and 1977 in *Digraphe*. Of *Glas* he says, "this text can only be *of interest* if one is assured that, beyond all the ruses and all the unassailable calculations, I am no longer aware of what is my own business *(je ne vois plus ce qui me regarde)*."[8] Indeed, in spite of the numerous calculations that inform the writing of *Glas,* "the important [one] (for me in any case) is to not succeed in the calculation in question."[9] The reason for risking such failure, for not wanting to be entirely responsible for the calculus, is not merely the desire to resist all possible appropriation, and hence to become unreceivable. Such a desire would require deliberate manipulation of a maximum of conditions of unacceptability—an infallible calculus, in short! If Derrida admits that "he likes to write precisely at that point where the calculus is lost absolutely,"[10] he does so because of a search for the absolute, more precisely the structural, limits of calculation as well as of the calculating subject. Of the calculations in *Glas,* Derrida remarks: "I am not fully responsible for them, the 'I' is not entirely responsible for them, and *the calculus succeeds only by failing.*"[11] Texts written from such a perspective give rise to effects of reading or non-reading that are "absolutely non-anticipatable, out of sight, structurally out of sight."[12] They are accessible not from the "I," but "only from the place of the Other," whether this place is that of the Other in the writing subject or his reader.[13] Rather than revealing a desire to become unacceptable and unreceivable, the relinquishing of the responsibility for control and mastery is testimony to a desire to open writing to unforeseeable effects, in other words, to the Other. It is a function of a responsibility for the Other—for managing in writing a place for the Other, saying *yes* to the call or demand of the Other, inviting a response. To write at the point where the calculus is lost for absolute reasons is to structurally inscribe into the text the possibility of the necessarily singular demand and response by the Other as Other. It is in not being entirely responsible for calculation that one begins to address the Other in self and the other self. Or, differently put, a writing that "calculates with the incalculable" is a writing that does justice if "justice [in contradistinction to the law] always addresses itself to singularity, to the singularity of the other, despite or even because it pretends to universality."[14] Since the response of the Other (as Other) is in principle characterized by incalculable singularity, and exceeds everything that could have been anticipated as a response, a writing that writes at the point where calculation absolutely fails is infinitely responsible. It is marked by "a responsibility without limits," as Derrida puts it in "Force of Law,"[15] that is itself incalculable because of the incalculable to which it responds. Yet such a writing, which in its very disposition is ethical in that it responds to the (in principle) excessive singularity of the Other, is not an invitation to licentious responding. Such a response would not be a response. It would lack all responsibility. Indeed, the place of the Other managed in a writing that calculates with the incalculable is an invitation to the Other in his or her necessarily singular response (as Other), and not a place for any calculable and predictable response in which the Other gives himself or herself away as such.

It will be important to keep in mind the foregoing statements about *Glas* as I now proceed to a reading of "Ulysses Gramophone," precisely because this text, which seems to deride Joycean scholarship and competence, might easily be construed as an irresponsible spinning out of private fantasies, wild jokes, and totally arbitrary associations—in other words, as a text of so-called deconstructive criticism where everything goes. Derrida's selective sampling of Joyce's work will certainly meet with disapproval as well, unless it is read as the positive expression of a genuine quest for private autonomy in defiance of the public, the universal.[16] And although "Ulysses Gramophone" certainly performs what it establishes through its argumentative procedures and thus has "literary" features, there is also ample evidence that this text belongs to philosophy.

If nothing else, the mere fact that, first in *Edmund Husserl's "Origin of Geometry": An Introduction* and later in "Two Words for Joyce," Husserl and Joyce are said to share the same project of trying "to grasp a pure historicity" should be sufficient evidence that there is a philosophical sweep to the text. To achieve this goal of a pure historicity, Husserl and Joyce mobilize "two great models, two paradigms with respect to thought," two parallel strategies, Derrida argues (*TWJ,* p. 149). Husserl seeks to "reach back and grasp again at its pure source a historicity or traditionality that no de facto historical totality will yield of itself," by methodically reducing empirical language, that is, a language characterized by equivocity, "to the point where its univocal and translatable elements are actually transparent" (*O,* p. 103). Absolute univocity and actual transparency, without which there would be no communication—they secure the *sameness* of language—"alone make pure history possible, i.e., as the transmission and recollection of sense" (*O,* p. 102). Husserl's project is "the transcendental 'parallel' to Joyce's," Derrida claims (*O,* p. 103). Indeed, rather than reducing equivocity to univocity, Joyce's endeavor consists in repeating and taking "responsibility for all equivocation, utilizing a language that could equalize the greatest possible synchrony with the greatest potential for buried, accumulated, and inter-woven intentions within each linguistic atom, each vocable, each word, each simple proposition, in all worldly cultures and their most ingenious forms" (*O,* p. 102). Yet "the equivocation generalized by Joyce" is not *symmetrically* parallel to Husserl's exigency of univocity (*O,* p. 104). Although absolute univocity in the Husserlian sense admits "an irreduc-ible, enriching, and always renascent equivocity," and is thus an infinite task, it is "the absolute horizon of equivocity," Derrida holds (*O,* pp. 103, 104). Univocity "is that without which the very equivocations of empirical culture and history would not be possible" (*O,* pp. 104–105). Hence, Joyce's project depends on the Husserlian project. The historicity and traditionality that it renders possible is also "always already presupposed by every Odyssean repetition of Joyce's type" (*O,* p. 103). Indeed, as Derrida argues, the Joycean project of resolute cul-tivation of equivocity can "only succeed by allotting its share to uni-vocity, whether it might draw from a given univocity or try to produce another. Otherwise, the very text of its repetition would have been unin-telligible; at least it would have remained so forever and for everyone" (*O,* p. 103). Therefore, the very endeavor to repeat through condensa-tion the totality of even the most distant historical cultures not only is directed in Joyce toward exhibiting "the structural unity of all empirical culture . . . in [precisely] the generalized equivocation of a writing . . . that circulates through all languages at once" (*O,* p. 102), but also pre-supposes, as Derrida emphasizes in "Two Words for Joyce," "that some minimal readability, an element of univocity or an analyzable equivo-cality, resist the Joycean overload and condensation for there to be a reading *(pour qu'une lecture commence à avoir lieu)*" (*TWJ,* p. 149). Some-thing must cross the "threshold of intelligibility" for there to be a history of the work (*TWJ,* p. 149). It comes therefore as no surprise that in "Ulysses Gramophone" Derrida is in search of "universal presupposi-tions" (*UL,* p. 303), a priori structures (*UL,* pp. 276, 288, 299), "tran-scendental conditions" (*UL,* p. 298), "a priori syntheses" (*UL,* p. 299), and "a priori synthetic judgements" (*UL,* p. 285), that is, elements that are unmistakably of a philosophical nature. But as will become clear hereafter, these minimal structures of intelligibility with which Derrida is concerned throughout "Ulysses Gramophone," and without which one could not hope to begin reading Joyce, or to respond to his work, reveal themselves to be the very limits from which such philosophical projects as a totalizing onto-encyclopedia, be it of Hegelian or Joycean style, become conceivable in the first place—and not only an onto-encyclopedia, but transcendental egology, speculative logic, fundamental ontology, and the thinking of Being, Derrida claims, thus establishing the range of philosophical implications of the ensuing analyses carried out in his text. Yet, what this concern with the structures of ideality and intelligibility that not only make such projects as Joyce's possible, but also mark their limits, also shows is that in "Ulysses Gramophone," Derrida operates from a position that is neither that of Husserl, nor that of Joyce, nor, for that matter, philosophical or literary. Derrida is intent on displacing what the recourse to intelligible structures is supposed to foreground, the totalizing venture of a literature of the Joycean kind. In the same process, however, the pure ideality of the intelligible structures becomes questioned as well. Derrida remains a stranger, as it were, to both the philosophical and the literary project. And yet the significance of his reading of Joyce, although not philosophical in the classical sense, can only be appreciated and assessed *from,* and *in view* of, philosophy.

Yet if these are (some of) the stakes of "Ulysses Gramophone"—stakes that are nothing less than "serious"—what is the status of Derrida's stories, puns, and plays in that text? Are they private jokes and stories, or is there something about their very singularity, as well as about the narrative in which they are embedded, that prevents them from being merely private? Do they indeed altogether escape the domain of the public? Let me first consider the following: If, as Derrida contends, echoing in this the vast majority of Joyce scholars, the Joycean project in *Ulysses* is (at least in intent) the project of totalizing the entirety of experience, not only of humankind, its history and its languages, but of all private scenes and affects as well, how then could there be an entirely private response to Joyce's text to begin with? Moreover, supposing that Joyce could have totalized, predated as it were, all possible private and singular responses, would that not be because they are not simply private in the first place? What if a singular event, or a so-called private experience, requires, for the constitution of its identity as a singular event, that it double or repeat itself *as such,* in other words, that it turn minimally ideal? Must it not be at least minimally intelligible in order for it to be recognized as what it is, a singular event, and in order to permit response to it as something singular? Yet, if the private, the singular, and even the idiosyncratic are not without minimal universal traits of intelligibility (which secure their readability), and hence are not entirely different (not simply in a relation of opposition to) from the universal, or public, the question of the possibility of the merely personal, private, takes on still another turn. Is a singular, and that also means a responsible, response, possible at all? Rather than a text positively studded with endless private puns and jokes or personal stories, "Ulysses Gramophone" might well represent an elaborate first attempt to secure the very possibility of something like singularity. Singularity, rather than being something that comes easily, lightly, playfully, might be something that has to be wrenched from forces that make it a very difficult thing to achieve, as for instance, if one is to *respond,* as an outsider moreover, to the Joyce scholars' invitation to open one of their annual international symposiums. If a response requires that it be an event, that is, singular, one that is not anticipatable, predictable, or derivable from a program, how then is one to respond to that invitation to respond to a corpus seemingly intended to preclude a response in the strict sense. What is at issue in "Ulysses Gramophone" is nothing less than how a response is possible to such an event as *Ulysses,* in other words, a singular event. It is the question of responsibility itself that this text thus attempts to elaborate. A genuinely philosophical theme is at the center of "Ulysses Gramophone." Yet if it is not simply a philosophical text—a text lecturing on the possibility of response, event, singularity, responsibility—that is because (and in this it is a text) it takes up the challenge of the Joyce Society to *respond*—and to respond in an event worthy of the name—to *Ulysses.* It is a text that also seeks *to be* a response, singular, and yet owed to the event "Joyce," hence responsible.

But let me return once again to the question of the readability of texts such as *Ulysses* and *Finnegans Wake,* which achieve their totalizing thrust largely through procedures of condensation that seem to render these texts both opaque to understanding and untranslatable into any given linguistic or cognitive idiom. These same texts, however, also demand to be read, they call for translation. Just as a reading response to their writing must consist in beginning to consent to the norms of minimal unequivocal intelligibility staged and repeated in these texts, so "translate one must" (*DMJ,* p. 45) by reenacting the law constitutive of these texts. To give an example, one must seek to translate the Joycean phrase "he war," although, as Derrida remarks, "to translate 'he war' into the system of a single language . . . is to erase the event of the mark, not only what is said in it but its very saying and writing, the mark of its law and the law of its mark" (*TWJ*, p. 155). Any such translation "would erase the simple fact: a multiplicity of idioms not only of meanings but of idioms, must have structured this event of writing which henceforth stands as law, and will have laid down the law *about itself (Il aura fait la loi à son propre sujet)*" (*TWJ*, p. 155). As the context in *Finnegans Wake* shows, in "he war" "war" functions simultaneously as an English noun and a German verb. Apart from all other semantic, phonic, and graphic virtualities which communicate with "he war" throughout the book, Joyce's phrase names YAHWEH's declaration of war on the Shem. In this sense of war, "he was it *(war)* by being himself this act of war which consisted in declaring, as he did, that he was the one he was *(war)*" (*TWJ*, p. 154), Derrida writes. Now, even if one could make all other implicit meanings and referrals of "he war" audible "the graft . . . of one language on the body of another" (*TWJ*, p. 155), the multiplicity of languages tied together in one event—in the singularity of a writing event—resists all translation. "The call to translate rejects you," Derrida notes (*TWJ*, p. 154). To respond to that call, and one must respond to it, would mean to do justice to precisely this unique event of being written at once in German and English, of tying together in one occurrence two heterogeneous idioms. Yet to respond to that demand forecloses the possibility of a repetition of the event in question since it is unique, singular, thus irreplaceable. To do justice to it, a response, a translation, must take upon itself the *law* that this event has laid down for itself, that has constituted this event in its very singularity and irreplaceability, and that causes it to be not translatable in the classical sense, or utterable, but readable. This minimal intelligibility that constitutes "he war" is the law of the singular "unity" in one writing performance of what cannot be spoken at the same time, two languages as different as English and German. The possibility of a responsible response to "he war," to its call to be read and translated, is grounded in this law that renders its opaqueness readable. In repeating this law, in enacting it in another singular event, one relates in a responding fashion to the uniqueness and singularity of the event constituted by it.

If this question of the minimal readability of texts such as *Ulysses* and *Finnegans Wake* stands at the center of Derrida's writings on Joyce it does so because the answer to this question determines the very possibility of responding to such texts. Yet what is true of Joyce's text is also true of "Ulysses Gramophone," and of Derrida's texts in general. The readability of "Ulysses Gramophone," of a text whose subtitle reads "Ouï-dire de Joyce," ("Hear Say Yes in Joyce") hinges on the singular status and the minimal law of intelligibility constitutive of the *hapax legomenon* "Ouï-dire." Not only does this unheard-of linguistic formation represent part (together with the "Oui-rire") of Derrida's *response* to *Ulysses,* but the demand for translation by this untranslatable event, whose minimal readability we must begin to establish in what follows, sets the stage for any response to Derrida's own text.

"Ulysses Gramophone" is admittedly a narrative text that poses its serious question, the question of the *yes* in Joyce, only in passing (*UL,* p. 263).[17] Indeed, in his communication to the Joyce Society, Derrida sets out to chronicle his *"experiences in Tokyo" UL,* p. 263), that is, events before and while preparing for the conference. "Ulysses Gramophone" recounts a series of random occurrences, coincidental experiences, seemingly personal affects and musings that, at first, look entirely insignificant and without the slightest relevance to the work and the question to be addressed. And yet, as the lecture proceeds, it becomes clear that even the apparently most insignificant and unrelated experiences are already pre-programmed, anticipated, recorded in *Ulysses.* Derrida remarks: "This is one of the things I wanted to demonstrate . . . in recounting all these stories, true ones moreover, about the postcard in Tokyo, the trip to Ohio, or the phone call from Rabaté. We have verified that all this had its narrative paradigm and was *already* recounted in *Ulysses.* Everything that happened to me, including the narrative that I would attempt to make of it, was already pre-dicted and pre-narrated, in its dated singularity, prescribed in a sequence of knowledge and narration: within *Ulysses,* to say nothing of *Finnegans Wake,* by a hypermnesic machine capable of storing in an immense epic work Western memory and virtually all the languages in the world *including traces of the future.* Yes, everything has already happened to us with *Ulysses* and has been signed in advance by Joyce" (*UL,* p. 281). Even the most insignificant occurrences evidence "the great circular return, the autobiographic-encyclopedic circumnavigation of Ulysses" (*UL,* p. 262). Or, differently put: one is always already "responding" to Ulysses. However haphazard one's experiences may be, one is always already at the conference, lecturing on the "long circular voyage around the Mediterranean lake" (*UL,* p. 263). Owing to its procedures of condensation and inscription of just about anything according to the minimal traits of intelligibility, including those of singularity, *Ulysses* reminds us of the fact that nothing is insignificant enough to escape its totalizing venture. It furthermore reminds us that any gesture to take the initiative and to respond to *Ulysses* is "already announced in an overpotentialized text that will remind you, at a given moment, that you are captive in a network of language, writing, knowledge, and *even narration*" (*UL,* p. 281). Narration itself is pre-programmed by the autobiographic encyclopedic circumnavigation of *Ulysses*. Not only narration, but also knowledge, academic competence, metadiscursive ingenuity! As Derrida remarks, no one has been more successful than Joyce at calculating "his feat *(son coup),* by modifying it in accordance with certain types of world research institutions prepared to use not only means of transport, of communication, of organizational programming allowing an accelerated capitalization, a crazy accumulation of interest in terms of knowledge blocked in Joyce's name, even as he lets you all sign in his name . . . but also modes of archivization and consultation of data unheard of for all the grandfathers," such as Homer, Plato, Shakespeare, Dante, Vico, Hegel (*UL,* p. 280). Conclusion: "nothing can be invented *on the subject* of Joyce" (*UL,* p. 281). It is impossible to imagine a response not already pre-programmed in Joyce's work. In short, although one is always already responding, always already embarked on the encyclopedic circumnavigation, be it in the narrative or the cognitive mode, one has not even yet begun to respond if all responses are already foretold. If with Joyce everything imaginable, even a chance encounter, "is always taken in hand by the law, by meaning, by the program, according to the overdetermination of figures and ruses" (*UL,* p. 258), as well as by the erudite and scholarly approach, thus precluding the possibility of any genuine response to his work—that is, a response not already pre-calculated and pre-programmed—that would address the Joycean text in its very singularity, how, then, can one hope to respond to such a work?

The paradox is thus the following: The event signed by Joyce, *Ulysses,* asks for a response, demands that it be counter-signed by other events, but "the singular novelty of any other *yes,* of any other signature, finds itself already programophoned in the Joycean corpus" (*UL,* p. 283). What thus *remains* to be done? How can one answer the call to respond responsibly and responsively if in advance all responses have already been pre-narrated and anticipated? How can there be a response if all response is precluded by having been pre-calculated?[18] Derrida's answer to this question, centering on the word *yes* in *Ulysses,* not only responds to the paradox of responding to Joyce's work, but itself begins a response to the Joycean text.

The question of the *yes* has "mobilized or traversed everything I have been trying to think, write, teach, or read" for a long time, Derrida writes (*UL,* p. 287). In *Ulysses* Derrida directs his attention to Molly's *yeses*—although his reading highlights their resonance with all the other *yeses* throughout the book—in particular to her first and last *yes,* the *yes* that "circumnavigates and circumcises, encircling the last chapter of *Ulysses*" (*UL,* p. 288). Now, Derrida holds that even though one can and must distinguish Molly's "eschatological final 'Yes' " from the signing Yes of Joyce, because after all in *Ulysses* Molly's "yes" is only a figure and moment, "they read each other and call out to each other. To be precise, they call to each other across a *yes,* which always inaugurates a scene of call and request: it confirms and countersigns. Affirmation demands *a priori* confirmation, repetition, safekeeping, and the memory of the *yes*" (*UL,* p. 288). The rationale for this argument will only become clear hereafter. For the moment, it is with the connection of the question of the *yes* to that of the signature that I am concerned. This curious connection becomes intelligible only if one realizes that a signature is not merely "the affixation of . . . [a] seal in the form of a surname or the play of signifiers, as they say, in which to reinscribe [for instance] the name 'Joyce' " (*UL,* p. 289).[19] Signature occurs, strictly speaking, only when the gesture with which one writes one's name is "the *synthetic* performative of a promise and a memory conditioning every commitment," in other words, when there is "the sense of *yes,* this is my name, I certify this, and, yes, yes, I will be able to attest to this again. I will remember later, I promise, that it is really I who signed" (*UL,* p. 279). A signature, consequently, always implies a *yes,* a double *yes* indeed, as we shall see, and only as such is it the required and obligating departure point of all discourse (*UL,* p. 279). Yet, when the signature is understood in this manner, as "the irreversible commitment of the person confirming, who *says* or *does* yes, the token of a mark left behind," the question of the signature, of its necessary uniqueness, overlaps with that of the singularity of the event (*UL,* p. 295). The "irreplaceable mark" of the signature is the mark of a continued engagement in the event in its very singularity. It constitutes it, so to speak, as an event, as a necessarily unique, singular happening. The question of the *yes* raised here is clearly a question that attempts to elucidate "what happens with *Ulysses,* or with the arrival of whatever" (*UL,* p. 295), in other words, with singular events as such, and thus how to respond to what arrives.

Yet what happens with *Ulysses* is also the unfolding of "the sum total of all sum totals," and a corresponding attempt to reconstitute it in and by "the totalizing hermeneutic that makes up the task of a worldwide and eternal institution of Joyce studies" (*UL,* p. 291). In short, what happens with *Ulysses* is an event that seems to have interiorized, and aborted, from the outset all possible response to it. How can this be, if *Ulysses* is an event, unique and singular, inaugurated by the *yes* of Joyce's signature? To understand how the *yes* of the signature can, while calling for a response, also prevent a response from happening, it is necessary to focus on the structure of the *yes* itself.

Listening to the word "yes" in Ulysses brings a very odd, more precisely a very *singular,* word into focus. "Yes" is a word about which "it is difficult to say something very definite, and certainly metalinguistic." It is an "odd *(singulier)* word . . . which names nothing, describes nothing, whose grammatical and semantic status is most enigmatic" (*UL,* p. 265). It would, therefore, of course, have been advisable, Derrida remarks, to precede all examination of this word "with a long, learned and thoughtful meditation on the meaning, the function, above all the pre-supposition of the *yes:* before language, in language, but also in an experience of the plurality of languages that perhaps no longer belongs to linguistics in the strict sense" (*UL,* p. 296). By contrast, one thing that seems to be beyond all doubt is that "yes" always must be taken as an answer. Indeed, does this word not always have the *form* of an answer? "It occurs after the other, to answer a request or a question, at least implicit, of the other, even if this is the other in me, the representation in me of another speech . . . *Yes* always has the meaning, the function, the mission of an *answer,* even if this answer . . . sometimes has the force of an originary and unconditional commitment" (*UL,* p. 265). Yet one of the books that Derrida picks up in the basement store of the Hotel Okura in Tokyo is entitled *Never Take Yes for an Answer.* (The other book's title was *Sixteen Ways to Avoid Saying No,* a book of commercial diplomacy about how not to say no even when one means it.) In the diplomatic-commercial context, a *yes* can indeed mean "no," or simply not be an answer at all (*UL,* pp. 264–265). It may not be prudent, Derrida concludes, to assume that a *yes* is always an answer. Such prudence is especially warranted in an examination of "what happens when the word *yes* is written, quoted, repeated, archived, recorded, gramophoned, or is the subject of translation or transfer" (*UL,* p. 266). As a matter of fact, as we shall see later, there is also—and Derrida notes its "curious designation"—"a question of the *yes.*" *Yes* also questions, demands, requests (*UL,* p. 288). It also asks for a *yes* to be said to it, or to be asked to say *yes.* "Yes," consequently, is a singular word because, in spite of everything that one may confidently affirm about it, it may be still more complex. But this small word is singular as well because it is not even sure that it is a word. Derrida writes: "We do not know whether this word shares anything at all with any other word in any language, even with the word *no,* which is most certainly not symmetrical to it. We do not know if a grammatical, semantic, linguistic, rhetorical, or philosophical concept exists capable of this event marked *yes*" (*UL,* p. 274). Any response to the word "yes" in *Ulysses,* must start out without the metalinguistic security of a theory regarding its operation in language. A response to this singular word, if it is one, thus requires a decision, that is, a noncalculable or non–pre-programmed risk. "Let us, and this is not merely a fiction, act *as if* this [lack of a theory] does not prevent us, on the contrary, from hearing what the word *yes* governs" (*UL,* p. 274). Indeed, the absence of a theory identifying the status of the word *yes* is what allows us to hear what that word does and says.

Listening to what the word *yes* commands makes it impossible not to hear that each *yes* "always appears as a *yes, yes*" (*UL,* p. 296). This is stated first about the *affirmative yes:* "In order for the *yes* of affirmation, assent, consent, alliance, of engagement, signature, or gift to have the value it has, it must carry the repetition within itself. It must *a priori* and immediately confirm its promise and promise its confirmation" (*UL,* p. 276). This "essential repetition" (*UL,* p. 276) and doubling of any *yes* is a transcendental condition for all affirmation, assent, consent, and so on. "*A priori* [the second *yes*] reproduces [the first *yes*] in the absence of all intentional presence of the affirmer." Even the most spontaneous, the most giving desire of the *yes* cannot but reaffirm itself instantly in order to preserve "as its truth the living *yes.*" Indeed, "such is the condition of a signed commitment. The *Yes* can only state *itself* by promising itself its own memory . . . *Yes* must preserve itself, and thus reiterate itself, archive its voice in order to allow it once again to be heard" (*UL,* p. 276). Even as an answer to the Other as a singular Other, a *yes* can be the affirmation that it promises only if it achieves a minimal ideality and identity by repeating itself. This idealizing, or what amounts to the same, universalizing repetition of the most singular *yes*—of a *yes* that responds to the Other as singular—is the transcendental condition for a *yes* to be *yes*, indeed, to be a response respectful of the singularity of the Other. This doubling of the *yes* secures the affirmation's minimal intelligibility even, and especially, if this affirmation is a genuinely singular, responsive, and responsible act.

But the essential repetition without which any *yes*, however spontaneous and singular, can meet what it promises also, and necessarily, grounds the possibility of mere mechanical repetition, of servile reproduction, and even of parody. I quote: "This essential repetition lets itself be haunted by an intrinsic threat, by an internal telephone which parasites it like its mimetic, mechanical double, like its incessant parody." Although only a repetition can preserve the living *yes*, and what it promises, this very repetition is fatally linked to the possibility "of a *yes* technique that persecutes the most spontaneous, the most giving desire of the *yes*" (*UL*, p. 276).

With this I return to the question of the possibility of responding to a work such as *Ulysses*. The response that such a work calls for, that must double and countersign its signature, can, indeed, become a mechanical and servile repetition, one that from the start lacks the genuine aspects of a response. Undoubtedly, the double *yes* is ambiguous: "one of them comes down to the Christian assumption of one's burden, the *Ja, Ja* of the donkey overloaded as Christ was with memory and responsibility, and the other light, airy, dancing, solar *yes, yes* is also a *yes* of reaffirmation, of promise, of oath, a *yes* to eternal recurrence," Derrida writes while referring to the double *yes* in Nietzsche's *Zarathustra* (*UL*, p. 287). Competent Joycean scholarship and the institution of Joyce studies correspond, for Derrida, to such a reproductive and servile *yes*. The Joyce scholar responds to *Ulysses* by memorizing, archiving, and institutionalizing the totality of knowledge, narrative, and effects of literary condensation that are pre-programmed by that work. Yet this non-response to Joyce is itself the mechanical reproduction of the burdensome and ambiguous *yes* with which Joyce's own signature invites or "gets going— some might say submits itself, at any rate restarts *for itself*, so that it might return to itself—the most competent and reliable production and reproduction machine" (*UL*, p. 282). Because the *yes* of the signature is always haunted by the possibility of mechanical reaffirmation, responding to it can always fail to take the singularity of the inaugurated event into account. Such is the case with Joyce, and Joyce himself is responsible for it. What the ambiguous *yes* signs is nothing less than the elimination of the place of the Other. Still, the servile *yes* is only one possible modification of the essential *yes,* which "at the limit . . . is co-extensive with every statement" (*UL,* p. 296), to quote Derrida. In search of what a responsible response to the event "Joyce" could be, it is thus necessary to return to the question of the *yes.*

What has been established up to this point is the a priori necessity of reaffirming a *yes* of affirmation. Without such essential repetition, the singularity of this event as a response would not be what it promises. But if any affirmation, more generally "any event brought about by a performative mark, any writing in the widest sense of the word involves a *yes,* whether this is phenomenalized or not, that is, verbalized or adverbalized as such" (*UL,* p. 298), it does so also because any act of *vouloir-dire,* of meaning, or signification, presupposes, prior to that act, a relating to or addressing of the Other. "A *yes* never comes alone, and we never say this word alone," Derrida remarks (*UL,* p. 298). Any affirmation of whatever kind, any phenomenal *yes,* any "manifest *yes* patently marked as a *word,* spoken or phonogramed" (*UL,* p. 297), requires—without therefore necessarily being spoken or written—"a *yes* more 'ancient' " (*UL,* p. 296). This pre-performative and "transcendental condition of all performative dimensions" (*UL,* p. 298) is "the minimal, primary *yes,* the telephonic 'hello' or tap through a prison wall, [which] marks, before meaning or signifying, 'I-here,' listen answer, there is some mark, there is some other" (*UL,* p. 298). This "*yes* indicates that there is address to the other" (*UL,* p. 299). It is a *yes* before all speech, and hence before all possible dialogue or interlocution; it is nothing but, in advance of all saying or demand, "the haste, in advance *(précipitation),* of a response that is already asking" (*UL,* p. 299). The 'presence' of an Other, for structural reasons, requires that all exchange with him or her be preceded by a response to the Other as Other—by a minimal and primary *yes.* It is this *yes* to the Other that prevents the Other from being reduced to me, becoming *my* Other, the Other of myself. Derrida writes: "For if there is some other, if there is some *yes,* then the Other no longer lets itself be produced by the same or by the ego. *Yes,* the condition of any signature and of any performative, addresses itself to some other which it does not constitute, and it can only begin by *asking* the other, in response to a request that has always already been made, to *ask* it to say *yes*" (*UL,* p. 299). The primary *yes* in question is, in essence, a demand that the response to the Other be demanded by the Other, that it be owed to the Other. It is the demanding response to the Other for a *yes,* for a request to be asked to be addressed. Indeed, if the Other is to be respected as Other, even the *yes* of the address to it must be owed by, or owed to, the Other. Derrida continues: "The *yes* says nothing and asks only for another *yes,* the *yes* of an other, which . . . is analytically—or by *a priori* synthesis—implied in the first *yes.* The latter only situates itself, advances itself, marks itself in the call for its confirmation, in the *yes, yes.* It begins with *yes, yes,* with the second *yes.*" (*UL,* p. 299).[20] Since the *yes* that addresses itself to the Other appeals to the Other to be asked to say *yes* to it, the primary and minimal *yes* is, structurally speaking, *only on the verge* of responding: "it begins by responding" (*UL,* p. 301). At the beginning there is a response, but that response is only *a beginning response.* Or, in the seemingly more playful language of "Ulysses Gramophone": "In the beginning, there must indeed have been some phone call. Before the act or the word, the telephone. In the beginning was the telephone. We can hear the telephone constantly ringing." (*UL,* p. 270). In other words, not unlike Bloom, who, in *Ulysses,* is constantly on the phone, before any particular act of meaning or signification, one always waits "for someone to say, 'hello, yes,' that is, for someone to say, 'Yes, yes,' beginning with the telephonic *yes* indicating that there is indeed another voice, if not an answering machine, on the other end of the line" (*UL,* p. 274).[21]

Yet this structure according to which the Other must be addressed in an appeal to say *yes* to the address prior to all possible acts or engagements can also lend itself to acts of negation or denegation of the Other. It must be remarked, however, that this possibility is not the symmetrical counterpart of the enabling fundamental structure in question. All negation or denegation of the Other presupposes it. It remains the condition of possibility—and hence unchallenged in its a prioriness—of its own "falling." Let us note that although the problematic of negation of the Other is explicitly broached in "Ulysses Gramophone" only under the rubric of the so-called monological structure of the last chapter of *Ulysses,* the context and the terms of the debate leave no doubt that this discussion pertains to the whole of *Ulysses,* to what Derrida called its autobiographic-encyclopedic thrust. And, consequently, the stakes of this debate also concern the possibility of responding to an event such as Joyce's work.

The *yes* requested from the Other to confirm the *yes* to the Other doubles the *yes* in still another *yes, yes.* The "*yes* says nothing but *yes:*

another *yes* that resembles the first even if it says *yes* to the advent of a completely other *yes*" (*UL*, pp. 299–300), Derrida writes. Although the second *yes* is the other *yes* in the structure in question, only a *yes* recalls itself. Consequently, this doubling can have the appearance of a monologue, of archi-narcissism and auto-affection. If this is so, it is because the structure of the *yes, yes* "opens up the position of the I, which is itself the condition for performativity" (*UL*, p. 300). It is the condition of possibility, or the "minimal *proposition*," "implied in every *cogito* as thought, self-positing, and will to self-positing" (UL, pp. 300–301). With the hetero-tautological *yes,* the movement of circular reappropriation commences, that is, the odyssey that can give rise to tautology, narcissism, egology, or, since Joyce's *Ulysses* is at issue here, to the encyclopedic synthesis of all knowledge through textual overdeterminacy. The very same structure that acknowledges the place of the Other also makes possible the speculative or imaginary project of a complete mastery of the Other, the reduction of the Other to an Other of self, to the Other of the same. The *yes, yes* opens up nothing less than the dream of a closure in which all Otherness would be comprehended, a closure inside or outside of which there would be no room for a response since, with this closure, the place of the Other would have been, it would seem, entirely eliminated. And yet, it must be reemphasized that, although the structure of the *yes, yes* is the condition of possibility of such a project or phantasm, it itself is neither tautological, nor narcissistic, nor egological. What this minimal *proposition* holds is, indeed, that *everything* "begins with the *yes, yes,* with the second *yes*" (*UL*, p. 299), the more ancient *yes.* The relay through an Other "holds open the circle that it institutes" (*UL*, p. 302). Whether this circle is that of the self-positing I or of the autobiographic-encyclopedic venture of *Ulysses,* it remains suspended from the confirmation by the Other. The Other's *yes inhabits*—I wish this word to resonate with the original meanings of *ethos*—the *yes* by which the self posits itself, or by which the circle of knowledge seeks to become self-inclusive. Derrida writes: "a *yes* to the *yes* inhabits the arrival of the 'first' *yes,* which is never therefore simply originary." The "first breath of *yes* . . . is suspended in the breath of the Other, it is already and always, a second breath" (*UL*, pp. 304–305).[22]

The analysis of the *yes, yes* thus yields two very distinct a priori conditions: (1) any event, however singular, and it is an event only if it is singular, requires repetition in order to be what it is; (2) any event can affirm itself only by being confirmed by an Other, by an entirely other event. *Yes, yes* is thus double itself. In "Ulysses Gramophone," Derrida responds to these two distinct structural necessities dramatized in *Ulysses* by drawing them together in an infrastructure of sorts, that is, in the singular linguistic construct, or *hapax legomenon,* "Ouï dire." Combining the meaning of "saying yes" *(oui dire)* and "hear say" *(ouï-dire)* in a synthetic condensation or constellation that "no etymological filiation between the two words 'oui' and 'ouï' " (*UL,* p. 291) justifies—Derrida takes pain to stress this lack of justification—*ouï-dire,* or *hear say yes,* is untranslatable, hence singular, since it fully works only in French, "which exploits the obscure, babelian homonomy of *oui* with just a dotted 'i,' and *ouï* with a diaresis" (*UL,* p. 267). Both this untranslatability and the forced interlinkage of *oui* and *ouï* cause "*ouï-dire*" to be a unique—single and singular—response to the "universal presuppositions" (*UL,* p. 303) exhibited in Derrida's reading of the Joycean *yeses.* What looks like a mere pun and irresponsible wordplay has the structure of a response in that it addresses what in the *yes* calls for its double doubling. But before further emphasizing this point, let us first see how *ouï-dire* succeeds in tying together, and thus "accounting" for, the two distinct structural necessities in question. Here is how Derrida unravels the meanings of "Ouï-dire de Joyce," the subtitle of "Ulysses Gramophone": "saying *yes* in Joyce but also the saying or the *yes* that is heard, the *saying yes* that travels round like a quotation or a rumor circulating, circumnavigating, via the ear's labyrinth, that which we know only by hearsay" (*UL,* p. 267). First, then, *ouï-dire* is the most economic rendering of the structural fact that any *yes* needs an idealizing repetition, that in *Ulysses yes* can only be "a mark at once written and spoken, vocalized as a grapheme and written as a phoneme, yes, *in a word, gramophoned*" (*UL,* p. 267). In its very brevity, *ouï-dire* signifies that the affirmation of a *yes* must "reiterate itself, archive its voice in order to once again be heard"—that *yes,* a priori, gramophones itself, that it hears itself always already say *yes* (*UL,* p. 276). Yet, second, *ouï-dire* inscribes the equally necessary structural fact that any *yes* must be confirmed by an other *yes,* the *yes* of an Other, the *yes* one knows from hear say, so to speak. In the crispness of its concision, *ouï-dire* remarks that one is never alone in saying *yes,* and that the affirmation that it enacts can affirm itself only in hearing the Other respond *yes* to what, in appearance, was the first *yes.*

Yet, in his essay on Joyce, Derrida flanks the investigation into the transcendental conditions of intelligibility—or minimal readability—of saying *yes,* of the signature that always implies a *yes,* with an inquiry into a "fundamental, quasi-transcendental tonality" (*UL,* p. 295) linked to the word *yes* in *Ulysses,* as well as to the event of the signature. This tonality is that of laughter, yet not of the various qualities, modalities, *genres* of laughter to be encountered in the book, or of, say, Joyce actually, factually laughing, but of a transcendental laughter, as it were, structurally tied up with saying *yes,* or signing an event. Compared with everything that has been said about laughter in Joyce, the tonality here in question is that of laughter precisely "as a remains" (*UL,* p. 291). Derrida writes: "Once one recognizes that, in principle, in *Ulysses* the virtual totality of experience . . . tends to unfold itself and reconstitute itself by playing out all its possible combinations, with writing that seeks to occupy virtually all the spaces, well, the totalizing hermeneutic that makes up the task of a worldwide and eternal institution of Joyce studies will find itself confronted with what I hesitatingly call a dominant effect, a *Stimmung* or a *pathos,* a tone which retraverses all the others yet which does not participate in the series of the others since it *re-marks (re-traverse)* all of them, adds itself to them without allowing itself to be added in or totalized, in the manner of a remainder that is both quasi-transcendental and supplementary" (*UL,* p. 291). This tonality is, according to Derrida, that of *oui-rire,* a *yes* that laughs, a laughing *yes,* a *yes-laughter.*

Before I embark on a more detailed elucidation of this quasi-transcendental tonality of yes-laughter, it needs to be recalled that the linkage of the question of laughter to that of the "yes" serves once again to think the singularity of the event, and the uniqueness of the signature. This time, however, what constitutes an event, an event such as *Ulysses* but, as Derrida also claims, "beyond even *Ulysses*" (*UL,* p. 292) is shown to be of the order of tonality, mood, or pathos. What constitutes the event in its singularity, apart from the intelligible structures discussed with *oui-dire,* is something that, to use classical terms, is of the order of the affects, the *pathe* or even the practical. What Derrida broaches under the title of yes-laughter is a kind of affect not unlike the few rational affects analyzed in classical philosophy (*respect,* for instance) which has an essential function in the arrival of an event. I read: "if laughter is a fundamental or abyssal tonality in *Ulysses,* if the analysis of this laughter is not exhausted by any of the available forms of knowledge precisely because it laughs at knowledge and from knowledge, then laughter bursts out in the event of signature itself" (*UL,* p. 295).

In Derrida's exploration of laughter in Joyce, "of who is laughing and how laughter comes about *with* Joyce—in Joyce, in an odd way—since *Ulysses,*" two kinds of yes-laughter come into view. Just as we saw with the *yes,* each one of the structures that characterizes it lends itself to a foreclosure precisely of what it opened. Yes-laughter is double, and commands a "double relationship" to it (*UL,* p. 292). First, Derrida distinguishes a reactive, even negative, yes-laughter in *Ulysses.* It is the laughter of "Nietzsche's Christian donkey, the one that cries *Ja, Ja*" (*UL,* p. 293), that is, a "yes-laughter of encircling reappropriation, of omnipotent Odyssean recapitulation" (*UL,* p. 294), a laughter in affirmation that "reaffirms control of a subjectivity that draws everything together as it draws itself together" (*UL,* p. 293). This is the yes-laughter of a Joyce "laughing at his omnipotence, at this great *tour joué:* a trick played and a grand tour completed" (*UL,* p. 292). Derrida continues: "But the eschatological tone of this yes-laughter also seems to me to be worked or traversed—I prefer to say *haunted*—joyously ventriloquised by a completely different music" (*UL,* p. 294). What haunts—in other words, *what belongs in,* in the way, for instance, animals belong in their haunts *(ethos)*—the reactive yes-laughter is "the yes-laughter of a gift without debt, light affirmation, almost amnesic, of a gift or abandoned event, which in classical language is called 'the work,' a lost signature without a proper name that reveals and names the cycle of reappropriation and domestication of all the paraphs only to delimit their fantasm, and does so in order to contrive the breach necessary for the coming of the other." (*UL,* pp. 294–295). As Derrida emphasizes, this second yes-laughter that haunts the first, reactive one is "very close to the other one *(tout près de l'autre)*" (*UL,* p. 294). Indeed, the reactive yes-laughter presupposes (for its possibility) "the other *yes* [which] laughs, the Other, yes, [who] laughs" (*UL,* p. 304). It is at the very place "where transcendental egology, ontoencyclopedia, great speculative logic, fundamental ontology and the thought on Being open onto a thought of the gift and sending *(envoi)* which they presuppose but cannot contain" (*UL,* p. 302) that the possibility of *yes* and yes-laughter must be situated. With the interlacing of *yes* and yes-laughter with the singular structure of *ouï-dire,* or *hear say yes,* which articulates an essential interrelatedness of addressing, giving, requesting, repeating, and so on, "we are in an area which is *not yet* the space where the large questions of the origin of negation, of affirmation or of denegation, can and must be unfolded," Derrida holds (*UL,* p. 298). With the *question* of the *yes,* and of yes-laughter, we are also in a space that is not yet the space where the question of Being, and the response to it, develop. We are here in an area in which only the quasi-transcendental conditions for these big questions are elaborated.

The second yes-laughter of the unconditional gift, of the renunciation

of reappropriation, is the laughing yes in the work which calls on another
yes, the *yes* of the Other, of its, his, or her response and countersignature
of the event of the gift. But what the yes–laughter of the light affirmation
requests is a responsible response, a response that affirms the uncondi-
tionality of the gift, as well as the singularity of its occurring in a singular
event. It demands a response free of all calculation, one that lets go,
absolutely, of all acts of reckoning and all desire for reappropriation.
What this yes–laughter of the gift requests of the Other for which, or
whom, it opens up the necessary space in the work is that it, he, or she
begin to respond, and that this beginning countersignature, in its turn,
appeal by its very singularity to the *yes* of still another Other. In short,
the light affirmation of yes–laughter affirms infinite responsibility, one
that remains suspended from the Other, and that does not suffer any
terminal fulfillment. All these are the conditions under which a response
is genuinely responsive and responsible. A genuine response to what in
a work is open to the arrival of the Other has thus all the allure of
irresponsibility: it is singular, untranslatable, affirming the chance of
encounters and the randomness of coincidences, never in its own, or
arriving at itself, always only beginning. A response that truly addresses
the Other cannot have the security, the certainty, of being an unconditional affirmation. This lack of safety in responding has its essential
reasons. It results from the closeness of the yes–laughter of light affirmation to the reactive one: "The *yes* of memory, with its recapitulating
control and reactive repetition, immediately doubles the light, dancing
yes of affirmation, the open affirmation of the gift" (*UL,* p. 308). Yet
this possible contamination of one *yes,* or one *oui-dire,* by the other is
not merely a fatal and regrettable necessity: "the relationship of a *yes* to
the Other, of a *yes* to the other and of one *yes* to the other yes, must be
such that the contamination of these two *yeses* remains inevitable" (*UL,*
p. 304). The two yeses *must* contaminate themselves precisely because
what seems to be a threat is also an opportunity, a chance, the only
chance of a responsible response. Without that risk, without the threat
of contamination, there could not possibly be a genuine response. The
lack of such a threat would make response impossible. It is thus not a
question of deciding or choosing between the two *yeses,* or the two yes-
laughters, the light and the negative one, either in *Ulysses* or in one's
response to them. In *Ulysses,* Derrida notes, "the two *yes-laughters* of
differing quality call one to the other, call for and imply each other
irresistibly" (*UL,* p. 307). As with the two *yeses* that Nietzsche distin-

guishes, the difference between the two yes-laughters "remains unstable, subtle, sublime. One repetition haunts the other" (*UL,* p. 287). They defy binarism, and hence, as far as *Ulysses* is concerned, "the two responses or two responsibilities refer to each other without having any relationship between them" (*UL,* p. 308). What these two responses achieve is to "prevent the signature from gathering itself together" (*UL,* p. 308). "But this failure is the chance of a response to them, of a countersigning *yes.* The two yes-laughters can only call up another *yes,* another signature" (*UL,* p. 308). Yet, as should be obvious from what has been established so far, this Other that *Ulysses* calls upon to countersign can always be "the head of the megaprogramotelephonic network" of derivative Joyce scholarship. Rather than "the unforeseeable other for whom a place must be kept"—Elijah, the Other—"Elija the great operator" may present himself. "But there we are," Derrida concludes, "this is a homonym, Elijah can always be one and the other at the same time, we cannot invite the one, without the risk of the other turning up. But this is a risk that must always be run" (*UL,* p. 295).

There is no responsible response to *Ulysses* without a double relationship to the two *yeses,* or the two yes-laughters. This double relationship "is instituted and requested, required by the Joycean signature itself" (*UL,* p. 292). Without the risk of the servile *yes* and the mastering laughter, without the threat of repetition and universal programmation, there would not even be a chance to respond. Derrida's reading and rewriting of Joyce in "Ulysses Gramophone" is instructed by this double relationship to both the *yes* and the *laughter* in Joyce, to both types of yes-laughter. In saying *ouï-dire/oui-rire,* Derrida responds to Joyce, to the one who, as he admits, "remains a stranger to me" (*UL,* p. 280). Estrangement, rather than familiarity—the familiarity of the Joyce scholars with Joyce—may well be the condition under which alone a genuine response may be possible: a singular response that is owed to and by the Other.

The reading of "Ulysses Gramophone" offered here should have dispelled its appearance of frivolity. The question of the *yes* that it poses is a "serious" question, a question that is significant only with respect to the great questions of philosophy, including the question of Being. Every "joke" or "pun" also works toward a solution of the question of the *yes.* Yet, in "Ulysses Gramophone," the search for a solution to the question of the *yes* is also a response to that question, a performance of a response. Ultimately, exposition and performance are indistinguishable here. As a

performance, however, the response to the question of the *yes* is necessarily singular, singular even to a degree bordering on the frivolous.
This is the risk that all response must inevitably run. It must be acknowledged, affirmed, abandoned to happen. This possibility, as well as the
response in its singularity, must be certified, signed. Derrida must say *yes*
to it in its (possibly frivolous) singularity. His signature must endorse his
chance encounter with Joyce, and endorse it in its very randomness. Such
signature occurs in "Ulysses Gramophone," in precisely the chance
encounter of *ouï-dire* and *oui-rire*. Speaking of both, Derrida notes "the
consonantal difference between *dire* and *rire,* that is, *d* and *r,*" and he
adds, between parentheses, these "are, moreover, the only consonants in
my name" (*UL,* p. 291).

Notes

Index

Notes

Introduction

1. Rodolphe Gasché, *The Tain of the Mirror* (Cambridge: Harvard University Press, 1986).
2. Christopher Norris, "Thinking the Unthought," in *The Times Literary Supplement,* December 18–24, 1987, p. 1407.
3. Richard Rorty, *Philosophical Papers,* vol. 2: *Essays on Heidegger and Others* (New York: Cambridge University Press, 1991), p. 128.
4. Richard Rorty, *Contingency, Irony, and Solidarity* (New York: Cambridge University Press, 1989), p. 123.
5. Ibid., pp. 123–124.
6. Rorty, *Philosophical Papers,* vol. 2., pp. 122–123, 127.
7. Ibid., p. 113.
8. Rorty, *Contingency,* p. 124.
9. Rorty, *Philosophical Papers,* vol. 2, p. 102.
10. For Derrida's own judgment of my use of the term "infrastructure," see, for instance, "This Strange Institution Called Literature: An Interview with Jacques Derrida," in Jacques Derrida, *Acts of Literature,* ed. D. Attridge (New York: Routledge, 1992), pp. 70–72.
11. Rorty, *Contingency,* p. 124.
12. Rorty, *Philosophical Papers,* vol. 2, p. 126.
13. Martin Heidegger, *On the Way to Language,* trans. P. D. Hertz (San Francisco: Harper, 1982), pp. 127–128.
14. Rorty, *Contingency,* p. 124.
15. Maurice Blanchot, *The Gaze of Orpheus and Other Literary Essays,* trans. L. Davis (Barrytown, N.Y.: Station Hill Press, 1981), p. 59.
16. Rorty, *Philosophical Papers,* vol. 2, p. 120.
17. Ibid., pp. 126, 117. See also Rorty, *Contingency,* p. 133.

18. Rorty, *Contingency*, p. 125.
19. Rorty, *Philosophical Papers*, vol. 2, p. 118.
20. Rorty, *Contingency*, p. 187.
21. Rorty, *Philosophical Papers*, vol. 2, pp. 93, 119.
22. Rorty, *Contingency*, pp. 125–127.
23. Rorty, *Philosophical Papers*, vol. 2, p. 118.
24. Rorty, *Contingency*, p. 133.
25. Jacques Derrida, "Psyche: Inventions of the Other," trans. C. Porter, in *Reading de Man Reading*, ed. L. Waters and W. Godzich (Minneapolis: University of Minnesota Press, 1989), p. 29.
26. Ibid., p. 28.
27. Ibid., p. 51.
28. Ibid., p. 28 See also Jacques Derrida, *Le Probleme de la genèse dans la philosphie de Husserl* (Paris: Presses Universitaires de France, 1990), where all invention is shown to require a verification. Derrida writes: "Ultimately, an invention without verification would negate the intentionality of consciousness. Such an invention would be an invention 'of' nothing, or an invention (of) itself (by) itself, which would destroy the very meaning of all invention which is synthetic. The paradox and the strangeness of transcendental intentionality reappear at the heart of all invention." (pp. 9–10). Unless otherwise indicated, translations are mine.
29. Rorty, *Contingency*, p. 127.
30. Ibid., p. 126.
31. Rorty, *Philosophical Papers*, vol. 2, p. 93.
32. Ibid., p. 128.
33. Ibid., p. 121.
34. Ibid., p. 128.
35. Ibid., pp. 100, 111.
36. Ibid., p. 100.
37. In Rorty's discussion of the public/private opposition and what he has called "noninferential association" (*Philosophical Papers*, vol. 2, p. 98), we are given the following example of what is, for instance, in *Glas*, public and what is private: "The association between 'Hegel' and 'Hegelian' or Hegel and Spirit, is public, Derrida's association between 'Hegel' and *aigle* is private" (Rorty, *Contingency*, p. 131). Yet, on the first page of *Glas*, Derrida evokes the French pronunciation (especially during the nineteenth and early twentieth centuries) of the name of Hegel as [eg(·)l], and which sounds almost exactly like aigle [egl(·)], as he argues that this pronunciation is only partially ludicrous, because it expresses the "magisterial coldness and impertubable seriousness" of Hegel's philosophy (*G*, p. 1).

Thus, rather than being a private fantasy "aigle" refers both to a linguistic fact and to the long tradition of the imagery (heraldic, numismatic, and so on) and metaphor of the eagle as expressive of mastery, power, sovereignty. *The Postal Card,* especially its first part, entitled "Envois," is for Rorty a representative text of the later Derrida, one that would make readings such as mine less and less possible. "Its form—a sequence of love letters . . . emphasizes the privacy of the work being done. Nothing is more private than a love letter . . . there is nothing to which general ideas are less relevant or more inappropriate," he remarks (p. 126). Since "Envois" produces no result or conclusion, "there will be no 'upshot'—nothing to carry away from 'Envois' . . . once one has finished reading it." It yields no infrastructures, and hence there is no certitude of having "hit rock bottom in the search for" them (p. 130). As two of the essays in the present volume demonstrate, one devoted to the Hegel column in *Glas* (a book whose pages are divided into two columns, one devoted to Hegel, the other to Jean Genet), the other to "Ulysses Gramophone," these seemingly playful and private texts lend themselves very well to a reading similar to the one sketched out for the earlier work of Derrida in *The Tain of the Mirror.* Although this is not the place to engage in a similar reading of "Envois," the very title of this text gives us a hint. In its plurality, "Envois" suggests that this text ties together not only the question of the truth of the letter discussed in "Le Facteur de la verité" (in Jacques Derrida, *The Post Card: From Socrates to Freud and Beyond,* trans. A. Bass [Chicago: University of Chicago Press, 1989], pp. 411–496), that is, the necessity that a letter remain intelligible in the absence of its addressee and the necessary possibility of its not reaching its destination, but also the Heideggerian question of *unterwegs, Weg, Spur* (on the way, way, trace), the relation to an Other, (perhaps) also the question of the voice, and so on. The difference between a text such as "Envois" and earlier works is only that the weaving of the public problematic into something resembling an infrastructure is acted out, taking on the form of a series of love letters. Indeed, if "Envois" is such a private production as Rorty claims, how can he then claim that this text which "does not issue in anything that could conceivably be called a philosophical *theory*" nevertheless does "count as 'philosophy'?" Apart from the reasons offered by Rorty—"only people who habitually read philosophy could possibly enjoy it"; and "it counts *philosophers,* rather than their doctrines, among its causes and topics" (pp. 135–136)—is it not rather because this text deliberates in a performative mode on the intelligibility of something as private as a love letter, and its connection to other, though at first sight unrelated, issues, such as Heidegger's notion of the way-fraying movement of language?

38. Rorty, *Contingency,* pp. 134–135.

39. Ibid., p. 130.
40. This review article of *The Tain of the Mirror* appeared first in *Diacritics,* Spring 1988. It has been reprinted as "Failing Reflection" in Mark C. Taylor, *Tears* (Albany: SUNY Press, 1990), pp. 87–103.
41. Ibid., p. 87.
42. Ibid., p. 99.
43. Ibid., p. 98. The quote is from Sylviane Agacinski, *Aparté: Conceptions and Deaths of Sören Kierkegaard,* trans. K. Newmark (Tallahassee: Florida State University Press, 1988).
44. Taylor, "Failing Reflection," p. 101.
45. Ibid., p. 87.
46. Ibid., pp. 101–102.
47. Ibid., p. 102.
48. Ibid., pp. 98, 102.
49. Derrida, *Acts of Literature,* p. 374.
50. Ibid., p. 379.
51. Ibid., p. 385.
52. Ibid., pp. 389–390.
53. Ibid., p. 398.
54. Taylor, "Failing Reflection," p. 98.
55. Jacques Derrida, "The Laws of Reflection: Nelson Mandela, in Admiration," in *For Nelson Mandela,* ed. J. Derrida and M. Tlili, (New York: Seaver Books, 1987), p. 26.
56. Ibid., p. 15.
57. Ibid., p. 176.
58. Ibid., pp. 15, 34.
59. Ibid., p. 22.
60. Ibid., p. 41.
61. Jacques Derrida, *Memoires for Paul de Man,* trans. C. Lindsay et al. (New York: Columbia University Press, 1986), p. 73.
62. Jacques Derrida, *Points de suspension: Entretiens* (Paris: Galilée, 1992), pp. 314–315.
63. Derrida, "The Laws of Reflection," p. 36.
64. Derrida, *Points de suspension,* p. 315.
65. Rorty, *Contingency,* p. 129.
66. Derrida, "The Laws of Reflection," p. 37.
67. Ibid., p. 42.
68. Ibid., p. 38.
69. Rorty, *Philosophical Papers,* vol. 2, p. 128.

1. Deconstruction as Criticism

1. Paul Feyerabend, *Against Method* (London: Verso, 1978), pp. 283–284.
2. Ibid., p. 167.
3. Ibid., p. 283.
4. Wayne C. Booth, "Preserving the Exemplar: or, How Not to Dig Our Own Graves," *Critical Inquiry,* 3, no. 2 (1977), 420.
5. Until recently "post-structuralism" has been an exclusively American label that reveals more about the departmentalizing spirit in power or in search of power than about the phenomenon in question, if we accept that there is such a thing as post-structuralism at all.
6. The notion of the epistemological break as a passage from sensible to scientific knowledge not only is a much more complex notion than is usually believed, but also cannot serve to conceptualize the incommensurability between theories. I will try to show this elsewhere.
7. See Edward W. Said, *Beginnings* (New York: Basic Books, 1975; Baltimore: Johns Hopkins University Press, 1978), pp. 202–203.
8. It is with the evidence of contemporary criticism that I am concerned here and not with the at least as questionable evidences of literary criticism in general. Of these evidences one can assert that they belong "to the deepest, the oldest, and apparently the most natural, the least historical layer of our conceptuality, that which best eludes criticism, and especially because it supports that criticism, nourishes it, and informs it; our historical ground itself" (*OG,* pp. 81–82).
9. See, for instance, the "Polemical Introduction" by Northrop Frye to his *Anatomy of Criticism* (Princeton: Princeton University Press, 1973), pp. 3–29.
10. Claude Lévi-Strauss, "Introduction à l'oeuvre de Marcel Mauss," in Marcel Mauss, *Sociologie et anthropologie* (Paris: Presses Universitaires de France, 1968).
11. It is precisely this self-undermining and self-canceling of the text's constituting oppositions that brings about what J. Hillis Miller in a first attempt to analyze what the anti-deconstruction's rhetoric calls "strong language" ("The Critic as Host," *Critical Inquiry,* 3, no. 2 [1977], 442). Indeed, the modern critic's approach to the text as a self-reflexive totality fills the traditional critic with strong moral, political, and religious indignation. The apocalyptic titles used by these critics, such as Abrams' "The Deconstructive Angel" and Booth's "Preserving the Exemplar: or, How Not to Dig Our Graves" (in the same issue), speak for themselves. Booth, moreover, in analyzing criticism in terms of a pluralistic (yet limited) community of critics, accuses the deconstructionists of a sacrilegious claim to superiority—a superiority which would spring forth from the nihilistic destruction of moral and aesthetic values. Booth, consequently,

demands the banishment (as foreign agents) of those who from the beginning refuse the openness demanded of them from the "country of debate" (Booth, pp. 420–423).

12. Besides this naive confusion as to the nature of deconstruction, Derrida foresaw in *Of Grammatology* the philosopher's critique of deconstruction as dialectics: since "the enterprise of deconstruction always in a certain way falls prey to its own work . . . the person who has begun the same work in another area of the same habitation does not fail to point [this] out with zeal. No exercise is more widespread today and one should be able to formalize its rules" (*OG*, p. 24). We might at this point note the erroneousness of the nonphilosopher's common identification of deconstruction with dialectics. Since deconstruction is precisely an operation on dialectics, this mistake nevertheless gives an inkling of the rigors of deconstruction. Deconstruction indeed vies with dialectics in what Hegel called the seriousness and the work of the concept.

13. Though not using the notion of deconstruction, Cary Nelson's approach in "Reading Criticism" (*PMLA* 91, no. 5 [1976]) to reading critical language as literary language rests also on the idea of the self-referentiality of language. Nelson's analysis provides provocative insights into the nature of criticism as a discourse, no doubt. Yet, since this approach leads, in particular in Nelson's analysis of the critical works of Susan Sontag, to a definition of criticism as an endless process of self-appropriation and self-actualization through the object and the Other at a distance, and consequently to dialectics in a genuinely Hegelian way (pp. 807–808), it is an excellent example of the presuppositions and implications of so-called deconstructive criticism.

14. Said, *Beginnings,* p. 237.

15. The major critics involved are Erich Auerbach and Georges Poulet. Poulet's notion of a harmony of vision that gives a sense of unity to the work of each individual writer, as well as Auerbach's germinal notion of a self-referring, self-interpreting, and self-criticizing text (see, in particular, Erich Auerbach, *Mimesis* [Princeton: Princeton University Press, 1953], p. 486), allowed for the transformation of the totalizing mode of formalism into a contextual unity based on the self-reflexivity of the text.

16. "Every time that, in order to hook writing up precipitously with some reassuring outside or in order to make a hasty break with idealism, one might be brought to ignore certain recent theoretical attainments . . . one would all the more surely regress into idealism, with all of what, as we have just pointed out, cannot but link up with it, singularly in the figures of empiricism and formalism" (*D,* pp. 43–44).

17. See also *D,* p. 62.

18. For the distinctions of the two steps of deconstruction, see *P*, p. 41.

19. See also *Of Grammatology,* where Derrida argues that Christianity privileged only a highly metaphorical notion of writing, as for instance God's or Nature's writing, while viewing all other forms of writing as derivative (*OG*, p. 15).

20. Jean-François Lyotard, *Discours, figure* (Paris: Klincksieck, 1971), pp. 13–14.

21. Jean-François Lyotard, *Phenomenology,* trans. B. Beakley (Albany: SUNY Press, 1991), p. 50.

22. Maurice Merleau-Ponty, *The Visible and the Invisible* (Evanston: Northwestern University Press, 1968), p. 9.

23. See also *SP*, pp. 78–79: "Every . . . form of auto-affection must either pass through what is outside the sphere of 'ownness' or forego any claim to universality. When I see myself, either because I gaze upon a limited region of my body or because it is reflected in a mirror, what is outside the sphere of 'my own' has already entered the field of this auto-affection, with the result that it is no longer pure. In the experience of touching and being touched, the same thing happens."

24. Merleau-Ponty, *The Visible and the Invisible,* p. 35.

25. Ibid., pp. 31–32.

26. It should already have become obvious that speaking of deconstruction versus reconstruction turns deconstruction erroneously into a moment of the speculative process.

27. Merleau-Ponty, *The Visible and the Invisible,* p. 33.

28. Ibid., p. 37.

29. Ibid., pp. 44–45.

30. Ibid., pp. 44.

31. Ibid., p. 38.

32. Ibid., p. 46.

33. Ibid., p. 38.

34. Ibid., p. 94.

35. Ibid., p. 92.

36. Ibid., p. 95.

37. Lyotard, *Discours, figure,* p. 56.

38. Ibid., p. 60.

39. Immanent criticism, as defined by Theodor W. Adorno in *Prisms,* trans. S. Weber (London: Neville Stearman, 1967), consists of measuring a culture or a discourse against its own ideal or concept *(Begriff)*. "Immanent criticism of intellectual and artistic phenomena seeks to grasp, through the analysis of their form and meaning, the contradiction between their objective idea and that

pretension. It names what the consistency or inconsistency of the work itself expresses of the structure of the existent" (p. 32). Yet, this notion of immanent criticism is not without "consciousness transcending the immanence of culture" (p. 29), and is "founded in the objectivity of the mind itself" (p. 28). This ensures that the immanent procedure is essentially dialectical or, to be more precise, negatively dialectic. Adorno writes: "A successful work, according to immanent criticism, is not one which resolves objective contradictions in a spurious harmony, but one which expresses the idea of harmony negatively by embodying the contradictions, pure and uncompromised, in its innermost structure" (p. 32). It is thus not so much through its procedure as through its perspective that what I call here immanent criticism in Derrida differs from Adorno's approach.

40. For indeed, as Wayne C. Booth points out, every skeptic shows "at his climatic moment of total doubt that valued enterprises need not end when conceptual doubt has done its worst, that . . . various enterprises including life itself are both more important than any one conceptual blind alley, and that they can be pursued and defended, once entered upon," as rational ("Preserving the Exemplar," p. 417). But that is precisely the question in deconstruction as the self-evidence of those ethical and pragmatic issues become problematic. Booth's assimilation of common sense and self-evidence, his valorization of the pragmatic of life over conceptual enterprises, moreover, does not diminish the conceptual status of his values, which, like the concept of life, are tributary to a metaphysics of presence.

41. Since these contradictions are an inevitable function of the ethico-theoretical decisions of philosophy, no renewal in terms of greater logical coherence can master them. For that same reason, deconstruction is no longer a simple attempt at mastery.

42. Although deconstruction provides a justifying analysis of the global situation of reflection, it does not account for this situation without residues. If an account is a record of debit and credit to be balanced, deconstruction is precisely an operation which makes such a mastery impossible.

43. Thus, if one still insists on using the notion of the self and of the auto (which to a certain extent is unavoidable), one has to account for everything that makes that self a decentered self.

44. See "Plato's Pharmacy," in *D.*

45. "Spacing (notice that this word speaks the articulation of space and time, the becoming-space of time and the becoming-time of space) is always the unperceived, the non-present, and the non-conscious. As such, if one can still use that expression in a non-phenomenological way; for here we pass the very limits

of phenomenology. Arche-writing as spacing cannot occur as such within the phenomenological experience of a presence" (*OG*, p. 68).

46. The arche-trace as arche-writing "does not depend on any sensible plenitude, audible or visible, phonic or graphic. It is on the contrary, the condition of such a plenitude" (*OG*, p. 62).

47. "The sound-image is the structure of the appearing of the sound which is anything but the sound appearing" and "being-heard is structurally phenomenal and belongs to an order radically dissimilar to that of the real sound in the world" (*OG*, p. 63).

48. Derrida responds to such a possible objection throughout the first part of *Of Grammatology (OG)*. Yet in *Edmund Husserl's "Origin of Geometry": An Introduction (O)* Derrida had already dealt most extensively with that question.

49. Defining deconstruction in this manner leaves the problem of its relation to notions like the text, textuality, literariness, and so forth, suspended. This relation is neither obvious nor self-evident.

50. Meyer H. Abrams thus mistakes the priority of writing over speech for a shift of elementary reference to the "black marks on white paper as the sole things that are actually present in reading" to "already existing marks"; and this leads him to accuse Derrida of "graphocentrism," as if such a concept did not already destroy its very name ("The Deconstructive Angel," pp. 439–440). Abrams "impudently makes of visibility the tangible, simple, and essential element of writing" (*OG*, p. 42).

51. "It should be recognized that it is in the specific zone of this imprint and this trace, in the temporalization of a *lived experience* which is neither *in* the world nor in 'another world,' which is not more sonorous than luminous, not more *in* time than *in* space, that differences appear among the elements or rather produce them, make them emerge as such and constitute the *texts,* the chains, and the systems of traces" (*OG*, p. 65).

52. Lyotard, *Discours, figure,* pp. 278–279.

53. Ibid., p. 324.

54. Ibid., p. 326.

55. Ibid., p. 296.

56. Ibid., p. 350.

57. Ibid., p. 387.

58. Paul de Man, *Blindness and Insight: Essays in the Rhetoric of Contemporary Criticism,* 2nd ed. (Minneapolis: University of Minnesota Press, 1983), p. 111.

59. Ibid., p. 119.

60. Ibid., pp. 139–140.

61. Ibid., p. 119.

62. Ibid., p. 136.
63. De Man also links this self-reflexibility and self-cognition of literary language to "the necessarily ambivalent nature of literary language" (ibid., p. 136). But *ambivalence* and *ambiguity* are not the presupposition of deconstruction. Ambiguity, says Derrida, "requires the logic of presence, even when it begins to disobey that logic" (*OG*, p. 71). Merleau-Ponty had already criticized ambivalence as a characteristic of negativist thought (such as Sartre's), as in fact something proper to the ventriloqual sophists, a thought that "always affirms or denies in the hypothesis what it denies or affirms in the thesis," oscillating between "absolute contradiction and the identity" (*The Visible and the Invisible,* p. 73). Moreover, since the idea of *simultaneity* always "coordinates two absolute presents, two points or instants of presence, and . . . [thus] remains a linear concept" (*OG*, p. 85), it fosters a kind of negative specularity and dialectics.
64. De Man, *Blindness and Insight,* p. 138.
65. Paul de Man, *Allegories of Reading: Figural Language in Rousseau, Nietzsche, Rilke, and Proust* (New Haven: Yale University Press, 1979), p. 131.
66. Properly speaking, this is no negative dialectics in the Adornian sense. For Adorno, in short, negative dialectics is a dialectics which for *historical* reasons cannot sublate its conflicting opposites. It is a dialectics without synthesis which tries to keep the conflict going. It refuses both *Aufhebung* and the annulment of the opposites. De Man's notion of negative dialectics is more precisely linked to Schelling's Romantic interpretation of dialectic as a neutralization, as a mutual annulment (and, actually, as constitutive of the *Witz*).
67. De Man, *Allegories of Reading,* p. 131.
68. Ibid., pp. 125–126.
69. Ibid., pp. 298–299.
70. Paul de Man, "Shelley Disfigured," in *The Rhetoric of Romanticism* (New York: Columbia University Press, 1984), pp. 92–93.
71. De Man, *Allegories of Reading,* p. 300.
72. Ibid., pp. 298–299.
73. Paul de Man, "The Epistemology of Metaphor," *Critical Inquiry,* 5, no. 1 (1978), 28.

2. The Law of Tradition

1. Jacques Derrida, *Memoires for Paul de Man,* trans. C. Lindsay et al. (New York: Columbia University Press, 1986), p. 15.
2. Jacques Derrida, "Some Statements and Truisms about Neologisms, Newisms, Postisms, Parasitisms, and Other Small Seismisms," trans. A. Tomiche, in *The*

States of Theory, ed. D. Caroll (New York: Columbia University Press, 1990), p. 74.

3. Ibid., See also Jacques Derrida, *Psyche: Inventions de l'autre* (Paris: Galilée 1987), p. 390.

4. Ibid., pp. 390–91.

5. Martin Heidegger, *Basic Writings,* ed. D. F. Krell (New York: Harper and Row, 1977), p. 67.

6. Martin Heidegger, *What Is Philosophy?* trans. W. Kluback and J. T. Wiede (Estover, Eng: Vision Press, 1989), pp. 31–34.

7. See, for example, Jacques Derrida, "Entre crochets," in *Points de suspension: Entretiens* (Paris: Galilée, 1992), p. 29.

8. Jacques Derrida, *Limited Inc* (Evanston: Northwestern University Press, 1988), p. 134.

9. Karl Jaspers, *Philosophische Autobiographie* (Munich: Piper, 1977), p. 100.

10. Ibid., p. 99.

11. Ibid., p. 100. See also in this context Hans Saner, "Aspekte der Heidegger-Kritik von Karl Jaspers," in *Martin Heidegger—Unterwegs im Denken,* ed. R. Wisser (Freiburg: Karl Alber, 1987), pp. 239–258.

12. Martin Heidegger, *The Metaphysical Foundation of Logic,* trans. Michael Heim (Bloomington: Indiana University Press), 1984, p. 141.

13. Heidegger, *Basic Writings,* p. 66.

14. Martin Heidegger, *Identity and Difference,* trans. J. Stambaugh (New York: Harper and Row, 1969), p. 41.

15. Heidegger, *Basic Writings,* p. 66.

16. Ibid., pp. 67–68.

17. Martin Heidegger, *An Introduction to Metaphysics,* trans. R. Manheim (New Haven: Yale University Press, 1959), p. 24.

18. Ibid., p. 27.

19. Otto Pöggeler, "Heideggers Neubestimmung des Phänomenbegriffs," in *Neuere Entwicklungen des Phänomenbegriffs,* ed. E. W. Orth (Munich: Karl Alber, 1980), p. 138.

20. Gérard Granel, *Traditionis Traditio* (Paris: Gallimard, 1972), p. 74. See also Gérard Granel, "L'Europe de Husserl," in *Ecrits logiques et philosophiques* (Paris: Galilée, 1990), where Granel recalls the fact that "Husserlian phenomenology describes itself explicitly as the heir to 'the Platonic foundation of logic,' according to the liminary declarations of *Formal and Transcendental Logic*" (p. 42).

21. Edmund Husserl, *The Crisis of European Sciences and Transcendental Phenomenology,* trans. D. Carr (Evanston: Northwestern University Press, 1970), pp. 17–18.

22. Ibid., p. 16 and p. 276.

23. Ibid., p. 16. For a discussion of this inevitable yet disturbing linkage of the absolute idea of theoretical universality to the concept of Europe, from rather opposite viewpoints, see Granel, "L'Europe de Husserl," and Klaus Held, "Husserls These von der Europäisierung der Menschheit," in *Phänomenologie im Widerstreit,* ed. C. Jamme and O. Pöggeler (Frankfort: Suhrkamp, 1989), pp. 13–39.

24. Husserl, *The Crisis,* p. 273. For a detailed discussion by Derrida of the aporias of the teleological and historical idea of "Europe," and their solution on the basis of a new ontology grounded in a nonmundane dialectic of originary temporality, see Jacques Derrida, *Le Problème de la genèse dans la philosophie de Husserl* (Paris: Presses Universitaires de France, 1990), pp. 249–258.

25. Husserl, *The Crisis,* pp. 276 and 280.

26. Ibid., p. 13.

27. Ibid., p. 279 and p. 14.

28. Ibid., p. 15 and p. 8.

29. Ibid., p. 280.

30. Held, "Husserls These," p. 24.

31. Ibid., p. 21.

32. Husserl, *The Crisis,* p. 8.

33. Martin Heidegger, *What Is Called Thinking?* trans. F. D. Wieck and J. Glenn Gray (New York: Harper and Row, 1968), p. 95.

34. If Heidegger's thought is thought in the eminent sense, as the thought of Being, then relations such as dependence, influence, anxiety (of influence), oedipal entanglement and so on, cannot serve to capture the nature of the relation with another thinker. What can be described in these terms is only something of the order of representation. As Heidegger notes, "The things which we conceive and assert *(vor- und fest-stellen)* to be the result *(Wirkungen)* of thinking, are the misunderstandings to which thinking ineluctably falls victim. Only they achieve publication *(Darstellung)* as alleged thought, and occupy those who do *not* think" (ibid., p. 169).

35. Christopher Fynsk, in *Heidegger: Thought and Historicity* (Ithaca: Cornell University Press, 1986), writes: "The new position gains its tenor from its relation to the initial position. The more the thinker enters into the position of his predecessor, the firmer his own position becomes and the more essential the relation to the predecessor. The new position can emerge only insofar as it stands forth against a tradition" (pp. 56–57).

36. Heidegger, *Introduction to Metaphysics,* p. 126.

37. Ibid., p. 46.

38. Heidegger, *Basic Writings,* pp. 86–87.

39. Heidegger, *Identity and Difference*, p. 71.

40. Ibid., p. 65.

41. Jacques Derrida, "Ja, ou le faux-bond," in Derrida, *Points de suspension,* pp. 76–77.

42. John Caputo, "Telling Left from Right: Hermeneutic, Deconstruction, and the Work of Art," *The Journal of Philosophy,* 86 (1988), 683.

43. Ibid., p. 684.

44. It should be obvious that this foregrounding can take place not in the mode of dialectical synthesis, but by establishing a law that calculates the (incalculable) commerce between both—by a law, consequently, that in a strange way is more universal than all universals, yet is at the same time singular.

3. The Eclipse of Difference

1. Gianni Vattimo, *Les Aventures de la différence* (Paris: Minuit, 1985).

2. Ibid., p. 88.

3. Ibid., pp. 160–161.

4. Ibid., pp. 161, 80.

5. The following outline is largely based on Silvian Nacht-Eladi, "Aristotle's Doctrine of the Differentia Specifica and Maimon's Law of Determinability," in *Scripta Hierosolymitana,* 6 (1960), 222–248, and on Josef Simon's entry "Differenz" in *Handbuch Philosophischer Grundbegriffe.* ed. H. Krings et al. (Munich: Kösel, 1973), pp. 309–320.

6. Aristotle, *Metaphysics,* trans. R. Hope (Ann Arbor: University of Michigan Press, 1975), p. 101.

7. Nacht-Eladi, "Aristotle's Doctrine," p. 228.

8. Ibid., p. 227.

9. Simon, "Differenz," p. 310.

10. The foregoing presentation of *differentia specifica,* which understands it as difference in genus, of course runs counter to the accustomed way of thinking of it as difference in species, which, historically speaking, has been the dominant interpretation. In either case, the intrinsic relation of difference to sameness remains the unquestionable presupposition.

11. Jacques Derrida, *Spurs: Nietzsche's Styles,* trans. B. Harlow (Chicago: University of Chicago Press, 1978), p. 63.

12. Martin Heidegger, *An Introduction to Metaphysics,* trans. R. Manheim (New Haven: Yale University Press, 1959), p. 204.

13. Martin Heidegger, *Identity and Difference,* trans. J. Stambaugh (New York: Harper and Row, 1969), p. 72.

14. Ibid., p. 70.

15. Martin Heidegger, *The Essence of Reasons*, trans. T. Malick (Evanston: Northwestern University Press, 1969), p. 3.

16. Heidegger, *Identity and Difference*, p. 62.

17. Ibid., p. 63.

18. Ibid., p. 62.

19. Jean-Luc Marion, *L'Idole et la distance* (Paris: Grasset, 1977), p. 280.

20. Jürgen Habermas, *The Philosophical Discourse of Modernity: Twelve Lectures*, trans. F. Lawrence (Cambridge: MIT Press, 1987), p. 135.

21. Heidegger, *Identity and Difference*, p. 47.

22. Heidegger, *The Essence of Reasons*, p. 39.

23. Martin Heidegger, *What Is Called Thinking?* trans. F. D. Wieck and J. Glenn Gray (New York: Harper and Row, 1968), p. 98 (trans. modified).

24. Heidegger, *The Essence of Reasons*, pp. 37, 27.

25. Jean-Luc Marion, *God without Being*, trans. T. A. Carlson (Chicago: University of Chicago Press, 1991), p. 45.

26. Undoubtedly, this is an urgent task. Yet, when Vattimo proposes not only to develop the ontological difference in terms of and in the direction of a theory of generalized communication based on the findings of psychology, the theory of information, studies in communication, and system theories, but to "start a new meditation on the ontological difference as the bringing-to-the-fore of nature as the natural ground-back-ground-un-ground *(fondo-sfondo-sfondamento)* of culture" (*Les Aventures de la différence,* p. 170), one cannot but wonder whether Vattimo does not himself dissolve difference in a manner similar to that employed by the thinkers of difference. Indeed, the philosophical differences between, spirit, consciousness, and culture on the one hand, and nature, on the other, are derivative of the ontological difference. To think that difference *as* the difference of nature and culture is not only not to think it anymore according to the elementary guiding words of philosophy, such as Being and beings, but, more than that, to obscure that difference by casting it in terms that refer to distinctions that ultimately *are* of the order of philosophical representation *(Vorstellen)*.

27. Martin Heidegger, *Being and Time*, trans. J. Macquarrie and E. Robinson (London: SCM, 1962), pp. 84–85.

28. Marion, *God without Being*, p. 105.

29. Marion, *L'Idole et la distance*, p. 185.

30. Marion, *God without Being*, p. 88.

31. Ibid., p. 89.

32. Ibid., p. 91.

33. Ibid., p. 93.

34. Ibid., p. 94.

35. Ibid., p. 95.

36. Ibid.

37. Ibid., pp. 101–102.

38. Ibid., pp. 109–110.

39. Martin Heidegger, "What Is Metaphysics?" in *Basic Writings*, ed. D. F. Krell (New York: Harper and Row, 1977), p. 101, and Heidegger, *Introduction to Metaphysics*, p. 1. But Marion seems to distance himself from Heidegger's claim in "What is Metaphysics?" that "boredom reveals beings as a whole" and from his claim in *An Introduction* that with such boredom "the question 'Why are there essents rather than nothing?' is evoked in a particular form." For an extensive analysis of boredom see Martin Heidegger, *Die Grundbegriffe der Metaphysik, Gesamtausgabe*, vol. 29/30 (Frankfort: Klostermann, 1983), pp. 111ff. See as well Parvis Emad, "Boredom as Limit and Disposition," *Heidegger Studies*, vol. 1 (Oak Brook, Ill.: Eterna Press, 1985), pp. 63–78.

40. Marion, *God without Being*, p. 116.

41. Ibid., p. 118.

42. Ibid., p. 85.

43. Ibid., p. 84 (translation amended).

44. Ibid.

45. For Marion, to be indifferent to both the ontic and the ontological difference in no way means to slide back into empiricism. Unlike empiricism, Marion's negative theology is not naively ignorant of these differences, and especially of the difference between both differences. On the contrary, it begins with a deliberate disregard of the importance of beings' existence, disregard of the fact *that* they are, in order to determine them in the perspective of the ab-solutely Other than Being, that is, of God. Indeed, if beings could be shown to be involved in a play in which they are no longer equivocal and twofold, no longer joined to Being, but, independently of their being (that is, also as nonbeings) turned toward God, they would lack the qualifications of beings altogether, and might have to be characterized in terms that are free of all suspicion of empiricity. Moreover, a relation of faith in which beings become liberated from the fold of Being, to enter into a communion with the distant Other, would also have to be thought from the difference that is more essential than ontological difference, rather than in purely ontic terms. See *God without Being*, p. 71.

46. Ibid., p. 115.

47. Ibid., p. 117.

48. Martin Heidegger, *Wegmarken, Gesamtausgabe*, vol. 9 (Frankfort: Klostermann, 1976), p. 307.

49. Marion, *God without Being*, p. 45.

50. Ibid., pp. 45–46.

51. Marion, *L'Idole et la distance,* p. 271.

52. Ibid., pp. 284–285.

53. Such anteriority therefore would also imply another notion of "older" and "earlier" than the one Heidegger claims for Being. See, for instance, Martin Heidegger, *The Metaphysical Foundations of Logic,* trans. M. Heim (Bloomington: Indiana University Press, 1984), pp. 184–186.

54. Aristotle, *Metaphysics,* p. 10.

55. Martin Heidegger, *On Time and Being,* trans. J. Stambough (New York: Harper and Row, 1977), p. 37.

56. Ute Guzzoni, *Identität oder nicht: Zur Kritischen Theorie der Ontologie* (Munich: Alber, 1981), p. 222.

57. Heidegger, *Identity and Difference,* pp. 64–65.

58. Ibid., pp. 50, 71.

59. Ibid., p. 65.

60. Ibid., p. 71.

61. Ibid., p. 64–65 (translation amended).

62. Vattimo, *Les Aventures de la différence,* pp. 92–93.

63. From early on, Heidegger attempted to foreground binary difference, the difference between two. Derrida has made this point in the essay "Geschlecht: Sexual Difference, Ontological Difference," in *Research in Phenomenology,* 13 (1983), 65–83. Derrida there seeks to demonstrate that if Heidegger insists on the genderlessness and asexuality of *Dasein,* on its neutrality, in short, he does so because sexuality is a dual difference that as such can only be derivative of what Heidegger calls "the transcendental dissemination proper to the metaphysical essence of neutral Dasein," and that represents "the binding possibility of each factical existential dispersion and division," sexual difference, first and foremost (Martin Heidegger, *The Metaphysical Foundations of Logic,* p. 138).

64. See, in this context, Derrida on "indifference" in *Of Spirit: Heidegger and the Question,* trans. G. Bennington and R. Bowlby (Chicago: University of Chicago Press, 1989), pp. 19–20.

65. Although differance does not structurally reduplicate the gestures characteristic of the ontological difference, or of "difference as such," but rather inscribes them within its own grid, the latter, with its tendency to withdraw into the two in the form of which it comes forth, and of thus having in itself no itself, has, undoubtedly, been a major stimulation to Derrida's conception of differance as the "space" of cohabitation of a multiplicity of heterogeneous differences.

66. In *Glas,* Derrida discusses the becoming different, or duality, of difference as a becoming that precedes the becoming *opposite* of difference, hence, the opening

up of difference to negativity (*G,* pp. 111, 168–169). For a discussion of the code "which immures everything for life in the figure 2," and in particular of sexual difference, see Jacques Derrida and Christie V. McDonald, "Choreographies," *Diacritics,* 12 (Summer 1982), 66–76.

4. Answering for Reason

1. See, for instance, in this context, Fred Dallmayer, "Habermas and Rationality," *Political Theory,* 16, no. 4 (November 1988), 553–579, as well as Bernhard Waldenfels, "Division ou dispersion? Un débat entre Habermas et Foucault," *Les Etudes Philosophiques,* 4 (1986), 473–484.
2. Jacques Derrida, "The Principle of Reason: The University in the Eyes of Its Pupils," *Diacritics,* 13, no. 3 (Fall 1983), 9.
3. Ibid.
4. Jurgen Habermas, *The Philosophical Discourse of Modernity: Twelve Lectures,* trans. F. Lawrence (Cambridge: MIT Press, 1987), p. 210.
5. See ibid., pp. 307 and 31.
6. Todd Gitlin, "Hip-Deep in Postmodernism," *The New York Times Book Review,* November 6, 1980, p. 36.
7. Albrecht Wellmer, *Zur Dialektik von Moderne und Postmoderne. Vernunftkritik nach Adorno* (Frankfort: Suhrkamp, 1985), p. 48.
8. Gianni Vattimo, *The End of Modernity: Nihilism and Hermeneutics in Postmodern Culture,* trans. J. R. Snyder (Baltimore: Johns Hopkins University Press, 1988), p. 2.
9. Wellmer, *Zur Dialektik,* p. 48.
10. Karl-Otto Apel, "Das Problem einer philosophischen Theorie der Rationalitätstypen," in *Rationalität: Philosophische Beiträge,* ed. Herbert Schnädelbach (Frankfort: Suhrkamp, 1984), p. 19.
11. Habermas, *The Philosophical Discourse of Modernity,* p. 210.
12. Ibid., p. 408.
13. *Historisches Wörterbuch der Philosophie,* ed. Joachim Ritter (Darmstadt: Wissenschaftliche Buchgesellschaft, 1971–), vol. 4, p. 583.
14. Jean-François Lyotard, *The Postmodern Condition: A Report on Knowledge,* trans. Geoff Bennington and Brian Massumi (Minneapolis: University of Minnesota Press, 1984), p. 43.
15. Jean-François Lyotard, "Re-writing Modernity," *Substance* 54 (1987), 3–9.
16. Lyotard, *The Postmodern Condition,* p. 54.
17. Ibid., p. 53.
18. Ibid., p. 40.

19. Ibid., pp. 54–55.
20. Ibid., pp. 43–44.
21. Ibid., p. 60.
22. Ibid., p. xxv.
23. Herbert Schnädelbach, "Einleitung," in *Rationälitat,* p. 8.
24. Charles Taylor, "Rationality," in *Rationality and Relativism,* ed. Martin Hollis and Steven Lukes (Oxford: Basil Blackwell, 1982), p. 88.
25. Lyotard, *The Postmodern Condition,* p. 59.
26. Vattimo, *The End of Modernity,* pp. 172–173.
27. This accusation is simply a convenient "argument" for evading an intellectual challenge, much as is the charge of free play. Whereas the first accusation is symptomatic of an inability to track the traditional modes of argumentation to the very displacement to which they become subjected in Derrida's writings, the incrimination of free play does not face the fact that truly patternless, truly arbitrary, truly random play is a highly complicated agenda only recently unraveled, it seems, by some mathematicians.
28. Habermas, *The Philosophical Discourse of Modernity,* p. 102.
29. Plato, *Sophist,* 242c, in *Plato: The Collected Dialogues,* ed. E. Hamilton and H. Cairns (Princeton: Princeton University Press, 1980), p. 986.
30. Although this rule is a most fundamental philosophical gesture, and thus binding for philosophical thought as such, it is possible to question the purity of the difference (between the ground and the grounded, between an essence and what it is the essence of) called for, yet not from an empiricist point of view (which would imply to entirely do away with this difference), but from an approach that both respects and questions such heterogeneity. Such is the case, for instance, when Derrida writes, in criticism of Heidegger's well-known statement that the essence of technology is nothing technological, that "the essence of technology and the thinking of this essence retain *something* technological." The awareness by Derrida of "the risk and gravity" of this apparently very trivial statement, namely, that it puts "into question, with all of the entailing consequences, the scope of even the most fundamental philosophical gesture," is clear indication of the fact that Derrida's questioning is not anti- or aphilosophical. If he can say that deconstruction, because it questions the purity of the difference between the essence of technology and technology itself, "is no longer 'Heideggerian,' " this does not mean that it would stand in no relation to Heidegger. "In terms of the thousands of ways imaginable, one can certainly not circumvent the necessity of all the Heideggerian trajectories, one cannot be any 'nearer' to this thinking, but one cannot also be any farther from it, nor can one be any more heterogeneous (this does not mean opposed) to it than by risking an

affirmation of this type: the essence of this is this, the essence of technology is (still) technological." Jacques Derrida, *Memoires for Paul de Man* (New York: Columbia University Press, 1986), pp. 139–140.

31. Jacques Derrida, *Limited Inc* (Evanston: Northwestern University Press, 1989), p. 93.
32. Habermas, *The Philosophical Discourse of Modernity,* p. 178.
33. Ibid., p. 102.
34. Ibid., p. 178.
35. Ibid., pp. 235–236.
36. In a letter to Gerald Graf entitled "Afterword: Toward an Ethic of Discussion," Derrida writes: "What has always interested me most, what has always seemed to me the most rigorous (theoretically, scientifically, philosophically, but also for a writing that would no longer be only theoretical- scientific-philosophical), is not indeterminacy in itself, but the strictest possible determination of the figures of play, of oscillation, of undecidability, which is to say, of the *differantial* conditions of determinable history, etc." (Derrida, *Limited Inc,* p. 145).
37. Habermas, *The Philosophical Discourse of Modernity,* p. 409.
38. Ibid., p. 189.

5. Structural Infinity

1. Jacques Derrida, "Living On: Borderlines," *Deconstruction and Criticism,* ed. H. Bloom et al. (New York: Seabury Press, 1979), pp. 139–140.
2. One could, therefore, continue beyond this question as follows: If one considers what the exigency of positive infinity represents in the classical tradition, and if one equates this requirement, as does Hegel, with the business of thought itself, what, then, does Derrida's interest in modes of nontotalization reveal about the very nature of his own philosophical enterprise? I can, of course, not hope to be able to answer here these questions with the same degree of accuracy. I will have to confine myself to a detailed response to the first question, and to providing some indications of how to proceed with respect to the other question.
3. Manfred Baum, "Zur Vorgeschichte des Hegelschen Unendlichkeitsbegriffs," *Hegel-Studien,* vol. 11 (Bonn: Bouvier, 1976), pp. 89–124.
4. Ibid., p. 107.
5. G. W. F. Hegel, *Faith and Knowledge,* trans. W. Cerf (Albany: SUNY Press, 1977), p. 186.
6. Ibid., p. 114.
7. G. W. F. Hegel, *Phenomenology of Spirit,* trans. A. V. Miller (Oxford: Oxford University Press, 1979), p. 144.

8. G. W. F. Hegel, *Lectures on the History of Philosophy,* vol. 1, trans. E. S. Haldane and E. F. Simson (New York: Humanities Press, 1968), p. 284.

9. See, for instance Gerard Genette, *Figures III* (Paris: Seuil, 1972), and Lucien Dällenbach, *Le Récit spéculaire. Essai sur la mise en abyme* (Paris: Seuil, 1977).

10. *Psychoanalysis and the Question of the Text,* ed. G. H. Hartman (Baltimore: Johns Hopkins University Press, 1978), p. 120.

11. Jacques Derrida, *Spurs,* trans. B. Harlow (Chicago: University of Chicago Press, 1979), p. 117; emphasis mine.

12. Jacques Derrida, *The Truth in Painting,* trans. G. Bennington and I. McLeod (Chicago: University of Chicago Press, 1987), pp. 33–34.

13. Ibid., p. 37.

In addition to the questions raised at the beginning of this essay, it would certainly have been in order to ask whether or not Derrida's notion of the text as characterized by a structure of infinite referral differs at all—and if so, how?—from the Romantic speculations on the figure of the literary abyss, and from Friedrich Schlegel's dream of transcendental poetry as an infinitely self-mirroring text. One could also have asked if the task of textual exegesis, which Derrida calls interminable, is to be demarcated from Schleiermacher's determination of the business of interpretation as an infinite task. Indeed, is it possible to fully sustain Manfred Frank's argument in "The Infinite Text" that Derrida's notion of the text is to be traced back to the speculations of the Romantics, who, Frank claims, were the first to produce an object of perception no longer inwardly oriented by meaning? It is undoubtedly the case that Friedrich Schlegel criticized the Kantian concept of the infinite for its mathematical and mechanical emptiness. But Schlegel himself is also subject to such reproof. Moreover, universality and infinity as the ultimate goal of Romantic transgression of everything particular and singular is, unquestionably, the object of a Kantian "ought." It is an aspiration in infinite approximation to the "whole" of the *menstruum universale* whose infinity and totality, though nothing extant belongs to it, is not for that matter "a vacant place." (See Manfred Frank, "The Infinite Text," *Glyph,* 7 [1980], 78) Hegel, therefore, could easily stigmatize the Romantic speculations as constricted by spurious infinity. Most of the critics who link Derrida's notion of text explicitly or implicitly to its Romantic conception do not seem to be bothered by Hegel's verdict, and thus make little or no attempt to shield the Romantic notion of the text from such criticism. Yet, unless it is shown that Hegel's objections are groundless, it remains impossible, it seems, to tie Derridean structural infinity in with the Romantic notion of infinity.

Hegel's debate with Romantic infinity as spurious infinity is undoubtedly a function of his classicism in aesthetics and in his philosophy as well. As it did for the Greeks, for whom the unlimited—the infinite in the sense of the indefinite and unrestricted—has no form, infinity remains incomplete, imperfect, and lacking true being for Hegel. Hegel's concept of infinity is, as has been seen, finite in a Greek sense inasmuch as it has form, and is a totality. The vehemence of his criticism of Romantic infinity reembodies what he termed the "absolute catastrophe," namely, the war in which the difference between the old and new gods becomes disclosed in Greek mythology as the difference between nature and spirit as the true totality. This victory of the new gods, as well as the dominion of the principle of spirituality and true infinity, is assured by the overthrow of the Titans, and by their subsequent banishment and subjection to many kinds of punishments. "Like the Titanic powers of nature themselves, these punishments are the inherently measureless, the bad infinite, the longing of the 'ought,' the unsatiated craving of subjective natural desire which in its continual recurrence never attains the final peace of satisfaction. For the Greek correct sense of the Divine, unlike the modern longing, did not regard egress into the boundless and the vague as what was supreme for men; the Greeks regarded it as a damnation and relegated it to Tartarus," writes Hegel (*A*, vol. 1, p. 466).

Derrida's notion of infinity tries to account for both true and spurious infinity, for true infinity's precipitation *(catastrophe)* of spurious infinity, as well as spurious infinity's eternal recurrence within its genuine counterpart. If Derrida's concept of infinity is indeed *structural* in the sense here elaborated, it is certainly impossible to view its roots as originating in Romantic thought. Romantic infinity, like spurious infinity, is at best its metaphysical ghost.

6. God, for Example

1. Mikel Dufrenne, *Le Poétique* (Paris: Presses Universitaires de France, 1973), pp. 7–57; Gianni Vattimo, *Les Aventures de la différence* (Paris: Minuit, 1985); Jean-Luc Marion, *L'Idole et la distance* (Paris: Grasset, 1977).

2. Jacques Derrida, "Violence and Metaphysics: An Essay on the Thought of Emmanuel Levinas," in *WD*, pp. 79–153; Jacques Derrida, "On a Newly Arisen Apocalyptic Tone in Philosophy," trans. J. Leavey, in *Raising the Tone of Philosophy: Late Essays by Immanuel Kant*, Transformative Critique by Jacques Derrida, ed. P. Fenves (Baltimore: Johns Hopkins University Press, 1993), pp. 117–171; Jacques Derrida, "How to Avoid Speaking: Denials," in *Languages of the Unsayable: The Play of Negativity in Literature and Literary Theory*, ed. Sanford Budich and Wolfgang Iser (New York: Columbia University Press, 1989), pp. 3–70.

3. Derrida, "On a Newly Arisen Apocalyptic Tone," p. 142–143 and p. 157.
4. Derrida, "How to Avoid Speaking," p. 40.
5. Ibid., p. 53.
6. Immanuel Kant, "On a Newly Arisen Superior Tone in Philosophy," in Fenves, ed., *Raising the Tone of Philosophy,* p. 64.
7. Jean-Luc Marion, *God without Being,* trans. Thomas A. Carlson (Chicago: University of Chicago Press, 1991), p. 41.
8. Jean-Luc Nancy, "Of Divine Places," in *Paragraph,* vol. 7 (Oxford: Oxford University Press, 1986), p. 7.
9. Martin Heidegger, *Identity and Difference,* (New York: Harper and Row, 1969), p. 60.
10. Ibid., p. 47.
11. Martin Heidegger, "Phenomenology and Theology," in *The Piety of Thinking* (Bloomington: Indiana University Press, 1976), pp. 5–21.
12. Martin Heidegger, *Hegel's Concept of Experience* (New York: Harper and Row, 1970), p. 135.
13. Marion, *L'Idole et la distance,* p. 292.
14. Marion, *God without Being,* p. 45.
15. Ibid. pp. 45–46.
16. Marion, *L'Idole et la distance,* p. 293.
17. Martin Heidegger, *Early Greek Thinking* (New York: Harper and Row, 1975), pp. 50–51.
18. Ibid.
19. Derrida, "On a Newly Arisen Apocalyptic Tone," p. 159.
20. Ibid., p. 160.
21. Ibid., p. 157.
22. Dufrenne, *Le Poétique,* pp. 19–20.
23. Derrida, "How to Avoid Speaking," pp. 31–34.
24. Ibid., pp. 34–36.
25. Ibid., pp. 37–38.
26. Ibid., p. 38.
27. Ibid., pp. 38–39.
28. Heidegger, *Identity and Difference,* p. 66.
29. Martin Heidegger, *An Introduction to Metaphysics* (New Haven: Yale University Press, 1959), p. 81.
30. Marion, *God without Being,* p. 45.

7. Strictly Bonded

1. G. W. F. Hegel, *Enzyklopädie der philosophischen Wissenschaften*, Part III, *Werke in Zwanzig Bänden,* vol. 10 (Frankfort: Suhrkamp, 1970), p. 188.

2. Ibid., p. 183.

3. Ibid., p. 188.

4. Ibid., p. 186.

5. Ibid., p. 189.

6. Ibid., p. 188.

7. Ibid., p. 186.

8. Ibid., p. 188.

9. G. W. F. Hegel, *Grundlinien der Philosophie des Rechts, Werke in Zwanzig Bänden,* vol. 7 (Frankfort: Suhrkamp, 1970), p. 302.

10. Hegel, *Grundlinien,* p. 331.

11. Ibid., p. 224.

12. Ibid., p. 101.

13. Ibid., p. 224.

14. Ibid., p. 90.

15. In the handwritten notes to paragraph 168, where Hegel explains why brother and sister cannot form a marriage in the ethical sense, he emphasizes that apart from not being different, because they are already unified, and therefore unable to enter a spiritual unity of marriage, siblings entertain an *"asexual* relation— not the conscious *living unity* that posits itself as inwardness *(Innigkeit),"* the specific form of the self-conscious mode relating in marriage (ibid., p. 322).

16. Ibid., p. 295,

17. Ibid., pp. 89–90.

18. Ibid., pp. 304–305.

19. Ibid., p. 321.

20. Ibid., p. 249. This passage, and a similar one in the margin of paragraph 142, refers, as the editors of the *Werke in Zwanzig Bänden* remind us in a footnote, to Goethe's distichs 76 and 77 from "Jahreszeiten," which I translate as follows: "What is sacred? It is that which binds together many souls even if it binds them only lightly as does the rush in the wreath. What is the most sacred? That which today and forever, being felt deeper and deeper, has rendered the minds more and more unified" (ibid., p. 249).

21. Ibid., p. 317.

22. Such limitation does not per se mean to privilege the philosophical column over the more literary, in particular, since the envisioned reading will also, implicitly, at least, elaborate on the modes of reading *Glas.* Yet, some brief and very sketchy

remarks on the construction of *Glas* might be warranted at this point. The way the two columns of *Glas* are laid out is indicative of how this text is to be approached. The virgin blank between the two columns sets both of them up as discrete and distinct columns erected *in themselves*. Consequently one has to read them, *at first,* independently and in distinction from each other, in and on their own terms, before "reading" the quasi-virtual texts of the cross-references that mark and re-mark the blank between the columns. What becomes emphasized in a thematic manner in the Hegel column is that certain modes of conceiving of the relation between the two columns, rather than putting philosophy in question, are ultimately philosophy's own modes of relating to *its* Others. That one column can be in the other, for instance (*G,* p. 36), presupposes the dialectical idea of negativity. It is precisely negativity that "erects one in the other" (*G,* p. 13), as Derrida argues on the occasion of his discussion of the paradigmatic familial relation of father and son in speculative thought. The same is the case with the assumption that one column would be the reverse of the other. "The possibility of turning upside down, of the upside-down erection, is inscribed in the cycle of the family stance," Derrida claims. It "describes the structure of the concept's nonconceptual conception" (*G,* p. 81). Any attempt to construe the movement between the two columns (can there be movement between columns?) in terms of a turning into each other, of a mutual canceling out (or what has become known as self-deconstruction), is rooted in speculative logic's possibility that "absolute appropriation is absolute expropriation," and the other way around. This logic can "(re)turn itself at each instant into its absolute other," as loss or spending without reserve, for instance (*G,* p. 167), to better be itself in absolute expropriation. In short, using such types of relation between the columns, one does not tamper with the economy of speculative philosophy. A reading of *Glas* that would mobilize such relations would be monolithic, and extend the Hegel column to the whole text of *Glas.* In contrast, the reading that *Glas* calls forth is one of the quasi-virtual text *from which* the two columns emerge in their mutual distinction, but which is also the backdrop against which certain exterior accidents (quions, judases, for example) *in* each distinct column become visible, as well as a number of mutual contaminations.

23. For how Hegel wishes to be read, see *G,* p. 105. For whether a bad reading of the text of absolute knowing could possibly entertain that text outside itself, in spite of its insignificance in the face of a correct reading, and what such a bad reading could *mean* in the first place, see *G,* pp. 231–232.

24. In an excellent essay, "Hegel's Antigone," Patricia Jagentowicz Mills (*The Owl of Minerva,* 17, no. 2 [Spring 1986], 131–152), explores the systematic difficulties

and inconsistencies that characterize Hegel's interpretation of Antigone. Hegel's misinterpretation, however, as well as his fascination with the figure, remains, and has to be accounted for as such.

25. The possibility of such double reading is what constitutes Hegel's text as a text.

26. On the function of such a "perhaps," see also Jacques Derrida, "En ce moment même dans cet ouvrage me voici," in *Psyche: Inventions de l'autre,* (Paris: Galilée, 1987), pp. 174–175.

27. Marian Hobson is the first (to my knowledge) to have drawn attention to the capital importance of this notion in Derrida's writings; see "History Traces," in *Post-structuralism and the Question of History,* ed. D. Attridge et al. (Cambridge: Cambridge University Press, 1987), pp. 108–109.

28. See in this context Derrida's elaborations on *de-stricturation* and *seriature* in "En ce moment même," pp. 180–181.

8. Yes Absolutely

1. G. W. F. Hegel, *Phenomenology of Spirit,* trans. A. V. Miller (New York: Oxford University Press, 1979), p. 409.

2. Ibid., p. 477.

3. Ibid., p. 448.

4. Ibid., p. 478.

5. Jacques Derrida, in *Points de suspension: Entretiens* (Paris: Galilée, 1992), p. 69.

6. Ibid., p. 49.

7. Ibid., p. 42.

8. Ibid., p. 56.

9. For a more detailed account of absolute identity, in particular of how it is different from Schelling's conception of the absolute, see Dieter Henrich, "Andersheit und Absolutheit des Geistes: Sieben Schritte auf dem Wege von Schelling zu Hegel," in *Selbstverhältnisse* (Stuttgart: Reclam, 1982), pp. 142–172.

10. Dieter Henrich, " 'Identität'—Begriffe, Probleme, Grenzen," in *Identität: Poetik und Hermeneutik,* vol. 8, ed. O. Marquard and K. Stierle (Munich: Fink, 1979), p. 138.

11. Ibid., p. 138.

12. Jean Hyppolite, *Logique et existence* (Paris: Presses Universitaires de France, 1953), p. 221.

13. Such a distinction, however, encounters some difficulties that arise from Hegel's inconsistent use of the term "absolute reflection" in *Science of Logic*. It signifies "the domain of the Notion," that is, "the region of free infinitude and truth"

(*SL,* p. 673), and is therefore sometimes called "infinite reflection-into-self" (*SL,* p. 580). But absolute reflection, at times, also simply means "reflection as such" (*SL,* p. 622) or "abstract reflection" (*SL,* p. 499).

14. Yet, it is precisely on such a misconception of Hegel's treatment of identity in the *Greater Logic* that Slavoj Zizek bases what he deems to be a refutation of the deconstructive approach to absolute identity. In "The Wanton Identity"—a chapter from *For They Know Not What They Do: Enjoyment as a Political Factor* (London: Verso, 1991)—he seeks to formulate "a Hegelian criticism of Derrida," as well as "a symptomatic impasse of the Derridean reading of Hegel." Not only does this project presuppose the reductionist interpretation of Hegel alluded to, but it looks for its evidence not in Derrida's writings themselves, but in secondary sources. In a gesture reminiscent of Habermas' recourse, in *The Philosophical Discourse of Modernity,* to Jonathan Culler's interpretation of deconstructive thought, and of his monological discourse, of which Heinz Kimmerle notes that in it "the Other does not truly appear as Other, but only as supplier of additional reasonable arguments" (Heinz Kimmerle, "Ist Derridas Denken Ursprungsphilosophie? Zu Habermas' Deutung der philosophischen' 'Postmoderne,' " in *Die Frage nach dem Subjekt,* ed. M. Frank et al. [Frankfort: Suhrkamp, 1988], p. 275), Zizek uses *The Tain of the Mirror* as the primary (if not sole) source for his understanding of Derrida's thinking. In the piece in question, he claims that "although the Derridean reading misses the crucial dimension of Hegelian dialectics, the very form of its criticism of Hegel is often uncannily 'Hegelian.' " First, then, Derrida (not to mention me) is dead wrong about Hegelian dialectics because he has a commonsensical and nonsensically simplified version of absolute identity, one that resurrects "worn-out textbook platitudes." While pretending to crack many a hard nut, nuts too hard "to crack even for those followers of Hegel who remain fascinated by the 'power of the Negative,' " Zizek opposes a nondoxical, if not exotic, interpretation of Hegelian identity to such a simplistic and academic rendering of this important issue. This more Hegelian version of Hegelian identity springs, in Zizek's words, from "the fact that identity as such is a 'reflective determination,' " an inverted presentation of its opposite. Paying little attention to the minimal conditions of reasoning spelled out in Hegel's discussion of the law of identity in the very chapters of the *Greater Logic* to which Zizek turns in order to make his point, he takes Hegel's discussion of identity in "Logic of Essence" for the latter's definite and final conception, thus creating the deceptive impression that Hegel's concept of identity is always already bereft of its absolute telos. With this thoroughly botched-up notion of identity, Zizek tries to argue that all Derridean attempts to "set heterogeneity free from the constraints of identity"

are pointless and self-defeating, since all such heterogeneities are always only inverted Others of identity itself. They have, consequently, always already "been *taken into account*" by it. Without bothering in the least to explain how, to begin with, after having radically overcome all the misguided textbook platitudes about absolute identity as the One, or whole, as well as the "notorious formulas" that define identity as the identity of identity and non-identity, he can still speak of relations of opposition, of inversions between identity and *its* Others, and especially of a coincidence of identity with *its* space of inscription, Zizek limits all possible Otherness with respect to identity to Otherness *in opposition to* identity, and hence to the Other *of* identity. Second, while saying that Derrida is wrong about Hegel's understanding of identity, and profoundly misled in thinking that a space of conditions of possibility and impossibility "exterior" to absolute identity can be discerned, Zizek also claims that the Derridean approach "systematically overlooks the Hegelian character of its own basic operation." The problem, according to Zizek, is that Derrida "is . . . thoroughly 'Hegelian.' " Indeed, he asserts that what Derrida supposedly unearthed "through the hard work of deconstructive reading" as conditions of possibility and impossibility is nothing other than the "empty place of its [identity's] 'inscription,' " with which identity, in a movement of reversal, coincides. Consequently, what is wrong with deconstruction is that it "seems unable to accomplish . . . the step" of recognizing that there is no escape from the logic of binary opposition. Rather than joyfully espousing the dialectic of opposition and inversion as an iron law, as Zizek does, deconstruction fools itself by believing in the possibility that the limits of dialectical mediation can be thought. This is the delusion of deconstruction that Zizek has set out to unground. For the champion of dialectics, any such attempt falls flat on its face in that it merely confirms the logic of opposition that it sought to delimit. It is here that the high price paid for having overlooked the dynamics of Hegel's critical treatment of identity, and especially its reformulation in a nonrepresentational mode toward the end of *Phenomenology,* or in *Science of Logic,* become evident. It is a price indicative of the extent to which, in Zizek's theory of identity, sociopsychological and psychoanalytical concepts of identity have become mixed up with its philosophical concept. The sphere beyond representation is, indeed, that of thinking. If thinking, as philosophical thinking, is the thinking of limits, then the step that Zizek's cheerful embrace of the logic of opposition is unable to accomplish is the step toward philosophical thinking.

15. Jacques Derrida, "Before the Law," *Acts of Literature,* ed. D. Attridge (New York: Routledge, 1992), p. 211.

16. Ute Guzzoni, *Identität oder nicht: Zur kritischen Theorie der Ontologie* (Freiburg:

Alber, 1981), p. 45. For an excellent discussion of what Hegel calls "moment," see pp. 38–41.

17. G. W. F. Hegel, "Wie der gemeine Menschenverstand die Philosophie nehme, dargestellt an den Werken des Herrn Krug," *Werke in zwanzig Bänden,* vol. 2 (Frankfort: Suhrkamp, 1970), p. 194.

18. Ibid., p. 196.

19. Ibid., p. 195.

20. Guzzoni, *Identität oder nicht,* p. 105.

21. Ibid., p. 39.

22. Ibid., pp. 44–45.

23. The problematic of what Hegel calls "the merely negative," "the harmless," "that which is devoid of all interest," and so forth, will be dealt with in greater detail on an other occasion.

24. *UL,* p. 291.

25. Jacques Derrida, *Spurs: Nietzsche's Styles,* trans. B. Harlow (Chicago: University of Chicago Press, 1978), p. 127.

26. Ibid., pp. 131–133 (modified trans.)

27. Ibid., p. 133.

28. *UL,* p. 298.

9. On Responding Responsibly

1. Jacques Derrida, "Force of Law: The 'Mystical Foundation of Authority,' " trans. M. Quaintance, *Cardozo Law Review,* 11, nos. 5–6 (July–August 1990), 955.

2. Jacques Derrida, *Limited Inc* (Evanston: Northwestern University Press, 1988), p. 122.

3. Reiner Schürmann, *Heidegger on Being and Acting: From Principles to Anarchy,* trans. C. M. Gros (Bloomington: Indiana University Press, 1987), pp. 262–263.

4. Martin Heidegger, *On the Way to Language,* trans. P. D. Hertz (New York: Harper and Row, 1982), pp. 75–76.

5. Jacques Derrida, *Of Spirit: Heidegger and the Question,* trans. G. Bennington and R. Bowlby (Chicago: University of Chicago Press, 1989), p. 130.

6. Jacques Derrida, *Ulysses Gramophone: Deux mots pour Joyce* (Paris: Galilée, 1987). The English translations of the two texts on Joyce that this volume contains have been published separately: "Ulysses Gramophone: Hear Say Yes in Joyce," here abbreviated *UL,* and "Two Words for Joyce," here abbreviated *TWJ.* The version of the latter text published in French is slightly different from the English translation; I abbreviate it as *DMJ.*

7. Derrida, "Force of Law," p. 955.

8. Jacques Derrida, "Entre crochets," in *Points de suspension: Entretiens* (Paris: Galilée, 1992), p. 29.

9. Jacques Derrida, "Ja, ou le faux-bond," in *Points de Suspension,* p. 50.

10. Ibid., p. 48.

11. Ibid., p. 50.

12. Ibid., p. 48.

13. Derrida, "Entre crochets," p. 29.

14. Derrida, "Force of Law," pp. 947 and 955.

15. Ibid., p. 953.

16. Geert Lernout's treatment of Derrida's reading of Joyce in *The French Joyce* (Ann Arbor: University of Michigan Press, 1990), pp. 56–72, is an excellent example of the kind of bewilderment that texts such as *Ulysses Gramophone* produce in the critic. In the face of this text, and other references in Derrida's work to Joyce, in which Derrida is said to use Joyce merely "for his own purposes" rather than being "concerned with an elucidation of the *Wake*" or *Ulysses,* Lernout is left with only one option: to try to demonstrate that "Derrida can hardly be seen as a reliable witness on Joyce" (p. 60), that he makes "extremely questionable" use of specific quotations (p. 59), and finally that the lecture in 1984 at the International Joyce Symposium in Frankfurt "contains a minor error" (p. 65).

17. "Difficult questions," Derrida writes, are postponed until later, and finally they are addressed in an "increasingly telegraphic style" (*UL,* pp. 274, 301). "If I am telling stories," he writes, "it is to put off speaking about serious things . . . nothing intimidates me more than a community of experts in Joycean matters" (*UL,* p. 279). But it is also acknowledged that any competent contribution about Joyce should not be "of a narrative type. In principle, one doesn't relate stories in a university" (*UL,* p. 282). Yet the possibility of such competence on Joyce is precisely one of the issues discussed in the essay.

18. This seemingly hopeless situation can lead to a dream about a position radically outside the text, not caught in the circumnavigation of the Mediterranean lake, in other words, of dreaming "of writing *on* Joyce and not *in* Joyce from the fantasy of some Far Eastern capital," such as Tokyo, for example. But as the most trivial encounters of Derrida in Tokyo demonstrate, they are already foretold by *Ulysses* as well (*UL,* p. 281). This is of course also the dream of the Joyce scholar, although he also knows well enough that such a dream is only an illusion. To confirm that there is no radical, exotic position from which the encyclopedic venture of Joyce could in turn be mastered, you invite outsiders, Derrida tells him. "Seeing that, you also have the feeling, given that nothing

new can take you by surprise from the inside, that something might eventually happen to you from an unforeseeable outside. And you have guests" (*UL,* pp. 283–284).

19. A signature is not to be confused "with a simple mention, apposition, or manipulation of the officially authorized name. For neither in its juridical capacity . . . nor in the essential complexity of its structure, does a signature amount to the mere mention of a proper name" (*UL,* pp. 283–284).

20. The Kantian (as well as Husserlian) language used by Derrida—"*a priori* synthesis"—to conceptualize the reference of any *yes* to another yes, the yes of the Other, should not mislead one into understanding this relation as one of judgment or cognition. Nor is the second yes, with which everything begins, necessarily an already constituted Other. Rather, what the first yes refers to is the place of the Other, and it refers to it according to a relation of *implication.* The first yes is *nothing but* implication of the Other; it is not yet the fulfillment of the relation of implication with which transcendental logic and hence cognition in a strict sense begin. Otherness is a priori implied by each yes, and as such this "a priori synthesis" precedes transcendental logic, constative theoreticity, or any knowledge in general.

21. My use throughout this chapter (and in the preceding one) of "genuine" to demarcate response different from normed, prescribed, mechanical response lends itself, of course, to an array of misunderstandings. No better qualification, however, is available. "According to its concept," "true," "real," or "authentic" would be worse. Yet "genuine" response implies no pathos of the Other. As the foregoing quotation reveals, no living voice, or real Other, needs to be at the end of the line—an answering machine will do as well. Indeed, the structures of what I have called genuine response are valid not only for the human being, for the living in general (see Jacques Derrida, " 'Eating Well,' or the Calculation of the Subject: An Interview with Jacques Derrida," in *Who Comes after the Subject,* ed. E. Cadarva et al. [New York: Routledge, 1991], pp. 108–111), but also for a device such as an answering machine. The structure of genuine response has nothing specifically human about it. On the contrary, it is ahuman. It is not primarily determined in view of the human Other, and is thus not ethical in a classical sense. Other, for Derrida, means singular, hence also plural, and plural to such a degree as to inscribe the human Other within a multitude of ontologically different Others. A priori, and general, is only the *structure* of response itself.

22. It follows from this that even the most totalizing, encyclopedic, or narcissistic self-closure and rejection of the Other has a chance to succeed only when it becomes confirmed by the yes of what it excludes, the yes of the Other. Its success is thus structurally linked to its failure.

Index